THE BEST OF

Gourmet

THE BEST OF

Gourmet

FROM THE EDITORS OF GOURMET

CONDÉ NAST BOOKS

RANDOM HOUSE, NEW YORK

Copyright © 2007
The Condé Nast Publications Inc. All rights reserved under International
and Pan-American Copyright Conventions. Published in the United States
by Random House, Inc., New York, and simultaneously in Canada by
Random House of Canada Limited, Toronto.
ISBN 978-1-4000-6638-4
ISSN 1046-1760

Random House website address: www.atrandom.com
Gourmet Books website address: www.Gourmetbks.com

All of the recipes in this work were published previously in
Gourmet Magazine.

Printed in the United States of America on acid-free paper.

987654321
First Edition

All informative text in this book was written by Diane Abrams, Kate
Winslow, Jane Daniels Lear, and Eric Hastie.

The text of this book was set in Trade Gothic. The four-color separa-
tions were provided by North Market Graphics and Quad/Graphics, Inc.
The book was printed and bound at R. R. Donnelley and Sons. Stock is
Sterling Ultra Web Gloss, MeadWestvaco.

Broccoli Rabe Crostini; Rigatoni with Tomato Sauce and Ricotta;
Marinara Sauce; Meatloaf, Old Naples Style; Neapolitan Potato Pie;
Sweet Peas with Lettuce and Mint; Easter Wheat-Berry Cake (pages
98–101). Reprinted by permission from *1,000 Italian Recipes*, by
Michele Scicolone (Wiley Publishing, Inc.). Copyright © 2004 by
Michele Scicolone.

Mill scene (pages 110–111); Rhubarb Ginger Cooler (page 112); Praline
Ice Cream Sandwiches (page 114); Double Crust Nectarine Raspberry
Pie (page 117). Photographs reprinted by permission from Gueorgui
Pinkhassov and Magnum Photos. All photographs © 2006 by Gueorgui
Pinkhassov.

FOR RANDOM HOUSE
Lisa Faith Phillips, Vice President/General Manager
Tom Downing, Marketing Director
Deborah Williams, Operations Director
Lyn Barris Hastings, Associate Marketing Director
Eric Killer, Direct Marketing Manager
Angela Donadic, Direct Marketing Associate
Richard Elman, Production Manager

FOR *GOURMET* BOOKS
Diane Abrams, Director
Kate Winslow, Senior Associate Editor

FOR *GOURMET* MAGAZINE
Ruth Reichl, Editor-in-Chief
Richard Ferretti, Creative Director
Zanne Early Stewart, Media Food Editor

Kemp Miles Minifie, Executive Food Editor
Alexis M. Touchet, Senior Food Editor
Ruth Cousineau, Test Kitchen Director
Paul Grimes, Food Editor/Stylist
Maggie Ruggiero, Food Editor/Stylist
Shelton Wiseman, Travel Food Editor
Gina Marie Miraglia Eriquez, Food Editor
Melissa Roberts, Food Editor
Lillian Chou, Food Editor
Ian Knauer, Food Editor
Andrea Albin, Assistant Food Editor

Erika Oliveira, Art Director
Romulo A. Yanes, Photographer

Index illustrations copyright © 2002 and 2005 by Tobie Giddio

Produced in association with Anne B. Wright and John W. Kern

Jacket: Black-Bean Shrimp with Chinese Broccoli (page 81)
Frontispiece: Port-and-Spice Poached Pears with Granita (page 280)

ACKNOWLEDGMENTS

This very special edition of *The Best of Gourmet*, which celebrates the magazine's sixty-fifth anniversary, would not exist without the hard work of many talented and creative people.

Special thanks go to creative director Richard Ferretti. It is his artistic vision that makes this volume—and every issue of the magazine—so very beautiful. Thanks also to photo editor Amy Koblenzer and her staff, Megan Re and Laurie Nelson, for enlisting the photographers who bring these pages to life. Throughout this book, you will see the work of in-house staff photographer Romulo Yanes, as well as John Kernick, Mikkel Vang, Richard Jung, Petrina Tinslay, Martyn Thompson, Gueorgui Pinkhassov, Hans Gissinger, Roland Bello, and Marcus Nilsson.

But what's a cookbook without fantastic recipes? The memorable dishes that you'll find here were developed and tested by our very discerning food editors, who prepare a recipe over and over again until it is just right: Alexis Touchet, Ruth Cousineau, Paul Grimes, Maggie Ruggiero, Shelley Wiseman, Gina Marie Miraglia Eriquez, Melissa Roberts, Lillian Chou, Ian Knauer, and Andrea Albin. As always, Zanne Stewart and Kemp Minifie lent their insight and remarkable expertise to the endeavor.

After that rigorous testing process, the recipes undergo a similarly thorough editorial review by senior features editor Hobby Coudert and recipe editor Shannon Rodgers Fox. This year, Shannon gave all the recipes an additional scrupulous look, and we appreciate her careful editing. You'll find many helpful and interesting "Kitchen Notes" laced throughout the Recipe Compendium. These were the work of senior articles editor Jane Daniels Lear and assistant editor Eric Hastie.

Once again, we thank production director Stephanie Stehofsky, who gathers electronic files for us, as well as Random House production director Richard Elman. The recipe index at the back of the book is the work of Marilyn Flaig, who has been part of our team for many years. And finally, we salute project director Anne Wright and production editor John Kern, who shepherd this book from start to finish with unflagging professionalism and good humor.

TABLE OF CONTENTS

TIPS FOR USING GOURMET'S RECIPES

MEASURE LIQUIDS in either glass or clear plastic liquid-measuring cups. **MEASURE DRY INGREDIENTS** in nesting dry-measuring cups that can be leveled off with a knife. **MEASURE FLOUR** by spooning (not scooping) it into a dry-measuring cup and leveling off with a knife without tapping or shaking cup. **SIFT FLOUR** only when specified in recipe. If sifted flour is called for, sift flour before measuring. (Many brands say "presifted;" disregard this.)

A SHALLOW BAKING PAN means an old-fashioned jelly-roll or four-sided cookie pan. **MEASURE SKILLETS AND BAKING PANS** across the top, not across the bottom. **METAL PANS** used for baking should be light-colored, unless otherwise specified. If using dark metal pans, including nonstick, your baked goods will likely brown more and the cooking times may be shorter.

A WATER BATH for baking is prepared by putting your filled pan in a larger pan and adding enough boiling-hot water to the larger pan to reach halfway up the side of the smaller pan.

FRESH HERBS OR GREENS are prepped by first removing the leaves from the stem, except cilantro, which has tender stems. Wash and dry **ALL PRODUCE** before using.

SALTED WATER for cooking requires 1 to 2 tablespoons of salt for every 4 quarts of water.

CHEESES should be grated just before using. To finely grate Parmigiano-Reggiano and similar cheeses, use the small (1/8-inch) teardrop-shaped holes (not ragged-edged holes) of a box grater. Other shaped holes, a Microplane rasp, and pregrated cheese yield different volumes.

TO TENDER-ROAST BELL PEPPERS preheat broiler. Halve bell peppers lengthwise, then discard stems and seeds. Put peppers, cut sides down, in 1 layer in an oiled shallow baking pan. Broil 2 inches from heat until charred and softened, 15 to 18 minutes. Transfer to a bowl. Cover and let steam 15 minutes, then peel.

CHILES require protective gloves when handling.

ZEST CITRUS FRUITS by removing colored part of rind only (avoid bitter white pith). For strips, use a vegetable peeler. For grated zest, we prefer a rasplike Microplane zester, which results in fluffier zest, so pack to measure.

TOAST SPICES in a dry heavy skillet over moderate heat, stirring, until fragrant and a shade or two darker. **TOAST NUTS** in a shallow baking pan in a 350°F oven until golden, 5 to 10 minutes. **TOAST SEEDS** as you would toast spices or nuts.

TO GRILL OVER DIRECT HEAT USING A CHARCOAL GRILL, open vents on bottom of grill. Light a large chimney starter full of charcoal (preferably hardwood). When coals are lit, dump them out across bottom rack, leaving a space free of coals on one side of grill equal to the size of the food to be grilled (as a respite from any flareups), and banking coals across the remaining space so that coals are about 3 times higher against opposite side of grill. When charcoal turns grayish white, about 15 minutes after lighting, the grill will be at its hottest, then it will begin to cool off. How long you can hold your hand 5 inches above the grill rack over thickest layer of coals will determine the heat of your grill as follows: **HOT**: 1–2 seconds; **MEDIUM-HOT**: 3–4 seconds; **LOW**: 5–6 seconds. **IF USING A GAS GRILL,** preheat burners on high, covered, 10 minutes, then, if necessary, reduce to heat specified.

TO GRILL OVER INDIRECT HEAT USING A CHARCOAL GRILL, open vents on bottom and lid of grill. Light a large chimney starter full of charcoal (preferably hardwood). When coals are lit, dump them out along two opposite sides of bottom rack, leaving a space free of charcoal in middle of rack equal to the size of food to be grilled. When charcoal turns grayish white, about 15 minutes after lighting, the grill will be at its hottest, then it will begin to cool off. How long you can hold your hand 5 inches above the grill rack over thickest layer of coals will determine the heat of your grill (see above for times). **IF USING A GAS GRILL,** preheat all burners on high, covered, 10 minutes, then adjust heat according to recipe. Just before grilling, turn off 1 burner (middle burner if there are 3).

INTRODUCTION

Recently, a survivor of Hurricane Katrina wrote a lovely piece that appeared in the food section of a national newspaper. It went something like this: The storm destroyed the contents of her home, and a treasured family recipe for her husband's favorite cake was lost. With his birthday just a few weeks away, she spent days in a makeshift kitchen trying to reconstruct the recipe from memory. Finally, the big day arrived, and the cake was a success, even though it wasn't exactly the one they remembered.

As all of us who love to cook know, favorite recipes are priceless, and we depend on them to get us through good times and bad. Imagine being hungry on a cool evening and having to do without the macaroni and cheese that you crave, or feeling sick and not being able to make your dependable soup. Or worse, as in this case, imagine losing even one of your family's most cherished recipes. What would Thanksgiving be like without your grandmother's turkey stuffing or your great-aunt's cranberry preserves?

Many of you are aware that the magazine recently celebrated its sixty-fifth anniversary, and we decided to put together a collection of our favorite recipes, one from each year. At first, this didn't sound difficult; in fact, it seemed like it would be fun. But the reality of scouring through twelve issues per calendar year for a single winner proved to be daunting, especially when the food editors discovered that they didn't even recognize some of the earliest dishes. The process was likened to an archeological dig, where, with patience and meticulous care, precious artifacts were unveiled, then restored. Many of the older recipes required weeks of delicate retooling to suit today's tastes. Recent recipes were another story. Since everyone in the food department knew these dishes intimately, there was often quite a discussion to see which ones would make it into the final lineup.

Producing our annual *The Best of Gourmet* allows us to give our very best recipes from the previous year a permanent home. This volume not only contains our selections from 2006, it also devotes a special section to these sixty-five winning favorites. Dozens of exquisite full-color photographs accompany these recipes, which begin on page 12.

As time went on, the woman who lost her recipe came to realize that thousands of other hurricane victims also were living without their most prized dishes. With the help of other survivors who were lucky enough to still have their family recipes intact, she put together a cookbook of Southern specialties to share with those less fortunate. In the same vein, we hope this collection will ensure that our most valued recipes are kept safe forever, and our wish is that everyone will make them their own.

THE EDITORS OF GOURMET BOOKS

SIXTY-FIVE YEARS, SIXTY-FIVE FAVORITE RECIPES

When we decided to celebrate *Gourmet*'s sixty-fifth anniversary by selecting one fabulous recipe from each year of the magazine's existence, we had no idea of the education we would receive. Who would have guessed that American palates were ready for the Indonesian *nasi goreng* recipe published in 1941, our inaugural year? Or that down-home fare such as oyster po' boys would be featured four years later? And we were amazed to learn that readers had clamored for an authentic recipe for Chinese egg rolls—in 1946!

Looking at our final selection, we realized that if the recipes' dates were removed we would be hard-pressed to guess the year they first appeared. They all seemed so timely. Take the Lady Curzon soup, from 1968. Foreshadowing the tiny cups of soup served by many chefs today as *amuse-bouches*, this curried mussel soup is incredibly current. It's so exquisitely rich that a sip is all you need.

Indeed, *Gourmet* has always been ahead of the curve, but its goal, first and foremost, is simply to present great food. And sifting through thousands of recipes from our sixty-five-year history proved to be a delicious exercise. The process reminded us of so many forgotten favorites, as well as recipes that deserved to become classics but somehow slipped from our memory.

We loved rediscovering bobotie (1960), a South African curried meatloaf enveloped by a voluptuous custard, and palacsinta (1958), delightful Austro-Hungarian jam-filled crêpes. And once you try *maccheroni quattro formaggi villa d'Este* (1970)—a very adult version of mac and cheese—no other version will do. It was also fun to revisit more recent recipes, like pan-seared curry-rubbed fish fillets in ginger broth (1994) and unctuous short ribs braised in coffee ancho chile sauce (2003; pictured opposite). Yet another treasure is the decadent chocolate soufflé cake with orange caramel sauce (2001). Not only is this crowd-pleaser the picture of sophistication, it boasts one of the shortest ingredient lists ever.

The grandeur of some recipes had faded over time and needed a little tinkering. The duck à l'orange recipe from 1945 was tweaked and tested five times before meeting unanimous approval. The secret? Using a gastrique (caramelized sugar and vinegar reduced to a syrup) for the orange sauce, which is then thickened with a *beurre manié*. The gastrique's brightness balances the richness of the duck and makes for a truly timeless dish.

We love the way these sixty-five recipes provide a glimpse into *Gourmet*'s past, while holding a place of honor at today's table. And we can't wait to taste whatever flavors the next sixty-five years will bring.

1941 NASI GORENG

Indonesian Fried Rice

SERVES 4 TO 6

ACTIVE TIME: 40 MIN   START TO FINISH: 9½ HR (INCLUDES CHILLING RICE OVERNIGHT)

Chicken, shrimp, and fried rice combine in this traditional version of the classic Indonesian one-dish meal, made intense and spicy with fish sauce and plenty of chiles. For help in finding Asian ingredients, see Sources.

1½   cups long-grain white rice (10 oz)
¾   cup water
1¾   cups reduced-sodium chicken broth (14 fl oz)
1   qt plus 3 tablespoons vegetable oil
8   *krupuk* (Indonesian shrimp crackers; optional)
2   cups thinly sliced shallots (¾ lb)
2   large garlic cloves, finely chopped
1   lb skinless boneless chicken breast, cut into ¾-inch pieces
1   lb medium shrimp in shell (31 to 35 per pound), peeled and deveined
2   to 3 (2½-inch) fresh hot red chiles, such as Thai or serrano, minced, including seeds
1¼   teaspoons salt
2   tablespoons *ketjap manis* (Indonesian sweet soy sauce)
1   tablespoon Asian fish sauce
4   scallions, thinly sliced

SPECIAL EQUIPMENT: a deep-fat thermometer; a large wok
ACCOMPANIMENTS: sliced cucumber; wedges of hard-boiled egg

▶ Rinse rice in a large sieve and drain well. Bring rice, water, and 1½ cups chicken broth to a full rolling boil in a 4-quart heavy saucepan. Cover pan, then reduce heat to very low and cook until liquid is absorbed and rice is tender, about 15 minutes. Remove pan from heat and let rice stand, covered, 5 minutes. Gently fluff with a fork, then transfer to a large shallow bowl or a large shallow baking pan and cool to room temperature, about 30 minutes. Chill rice, covered, 8 to 12 hours.

▶ Heat 1 quart of oil in a 4-quart pot over high heat until thermometer registers 375°F. Gently drop 2 *krupuk* into oil, then fry until they float to the surface, curl up, and expand, about 20 seconds. Turn *krupuk* over and fry until pale golden, about 10 seconds, then transfer with a slotted spoon to paper towels to drain. Fry remaining *krupuk* in 3 batches in same manner, transferring to paper towels to drain, then cool and break into pieces.

▶ Break up rice into individual grains with your fingers.

▶ Heat remaining 3 tablespoons oil in wok over high heat until hot but not smoking, then add shallots and stir-fry 1 minute. Add garlic and stir-fry 30 seconds. Add chicken and stir-fry until outside is no longer pink, about 2 minutes. Add shrimp, chiles, and salt and stir-fry until shrimp are just cooked through, 2 to 3 minutes. Add remaining ¼ cup broth with *ketjap manis* and rice and stir-fry until rice is heated through, about 2 minutes. Remove wok from heat and stir in fish sauce and scallions until combined well.

▶ Serve *nasi goreng* on a platter with *krupuk*, cucumber slices, and hard-boiled eggs.

COOKS' NOTE: *Krupuk* can be fried 1 day ahead and cooled completely, then kept in an airtight container at room temperature.

1942 PHILADELPHIA CLAM PIES
SERVES 6
ACTIVE TIME: 45 MIN   START TO FINISH: 1¼ HR

Clam pie is a superlative potpie, hearty with chunks of vegetables and bacon and sweet with briny clams. Inspired by legendary French chef Paul Bocuse, we updated these pies by substituting puff pastry for piecrust.

1½	lb boiling potatoes
½	stick (¼ cup) unsalted butter
1	bacon slice, chopped

1	large onion, chopped
1	garlic clove, finely chopped
½	teaspoon salt
1	Turkish or ½ California bay leaf
1	sprig fresh thyme
1	whole clove
3	medium carrots, cut into ¼-inch dice
2	celery ribs, cut into ¼-inch dice
2	tablespoons dry white wine
1	(8-oz) bottle clam juice
2	teaspoons cornstarch
24	small clams (1½ to 2 inches across), shucked, reserving their liquor, and chopped if desired
1	(17½-oz) package frozen puff pastry, thawed
1	large egg, lightly beaten

SPECIAL EQUIPMENT: 6 (12- to 14-oz) deep ovenproof soup bowls

▶ Peel potatoes and cut into ¼-inch dice.

▶ Heat butter and bacon in a 12-inch heavy skillet over moderately high heat until foam subsides, then add onion, garlic, and salt and cook, stirring occasionally, until onion is pale golden, about 5 minutes. Add bay leaf, thyme, clove, carrots, celery, and potatoes and reduce heat to moderate, then cook, stirring occasionally, until vegetables are golden and almost tender, about 15 minutes (be careful not to let them burn). Add wine, scraping up any brown bits.

▶ Stir together clam juice and cornstarch. Add to vegetables in skillet and bring to a simmer. Cover skillet and simmer until vegetables are tender, about 5 minutes. Remove lid and stir in clams with their liquor. Bring to a simmer and cook 1 minute, then remove from heat and cool to warm, uncovered. Discard bay leaf and clove.

▶ Put oven rack in middle position and preheat oven to 425°F.

▶ Roll out 1 pastry sheet into a 12-inch square on a lightly floured surface with a lightly floured rolling pin. Cut out 3 squares of pastry that are at least 1 inch larger all around than tops of soup bowls. Repeat with remaining pastry sheet.

▶ Divide clam filling among soup bowls (leaving at least a ¾-inch space between surface of filling and tops of bowls). Brush 1 pastry square with egg and cover 1 bowl with it, egg side down, pressing edges of pastry firmly onto outside of bowl. Repeat with remaining squares of pastry and bowls. Brush tops of pastry with remaining egg.

▶ Bake pies in bowls in a large shallow baking pan until pastry is golden and puffed, about 20 minutes.

1943 DUCK À L'ORANGE

SERVES 4

ACTIVE TIME: 45 MIN   START TO FINISH: 2¼ HR

We had always thought of duck à l'orange as a tired cliché of the 1960s, so it was a surprise to find out how delightful this old recipe actually is. We have reduced the original quantity of sugar and caramelized it (along with the aromatic vegetables which balance out the sweetness) for a rich sauce with layers of flavor.

FOR DUCK

- 1 tablespoon kosher salt
- 1 teaspoon ground coriander
- ½ teaspoon ground cumin
- 1 teaspoon black pepper
- 1 (5- to 6-lb) Long Island duck (also called Pekin)
- 1 juice orange, halved
- 4 fresh thyme sprigs
- 4 fresh marjoram sprigs
- 2 fresh flat-leaf parsley sprigs
- 1 small onion, cut into 8 wedges
- ½ cup dry white wine
- ½ cup duck stock, duck and veal stock (see Sources), chicken stock, or reduced-sodium chicken broth
- ½ carrot
- ½ celery rib

FOR SAUCE

- ⅓ cup sugar
- ⅓ cup fresh orange juice (from 1 to 2 oranges)
- 2 tablespoons white-wine vinegar
- ⅛ teaspoon salt
- 2 to 4 tablespoons duck or chicken stock or reduced-sodium chicken broth
- 1 tablespoon unsalted butter, softened
- 1 tablespoon all-purpose flour
- 1 tablespoon fine julienne of fresh orange zest, removed with a vegetable peeler

SPECIAL EQUIPMENT: **an instant-read thermometer; a 13- by 9-inch flameproof roasting pan**

ROAST DUCK:

▶ Put oven rack in middle position and preheat oven to 475°F.

▶ Stir together salt, coriander, cumin, and pepper. Pat duck dry and sprinkle inside and out with spice mixture. Cut 1 half of orange into quarters and put in duck cavity with thyme, marjoram, parsley, and 4 onion wedges.

▶ Squeeze juice from remaining half of orange and stir together with wine and stock. Set aside.

▶ Spread remaining 4 onion wedges in roasting pan with carrot and celery, then place duck on top of vegetables and roast 30 minutes.

▶ Pour wine mixture into roasting pan and reduce oven temperature to 350°F. Continue to roast duck until thermometer inserted into a thigh (close to but not touching bone) registers 170°F, 1 to 1¼ hours more. Turn on broiler and broil duck 3 to 4 inches from heat until top is golden brown, about 3 minutes.

▶ Tilt duck to drain juices from cavity into pan and transfer duck to a cutting board, reserving juices in pan. Let duck stand 15 minutes.

MAKE SAUCE:

▶ While duck roasts, cook sugar in a dry 1-quart heavy saucepan over moderate heat, undisturbed, until it begins to melt. Continue to cook, stirring occasionally with a fork, until sugar melts into a deep golden caramel. Add orange juice, vinegar, and salt (use caution; mixture will bubble and steam vigorously) and simmer over low heat, stirring occasionally, until caramel is dissolved. Remove syrup from heat.

▶ Discard vegetables from roasting pan and pour pan juices through a fine-mesh sieve into a 1-quart glass measure or bowl, then skim off and discard fat. Add enough stock to pan juices to total 1 cup liquid.

▶ Stir together butter and flour to form a beurre manié. Bring pan juices to a simmer in a 1- to 2-quart heavy saucepan, then add beurre manié, whisking constantly to prevent lumps. Add orange syrup and zest and simmer, whisking occasionally, until sauce is thickened slightly and zest is tender, about 5 minutes. Serve with duck.

1944 CHICKEN À LA KING

SERVES 6

ACTIVE TIME: 45 MIN   START TO FINISH: 45 MIN

In 1944, E. Clarke King of Dayton, Ohio, sent us "the original recipe" for this dish, which he claimed had been invented by George Greenwald, head chef at New York's Brighton Beach Hotel in the early 1900s. This time, we've lightened Greenwald's dish with stock and added red, yellow, and orange bell peppers.

- 1¾ cups chicken broth (14 fl oz)
- 1½ lb skinless boneless chicken breast halves
- 5 tablespoons unsalted butter
- ½ each yellow, red, and orange bell peppers, cut into ½-inch pieces (2 cups)
- 1¼ teaspoons salt, or to taste
- ½ teaspoon black pepper
- ½ cup finely chopped onion

2 tablespoons all-purpose flour

1¼ cups heavy cream

¼ lb white mushrooms, trimmed and quartered

3 large egg yolks

1 tablespoon fresh lemon juice, or to taste

2 tablespoons dry Sherry, or to taste

½ teaspoon paprika (not hot)

6 (½-inch-thick) slices firm white sandwich bread (preferably Pullman), toasted

¼ cup chopped fresh flat-leaf parsley

▶ Put broth and chicken in a 2- to 3-quart heavy saucepan and bring just to a simmer over moderate heat, uncovered. Turn chicken over and gently poach at a bare simmer, uncovered, until just cooked through, about 5 minutes more.

▶ Transfer chicken to a cutting board. Pour broth through a fine-mesh sieve into a heatproof 2-cup measure and reserve for sauce.

▶ Heat 2 tablespoons butter in a 4- to 5-quart wide heavy pot over moderately high heat until foam subsides, then cook peppers, stirring, until softened (do not brown), 6 to 8 minutes. Transfer peppers to a bowl and stir in ¼ teaspoon salt and ¼ teaspoon pepper.

▶ Add onion and remaining 3 tablespoons butter to pot and cook over moderately low heat, stirring, until softened, 3 to 5 minutes. Add flour and remaining teaspoon salt and ¼ teaspoon pepper and reduce heat to low, then cook, stirring, 2 minutes. Whisk in ¾ cup broth, then all of cream and mushrooms, and simmer until mushrooms are tender, about 5 minutes.

▶ Meanwhile, whisk together yolks, lemon juice, Sherry, and paprika in a small bowl. Whisk in ½ cup sauce, then stir yolk mixture back into sauce remaining in pot. Cook over low heat, stirring (do not simmer, or sauce will curdle), until sauce is slightly thickened, about 2 minutes. Remove from heat and reserve.

▶ Cut chicken crosswise into ⅓-inch-thick slices and add along with peppers to sauce, then cook over low heat (do not simmer, or sauce will curdle), stirring occasionally, until chicken and peppers are just heated through. Add more broth to thin if desired.

▶ Spoon chicken à la king over toast on 6 plates, then sprinkle with parsley.

COOKS' NOTES: Chicken can be poached 1 day ahead and cooled completely in broth, uncovered, then chilled, covered. Reheat chicken in broth over low heat before proceeding.

• Sauce, without yolk mixture, can be made 1 day ahead and chilled, covered. Bring sauce slowly to a simmer before proceeding.

1945 OYSTER PO' BOYS

SERVES 4

ACTIVE TIME: 30 MIN   START TO FINISH: 30 MIN

There are many ways to stuff these iconic New Orleans sandwiches, but doing it with fried oysters is arguably the best.

1 large egg

½ cup milk

2 teaspoons salt

2 teaspoons black pepper

1 cup all-purpose flour

1½ cups yellow cornmeal

2 teaspoons cayenne

3 dozen shucked small oysters such as Kumamoto, drained

1 qt vegetable oil

1 (20-inch) loaf soft French or Italian bread (about 3½ inches wide)

¾ cup mayonnaise

2 cups thinly sliced iceberg lettuce

SPECIAL EQUIPMENT: a deep-fat thermometer

ACCOMPANIMENT: Tabasco

▶ Put oven rack in middle position and preheat oven to 350°F.

▶ Lightly beat together egg, milk, ½ teaspoon salt, and 1 teaspoon black pepper in a bowl. Whisk together flour, ½ teaspoon salt, and remaining teaspoon black pepper in a shallow baking dish. Whisk together cornmeal, remaining teaspoon salt, and cayenne in another shallow baking dish.

▶ Dredge 8 oysters in flour, knocking off excess, then dip into egg mixture, letting excess drip off, and dredge in cornmeal mixture, knocking off excess. Transfer to a large rack, then coat remaining oysters in batches of 6 to 8 in same manner, transferring to rack.

▶ Heat oil in a 4-quart pot over high heat until thermometer registers 375°F.

▶ While oil is heating, halve bread crosswise, then cut each piece in half horizontally, cutting all the way through. Put bread halves back together and heat bread in oven (directly on oven rack) until warm, about 5 minutes.

▶ While bread is heating, gently drop one third of oysters into hot oil and fry, stirring occasionally, until golden, 45 seconds to 1 minute, then transfer to paper towels to drain. Fry remaining oysters in 2 batches in same manner, returning oil to 375°F between batches.

▶ Spread mayonnaise on cut sides of bread, then make sandwiches, topping lettuce with oysters. Halve each sandwich crosswise for a total of 4 sandwiches.

1946 CHINESE EGG ROLLS

MAKES ABOUT 24
ACTIVE TIME: 1¾ HR   START TO FINISH: 2¼ HR

In the 1940s, Gourmet *readers clamored for a genuine version of this "Chinese delicacy." Our answer was fragrant with garlic, scallions, shiitakes, shrimp, and roast pork. For help in finding Asian ingredients, see Sources.*

- 2   tablespoons oyster sauce
- 1   tablespoon soy sauce
- 2   teaspoons Asian sesame oil
- 2   teaspoons sugar
- ½   teaspoon salt
    About 4 cups peanut or vegetable oil
- 2   teaspoons finely chopped peeled fresh ginger
- 2   teaspoons finely chopped garlic
- 1½ bunches scallions (about 10), white and pale green parts cut into 2-inch lengths, then cut lengthwise into very thin matchsticks (2½ cups)
- 2   celery ribs, cut into very thin matchsticks (2 cups)
- 2   medium carrots, cut into very thin matchsticks (1 cup)
- 8   large fresh shiitake mushrooms, stems discarded and caps sliced ¼ inch thick (3 cups)
- 1   lb medium shrimp in shell (31 to 35 per lb), peeled, deveined, and coarsely chopped

- ¼   lb Chinese roast pork (*char siu*) or leftover roast pork, cut into 2-inch lengths, then cut lengthwise into very thin matchsticks
- 1   (1-lb) package Asian egg roll or spring roll wrappers
- 1   large egg, lightly beaten

SPECIAL EQUIPMENT: **a deep-fat thermometer**
ACCOMPANIMENTS: **Asian sweet chile sauce; Chinese mustard**

MAKE FILLING:

▶ Stir together oyster sauce, soy sauce, sesame oil, sugar, and salt in a small bowl until sugar and salt are dissolved.
▶ Heat a dry 12-inch heavy skillet (not nonstick) over moderately high heat until hot but not smoking, then add 2 tablespoons peanut oil, swirling skillet to coat. Stir-fry ginger, garlic, and scallions until scallions are wilted, about 1 minute. Add celery, carrots, and mushrooms and stir-fry until vegetables are softened, 4 to 6 minutes. Push vegetables toward edge of skillet, then add shrimp to center and stir-fry until shrimp are just cooked through, 3 to 5 minutes. Add pork and oyster sauce mixture and stir together all ingredients in skillet until combined. Season with salt and transfer to a large shallow bowl. Cool, stirring occasionally, about 30 minutes.

MAKE EGG ROLLS:

▶ Gently peel apart wrappers to separate if necessary (wrappers may not be perfectly square).
▶ Put 1 wrapper on a work surface, arranging wrapper with a corner nearest you and keeping remaining wrappers covered with plastic wrap. Stir filling, then spread a scant ¼ cup filling horizontally across center of wrapper to form a 4-inch log. Fold bottom corner over filling, then fold in side corners. Brush top corner with egg and roll up wrapper tightly to enclose filling, sealing roll closed with top corner. Transfer roll, seam side down, to a paper-towel-lined baking sheet and loosely cover with plastic wrap. Make more egg rolls in same manner, transferring to baking sheet as formed (you may have some filling left over).
▶ Put oven rack in middle position and preheat oven to 250°F. Line a large colander with paper towels. Heat 1 inch peanut oil in a 5- to 6-quart wide heavy pot until it registers 350°F on thermometer, then fry 4 or 5 egg rolls (don't crowd pot), turning with a slotted spoon, until golden brown, 3 to 5 minutes. Transfer with slotted spoon to colander and drain rolls upright 2 to 3 minutes, then keep warm on a rack set on a large baking sheet in oven. Fry remaining egg rolls in batches, transferring to colander and then to rack in oven.

OPPOSITE: 1947 Sauternes and sage jelly

1947 SAUTERNES AND SAGE JELLY

MAKES ABOUT 2 CUPS
ACTIVE TIME: 20 MIN   START TO FINISH: 1 DAY (INCLUDES TIME FOR
FLAVORS TO DEVELOP)

We ran many jelly recipes in the 1940s, but this one impressed us the most. Sophisticated and subtle, it is delicious with any roasted or grilled meat.

½ cup boiling-hot water
2 tablespoons chopped fresh sage
    Pinch of turmeric (for yellow color; optional)
1½ cups Sauternes (from a 375-ml bottle)
3½ cups sugar
⅛ teaspoon salt
1 Turkish or ½ California bay leaf
½ cup liquid fruit pectin

SPECIAL EQUIPMENT: **4 (½-pint) canning jars with lids and screw bands; an instant-read thermometer**

▶Wash jars, lids, and screw bands in hot soapy water, then rinse well. Dry screw bands. Put empty jars on a rack in a boiling-water canner or an 8- to 10-quart deep pot and add enough water to cover by 2 inches. Bring to a boil, covered, then boil 10 minutes. Remove canner from heat, leaving jars in water. Heat lids in water to cover by 2 inches in a small saucepan until thermometer registers 180°F (do not let boil). Remove from heat. Keep jars and lids submerged in hot water, covered, until ready to use.
▶Pour ½ cup boiling-hot water over sage and turmeric in a cup and let steep, covered, 15 minutes. Pour sage water through a fine-mesh sieve into a bowl, pressing on solids, then add enough extra water to bring total to ½ cup.
▶Carefully remove jars with tongs, then drain jars upside down on a clean kitchen towel.
▶Bring sage water, Sauternes, sugar, salt, and bay leaf to a boil in a 2- to 2½-quart heavy saucepan. Whisk in pectin until dissolved and bring to a boil. Boil 1 minute, then remove from heat. Invert jars. Immediately divide jelly among jars, leaving ¼ inch of space at top. Wipe off rims of filled jars with a clean damp kitchen towel, then top with lids and firmly screw on screw bands.
▶Put sealed jars on rack in canner or deep pot and add enough water to cover by 2 inches. Bring to a boil, covered, then boil 10 minutes. Transfer jars with tongs to a towel-lined surface to cool. Jars will seal; if you hear a ping, that means that the

vacuum formed above the cooling jelly has made the lid concave. Remember that you may or may not be around to hear the ping. The important thing is for the jars to eventually have concave lids. Jelly will thicken as it cools.

▸ After jars have cooled 12 to 24 hours, press center of each lid to check that it's concave, then remove screw band and try to lift off lid with your fingertips. If you can't, the lid has a good seal. Replace screw band. Put any jars that haven't sealed properly in the refrigerator and use them first.

COOKS' NOTES: Be sure to check the expiration date on your pectin to ensure freshness.
• Let jelly stand in jars at least 1 day for flavors to develop.
• Jelly keeps in sealed jars in a cool dark place 5 to 6 months.

1948 CHICKEN CACCIATORE

SERVES 6
ACTIVE TIME: 45 MIN   START TO FINISH: 1½ HR

The moist, tender meat takes on a deep tomatoey flavor that suggests it's been slowly cooking for days rather than for less than 2 hours.

1 (3½- to 4-lb) chicken, cut into 8 serving pieces
1¾ teaspoons salt
¾ teaspoon black pepper
2 tablespoons olive oil
1 large onion, chopped
1 green bell pepper, chopped
4 garlic cloves, chopped
½ cup dry red wine
1 (28-oz) can whole tomatoes in juice
½ cup chicken stock or reduced-sodium chicken broth

ACCOMPANIMENT: cooked white rice or buttered noodles

▸ Pat chicken dry and sprinkle on all sides with 1¼ teaspoons salt and pepper. Heat oil in a deep 12-inch heavy skillet over moderately high heat until hot but not smoking, then brown chicken in 2 batches, turning over once, about 10 minutes per batch. Transfer chicken to a plate.
▸ Reduce heat to moderate and add onion, bell pepper, and garlic to skillet. Cook, stirring occasionally and scraping up any brown bits, until onion and garlic are golden, 8 to 10 minutes. Add wine and simmer, scraping up brown bits, until liquid is reduced by half, 1 to 2 minutes. Add tomatoes with their juice and simmer, breaking up tomatoes with a wooden spoon, 5 minutes. Add stock and nestle chicken pieces in sauce.

▸ Simmer, loosely covered with foil, until chicken is cooked through, 35 to 45 minutes. Season with remaining ½ teaspoon salt. For a thicker sauce, transfer cooked chicken to a platter and keep warm, covered, then boil sauce until it reaches desired consistency.

1949 ESCARGOTS À LA BOURGUIGNONNE

SERVES 4 (FIRST COURSE)
ACTIVE TIME: 25 MIN   START TO FINISH: 30 MIN

When we ran this recipe in 1949, it took a full day's work, most of it cleaning and prepping the fresh snails. We found that canned snails work just as well and turn this appetizer into one that can be whipped up anytime.

1 small garlic clove
⅜ teaspoon table salt
1 stick (½ cup) unsalted butter, softened
1½ teaspoons finely minced shallot
1 tablespoon finely chopped fresh flat-leaf parsley
¼ teaspoon black pepper
1 tablespoon dry white wine
12 to 16 snails (from a 7- to 8-oz can; see Sources)
    About 2 cups kosher salt (for stabilizing snail shells)

SPECIAL EQUIPMENT: 12 to 16 sterilized escargot shells (see Sources)
ACCOMPANIMENT: French bread

▸ Put oven rack in middle position and preheat oven to 450°F.
▸ Using a heavy knife, mince and mash garlic to a paste with ⅛ teaspoon table salt.
▸ Beat together butter, shallot, garlic paste, parsley, remaining ¼ teaspoon table salt, and pepper in a small bowl with an electric mixer until combined well. Beat in white wine until combined well.
▸ Divide half of garlic butter among snail shells. Stuff 1 snail into each shell and top snails with remaining butter. Spread kosher salt in a shallow baking dish and nestle shells, butter sides up, in salt.
▸ Bake snails until butter is melted and sizzling, 4 to 6 minutes. Serve immediately.

COOKS' NOTE: The escargots can be prepared, but not baked, up to 30 minutes ahead and kept at room temperature until ready to bake.

OPPOSITE: 1949 escargots à la Bourguignonne

1950 LOG CABIN PIE

SERVES 8 TO 10

ACTIVE TIME: 25 MIN   START TO FINISH: 3½ HR (INCLUDES COOLING)

*Don't be concerned if the pie appears thin—this makes for a
good balance between filling and pastry.*

FOR PASTRY DOUGH

1¼ cups all-purpose flour
¾ stick (6 tablespoons) cold unsalted butter, cut into
     ½-inch cubes
 2 tablespoons cold vegetable shortening (preferably
     trans-fat-free)
¼ teaspoon salt
 3 to 4 tablespoons ice water

FOR FILLING

 4 large egg yolks
   Rounded ¼ teaspoon salt
1¼ cups pure maple syrup (preferably dark amber or Grade B)
 2 teaspoons fresh lemon juice
 2 cups pecan halves (7 oz), toasted (see Tips, page 8)
     and cooled

SPECIAL EQUIPMENT: a pastry or bench scraper
ACCOMPANIMENT: unsweetened whipped cream

MAKE DOUGH:

▸Blend together flour, butter, shortening, and salt in a bowl with
your fingertips or a pastry blender (or pulse in a food processor)
just until mixture resembles coarse meal with some small
(roughly pea-size) butter lumps. Drizzle 3 tablespoons ice water
evenly over mixture and gently stir with a fork (or pulse) until
incorporated.
▸Squeeze a handful of dough: If it doesn't hold together, add
more ice water, ½ tablespoon at a time, stirring (or pulsing) until
incorporated. (Do not overwork dough or pastry will be tough.)
▸Turn dough out onto a work surface and divide dough into
4 portions. With heel of your hand, smear each portion once or
twice in a forward motion to help distribute fat. Gather all dough
together with pastry scraper and press into a ball, then flatten
into a 5-inch disk. If dough is sticky, dust lightly with additional
flour. Wrap disk in plastic wrap and chill until firm, at least
1 hour.

MAKE PIE SHELL:

▸Put oven rack in middle position and preheat oven to 350°F.
▸Roll out dough into a 13-inch round on a lightly floured surface
with a lightly floured rolling pin. Fit dough into a 9-inch pie plate
and trim, leaving a ½-inch overhang, then fold overhang under
slightly. Crimp edge decoratively. Chill shell until firm, about
30 minutes.

▸Lightly prick shell all over with a fork. Line shell with foil and
fill with pie weights. Bake until pastry is pale golden along rim
and set underneath weights, 15 to 20 minutes. Carefully remove
foil and weights and bake shell until bottom and side are golden,
about 15 minutes more. Cool completely in pie plate on a rack,
about 20 minutes.

MAKE FILLING AND BAKE PIE:

▸Whisk together egg yolks and salt in a bowl until blended,
then whisk in syrup and lemon juice. Stir in pecans and pour
filling into pie shell, spreading nuts evenly. Cover edge of
shell with a pie shield or foil and bake just until filling is set,
20 to 30 minutes. Cool to warm or room temperature on rack.

COOKS' NOTE: Pie can be made 6 hours ahead and kept at room
temperature.

1951 BRAISED PORK LOIN WITH PRUNES

SERVES 8

ACTIVE TIME: 40 MIN   START TO FINISH: 1½ HR

*Infused with the deep sweetness of prunes, pork loin takes on the
rich, robust flavors of southwestern France.*

¼ cup olive oil
 2 lb onions (6 to 8 medium), halved lengthwise, then thinly
     sliced lengthwise
 1 head of garlic, cloves separated and peeled
1¼ teaspoons salt
½ teaspoon black pepper
 2 cups pitted prunes (14 oz)
 1 cup Armagnac
 1 (3- to 3½-lb) boneless center-cut pork loin roast (3 to
     4 inches in diameter), tied
10 fresh parsley stems
 2 large fresh thyme sprigs
 1 large fresh sage sprig
 1 California bay leaf or 2 Turkish
¼ teaspoon black peppercorns
 2 whole cloves
⅓ cup Dijon mustard
⅓ cup packed light brown sugar
 1 cup dry white wine
 1 cup reduced-sodium chicken broth (8 fl oz)
 2 to 3 tablespoons red-wine vinegar

SPECIAL EQUIPMENT: a 5-qt heavy pot with lid (round or oval
to accommodate a 12-inch roast; see cooks' note, below); a
6-inch square of cheesecloth; kitchen string; an instant-read
thermometer; heavy-duty foil

▸ Heat 2 tablespoons oil in 5-quart pot over moderate heat until hot but not smoking, then cook onions, garlic, ½ teaspoon salt, and ¼ teaspoon pepper, stirring occasionally, until onions are soft and golden, about 20 minutes. Transfer onions to a bowl and reserve pot.

▸ Simmer prunes and Armagnac in a 1- to 2-quart saucepan 5 minutes. Remove from heat and set aside.

▸ Make a hole for stuffing: Insert a long thin sharp knife into middle of one end toward center of loin, then repeat at opposite end to make an incision that runs lengthwise through roast. Enlarge incision with your fingers, working from both ends, to create a ¾-inch-wide opening.

▸ Pack about 20 prunes into pork, pushing from both ends toward center (reserve remaining Armagnac and prunes). Pat pork dry and season with ½ teaspoon salt and remaining ¼ teaspoon pepper.

▸ Put oven rack in middle position and preheat oven to 375°F.

▸ Wrap parsley, thyme, sage, bay leaf, peppercorns, and cloves in cheesecloth and tie into a bundle with kitchen string.

▸ Brush pork with mustard, then evenly coat with brown sugar. Heat remaining 2 tablespoons oil in reserved pot over high heat until hot but not smoking, then brown meat on all sides (not ends), reducing heat if necessary to keep from burning, about 6 minutes total.

▸ Transfer pork with tongs to a plate, then add white wine and reserved Armagnac (but not prunes) to pot. Bring to a boil, then remove from heat.

▸ Add broth, onions, and cheesecloth bundle to pot with Armagnac mixture, then add pork with any juices accumulated on plate and turn pork fat side up. Bring to a boil over high heat, covered, then transfer to oven and braise 30 minutes.

▸ Add remaining prunes and braise until thermometer inserted diagonally 2 inches into meat (avoid stuffing) registers 150°F, about 15 minutes.

▸ Transfer pork to a cutting board and cut off and discard string, then cover with heavy-duty foil (temperature of pork will rise as it stands).

▸ While pork stands, skim fat from surface of sauce (if necessary) and remove and discard cheesecloth bundle, then stir in vinegar and remaining ¼ teaspoon salt and pepper to taste.

COOKS' NOTE: If you don't have a 5-quart heavy pot, onions and pork can be browned separately in a 12-inch heavy skillet, then transferred with remaining ingredients to a deep 13- by 9-inch roasting pan, tightly covered with heavy-duty foil, and braised in oven.

1952 GERMAN APPLE PANCAKES

SERVES 4 TO 6 (ABOUT 12 PANCAKES)
ACTIVE TIME: 1 HR   START TO FINISH: 1 HR

These tender and not-too-sweet cakes fall somewhere between an American flapjack and a crêpe. Though they're traditionally served for dessert, we love them for a special winter breakfast, generously dusted with cinnamon sugar.

¼   cup plus 2 teaspoons sugar
½   teaspoon cinnamon
 1   cup all-purpose flour
½   teaspoon salt
1½ cups whole milk
 4   large eggs
1½ lb Gala apples (3 or 4)
 2   tablespoons fresh lemon juice
¾   stick (6 tablespoons) unsalted butter, cut into
        12 pieces

SPECIAL EQUIPMENT: an adjustable-blade slicer

▸ Preheat oven to 200°F.

▸ Stir together ¼ cup sugar and cinnamon and set aside.

▸ Whisk together flour, salt, and remaining 2 teaspoons sugar in a large bowl. Add milk in a slow stream, whisking, then add eggs, 1 at a time, whisking well after each addition.

▸ Peel apples, then cut into ⅛-inch thick slices with slicer, rotating around core (discard core). Cut apple slices into ⅛-inch-thick matchsticks and toss with lemon juice in a bowl. Fold apples and juice into batter.

▸ Heat 1 piece butter (½ tablespoon) in a 6-inch nonstick skillet over moderate heat until foam subsides, then add ⅓ cup batter, spreading evenly to cover bottom. Cook, reducing heat if browning too quickly and turning pancake over once with a thin flexible heatproof spatula, until golden on both sides, about 4 minutes total. Slide pancake onto a platter and keep warm in oven. Make more pancakes with remaining butter and batter in same manner. Sprinkle with cinnamon sugar and serve immediately.

COOKS' NOTE: Batter, with apples, can be made 3 hours ahead and kept chilled, covered. Stir before using.

ACCOMPANIMENTS: rice; toasted coconut; ½-inch cubes fresh pineapple; lime wedges; mango chutney; chopped salted roasted cashews or peanuts; chopped fresh cilantro leaves

▸ Pat chicken dry and sprinkle with ½ teaspoon salt.
▸ Heat oil in a 6- to 8-quart heavy pot over moderately high heat until hot but not smoking, then brown chicken in batches (without crowding), turning over occasionally, 8 to 10 minutes per batch. Transfer to a plate as cooked, reserving fat in pot.
▸ Add onion, ginger, garlic, cinnamon sticks, and bay leaf to fat in pot and cook, stirring occasionally, until onion is browned, about 5 minutes. Add curry powder and flour and cook over moderately high heat, stirring, 1 minute. Stir in sugar (if using), coconut milk, and remaining ½ teaspoon salt and bring to a boil, stirring and scraping up any brown bits from bottom of pot. Return chicken and any juices accumulated on plate to pot, then reduce heat and simmer, covered, stirring occasionally, until chicken is cooked through, about 20 minutes. Discard cinnamon sticks and bay leaf. Season with salt, then transfer to a shallow serving dish.
▸ Serve chicken over rice and topped with remaining accompaniments.

1953 CHICKEN HAWAII

SERVES 4
ACTIVE TIME: 40 MIN   START TO FINISH: 1 HR

For a festive, interactive meal, serve our version of the Aloha State's take on curried chicken. Let your guests customize their plates with a choice of toppings—from toasted coconut to fresh pineapple.

1   (3- to 3½-lb) chicken, cut into 8 serving pieces
1   teaspoon salt
2   tablespoons vegetable oil
1   large onion, chopped (1¼ cups)
3   tablespoons finely chopped peeled fresh ginger
1   tablespoon finely chopped garlic (2 cloves)
2   (3-inch) cinnamon sticks
1   Turkish or ½ California bay leaf
1   tablespoon curry powder (preferably Madras)
2   teaspoons all-purpose flour
2   teaspoons sugar (optional)
1   (13½- to 15-oz) can unsweetened coconut milk
    (not low-fat)

1954 GALETTE DES ROIS

Almond Butter Cake
SERVES 8 TO 10
ACTIVE TIME: 1¼ HR   START TO FINISH: 5¼ HR

You can bake this cake to celebrate Epiphany, as they've done in parts of France since the Middle Ages, and bury a trinket (called a fève, *after the fava bean that was originally used) in its filling. Whoever finds it will be king or queen for the day. Serving a dessert this buttery, flaky, and downright delicious, however, doesn't require a holiday (or a hidden surprise).*

FOR PASTRY
1⅔ cups all-purpose flour
¼   teaspoon salt
1   tablespoon granulated sugar
2   sticks (1 cup) unsalted butter, frozen
½   cup ice water
FOR FILLING
¼   cup pure almond paste (2 oz)
¼   cup granulated sugar
2   tablespoons unsalted butter, softened
1   large egg
¼   teaspoon vanilla
¼   teaspoon almond extract

    2   tablespoons all-purpose flour
    1   whole almond or a dried bean, such as a lima bean

FOR GLAZE
    1   large egg
    1   tablespoon milk
    ½   tablespoon confectioners sugar for dusting

SPECIAL EQUIPMENT: **a pastry or bench scraper; 2 large baking sheets (at least 12 inches wide), not dark metal (or pastry may overbrown)**

MAKE DOUGH (ROUGH PUFF PASTRY):

▸ Sift together flour, salt, and sugar into a chilled large metal bowl. Set a grater over flour mixture and coarsely grate frozen butter into flour, gently lifting flour and tossing to coat butter.

▸ Drizzle ice water evenly over flour mixture and gently stir with a fork until incorporated. Turn out mixture onto a lightly floured surface and divide into 6 portions. With heel of your hand, smear each portion once or twice in a forward motion to help distribute fat. Gather dough together with scraper and form into a 6- to 7-inch square. Wrap in plastic wrap and chill at least 1 hour. (Dough will be lumpy and streaky.)

MAKE FILLING WHILE PASTRY CHILLS:

▸ Purée almond paste, sugar, butter, and a pinch of salt in a food processor until smooth. Add egg, vanilla, and almond extract and purée until incorporated. Add flour and pulse until incorporated. Transfer to a small bowl and chill, covered, to firm at least 1 hour.

ROLL OUT PASTRY:

▸ Roll out dough on a well-floured surface with a floured rolling pin into a 21- by 7-inch rectangle and arrange rectangle with a short side nearest you. Fold into thirds, first the top down and then the bottom up (like a letter), brushing off excess flour, to form a roughly 7-inch square. Rewrap dough and chill 20 minutes.

▸ Arrange square on floured surface so that a side with 3 layers visible is nearest you and roll into a 21- by 7-inch rectangle, rolling lengthwise away from and toward yourself, but not side to side. Fold in thirds, brush off excess flour, and chill 20 minutes. Repeat rolling out, folding in thirds, and chilling 3 more times. After last round of rolling and folding, chill rewrapped dough 1 hour.

ASSEMBLE AND GLAZE GALETTE:

▸ Roll out dough in same manner into a rectangle 24 inches long, then cut in half crosswise. On a floured surface, roll out each piece of pastry into a 12-inch square and transfer to separate baking sheets by rolling pastry around rolling pin, brushing off excess flour, then unrolling onto baking sheets. Chill squares until firm, about 10 minutes in freezer or 30 minutes in refrigerator.

▸ Put an oven rack in lowest position and another in top third of oven and preheat oven to 450°F.

▸ Stir together egg and milk in a small bowl with a fork to make an egg wash.

▸ Using a plate as a guide, cut 1 pastry square on baking sheet into an 11-inch round, reserving excess dough for another use. Using tip of a knife and a smaller plate as a guide, score a 9-inch circle, leaving a 1-inch border all around. (If at any time pastry becomes too soft to work with, chill until firm.) Cut a ½-inch circle in center of round to serve as a steam vent, then score curved lines close together inside 9-inch circle in a pinwheel design and lightly brush pastry all over with egg wash. Chill scored pastry on a baking sheet while preparing remaining pastry.

▸ Cut remaining square into an 11-inch round in same manner. Brush some of egg wash in a 1-inch wide border around edge of round and mound chilled filling in center, spreading to about 1½ inches from edge. Bury almond or bean anywhere in filling. Slide chilled pastry round gently over filling, scored side up, and press edges of rounds together to seal. Cut decorative notches, 1 inch apart, around sealed edge of galette.

▸ Using a fine-mesh sieve, dust top of galette lightly with confectioners sugar.

BAKE GALETTE:

▸ Bake on baking sheet on bottom rack of oven until puffed and golden, 15 to 20 minutes. Transfer galette to upper third of oven and continue baking until very puffed and deep golden brown, 10 to 15 minutes more. Transfer to a rack to cool slightly, 5 to 10 minutes (galette will deflate slightly). Serve warm.

COOKS' NOTES: **Dough can be chilled up to 1 day at any step in the procedure.**

• Filling can be chilled up to 1 day.

• Galette can be assembled, but not baked, 6 hours ahead and chilled, loosely covered. Transfer directly to oven to bake.

1955 STEAK AU POIVRE

SERVES 4
ACTIVE TIME: 35 MIN START TO FINISH: 35 MIN

Although we've run at least a dozen different recipes for steak au poivre since our first one, in 1953, we continue to return to this dish because it's so darn good. Use fine-quality peppercorns, such as Tellicherry or the smoky, meaty Talamanca del Caribe.

- 4 (¾- to 1-inch-thick) boneless beef top-loin (strip) steaks (8 to 10 oz each)
- 1 tablespoon kosher salt
- 2 tablespoons whole black peppercorns
- 1 tablespoon vegetable oil
- ⅓ cup finely chopped shallots
- ½ stick (¼ cup) unsalted butter, cut into 4 pieces
- ½ cup Cognac or other brandy
- ¾ cup heavy cream

▸ Preheat oven to 200°F.
▸ Pat steaks dry and season both sides with kosher salt.
▸ Coarsely crush peppercorns in a sealed plastic bag with a meat pounder or bottom of a heavy skillet, then press pepper evenly onto both sides of steaks.

▸ Heat a 12-inch heavy skillet (preferably cast-iron) over moderately high heat until hot, about 3 minutes, then add oil, swirling skillet, and sauté steaks in 2 batches, turning over once, about 6 minutes per batch for medium-rare.
▸ Transfer steaks as cooked to a heatproof platter and keep warm in oven while making sauce.
▸ Pour off fat from skillet, then add shallots and half of butter (2 tablespoons) to skillet and cook over moderately low heat, stirring and scraping up brown bits, until shallots are well-browned all over, 3 to 5 minutes.
▸ Add Cognac (use caution; it may ignite) and boil, stirring, until liquid is reduced to a glaze, 2 to 3 minutes. Add cream and any meat juices accumulated on platter and boil sauce, stirring occasionally, until reduced by half, 3 to 5 minutes. Add remaining 2 tablespoons butter and cook over low heat, swirling skillet, until butter is incorporated. Serve sauce with steaks.

1956 BUTTERSCOTCH CHIFFON PIE

SERVES 8 TO 10

ACTIVE TIME: 45 MIN   START TO FINISH: 5 HR (INCLUDES COOLING
AND FREEZING)

*The lighter-than-air quality of the creamy filling, along with the
crunch of the pecan topping, make every bite of this pie a treat.*

FOR PASTRY DOUGH

1¼ cups all-purpose flour
¾ stick (6 tablespoons) cold unsalted butter, cut into
    ½-inch cubes
2 tablespoons cold vegetable shortening (preferably
    trans-fat-free)
¼ teaspoon salt
3 to 4 tablespoons ice water

FOR FILLING

3 tablespoons light corn syrup
¾ cup plus 1 tablespoon sugar
¼ cup water
½ stick (¼ cup) unsalted butter
1 teaspoon cider vinegar
1⅓ cups chilled heavy cream
1½ teaspoons vanilla
2 teaspoons unflavored gelatin (from 1 envelope)
3 large egg whites

FOR TOPPING

1 cup chopped pecans (3½ oz)
1 tablespoon unsalted butter
⅛ teaspoon salt

SPECIAL EQUIPMENT: a pastry or bench scraper; pie weights
or raw rice

MAKE DOUGH:

▶ Blend together flour, butter, shortening, and salt in a bowl with
your fingertips or a pastry blender (or pulse in a food processor)
just until mixture resembles coarse meal with some small
(roughly pea-size) butter lumps. Drizzle 3 tablespoons ice
water evenly over mixture and gently stir with a fork (or pulse)
until incorporated.

▶ Squeeze a small handful of dough: If it doesn't hold together,
add more ice water, ½ tablespoon at a time, stirring (or pulsing)
until incorporated, then test again. Do not overwork dough, or
pastry will be tough.

▶ Turn out dough onto a work surface and divide into 4 portions.
With heel of your hand, smear each portion once or twice in a
forward motion to help distribute fat. Gather all dough together
with pastry scraper and press into a ball, then flatten into a

5-inch disk. If dough is sticky, dust lightly with additional flour.
Wrap disk in plastic wrap and chill until firm, at least 1 hour.

▶ Roll out dough into a 13-inch round on a lightly floured surface
with a lightly floured rolling pin. Fit dough into a 9-inch pie plate
and trim, leaving a ½-inch overhang, then fold overhang under
slightly. Crimp edge decoratively. Chill shell until firm, about
30 minutes.

▶ Put oven rack in middle position and preheat oven to 375°F.

▶ Lightly prick shell all over with a fork. Line shell with foil and
fill with pie weights. Bake until pastry is pale golden along rim
and set underneath weights, 15 to 20 minutes. Carefully remove
foil and weights and bake shell until bottom and side are golden,
about 15 minutes more. Cool completely in pie plate on a rack,
about 20 minutes.

MAKE BUTTERSCOTCH FILLING:

▶ Bring corn syrup, ¾ cup sugar, and 2 tablespoons water to a
boil in a 1½- to 2-quart heavy saucepan over moderate heat,
stirring until sugar is dissolved. Boil mixture, without stirring,
swirling pan occasionally, until it melts into a deep golden
caramel, 7 to 9 minutes.

▶ Remove saucepan from heat and add butter, vinegar, and a
pinch of salt, swirling pan until butter is melted. Add ⅓ cup
cream and vanilla and simmer, stirring, 1 minute (sauce will
be golden brown). Cool sauce to warm.

▶ While sauce is cooling, sprinkle gelatin over remaining
2 tablespoons water in a small saucepan and let stand
1 minute to soften, then heat over low heat until dissolved.
Stir into butterscotch sauce and cool to room temperature.

▶ Beat egg whites with a pinch of salt in a large bowl with an
electric mixer until they hold soft peaks, then add remaining
tablespoon sugar and continue to beat until whites just hold stiff
glossy peaks. Fold in butterscotch sauce gently but thoroughly.

▶ Beat remaining cream with cleaned beaters until it just holds
stiff peaks, then fold into butterscotch mixture gently but
thoroughly. Gently pour chiffon into cooled pastry shell, letting
it mound, and chill, uncovered, until set, at least 2 hours.

MAKE TOPPING:

▶ Cook pecans in butter with salt in a small heavy skillet over
moderate heat, stirring frequently, until golden, about
5 minutes. Remove from heat and cool nuts completely.

▶ Let pie stand at room temperature, about 30 minutes.
Just before serving, sprinkle cooled nuts over top of pie.

COOKS' NOTES: The egg whites in this recipe are not cooked,
which may be of concern if salmonella is a problem in your area.

• Chiffon pie, without nut topping, can be made 1 day ahead
and chilled, loosely covered once set. Let pie stand at room
temperature 30 minutes before sprinkling with nuts and serving.

½ cup all-purpose flour

2 large eggs

FOR FRYING

About 4 cups vegetable oil

SPECIAL EQUIPMENT: **a potato ricer; a pastry bag fitted with a ½-inch star tip; a deep-fat thermometer**

MAKE *DUCHESSE* POTATOES:

▸ Peel potatoes and cut into 1-inch pieces. Cover potatoes with cold salted water (see Tips, page 8) by 1 inch in a 2-quart pot, then simmer, uncovered, until tender, about 15 minutes.

▸ Drain potatoes in a colander and return to pot. Dry potatoes by shaking pot over low heat until all moisture is evaporated and a film begins to appear on bottom of pot, about 2 minutes.

▸ Force potatoes through ricer into a bowl. Add butter, whole egg and yolk, salt, and pepper and stir with a wooden spoon until very smooth. Keep potato mixture warm, covered.

MAKE *PÂTE À CHOUX:*

▸ Bring water, butter, salt, pepper, and nutmeg to a boil in a 1-quart heavy saucepan over high heat, then reduce heat to moderate.

▸ Add flour all at once and stir briskly with a wooden spoon until mixture pulls away from side of pan, 1 to 2 minutes. Remove from heat and cool slightly, about 3 minutes. Add eggs 1 at a time, stirring well after each addition. Add potato mixture and stir until combined well. Transfer mixture to pastry bag.

FORM AND FRY POTATOES:

▸ Put oven rack in middle position and preheat oven to 200°F.

▸ Heat 2 inches oil in a 5- to 6-quart heavy pot over moderately high heat until thermometer registers 370°F.

▸ Resting metal tip of pastry bag on edge of pot, pipe 8 (2-inch) lengths of potato mixture directly into oil (use caution when piping into hot oil), using a small knife or kitchen shears to cut off each length of dough at tip of bag. Fry potatoes, turning over once with a slotted spoon, until crisp, golden, and cooked through, 2 to 3 minutes. Transfer to paper towels to drain briefly. Fry remaining potato mixture in batches in same manner.

▸ Transfer potatoes as fried and drained to a metal rack set in a large shallow baking pan in oven to keep them crisp and warm until ready to serve.

COOKS' NOTES: Potato batter can be made, but not formed or fried, 1 day ahead and chilled in pastry bag, with tip covered.

• Potatoes can be fried 2 hours ahead and kept at room temperature, on rack in baking pan and loosely covered with paper towels. Remove paper towels and reheat in a 400°F oven until heated through and slightly crisp, about 5 minutes.

1957 POMMES DE TERRE LORETTE

SERVES 6 TO 8

ACTIVE TIME: 50 MIN START TO FINISH: 1½ HR

These are the most elegant fried potatoes in the world. Don't expect the crunchy snap of a french fry but, instead, a soft, light crispness concealing an ethereally fluffy interior.

FOR *DUCHESSE* POTATOES

1 lb medium boiling potatoes

1 tablespoon unsalted butter

1 whole large egg

1 large egg yolk

1¼ teaspoons salt

⅛ teaspoon black pepper

FOR *PÂTE À CHOUX*

½ cup water

1 tablespoon unsalted butter

½ teaspoon salt

⅛ teaspoon black pepper

⅛ teaspoon freshly grated nutmeg

1958 PALACSINTA

Jam-Filled Crêpes
SERVES 8
ACTIVE TIME: 25 MIN   START TO FINISH: 1 HR 25 MIN (INCLUDES RESTING BATTER)

This Austro-Hungarian dessert strikes just the right balance of lightness and sweetness.

      1   cup plus 2 tablespoons whole milk
      2   large eggs
      1   cup all-purpose flour
      2   tablespoons granulated sugar
      3   tablespoons plus 1 teaspoon unsalted butter, melted
            and cooled slightly
    ¼   teaspoon salt
            About ⅔ cup apricot or strawberry jam (from a
            10- to 12-oz jar)
      1   tablespoon brandy
            Confectioners sugar (preferably vanilla sugar) for
            dusting (see cooks' note)

SPECIAL EQUIPMENT: **a 10-inch nonstick skillet**

▶ Blend milk, eggs, flour, granulated sugar, 2 tablespoons butter, and salt in a blender, scraping down side once or twice, until batter is smooth, about 1 minute. Let batter stand at room temperature 1 hour (this prevents tough crêpes). Stir together jam and brandy in a small bowl.
▶ Preheat oven to 250°F.
▶ Add ½ teaspoon butter to skillet and brush to coat bottom. Heat over moderate heat until hot, about 30 seconds, then pour ¼ cup batter into skillet, tilting to coat bottom evenly. Cook until underside is pale golden, 1½ to 2 minutes, then jerk skillet to loosen crêpe and flip crêpe with a spatula. Cook until underside is pale golden, 30 seconds to 1 minute. Transfer crêpe with spatula to a work surface, turning over so that side cooked first is facedown. Spread crêpe all over with 1 tablespoon jam and roll up jelly-roll style. Transfer to a heatproof platter and keep warm in oven. Make 7 more crêpes in same manner, transferring to oven (rolled crêpes can be arranged side by side or stacked like logs). Dust generously with vanilla sugar.

COOKS' NOTES: To make vanilla sugar, combine 2 cups confectioners sugar with 1 vanilla bean, halved lengthwise and chopped, in an airtight container and let stand, covered, at least 24 hours. Sift to remove vanilla bean before using. Vanilla sugar keeps, in an airtight container at room temperature, indefinitely.

• Crêpes (without jam) can be made 1 day ahead and kept chilled, separated between layers of wax paper, in an airtight container. Reheat crêpes in a 350°F oven in batches on a large baking sheet in middle of oven until hot, about 1 minute, then spread with jam and roll up. Heat all rolled crêpes on baking sheet in oven until hot, 1 to 2 minutes. Dust with vanilla sugar.

1959 BULGARIAN POTATOES

SERVES 10 TO 12
ACTIVE TIME: 10 MIN   START TO FINISH: 1¾ HR

Pouring an egg-and-yogurt mixture over a gratin of potatoes creates a thin layer of tangy custard that just melts into the gratin. Like a much more sumptuous version of the sour-cream-topped baked potato, this dish is a welcome change of pace.

      2   cups 4% cottage cheese (1 lb)
      1   stick (½ cup) unsalted butter, melted and cooled slightly
  1¼   teaspoons salt
    ¾   teaspoon black pepper
      3   lb russet (baking) potatoes (6 medium)
      2   large eggs
      1   cup plain whole-milk yogurt (8 oz)

SPECIAL EQUIPMENT: **an adjustable-blade slicer; a 2½-qt baking dish (about 12 by 10 by 2 inches)**

▶ Put oven rack in middle position and preheat oven to 375°F. Butter baking dish.
▶ Purée cottage cheese in a food processor until as smooth as possible, about 1 minute, then add butter, 1 teaspoon salt, and ½ teaspoon pepper and blend until combined well. Peel potatoes and cut crosswise using slicer into ⅛-inch-thick slices. Spread one third of potatoes evenly in 1 layer in dish and top with one third (a scant cup) cottage cheese mixture (mixture will not cover potatoes completely). Continue layering potatoes and cottage cheese mixture, ending with mixture. Cover tightly with foil and bake until potatoes are tender, 1 to 1¼ hours.
▶ Whisk together eggs, yogurt, remaining ¼ teaspoon salt, and remaining ¼ teaspoon pepper in a bowl. Pour egg mixture evenly over potatoes and bake, uncovered, until custard is set, about 20 minutes.

COOKS' NOTE: Potatoes with custard can be baked 1 day ahead and cooled completely, then chilled, covered with foil. Reheat, covered, in a 375°F oven until hot, about 30 minutes.

1960 BOBOTIE

South African Curried Lamb Meatloaf
SERVES 6
ACTIVE TIME: 30 MIN   START TO FINISH: 1¼ HR

Curried lamb spiked with raisins and apples and framed by a smooth egg custard is our idea of how meatloaf would be if we had to reinvent it. Although tasty on its own, bobotie is ideal when served with a dollop of chutney—mango for a sweet touch or cilantro for an herby, savory note.

  1 cup coarse fresh bread crumbs (from 2 slices firm white sandwich bread)
1½ cups whole milk
  2 medium onions, finely chopped (2 cups)
  1 Granny Smith apple, peeled, cored, and finely chopped (1½ cups)
1¾ teaspoons salt
  3 tablespoons unsalted butter
⅓ cup raisins (1½ oz)
¼ cup slivered blanched almonds (1 oz)
  2 tablespoons curry powder (preferably Madras)
  1 teaspoon sugar
  3 large eggs
  2 lb ground lamb or beef (not lean)
  2 tablespoons fresh lemon juice
½ teaspoon finely grated fresh lemon zest
¼ teaspoon black pepper

SPECIAL EQUIPMENT: **a 9- by 9- by 2-inch baking dish (3-qt capacity)**
ACCOMPANIMENT: **cooked white rice; mango or cilantro chutney (preferably Swad brand; see Sources)**

▶ Soak bread crumbs in milk in a small bowl until very soft, about 15 minutes, then drain in a sieve set over a bowl, lightly pressing to remove excess milk. Reserve milk.
▶ Put oven rack in middle position and preheat oven to 350°F. Butter baking dish.
▶ Cook onions, apple, and ¼ teaspoon salt in butter in a 12-inch heavy skillet over moderately low heat, stirring occasionally, until onions and apple are softened, about 12 minutes (do not brown). Add raisins, almonds, curry powder, and sugar and cook, stirring, 1 minute, then remove from heat. Lightly beat 1 egg in a large bowl, then add bread crumbs, lamb or beef, raisin mixture, lemon juice and zest, 1¼ teaspoons salt, and pepper and blend with your hands until combined well; do not overmix. Spread meat mixture evenly in baking dish and bake 30 minutes.
▶ While meatloaf bakes, whisk together remaining 2 eggs, reserved milk, and remaining ¼ teaspoon salt.

▶ Pour off excess fat from meatloaf (still in baking dish). Pour egg mixture over meatloaf (much of egg will fill space that has formed around meatloaf), then return to oven and bake until custard is just set, about 15 minutes more.

1961 VEAL CORDON BLEU

SERVES 4
ACTIVE TIME: 25 MIN   START TO FINISH: 2 HR (INCLUDES RESTING MEAT)

Making the veal and the layers of cheese and ham very thin results in a truly refined version of this classic dish.

  8 (⅛-inch-thick) veal cutlets (also called scaloppine; all the same size, about 2½ oz each)
  1 (½-lb) piece Gruyère
  4 (⅛-inch-thick) slices baked ham such as Virginia
  1 cup plain dry bread crumbs
  2 teaspoons salt
¾ teaspoon black pepper
¾ cup all-purpose flour
  2 large eggs
  2 tablespoons unsalted butter
  2 tablespoons olive oil

SPECIAL EQUIPMENT: **a meat pounder; a cheese plane**
GARNISH: **lemon wedges; fresh parsley sprigs**

▶ If cutlets are thicker than ⅛ inch, pound them between sheets of plastic wrap with flat side of meat pounder. Using cheese plane, shave enough cheese to make a double layer for each of 4 cutlets.
▶ Pat dry 2 cutlets of the same shape and arrange 1 cutlet on a work surface. Put 1 slice of ham on cutlet, trimming ham to leave a ¼-inch border of veal around the ham, then arrange a double layer of cheese on ham and top with second cutlet. Lightly pound ¼-inch border around cutlets' outer edges to seal veal sandwich. Make 3 more sandwiches in same manner.
▶ Line a baking sheet with wax paper. Stir together bread crumbs, 1 teaspoon salt, and ¼ teaspoon pepper in a large shallow baking dish. Stir together flour, ¾ teaspoon salt, and ¼ teaspoon pepper in another large baking dish. Whisk together eggs, remaining ¼ teaspoon salt, and remaining ¼ teaspoon pepper in a third large baking dish.
▶ Dredge 1 veal sandwich in flour, knocking off excess, then dip in egg to coat, letting excess drip off, and dredge in bread crumbs, patting to help them adhere. Transfer coated sandwich to a rack set on a baking sheet. Dredge and coat remaining sandwiches in same manner. Chill, uncovered, 1 hour, and let stand at room temperature 30 minutes before cooking.

▶ Heat 1 tablespoon butter and 1 tablespoon oil in a 12-inch heavy skillet over moderately high heat until foam subsides. Add 2 veal sandwiches, then reduce heat to moderate and cook, turning over once, until golden, about 4 minutes total. Transfer to plates and wipe out skillet with paper towels. Cook remaining sandwiches in remaining butter and oil in same manner.

COOKS' NOTE: Chilling coated cutlets helps the coating to adhere when cooking.

1962 RICE PUDDING '21'

SERVES 8
ACTIVE TIME: 25 MIN START TO FINISH: 1¾ HR (INCLUDES COOLING)

If you love rice pudding, you'll swoon over this unusual version from the '21' Club in New York City. Whipped heavy cream lends body and creates a browned top that suggests toasted marshmallow.

  ½ cup plus 2 tablespoons (5 oz) sushi rice (see Sources)
  1 qt whole milk
  ⅛ teaspoon salt
  ½ cup sugar
  1 teaspoon vanilla
  ⅔ cup chilled heavy cream

SPECIAL EQUIPMENT: an 11- by 8- by 2-inch flameproof gratin dish (2-qt capacity)

▶ Rinse rice in a fine-mesh sieve and drain well. Bring milk and salt just to a simmer in a 3-quart heavy saucepan over moderately high heat, stirring occasionally. Stir in rice, then reduce heat to very low and cook, covered, stirring occasionally, until rice is very soft and creamy, 45 to 50 minutes. Pour rice into a large bowl, then stir in sugar until dissolved. Cool to room temperature, stirring occasionally to prevent a skin from forming on top, about 1 hour. Stir in vanilla.
▶ Preheat broiler.
▶ Beat cream with an electric mixer until it holds soft peaks, then fold half of cream into pudding. Pour pudding into gratin dish, smoothing top. Spread remaining cream evenly over pudding and broil 1 to 2 inches from heat until top is browned, about 1 minute. Serve immediately.

COOKS' NOTE: Rice pudding can also be portioned into 8 (8-ounce capacity) flameproof dishes.

1963 SPINACH WITH SESAME SHOYU DRESSING

SERVES 6 (FIRST COURSE)
ACTIVE TIME: 30 MIN   START TO FINISH: 30 MIN

With their light, tangy sesame dressing, these delicious little spinach cakes needn't only accompany a Japanese meal. They also make a delightful prelude to a hearty entrée like steak or chops.

  2 lb baby spinach
  2 tablespoons sesame seeds, lightly toasted (see Tips, page 8) and cooled
  ¼ cup peanut oil
  1½ tablespoons rice vinegar (not seasoned)
  2 tablespoons mirin (Japanese sweet rice wine)
  2 teaspoons shoyu (Japanese all-purpose soy sauce)
  ½ teaspoon Asian sesame oil
  ⅛ teaspoon salt

▶ Rinse spinach and drain lightly. With water still clinging to leaves, cook in 3 batches in an 8-quart pot over moderately high heat, covered, turning occasionally with tongs, until wilted and bright green, 2 to 3 minutes per batch. Transfer as cooked to a colander, then rinse under cold water until cool and drain well. Squeeze small handfuls of spinach to remove as much moisture as possible, then in 3 batches wrap spinach in several layers of paper towels and squeeze to remove even more moisture. Coarsely chop spinach.
▶ On a 16-inch sheet of plastic wrap, form half of spinach into a 13½- by 1 ½-inch log. Repeat with remaining spinach on another sheet of plastic wrap. Use plastic wrap and your hands to roll, compact, and smooth sides of logs. Remove and discard plastic wrap. With a sharp knife, cut each spinach log crosswise into 9 (1½-inch) pieces (18 total), then arrange, cut sides up, on a platter, reshaping and smoothing mounds with your fingers.
▶ Finely grind 2 teaspoons sesame seeds in a blender, then add peanut oil, vinegar, mirin, shoyu, sesame oil, and salt and blend until combined well. Spoon 1 teaspoon dressing over each spinach mound, stirring dressing occasionally (it will separate as it stands), and sprinkle mounds with remaining 4 teaspoons sesame seeds.

COOKS' NOTES: Spinach can be cooked 1 day ahead, then cooled, drained, and kept in a bowl, covered and chilled. Bring to room temperature before proceeding, about 1 hour.
• Shoyu dressing can be made 1 day ahead and chilled, covered. Bring to room temperature, about 1 hour, and whisk to combine before using.

1964 DRUNKARD'S SOUP WITH EGG BARLEY

SERVES 6 TO 8

ACTIVE TIME: 30 MIN   START TO FINISH: 1½ HR

Rich with sausage, bacon, and egg barley, this restorative Hungarian soup comes from Eugene Lux's article "Memories of a Magyar." You can find egg barley in the pasta aisle or kosher foods section of many supermarkets.

      3 bacon slices
    ¾ cup (5½ oz) barley-shaped egg noodles (also called
            egg barley)
      1 medium onion, chopped
      1 tablespoon all-purpose flour
  1½ teaspoons sweet Hungarian paprika
      4 cups canned beef broth (32 fl oz)
      4 cups water
      1 lb packaged sauerkraut, rinsed, drained, and finely chopped
      1 teaspoon salt
    ½ Turkish or ¼ California bay leaf
    ½ lb kielbasa (Polish smoked sausage), cut into ½-inch pieces

ACCOMPANIMENTS: **sour cream; chopped fresh dill**

▸ Cook bacon slices in a 5- to 6-quart heavy pot over moderate heat, stirring occasionally, until crisp. Transfer bacon to paper towels to drain, then pour off all but 2 tablespoons fat from pot. Crumble bacon.
▸ Add egg noodles to pot and cook, stirring frequently, until they begin to turn golden, 1 to 3 minutes. Add onion and cook, stirring frequently, until egg noodles are golden and onion is softened, 3 to 4 minutes. Stir in flour and paprika and cook, stirring, 1 minute, then add 1 cup broth in a stream, stirring. Bring to a boil, stirring.
▸ Add water, sauerkraut, crumbled bacon, salt, bay leaf, and remaining 3 cups broth and return to a boil, then simmer, covered, 1½ hours. Stir in kielbasa and simmer just until heated through, about 1 minute. Discard bay leaf before serving.

1965 BAKED INDIAN PUDDING

SERVES 8 TO 10

ACTIVE TIME: 10 MIN   START TO FINISH: 1½ HR

At the famous Boston restaurant Durgin-Park, solid New England fare such as this has been served up in brusque Yankee style since before any of us were born. The earthy molasses and down-home corn flavor of this warm dessert is enhanced by a scoop of vanilla ice cream.

    ½ stick (¼ cup) unsalted butter plus additional
            for greasing
      6 cups whole milk
      1 cup yellow cornmeal (preferably stone-ground)
    ½ cup robust molasses (not blackstrap)
    ⅓ cup packed dark brown sugar
    ½ teaspoon salt
      2 large eggs
    ¼ teaspoon baking soda

ACCOMPANIMENT: **vanilla ice cream**

▸ Put oven rack in middle position and preheat oven to 350°F. Butter a shallow 11- by 7-inch (2½-quart) baking or gratin dish.
▸ Bring 3 cups milk to a boil with cornmeal, molasses, brown sugar, salt, and butter in a 4- to 5-quart heavy pot over moderate heat, whisking constantly. Remove from heat and whisk in remaining 3 cups milk.
▸ Beat eggs with baking soda in a small bowl until combined, then whisk into cornmeal mixture.
▸ Pour batter into buttered dish and bake until puffed but still wobbly in center, 45 to 60 minutes. (Pudding will sink slightly and set as it cools.) Cool to warm on a rack.

1966 EGGPLANT KUKU

SERVES 4 TO 6 (MAIN COURSE OR SIDE DISH)

ACTIVE TIME: 10 MIN   START TO FINISH: 1½ HR

Persian in origin, this wonderfully airy soufflé is like a warm, puffy baba ghanouj.

- 1 (1½- to 1¾-lb) eggplant, halved lengthwise
  Olive oil for greasing
- 6 large eggs, separated
- ½ oz Parmigiano-Reggiano, finely grated with a rasp (½ cup)
- 1 garlic clove, minced
- 2½ tablespoons fresh lemon juice
- ¼ teaspoon black pepper
- 1 teaspoon salt
- 2 tablespoons unsalted butter, melted

ACCOMPANIMENTS: **whole-milk yogurt; chopped fresh mint**

▶ Put oven rack in middle position and preheat oven to 350°F.

▶ Bake eggplant, cut sides down, in an oiled shallow baking pan until very tender, about 30 minutes. When cool enough to handle, scrape flesh into a food processor, discarding skin, and purée until smooth. Add egg yolks, cheese, garlic, lemon juice, pepper, and ¾ teaspoon salt and pulse until blended. Transfer to a bowl.

▶ Pour melted butter into a 6-cup (1½-quart) gratin dish or a 9½-inch deep-dish pie plate and tilt to coat bottom. Beat egg whites with remaining ¼ teaspoon salt using an electric mixer at medium speed until they just hold stiff peaks. Fold one third of whites into eggplant mixture to lighten, then fold in remaining whites gently but thoroughly. Spoon into gratin dish. Bake until golden and puffed, 25 to 30 minutes.

1967 BOUILLABAISSE OF PEAS

SERVES 6

ACTIVE TIME: 20 MIN   START TO FINISH: 55 MIN

Originally introduced in our pages as "an ancient Provençal way of dressing up little green peas," this soup may not qualify as a true bouillabaisse (there is no seafood in sight), but it is comfort in a bowl. And since it uses frozen rather than fresh peas, it can be made at any time of year.

FOR BOUQUET GARNI

- 1 (4-inch) piece celery
- 1 Turkish or ½ California bay leaf
- 3 fresh thyme sprigs
- 2 fresh parsley sprigs
- 8 black peppercorns
- ¼ teaspoon slightly crushed fennel seeds

FOR SOUP

- 1 qt water
- 5 tablespoons extra-virgin olive oil
- 6 (1-inch-thick) slices baguette
- 1 medium onion, finely chopped
- 1 lb medium boiling potatoes
- 4 garlic cloves, minced
- 1 (10-oz) package frozen baby peas (not thawed)
- 1½ teaspoons salt
- ½ teaspoon black pepper
- 6 large eggs

SPECIAL EQUIPMENT: **an 8-inch square of cheesecloth; kitchen string**

MAKE BOUQUET GARNI:

▶ Wrap bouquet garni ingredients in cheesecloth and tie with kitchen string.

MAKE SOUP:

▶ Bring water and bouquet garni to a boil in a 1½-quart heavy saucepan.

▶ Meanwhile, heat 2 tablespoons oil in a 12-inch heavy skillet over moderate heat until hot but not smoking and cook bread slices, turning over once, until golden, 3 to 5 minutes. Transfer bread to 6 soup bowls. Add remaining 3 tablespoons oil to skillet and cook onion over moderate heat, stirring frequently, until softened, 4 to 5 minutes. Peel potatoes, then cut crosswise into ⅓-inch-thick slices. Add potatoes to onion and cook, turning occasionally, until onion is translucent, 3 to 4 minutes. Add garlic, peas, salt, pepper, and hot water with bouquet garni and simmer, covered, until potatoes are tender, about 7 minutes. Discard bouquet garni.

▶ Break eggs into simmering soup and poach, uncovered, spooning broth over eggs occasionally, until softly set, about 6 minutes. Transfer eggs with a slotted spoon to toasts and divide soup among soup bowls.

COOKS' NOTE: Egg yolks will not be fully cooked, which may be of concern if there is a problem with salmonella in your area.

OPPOSITE: 1967 bouillabaisse of peas

1968 **LADY CURZON SOUP**

SERVES 8 TO 10 (HORS D'OEUVRE)
ACTIVE TIME: 15 MIN START TO FINISH: 20 MIN

Introduced to England at the beginning of the 20th century by the wife of the British viceroy of India, this soup, enhanced with cream and a touch of curry, was soon turning up in dining rooms across Europe.

FOR BROTH
- 2 lb mussels (preferably cultivated), scrubbed and beards removed
- 1½ cups water
- 1 large onion, chopped
- 1 garlic clove, smashed
- 2 Turkish bay leaves or 1 California

FOR SOUP
- 1½ tablespoons unsalted butter
- ½ teaspoon Madras curry powder
- 1 tablespoon Sercial Madeira
- ½ cup heavy cream
- 1 large egg yolk

SPECIAL EQUIPMENT: **an instant-read thermometer; 8 to 10 (1-oz) shot glasses or demitasse or espresso cups**

MAKE BROTH:
▶ Cook all broth ingredients, covered, in a 4- to 5-quart heavy pot over moderately high heat until mussels just open wide, 4 to 6 minutes. Transfer mussels with a slotted spoon to a bowl and reserve for another use. (Discard any unopened mussels.) Pour broth through a coffee-filter-lined sieve into a bowl, discarding solids. Strain broth again through same lined sieve into a 2-cup glass measure and reserve 1 cup for soup. (Freeze remainder if desired.)

MAKE SOUP:
▶ Heat butter in a 1-quart heavy saucepan over moderately low heat until foam subsides. Add curry powder and cook, stirring constantly, until just a shade darker, about 1 minute. Add Madeira and bring to a boil. Add mussel broth and bring to a boil. Whisk together cream and yolk in a bowl, then add broth mixture in a slow stream, whisking constantly. Return soup to saucepan and cook over moderately low heat, stirring, until just slightly thickened and registers 170°F on thermometer, about 2 minutes. (Do not simmer.) Divide among glasses.

COOKS' NOTE: Soup can be made 1 day ahead and cooled, uncovered, then chilled, covered. Carefully reheat (do not let simmer) before serving.

1969 MEN'S FAVORITE SALAD

SERVES 8 TO 10
ACTIVE TIME: 20 MIN   START TO FINISH: 35 MIN

Barbara Edwards, the reader who sent us this recipe, wrote that every time she served this salad, the men in the group would "lick the platter clean." The creaminess and tang of cottage cheese and mayonnaise offset the edge of onion and the crispness of cabbage.

- 1 (2½-lb) green cabbage, outer leaves discarded
- 1 medium onion, halved lengthwise, then thinly sliced crosswise
- 2 tablespoons chopped fresh flat-leaf parsley
- 2 cups 4% cottage cheese (preferably small-curd; 16 oz)
- ½ cup plus 2 tablespoons mayonnaise
- 1 teaspoon fresh lemon juice, or to taste
- 1 teaspoon salt
- ½ teaspoon black pepper

▶ Cut cabbage into 2-inch wedges and core, then very thinly slice crosswise. Transfer to a large bowl. Add remaining ingredients and toss to coat. Let stand 15 minutes (or chill up to 2 hours) to allow flavors to meld.

1970 MACCHERONI QUATTRO FORMAGGI VILLA D'ESTE

Macaroni with Four Cheeses
SERVES 8 TO 10 (FIRST COURSE) OR 6 (MAIN COURSE)
ACTIVE TIME: 30 MIN   START TO FINISH: 30 MIN

This very grown-up pasta dish, adapted from a story about the historic hotel Villa d'Este, on Italy's Lake Como, is seriously cheesy. However, the bacon, herbs, and touch of tomato sauce add refinement and complexity as well.

- 6 bacon slices (6 oz), diced
- 1½ lb dried elbow macaroni
- 6 oz Italian Fontina, cut into ⅓-inch dice (1 cup)
- 6 oz Bel Paese cheese, cut into ⅓-inch dice (1 cup)
- 6 oz Gruyère, cut into ⅓-inch dice (1 cup)
- 3 tablespoons tomato sauce
- ¼ cup heavy cream plus additional if necessary to thin sauce
- ½ teaspoon minced fresh rosemary
- ½ teaspoon minced fresh sage
- ½ teaspoon minced fresh oregano
- 1 large egg yolk
- 2 oz finely grated Parmigiano-Reggiano (1 cup; see Tips, page 8)

▶ Cook bacon in a 10-inch heavy skillet over moderate heat, stirring frequently, until browned and crisp, about 5 minutes. Transfer with a slotted spoon to paper towels to drain.
▶ Cook macaroni in an 8-quart pot of boiling salted water (see Tips, page 8) until al dente, then drain pasta in a colander.
▶ While pasta cooks, heat first three cheeses with tomato sauce, cream (¼ cup), and herbs in a 5- to 6-quart heavy pot over moderately low heat, stirring, until melted and smooth. Put egg yolk in a cup and stir in ½ cup sauce (to temper), then whisk into remaining sauce in pot.
▶ Remove from heat and add macaroni, bacon, and parmesan to sauce, tossing to combine well. Season with salt and pepper and stir in more cream to thin sauce if necessary.

COOKS' NOTE: The egg yolk in this recipe may not be fully cooked, which could be of concern if salmonella is a problem in your area.

OPPOSITE: 1970 maccheroni quattro formaggi Villa d'Este

1971 **TURKEY MOLE**

Mole Poblano de Guajolote

SERVES 10 TO 12

ACTIVE TIME: 1¾ HR   START TO FINISH: 3½ HR

Today, everyone recognizes that Mexican cuisine can be sophisticated; mole poblano de guajolote was the dish that first opened many Americans' eyes to that fact. A magical alchemy occurs when chocolate's deep flavors meld with chiles and nuts. This recipe was adapted from Elisabeth Lambert Ortiz. For help in finding the chiles, see Sources.

1	(10- to 12-lb) turkey, cut into 10 to 12 serving pieces
3	tablespoons plus ½ teaspoon salt
6	tablespoons pork lard or vegetable oil
12	to 18 cups cold water
6	dried ancho chiles (4 by 2½ inches; 3 oz total)
4	dried *mulato* chiles (4 by 2½ inches; 2 oz total)
4	dried *pasilla* chiles (not *pasilla de Oaxaca*; about 6 by 1½ inches; 1½ oz total)
2	cups boiling water
1	lb tomatoes (3 medium) or 1 (14- to 16-oz) can whole tomatoes in juice
3	cups chopped white onion (1 lb)
1	tablespoon chopped garlic (3 large cloves)
2	(6- to 7-inch) corn tortillas, torn into pieces
1	cup whole blanched almonds (6 oz)
½	cup (3 oz) shelled and skinned peanuts (preferably raw)
½	cup raisins
½	teaspoon coriander seeds
½	teaspoon anise seeds
2	whole cloves
1	(½-inch) cinnamon stick (preferably Mexican *canela*), crumbled
¼	cup sesame seeds, toasted (see Tips, page 8)
1½	oz unsweetened chocolate, chopped
1	tablespoon sugar, or to taste

ACCOMPANIMENT: white rice

COOK TURKEY AND MAKE BROTH:

▶ Pat turkey pieces dry and season with 1½ teaspoons salt. Heat lard in a 12-inch heavy skillet over moderately high heat until hot but not smoking, then cook turkey pieces in 3 or 4 batches until browned on all sides, about 6 minutes per batch. Transfer turkey pieces as browned to a 10-quart pot. Pour lard into a heatproof measuring cup and reserve.

▶ Add enough cold water to just cover turkey (12 to 18 cups) and 2 tablespoons salt. Bring to a boil, skimming any foam, then simmer, uncovered, until turkey is tender and cooked through, 1 to 1½ hours. Transfer turkey pieces to a bowl and broth to another bowl. Skim fat from surface of broth.

PREPARE CHILES AND TOMATOES WHILE BROTH SIMMERS:

▶ Discard stems, seeds, and ribs from chiles (see Tips, page 8) and tear chiles into pieces. Soak chiles in 2 cups boiling water in a large bowl, keeping submerged with a sieve or plate, 30 minutes.

▶ Cut an X in the end opposite stem of each fresh tomato, if using, and immerse in a 2- to 3-quart pot of boiling water 10 seconds, then transfer to a bowl of ice and cold water to stop cooking. Peel and seed fresh tomatoes when cool, then coarsely chop.

MAKE *MOLE*:

▶ Purée chiles with soaking liquid, onions, garlic, tomatoes (including juice if canned), tortillas, and 2 cups turkey broth in a blender (use caution when blending hot liquids) in 2 to 3 batches until smooth, about 2 minutes per batch, and transfer to a large bowl.

▶ Grind almonds, peanuts, raisins, coriander, anise seeds, cloves, cinnamon, and 2 tablespoons sesame seeds in a food processor until finely ground, about 2 minutes. Add ¼ cup turkey broth and process until mixture forms a paste, about 2 minutes more. Stir paste into chile purée.

▶ Heat ¼ cup reserved lard in a wide 8- to 9-quart heavy pot over moderate heat until hot but not smoking, then carefully add chile-nut mixture (use caution; mixture will spatter) and bring to a boil over high heat, stirring with a long-handled wooden spoon. Reduce heat to moderate and cook, stirring, until thickened (and to help flavors develop), 8 to 10 minutes. Stir in chocolate and enough turkey broth (about 4 cups) to thin *mole* to consistency of heavy cream, and bring to a simmer, stirring until chocolate is melted. Stir in sugar and remaining 2 teaspoons salt and simmer, partially covered (leave only a small gap), stirring occasionally, 30 minutes. Add turkey pieces to *mole* and simmer, covered, stirring occasionally, until heated through, 15 to 20 minutes. Season with salt and sugar and add more turkey broth as necessary (sauce should be thick enough to coat turkey, but not gloppy; sauce will continue to thicken as it stands). Serve sprinkled with remaining 2 tablespoons sesame seeds.

COOKS' NOTES: Turkey and broth can be cooked 1 day ahead. Cool turkey completely in broth, uncovered, then chill in broth, covered. Discard solidified fat.

• *Mole*, without turkey, can be prepared 1 day ahead. Cool completely, uncovered, then chill, covered. Chill turkey in remaining broth. Add turkey to *mole* and gently reheat in heavy pot over low heat, stirring frequently to prevent scorching. Add more broth to thin if necessary.

1972 STUBENKÜKEN ANGOSTURA
Squab with Bitters
SERVES 6
ACTIVE TIME: 1¾ HR   START TO FINISH: 2½ HR

Bitters, the magic ingredient in so many cocktails, adds a complexity to the stuffing of this dish, adapted from Hotel Vier Jahreszeiten of Hamburg, Germany. Squab is a dark meat best served when still pink, since well-done squab tends to be tough.

  6 (1-lb) squabs with their livers, if included
  3 tablespoons vegetable oil
1¼ sticks (½ cup plus 2 tablespoons) unsalted butter, cut into tablespoon pieces
  1 small onion, halved lengthwise then sliced
  1 Turkish or ½ California bay leaf
  3 sprigs fresh thyme
  3 sprigs fresh flat-leaf parsley plus 2 tablespoons finely chopped
  1 (3-inch) piece celery
  1 cup dry white wine
1¾ cups reduced-sodium chicken broth (14 fl oz)
2¼ cups water
  3 cups coarse fresh bread crumbs (from ½ baguette, including crust)
  3 chicken livers (6 if there are no squab livers), trimmed and rinsed
½ cup finely chopped shallots
  2 teaspoons salt
  1 teaspoon black pepper
¼ cup heavy cream
  1 teaspoon Angostura bitters
  1 teaspoon cornstarch
  1 teaspoon brandy

SPECIAL EQUIPMENT: 6 (28-inch-long) pieces of kitchen string plus additional for bouquet garni; an instant-read thermometer

MAKE STOCK:
▶ Rinse squabs, trimming and rinsing livers and other giblets if inside. Cut off necks and last joint of wings and reserve for stock. Chill squabs and any livers and giblets.
▶ Pat necks and wing tips dry. Heat 1 tablespoon oil and 1 tablespoon butter in a 12-inch heavy skillet over moderately high heat until foam subsides, then sauté necks, wing tips, and onion, stirring frequently, until well browned, 6 to 8 minutes. Tie bay leaf and herb sprigs to celery with kitchen string to make a bouquet garni. Add wine to onion mixture and boil to deglaze, scraping up brown bits, until wine is reduced to about ¼ cup,

about 10 minutes. Transfer mixture to a 3-quart pot, then add broth, water, any giblets (except livers), and bouquet garni and simmer, uncovered, 1 hour. Pour stock through a fine-mesh sieve into a heatproof 1-quart measure, pressing on and then discarding solids. Let stand until fat rises to top, 1 to 2 minutes, then skim fat. Transfer stock to a 2-quart heavy saucepan and boil until reduced to 1 cup.

MAKE STUFFING AND BROWN SQUABS WHILE STOCK SIMMERS:
▶ Put oven rack in middle position and preheat oven to 400°F.
▶ Melt 3 tablespoons butter in cleaned skillet over moderate heat, then remove from heat and add bread crumbs, tossing to coat. Transfer crumbs to a shallow baking pan (reserve skillet) and bake until dry and pale golden, about 5 minutes. Transfer pan to a rack and cool crumbs completely. Leave oven on.
▶ Coarsely chop chilled squab livers and chicken livers.
▶ Add 3 tablespoons butter to skillet and cook shallots over moderately low heat, stirring, until softened, about 3 minutes. Add livers and increase heat to moderately high, then cook until livers are no longer pink on the outside, about 3 minutes. Stir in 1 teaspoon salt and ½ teaspoon pepper and remove from heat.
▶ Stir together cream and bitters in a large bowl, then stir in liver mixture and cool to room temperature, about 10 minutes. Stir in bread crumbs and chopped parsley.
▶ Pat squabs dry and fill each cavity with stuffing. Truss each squab with kitchen string. Season 3 squabs with a total of ½ teaspoon salt and ¼ teaspoon pepper.
▶ Heat 1 tablespoon oil and ½ tablespoon butter in cleaned skillet over moderately high heat until foam subsides, then brown seasoned squabs on all sides, about 8 minutes total, transferring with tongs to a large shallow baking pan. Clean skillet, then season and brown remaining 3 squabs in ½ tablespoon butter and remaining tablespoon oil in same manner and transfer to baking pan.

ROAST SQUABS:
▶ Roast squabs until thermometer inserted diagonally into thickest part of breast (without touching bone) registers 140°F (meat will be pink), 25 to 30 minutes. Spoon juices over squabs and let squabs stand in pan on a rack 5 minutes (temperature will rise to 145 to 150°F). Cut off and discard strings.
▶ Bring reduced stock to a boil in saucepan over moderate heat. Stir together cornstarch and brandy in a cup, then whisk mixture into stock and boil 1 minute. Season sauce with salt and pepper and remove from heat. Add remaining 2 tablespoons butter, swirling pan until butter is completely incorporated. Serve squabs with sauce.

COOKS' NOTE: Stock can be made 1 day ahead and cooled completely, uncovered, then chilled, covered. Fat will be easier to remove once stock is cold.

1973 SWEETBREADS MEUNIÈRE

SERVES 8 (FIRST COURSE) OR 4 (MAIN COURSE)
ACTIVE TIME: 1¾ HR   START TO FINISH: 3¾ HR

The Sherry in this preparation, adapted from The Compound in Santa Fe, enhances sweetbreads' nutty flavor.

  2 lb veal sweetbreads
1¼ sticks (½ cup plus 2 tablespoons) unsalted butter, cut into tablespoon pieces
  2 qt water
  1 medium onion, sliced
  1 Turkish or ½ California bay leaf
  1 whole clove
  1 tablespoon plus ¾ teaspoon salt
  ½ lb fresh chanterelle or cremini mushrooms, trimmed
  ¾ teaspoon black pepper
  ⅓ cup finely chopped shallots (about 2 medium)
  ⅓ cup dry Sherry, or to taste
  2 tablespoons fresh lemon juice, or to taste
  ¼ cup chopped fresh flat-leaf parsley

SOAK SWEETBREADS:
▶ Rinse sweetbreads under cold running water, then soak in a

large bowl of ice and cold water in the refrigerator, changing water once or twice if water becomes pink, at least 2 hours, then drain sweetbreads.

MAKE BROWN BUTTER:
▶ Melt 1 stick (½ cup) butter in a 2-cup to 1-quart heavy saucepan over moderate heat, then cook, stirring occasionally, until butter turns golden with a nutlike fragrance and flecks on bottom of pan turn a rich caramel brown, 10 to 20 minutes. (Butter will initially foam, then subside. A thicker foam will appear and cover the surface just before butter begins to brown; stir more frequently toward end of cooking.) Pour through a fine-mesh sieve into a heatproof measuring cup (you will have 5 to 6 tablespoons brown butter).

COOK SWEETBREADS AND MUSHROOMS:
▶ Bring water to a simmer in a 3- to 4-quart saucepan with onion, bay leaf, clove, and 1 tablespoon salt. Add sweetbreads and poach, uncovered, at a bare simmer 20 minutes.
▶ Transfer sweetbreads with a slotted spoon to a bowl of cold water to stop cooking. Pour 1 cup poaching liquid through a sieve into a small bowl and reserve for sauce, discarding remaining poaching liquid and solids.
▶ Drain sweetbreads and pat dry. Using a paring knife, cut away any fat and pull away as much membrane and connective tissue as possible, separating sweetbreads into roughly 2-inch pieces.

Arrange sweetbreads on a tray lined with paper towels to keep dry, blotting tops with more paper towels.

▶ Tear any large chanterelles lengthwise into 2 or 4 pieces, or quarter creminis (into ¾-inch wedges).

▶ Put oven rack in middle position and preheat oven to lowest temperature (175 to 200°F).

▶ Heat a 12-inch heavy skillet over high heat until a bead of water dropped onto cooking surface evaporates immediately, 2 to 3 minutes.

▶ Meanwhile, season half of sweetbreads on both sides with ¼ teaspoon salt and ¼ teaspoon pepper.

▶ Add 2 tablespoons brown butter to skillet, swirling to cover bottom (butter will smoke), then add seasoned sweetbreads without crowding. Reduce heat to moderately high, then cook, undisturbed, until undersides are golden brown, 2 to 3 minutes. Turn sweetbreads and cook, undisturbed, until all flat sides are golden brown, 2 to 3 minutes per side. Remove from heat and transfer browned sweetbreads with tongs to a shallow baking pan, arranging them in 1 layer. Keep warm in oven.

▶ Wipe skillet clean and repeat procedure, seasoning remaining sweetbreads and browning them in 2 more tablespoons brown butter. Transfer to baking pan.

▶ Add all remaining brown butter to hot skillet. Add mushrooms and sauté, stirring occasionally, until browned on edges, 3 to 5 minutes. Add shallots and remaining ¼ teaspoon each of salt and pepper and sauté, stirring, 1 minute. Add Sherry, lemon juice, and reserved poaching liquid and boil, scraping up brown bits, until mushrooms are tender and liquid is reduced by half, about 5 minutes. Add parsley and remaining 2 tablespoons butter (not brown butter), then remove from heat and swirl skillet or stir mixture until butter is incorporated into sauce. Serve sweetbreads immediately, topped with mushrooms and sauce.

COOKS' NOTES: Sweetbreads can be soaked up to 1 day.
• Sweetbreads can be poached and trimmed 1 day ahead. Chill cooled sweetbreads, wrapped in plastic wrap, and chill reserved poaching liquid separately.
• Brown butter keeps, covered and chilled, up to 2 weeks.

1974 CHICKEN WITH VINEGAR

SERVES 4

ACTIVE TIME: 1 HR   START TO FINISH: 1½ HR

Nouvelle cuisine, for all its fussiness, did return acidity to the table, exciting the senses with the interplay of sweet and sour.

- 1 (3½- to 4-lb) chicken, cut into 8 serving pieces
- 2 teaspoons salt
- 1 teaspoon black pepper

- 1 tablespoon vegetable oil
- 3 tablespoons unsalted butter
- 4 large garlic cloves, finely chopped
- ⅓ cup finely chopped shallots (about 2 medium)
- 1 medium carrot, finely chopped
- 2 fresh thyme sprigs
- 2 Turkish bay leaves or 1 California
- 1 tablespoon tomato paste
- 1 cup dry red wine
- ½ cup red-wine vinegar
- 2 tablespoons sugar
- 1 cup reduced-sodium chicken broth (8 fl oz)

GARNISH: **fresh thyme sprigs**

COOK CHICKEN:

▶ Put oven rack in middle position and preheat oven to 350°F.

▶ Pat chicken pieces dry and sprinkle with 1 teaspoon salt and ½ teaspoon pepper. Heat oil and 1 tablespoon butter in a 10- to 12-inch heavy skillet over moderately high heat until foam subsides, then brown chicken in 2 batches, turning over once, 8 to 10 minutes per batch. Transfer chicken as browned to a small (13- by 9-inch) flameproof roasting pan, arranging it in 1 layer. Once all chicken is browned, roast, uncovered, in oven 15 minutes.

MAKE SAUCE WHILE CHICKEN ROASTS:

▶ Discard all but 2 tablespoons fat from skillet, then add garlic, shallots, carrot, thyme sprigs (2), and bay leaves and cook over moderately high heat, stirring and scraping up brown bits, until vegetables are browned, 3 to 6 minutes. Add tomato paste and cook, stirring, 1 minute. Add wine, vinegar, sugar, and remaining teaspoon salt and ½ teaspoon pepper and boil, stirring occasionally, until reduced by half, 5 to 10 minutes.

FINISH SAUCE AND CHICKEN:

▶ Add chicken broth to sauce along with any juices from roasting pan and bring to a boil. Pour through a fine-mesh sieve onto chicken in roasting pan, pressing on and then discarding solids. Continue to roast chicken, uncovered, until just cooked through, about 15 minutes more.

▶ Transfer chicken with tongs to an ovenproof serving dish and keep warm, uncovered, in turned-off oven.

▶ Meanwhile, boil sauce in roasting pan over high heat, stirring occasionally, until reduced to a scant cup, then remove sauce from heat and swirl in remaining 2 tablespoons butter. Season with salt and pepper and pour sauce over chicken.

OPPOSITE: 1973 sweetbreads meunière (left); 1974 chicken with vinegar (right)

1975 CHAWAN MUSHI

Japanese Savory Egg Custards
SERVES 6 (FIRST COURSE)
ACTIVE TIME: 20 MIN START TO FINISH: 40 MIN

The best of Japanese cooking combines subtle flavors and textures in a magnificent way. You'll taste mushrooms for the first time in these brilliant custards, adapted from Elizabeth Andoh. Don't be put off by ingredients' exotic-sounding names, as all are available at any Asian market (see Sources).

FOR DASHI (JAPANESE SEA STOCK)
- 3 cups cold water
- 1 (8- by 4-inch) piece *kombu* (dried kelp; 15 g)
- 1 (5-g) package *katsuo bushi* (dried bonito flakes; about ½ cup)

FOR CUSTARDS
- 3 large eggs
- 1¼ teaspoons mirin (Japanese sweet rice wine)
- 1 teaspoon *usukuchi shoyu* (Japanese light soy sauce)
- ½ teaspoon salt
- 3 small fresh shiitake mushrooms, stems discarded
- 6 medium shrimp in shell (31 to 35 per lb), peeled and deveined
- 6 fresh or thawed frozen ginkgo nuts (optional)
- 1 scallion, very thinly sliced diagonally

SPECIAL EQUIPMENT: **6 (4-oz) ramekins; a 2-tiered 10-inch bamboo steamer with lid, soaked in water 10 minutes, or a pasta pot with 2 inserts (deep and shallow)**

MAKE DASHI:
▶Bring cold water and *kombu* just to a boil in a 2-quart saucepan, then remove from heat and discard *kombu*. Sprinkle *katsuo bushi* over liquid in pan and let stand 3 minutes (stir if necessary to make *katsuo bushi* sink). Pour through a sieve lined with a dampened paper towel or coffee filter into a bowl.
MAKE CUSTARDS:
▶Whisk together eggs in a bowl, then whisk in mirin, soy sauce, salt, and 1½ cups dashi. Pour mixture through a fine-mesh sieve into another bowl.
▶Thinly slice mushrooms and divide among ramekins along with shrimp, ginkgo nuts, and scallion. Divide egg mixture among ramekins and cover each ramekin with a piece of foil. Arrange 3 ramekins on rack of each tier of steamer or in pasta-pot inserts (off heat), then stack tiers and cover with lid.
▶Add enough water to a 12-inch skillet (or bottom of pasta pot, if using) to measure 1 inch and bring to a boil over high heat. Set steamer in or above water (water should not touch rack of bottom tier) and steam 2 minutes. Reduce heat to moderate and

continue to steam until custards are just set, 10 to 13 minutes more. Serve immediately.

COOKS' NOTES: Custards can be assembled in ramekins, but not steamed, 2 hours ahead and chilled, covered.

1976 RISOTTO AL GORGONZOLA

SERVES 8 TO 10 (FIRST COURSE OR SIDE DISH)
ACTIVE TIME: 25 MIN START TO FINISH: 35 MIN

Dishes like this lush, creamy risotto helped move Northern Italian food (and the Ristorante Bice empire) from the back to the front burner. Originally a first course, it may be too rich for that role today, but it is a great side dish for beef, grilled chicken, or veal.

- 5 cups chicken stock or reduced-sodium chicken broth (40 fl oz)
- ¾ stick (6 tablespoons) unsalted butter, cut into tablespoon pieces
- 2 tablespoons olive oil
- 2½ cups Arborio rice (14 oz)
- 1⅓ cups heavy cream
- 6 oz Gorgonzola *dolce*, cut into ¼-inch pieces (see Sources)
- ½ teaspoon salt
- ½ teaspoon black pepper
- 1 oz finely grated Parmigiano-Reggiano (½ cup; see Tips, page 8)
- 2 tablespoons chopped fresh flat-leaf parsley

▶Bring stock to a simmer in a 3-quart heavy saucepan, then turn off heat.
▶Meanwhile, heat 2 tablespoons butter and oil in a 4- to 5-quart heavy pot over moderately high heat until foam subsides, then stir in rice and cook, stirring, 3 minutes.
▶Add all of stock to rice at once and cook over moderately high heat, stirring frequently to prevent rice from sticking and to let rice absorb liquid, 12 minutes.
▶Meanwhile, heat cream and Gorgonzola in cleaned 3-quart heavy saucepan over moderately low heat, stirring, until cheese is completely melted, then stir in salt and pepper.
▶Add cream mixture to cooked rice and simmer, stirring, until sauce has been absorbed, rice is very tender, and mixture is thickened, 8 to 10 minutes.
▶Remove from heat and stir rice with a fork, then stir in remaining 4 tablespoons butter and parmesan until incorporated. Serve sprinkled with parsley.

OPPOSITE: 1975 chawan mushi

1977 PASTA CON PESCE

Spaghetti with Seafood

SERVES 4 TO 6

ACTIVE TIME: 30 MIN   START TO FINISH: 40 MIN

Operated by the Bommarito family for three generations, Tony's is a St. Louis legend. One taste of this seafood cornucopia will convince you that the restaurant's reputation is richly deserved.

1½ lb tomatoes
1 cup water
12 small hard-shelled clams (about 2 inches in diameter), scrubbed well
1 lb dried spaghetti
1 stick (½ cup) unsalted butter, cut into tablespoon pieces
1 cup thinly sliced mushrooms (3 oz)
5 garlic cloves, finely chopped
¼ lb medium shrimp in shell (31 to 35 per lb), peeled, deveined, and cut into ½-inch pieces
¼ lb lump crabmeat, picked over
¼ lb cooked lobster meat, picked over
¼ cup chopped fresh parsley

ACCOMPANIMENT: **grated parmesan**

► Cut an X in the end opposite stem of each tomato. Blanch tomatoes in a saucepan of boiling water 10 seconds, then transfer tomatoes with a slotted spoon to a bowl of ice water. Peel and core tomatoes, then finely chop, removing and discarding seeds.

► Bring water (1 cup) to a boil over moderately high heat in a 3- to 4-quart heavy pot, then add clams and cook, covered, stirring occasionally, until clams just open wide, 6 to 10 minutes. (Discard any clams that remain unopened after 10 minutes.) Transfer clams as they open to a cutting board and let stand until cool enough to handle. Remove clams from shells and finely chop, discarding shells.

► Cook pasta in a 6- to 8-quart pot of boiling salted water (see Tips, page 8) until al dente, then reserve ¼ cup pasta cooking water and drain pasta in a colander.

► While pasta cooks, heat 4 tablespoons butter in a 12-inch skillet over moderate heat until foam subsides, then cook mushrooms, stirring, until pale golden, 3 to 5 minutes. Stir in garlic and cook, stirring, until golden, about 2 minutes. Stir in tomatoes and increase heat to moderately high, then cook until most of liquid is evaporated, about 5 minutes. Stir in shrimp and cook, stirring, until just cooked through, about 2 minutes. Stir in remaining 4 tablespoons butter, chopped clams, crab, lobster, parsley, spaghetti, and reserved cooking water and cook until heated through, about 5 minutes. Season with salt and pepper.

1978 SESAME TWISTS

MAKES 16 TWISTS

ACTIVE TIME: 30 MIN   START TO FINISH: 45 MIN

There may be no better way to put a fetching basket of fresh bread on the table. The secret is a biscuit dough so simple to make and handle that you'll find yourself baking these twists for weekday family meals as well as special dinners.

2½ cups all-purpose flour
2 teaspoons baking powder
1 teaspoon salt
½ teaspoon baking soda
¾ stick (6 tablespoons) unsalted butter, melted and cooled
2 large eggs, each in a separate bowl, lightly beaten
1 cup sour cream
¼ cup sesame seeds, toasted (see Tips, page 8)

► Put oven racks in upper and lower thirds of oven and preheat oven to 450°F.

► Whisk together flour, baking powder, salt, and baking soda in a large bowl. Whisk together butter, 1 egg, and sour cream in another bowl, then add to flour mixture and stir with a fork until a dough just begins to form (dough will be very moist).

▶ Turn dough out onto a well-floured surface and knead gently 6 times. Pat out dough on a floured surface with floured hands, reflouring surface if necessary, and form into a 12-inch-long log.
▶ Cut dough into 16 equal pieces. Roll each piece into an 8-inch-long rope using well-floured hands, then fold rope loosely in half and twist it once, holding both ends of twist.
▶ Arrange twists 2 inches apart on 2 ungreased large baking sheets, pressing ends against baking sheet to prevent them from coming apart.
▶ Brush tops of twists with remaining egg and sprinkle generously with sesame seeds. Bake until golden, 12 to 15 minutes. Transfer twists to metal racks and cool completely.

1979 FROZEN LEMON MERINGUE CAKE

SERVES 8
ACTIVE TIME: 1½ HR   START TO FINISH: 8 HR (INCLUDES FREEZING)

Three cheers for any dessert that can be made two days ahead, frozen, and then softened in the fridge while guests and cook alike enjoy dinner.

FOR MERINGUE LAYERS
- 4 large egg whites at room temperature for 30 minutes
- ½ teaspoon cream of tartar
- ⅛ teaspoon salt
- ½ cup sugar

FOR FILLING
- 1 pint (2 cups) vanilla ice cream (preferably premium)
- ½ cup fresh lemon juice (from 2 medium lemons)
- 1½ tablespoons fresh lemon zest (from 2 medium lemons; see Tips, page 8)
- ⅔ cup sugar
- 4 large egg yolks
- 2 whole large eggs
- ¼ teaspoon salt
- ¾ stick (6 tablespoons) unsalted butter, cut into tablespoon pieces

SPECIAL EQUIPMENT: **2 (15- by 12-inch) sheets of parchment paper; an 8-inch (20-cm) springform pan**

MAKE MERINGUE LAYERS:
▶ Put oven racks in upper and lower thirds of oven and preheat oven to 200°F.
▶ Using the bottom of the springform pan as a guide, draw 2 (8-inch) circles on one sheet of parchment and a third (8-inch) circle on the second sheet of parchment. Turn paper over (circles will be visible).

▶ Beat whites with cream of tartar and salt in a large bowl with an electric mixer at medium speed until they hold soft peaks. Beat in sugar, 1 tablespoon at a time, then increase speed to high and continue beating until whites hold stiff, glossy peaks, about 4 minutes in a stand mixer or 8 to 10 minutes with a handheld. Divide meringue mixture among 3 circles, spread evenly within lines, and gently smooth tops. Bake until firm and very pale golden, about 2 hours, then let stand in turned-off oven (door closed) until firm, about 1 hour.
▶ While meringues bake, put ice cream in refrigerator to soften.
▶ Slide parchment sheets with meringue layers onto racks to cool completely. Carefully lift meringue and peel off parchment.

MAKE CURD WHILE MERINGUES BAKE:
▶ Whisk together lemon juice, zest, sugar, yolks, whole eggs, and salt in a 2-quart heavy saucepan. Stir in butter and cook over moderately low heat, whisking frequently, until mixture is thickened and just reaches a boil, about 6 minutes. Transfer lemon curd to a bowl and chill, its surface covered with plastic wrap, until cold, at least 1 hour.

ASSEMBLE CAKE:
▶ Line springform pan with 2 crisscrossed sheets of plastic wrap. Arrange 1 meringue layer (trimming if necessary) flat side down in springform pan and spread 1 cup ice cream over it, then evenly spread half of lemon curd over ice cream. Cover curd with another meringue layer, then spread remaining cup ice cream over meringue. Spread remaining curd on top, then cover curd with remaining meringue layer, flat side down. Cover with plastic wrap and freeze until firm, at least 4 hours.
▶ About 1 hour before serving, put cake in refrigerator to soften slightly. Remove side of pan and transfer cake to platter, then cut into wedges with a long serrated knife.

COOKS' NOTE: Cake can be frozen up to 2 days. Once cake is firm, cover with plastic wrap; remove plastic wrap before softening cake in refrigerator.

1980 KEFTA AND ZUCCHINI KEBABS

SERVES 6

ACTIVE TIME: 45 MIN START TO FINISH: 1 HR

With these distinctly Middle Eastern kebabs, the minty coolness of the yogurt sauce offsets the allspice, pepper, and cinnamon in some of the most succulent meatballs you have ever tasted.

FOR SAUCE
- 1 cup plain yogurt (preferably whole-milk)
- 2 tablespoons chopped fresh mint
- 1 teaspoon minced garlic
- ⅛ teaspoon salt

FOR ZUCCHINI
- 3 tablespoons fresh lemon juice
- 1 teaspoon sugar
- ¼ teaspoon salt
- ¼ teaspoon black pepper
- ⅓ cup olive oil
- 2 medium zucchini (1¼ lb total), cut crosswise into ½-inch-thick slices

FOR *KEFTA* (LAMB MEATBALLS)
- 2 slices firm white sandwich bread, torn into small pieces
- 1 small onion, finely chopped (about 1 cup)
- ¼ cup loosely packed fresh parsley leaves
- ¼ cup loosely packed fresh cilantro leaves
- 1 lb ground lamb (from shoulder)
- 1 teaspoon salt
- ½ teaspoon ground allspice
- ½ teaspoon cayenne
- ¼ teaspoon cinnamon
- ¼ teaspoon black pepper
- ⅓ cup pine nuts, toasted (see Tips, page 8) and finely chopped

SPECIAL EQUIPMENT: **12 (10-inch) wooden skewers, soaked in cold water for 30 minutes**

MAKE SAUCE:
▶ Stir together yogurt, mint, garlic, and salt in a small bowl and chill.

PREPARE ZUCCHINI:
▶ Whisk together lemon juice, sugar, salt, pepper, and oil in a large bowl and stir in zucchini slices. Marinate at room temperature while making meatballs.

MAKE MEATBALLS:
▶ Cover bread with water in a bowl and soak 10 minutes. Squeeze handfuls of bread to remove as much excess water as possible, then transfer to a bowl.
▶ Pulse onion and herbs in a food processor until finely chopped, then add to bread along with lamb, salt, spices, and pine nuts. Mix with your hands until well blended. Form lamb mixture into 36 balls (1 scant tablespoon each).

ASSEMBLE AND GRILL KEBABS:
▶ Prepare grill for cooking over medium-hot charcoal (moderate heat for gas; see Tips, page 8). For indoor cooking instructions, see cooks' note below.
▶ Thread 6 meatballs ¼ inch apart onto each of 6 skewers. Thread zucchini lengthwise onto remaining 6 skewers (5 slices per skewer), so cut sides are on the grill, leaving ¼ inch between slices. Grill zucchini and lamb on oiled grill rack, turning over once, until golden and just cooked through, 4 to 6 minutes. Serve warm, with yogurt sauce.

COOKS' NOTE: Kebabs can be broiled on 2 large shallow baking pans 5 inches from heat, turning over once, until golden and just cooked through, 4 to 6 minutes.

OPPOSITE: **1982 apricot almond tart**

1981 SAUTÉED GREEN BEANS WITH COCONUT

SERVES 4
ACTIVE TIME: 20 MIN   START TO FINISH: 1½ HR (INCLUDES SOAKING COCONUT)

If you're tired of serving the same old green bean dishes, here's a way to give them a South Indian spin.

½ cup finely grated unsweetened coconut (1½ oz; see Sources)
⅓ cup water
1 lb green beans, trimmed
3 tablespoons vegetable oil
2 teaspoons black mustard seeds (see Sources)
1 (1½-inch) dried hot red chile, seeded and crumbled
1 Turkish bay leaf or ½ California
¼ teaspoon salt
¼ teaspoon black pepper

▸Stir together coconut and water in a bowl. Let soak at room temperature until water is absorbed, about 1 hour.
▸Cook beans in a 6-quart heavy pot of boiling salted water (see Tips, page 8), uncovered, until crisp-tender, 6 to 7 minutes. Transfer beans to a colander set in a bowl of ice and cold water to stop cooking, then drain well.
▸Heat oil in a 12-inch heavy skillet over moderately high heat until hot but not smoking, then add mustard seeds, chile, and bay leaf and sauté, stirring, until mustard seeds make popping sounds, about 1 minute. Add beans and stir until coated with oil. Add coconut mixture and cook, stirring, until heated through, 2 to 3 minutes. Discard bay leaf and season with salt and pepper.

1982 APRICOT ALMOND TART

SERVES 10 TO 12
ACTIVE TIME: 35 MIN   START TO FINISH: 4¼ HR (INCLUDES COOLING)

Roasted canned apricots combined with frangipane filling make for one sweet dream in the middle of winter.

Pastry dough (see log cabin pie recipe, page 20)
18 to 20 drained canned apricot halves (from 2 [1-lb] cans)
1 cup whole blanched almonds (5 oz)
6 tablespoons plus 2 teaspoons sugar
1 stick (½ cup) unsalted butter, softened
2 large eggs
1 teaspoon vanilla
¼ teaspoon almond extract

SPECIAL EQUIPMENT: an 11- by 1-inch fluted tart pan with a removable bottom; pie weights or raw rice

MAKE TART SHELL:
▸Put oven rack in middle position and preheat oven to 375°F.
▸Roll out dough on a lightly floured surface with a lightly floured rolling pin into a 14-inch round and fit into bottom and side of tart pan, then trim flush with top of rim. Chill until firm, about 30 minutes.
▸Lightly prick bottom of shell all over with a fork, then line with foil and fill with weights. Bake until pastry is pale golden along rim and set underneath weights, 18 to 20 minutes. Carefully remove foil and weights and bake shell until bottom and side are golden, about 10 minutes more. Cool completely in pan on a rack, about 30 minutes. Leave oven on.

FILL AND BAKE TART:
▸While shell cools, roast apricots in 1 layer, cut sides up, in a 13- by 9-inch baking dish 30 minutes, then set aside.
▸Reduce oven temperature to 350°F.
▸Pulse almonds with 2 tablespoons sugar and a pinch of salt in a food processor until finely ground.
▸Beat together butter and ¼ cup sugar with an electric mixer at medium-high speed until pale and fluffy. Add eggs, 1 at a time, beating well after each addition, then beat in almond mixture, vanilla, and almond extract until just combined.
▸Spread frangipane evenly in tart shell. Arrange apricots, cut sides up, on top of frangipane. (Frangipane will puff up around apricots when baked.) Bake until frangipane is golden brown and just firm to the touch, about 45 minutes.
▸Preheat broiler.
▸Sprinkle top of tart with remaining 2 teaspoons sugar and broil about 6 inches from heat until sugar is melted and top of tart is browned, 1 to 2 minutes (watch carefully). Cool to warm or room temperature in pan on a rack, at least 30 minutes.

COOKS' NOTES: Apricots can be roasted 1 day ahead and chilled, covered.
• Tart can be baked 6 hours ahead and kept at room temperature.

1983 CHICKEN WITH RAISINS, ALMONDS, AND OLIVES

SERVES 4

ACTIVE TIME: 40 MIN   START TO FINISH: 1¾ HR

With a healthy dose of Sherry and an orange juice marinade, this dish invites the sophistication of Barcelona to join the tropical brightness of the Caribbean. This recipe came from La Zaragozana in San Juan, Puerto Rico.

- 3 tablespoons raisins
- ⅓ cup dry Sherry
- 3 lb chicken pieces with skin and bones
- 1 garlic clove, chopped
- ¼ cup chopped fresh flat-leaf parsley
- 3 tablespoons fresh orange juice
- ½ teaspoon salt
- ¼ teaspoon black pepper
- ¼ cup all-purpose flour
- ¼ cup olive oil
- ¾ cup reduced-sodium chicken broth (6 fl oz)
- 3 tablespoons sliced almonds, toasted (see Tips, page 8)
- ½ cup brine-cured green olives, pitted
- 2 tablespoons cold unsalted butter, cut into several pieces

MACERATE RAISINS AND MARINATE CHICKEN:

▶ Stir together raisins and Sherry in a small bowl and let stand 1 hour.

▶ Place chicken in a sealable plastic bag and put bag in a shallow baking dish (in case of leakage). Purée garlic, parsley, and juice in a blender, then pour over chicken in bag and seal bag, pressing out excess air. Marinate, chilled, 1 hour.

SAUTÉ CHICKEN:

▶ Drain raisins in a sieve set over a small bowl, reserving raisins and Sherry. Pat chicken dry and sprinkle all over with salt and pepper. (Discard marinade.) Dredge chicken lightly in flour, shaking off excess. Heat oil in a 12-inch heavy skillet over moderately high heat until hot but not smoking, then brown chicken in 2 batches, starting with skin sides down and turning over once, 8 to 10 minutes per batch. Transfer chicken as browned to a plate and discard oil from skillet.

▶ Add Sherry to skillet (use caution; it may ignite) and cook over moderately high heat, stirring and scraping up brown bits, 1 minute. Return chicken, skin sides up, to skillet along with any juices accumulated on plate, then add broth, almonds, olives, and raisins. Reduce heat and gently simmer, covered, until

chicken is cooked through, 15 to 20 minutes. Transfer chicken with tongs to a serving dish and, if sauce is too thin, boil, uncovered, stirring occasionally, until thickened, 1 to 2 minutes. Remove from heat and stir in butter until incorporated, then stir in salt and pepper to taste. Pour sauce over chicken.

1984 EGG NOODLES WITH CABBAGE AND ONIONS

SERVES 4

ACTIVE TIME: 30 MIN   START TO FINISH: 1¾ HR

Crunchy with poppy seeds, and rich with browned onions, this simple dish, from cookbook author Faye Levy, makes a great side for pot roast or roast chicken—or a homey vegetarian meal in itself.

- 1½ lb green cabbage, quartered, cored, and cut crosswise into ½-inch-wide strips
- 2 teaspoons salt
- 1 large onion, finely chopped (about 2 cups)
- 5 tablespoons unsalted butter
- 1 teaspoon sugar
- ¼ teaspoon black pepper
- 4 oz wide egg noodles (about 2½ cups)
- 1 teaspoon poppy seeds (optional)

▶ Toss cabbage with salt in a large bowl and let stand, tossing occasionally, 45 minutes. Squeeze cabbage by handfuls to remove as much liquid as possible.

▶ Cook onion in 4 tablespoons butter in a 12-inch heavy skillet over moderate heat, stirring occasionally, until softened, about 5 minutes. Stir in cabbage, sugar, and pepper, then cover, reduce heat to low, and cook, stirring occasionally, until cabbage is very tender, about 30 minutes.

▶ Remove lid and increase heat to moderately high, then cook, stirring frequently, until onion and cabbage are golden, 6 to 8 minutes.

▶ While cabbage is browning, cook noodles in a 4- to 5-quart pot of boiling salted water (see Tips, page 8) until al dente. Drain noodles well and add to browned cabbage along with remaining tablespoon butter, then cook over low heat, stirring occasionally, until butter is completely melted. Add salt and pepper to taste, then sprinkle with poppy seeds, if using.

1985 **MASALA DOSAS**

Rice and Lentil Crêpes with Potato Filling

SERVES 4

ACTIVE TIME: 1½ HR   START TO FINISH: 1½ DAYS (INCLUDES SOAKING
AND FERMENTING)

With its fermented dough whirled into a crêpe-like exterior and
its rich filling of curried potato, this classic Indian dish achieves
a unique balance. For help in finding the urad dal, black mustard
seeds, and curry leaves, see Sources.

FOR DOSAS

1½ cups long-grain white rice (not converted; 10 oz)
¾ cup *urad dal* (white split lentils; 5 oz)
1½ cups plus ⅓ cup water
1 teaspoon salt
  About ½ cup vegetable oil for cooking

FOR POTATO FILLING

1½ lb Yukon Gold potatoes, all about the same size (4 medium)
¼ cup vegetable oil
1 teaspoon black mustard seeds
8 fresh or thawed frozen curry leaves
½ teaspoon cumin seeds
1 medium onion, chopped
1 fresh green chile (such as Thai or serrano; 2½ inches),
  minced, including seeds
½ teaspoon turmeric
1 cup water
¾ teaspoon salt

SPECIAL EQUIPMENT: a well-seasoned 10-inch round cast-iron
griddle or a 10-inch nonstick heavy skillet
ACCOMPANIMENT: bottled mango chutney

MAKE DOSA BATTER:

▶ Place rice and lentils in separate bowls. Fill each with water to
cover by 2 inches and soak 4 hours.

▶ Drain lentils in a sieve and purée in a food processor with
¾ cup water until light and fluffy, 3 to 5 minutes. Transfer to a
large bowl. Drain rice in a sieve and purée in food processor with
⅓ cup water until a gritty paste forms, about 1 minute. (Rice
paste will not be as smooth as lentil paste.) Stir rice paste and
¾ teaspoon salt into lentil paste.

▶ Let mixture ferment, covered with plastic wrap, in a warm
(about 80°F) draft-free place until doubled in bulk, about
24 hours. (Mixture will be light and foamy.) Stir in remaining
¾ cup water and ¼ teaspoon salt. Let batter stand, covered, in
a warm (about 80°F) draft-free place 2½ hours.

MAKE FILLING WHILE BATTER STANDS:

▸ Combine potatoes with cold salted water (see Tips, page 8) to cover by 2 inches in a 2½- to 3-quart saucepan and simmer, uncovered, until potatoes are just tender, 15 to 25 minutes. Drain potatoes in a colander. When cool enough to handle, peel potatoes and cut into ½-inch cubes.

▸ Heat oil in a 10- to 12-inch heavy skillet over moderately high heat until hot but not smoking, then cook mustard seeds, partially covered with lid, until they just begin to pop, 15 to 30 seconds. Add curry leaves and cumin and cook, stirring, until cumin turns a shade darker, 10 to 15 seconds. Reduce heat to moderately low, then add onion and cook, stirring occasionally, until softened but not browned, 8 to 10 minutes. Stir in chile and turmeric and cook, stirring, 1 minute. Add potatoes, water, and salt and bring to a boil. Reduce heat to moderately low, then simmer, covered, stirring occasionally and mashing potatoes slightly, until sauce is thickened, 8 to 10 minutes. Discard curry leaves.

COOK DOSAS:

▸ Put oven rack in middle position and preheat oven to 250°F.

▸ Spread 1 teaspoon oil on griddle using a paper towel, then heat over moderate heat until hot but not smoking. Dip a ⅓-cup dry measure into batter, scooping gently to fill without deflating batter, and pour into center of griddle (scrape out batter remaining in measure). Quickly spread batter with back of a small spoon in a circular motion to thinly cover griddle. (Dosa may be lacy around edge.) Drizzle edge and top of dosa with 1 teaspoon oil and cook until underside is golden and crisp, 1½ to 2 minutes. Turn dosa over with a metal spatula and cook, pressing occasionally, until underside is pale golden, about 1 minute more. (Adjust heat up or down if necessary to prevent overbrowning.) Transfer dosa to a foil-lined large baking sheet and keep warm, loosely covered with foil, in oven.

▸ Make 9 to 11 more dosas in same manner, transferring as cooked to baking sheet in 1 layer and separating additional layers of dosas with foil.

ASSEMBLE DOSAS:

▸ Spread ⅓ cup hot potato filling in a line across middle of each dosa and loosely fold dosa over filling in thirds like a letter.

COOKS' NOTES: Batter, after fermenting (24 hours) and standing (2½ hours), can be chilled up to 24 hours more. Let stand at room temperature 30 minutes and gently stir to combine before cooking.

• Dosas, without filling, can be cooked up to 1 hour ahead and kept, covered with foil, at room temperature. Reheat dosas in a 350°F oven between layers of foil until warm, about 10 minutes.

• Filling can be made 1 day ahead and chilled, covered. Reheat, adding water to loosen filling if necessary.

1986 MÂCHE SALAD WITH TAPENADE AND HARD-BOILED EGGS LA SARA

SERVES 6
ACTIVE TIME: 20 MIN   START TO FINISH: 20 MIN

Nathalie Waag, who taught cooking at La Sara, her farmhouse in Provence, gave us this recipe. We've taken the original dollop of tapenade and mixed it with the dressing to add an engaging tartness to each bite.

  3 large eggs
  3 tablespoons extra-virgin olive oil (see cooks' note, below)
  1 tablespoon red-wine vinegar
  ⅛ teaspoon salt
  ⅛ teaspoon black pepper
  1 tablespoon black-olive tapenade
  8 cups loosely packed *mâche* (lamb's lettuce; 2 oz)

▸ Cover eggs with cold water by 1½ inches in a heavy saucepan and bring to a boil, partially covered. Reduce heat to low and cook eggs, covered, 30 seconds. Remove from heat and let stand, covered, 12 minutes. Transfer to a bowl of ice and cold water and let stand 5 minutes. Peel and cut each egg into 6 wedges.

▸ Whisk together oil, vinegar, salt, and pepper in a small bowl. Stir together 3 tablespoons vinaigrette with tapenade in another small bowl.

▸ Just before serving, drizzle 6 plates with a teaspoon of tapenade mixture each (dressing will appear separated). Toss *mâche* with remaining vinaigrette and divide among plates. Divide eggs among salads and drizzle with remaining tapenade mixture.

COOKS' NOTE: If your tapenade is very oily, cut back on the oil in the vinaigrette.

OPPOSITE: 1985 masala dosas (left); 1984 egg noodles with cabbage and onions (right)

1987 YELLOW CAKE WITH CHOCOLATE FROSTING

SERVES 10 TO 12

ACTIVE TIME: 1¼ HR   START TO FINISH: 6¼ HR (INCLUDES COOLING FROSTING)

The bittersweet-chocolate ganache that we use as frosting gives this whisper-light cake, from cookbook author Barbara Kafka, a truly heavenly richness.

FOR CAKE

- 2 cups sifted cake flour (not self-rising; sift before measuring)
- 2 teaspoons baking powder
- ¾ teaspoon salt
- 1½ sticks (¾ cup) unsalted butter, softened
- 1½ cups sugar
- 3 large eggs, at room temperature for 30 minutes
- 1½ teaspoons vanilla
- ¾ cup whole milk

FOR FROSTING

- 2 cups heavy cream
- 10 oz bittersweet chocolate (not more than 60% cacao if marked), finely chopped
- 6 oz 70% cacao bittersweet chocolate, finely chopped
- 1 tablespoon corn syrup
- 1 teaspoon vanilla

SPECIAL EQUIPMENT: **3 (8-inch) round cake pans**

MAKE CAKE LAYERS:

▶ Put oven rack in middle position and preheat oven to 350°F. Butter and flour cake pans, knocking out excess flour.

▶ Sift together flour (2 cups), baking powder, and salt into a bowl.

▶ Beat together butter (1½ sticks) and sugar with an electric mixer (fitted with paddle attachment if using a stand mixer) at medium-high speed until pale and fluffy, 3 to 5 minutes. Add eggs 1 at a time, beating well after each addition, then add vanilla and beat 5 minutes more. Reduce speed to low, then add flour mixture alternately with milk in 3 batches, beginning and ending with flour mixture and mixing until just smooth. Divide among cake pans (about 1¼ cups per pan), spreading evenly, then rap each pan against work surface once or twice to eliminate air bubbles.

▶ Bake cake layers, rearranging pans in oven halfway through baking time to allow for even baking, until barely pulling away from sides of pans and a wooden pick or skewer inserted in center of each comes out clean, 15 to 20 minutes total. Cool 5 minutes in pans on racks, then run a thin knife around inside edge of pan and invert layers onto racks to cool completely.

MAKE FROSTING WHILE LAYERS BAKE:

▶ Bring cream to a simmer in a 3- to 4-quart saucepan and remove from heat. Add chocolate and let stand 1 minute, then whisk mixture until smooth and chocolate is completely melted. Stir in corn syrup, vanilla, and a pinch of salt. Transfer frosting to a bowl and chill, its surface covered with wax paper, stirring occasionally, until thickened but spreadable, about 4 hours. (If frosting becomes too thick, let stand at room temperature until softened enough to spread.)

ASSEMBLE CAKE:

▶ Put 1 cake layer on a cake stand or plate and spread ¾ cup frosting evenly over top. Top with another cake layer and ¾ cup frosting, spreading evenly. Top with third cake layer.

▶ Spread a thin layer of frosting over top and sides of cake to seal in crumbs, then chill cake 1 hour, leaving remaining frosting at room temperature. Spread remaining frosting evenly over top and side of cake.

COOKS' NOTES: Cake layers can be made 1 day ahead and cooled completely, then chilled, wrapped well in plastic wrap.

• Frosting can be made 1 day ahead and chilled, covered. Let stand at room temperature 2 to 3 hours to soften to a spreadable consistency.

• Cake can be frosted 1 day ahead and kept in a cake keeper at cool room temperature.

1988 CAVIAR TART

SERVES 8 TO 10
ACTIVE TIME: 30 MIN   START TO FINISH: 3½ HR

Hard-boiled eggs, sour cream, and onion are traditional accompaniments for caviar. In this longtime staple of community cookbooks, they are turned into a shallow cake and spread with caviar. We used supermarket lumpfish caviar, but if you're feeling flush, use the good stuff, or even Japanese tobiko *(flying-fish roe).*

¾ cup sour cream
8 hard-boiled large eggs, finely chopped
½ cup finely chopped onion (1 medium)
¾ stick (6 tablespoons) unsalted butter, melted and cooled
2 tablespoons finely chopped fresh dill
2 teaspoons finely grated fresh lemon zest (see Tips, page 8)
¼ teaspoon salt
¼ teaspoon black pepper
3 tablespoons finely chopped fresh chives
7 oz black lumpfish caviar (see cooks' note below)

SPECIAL EQUIPMENT: **a 9-inch nonstick springform pan; a small offset spatula**

ACCOMPANIMENTS: **lemon wedges; 16 thin slices whole-wheat toast, buttered, then halved or quartered diagonally**

▶ Put ½ cup sour cream in a paper-towel-lined sieve set over a bowl, then let drain, covered with plastic wrap and chilled, 3 hours.

▶ Stir together remaining ¼ cup sour cream, hard-boiled eggs, onion, butter, dill, zest, salt, pepper, and 1 tablespoon chives until combined well.

▶ Invert bottom of springform pan (so that turned-up edge is underneath for easy removal of tart) and close side of pan around bottom. Spread egg mixture evenly in pan with offset spatula, smoothing top. Cover surface with plastic wrap, pressing gently, and chill until firm, at least 3 hours.

▶ Carefully remove plastic wrap from egg mixture and spread drained sour cream evenly over egg mixture with offset spatula.

▶ Gently spread half of caviar on several sheets of paper towels to absorb excess cuttlefish ink. Carefully lift caviar from paper towels and spread on top of egg mixture (be careful not to smash caviar). Repeat method with remaining caviar. Serve cut into wedges and sprinkled with remaining chives, if desired.

COOKS' NOTE: Draining the black lumpfish caviar removes excess fish ink, which stains the cream. This is not necessary for higher-quality caviar or *tobiko*. For a caviar alternative, see Sources.

1989 SOLE WITH SALMON MOUSSELINE AND PARSLEY SAUCE

SERVES 4

ACTIVE TIME: 1 HR   START TO FINISH: 2¼ HR

In the '80s, every caterer had a dish like this in his hip pocket, and for good reason: It's easy and beautiful. This version, from cookbook author Faye Levy, is particularly delicate, with a bright green herbaceous sauce.

FOR SALMON MOUSSELINE

- 1 (6-oz) piece salmon fillet, skinned
- 1 large egg white
- ⅛ teaspoon freshly grated nutmeg
- ¼ teaspoon salt
- ⅛ teaspoon black pepper
- ¾ cup well-chilled heavy cream

FOR SOLE

- 5 cups loosely packed fresh parsley sprigs, plus additional for garnish
- 1¼ cups heavy cream
- 4 (4- to 6-oz) gray sole fillets
- 1 tablespoon unsalted butter, softened
- 1 tablespoon finely chopped shallot
- ¼ cup dry white wine
- ¼ cup white fish stock (recipe follows), at room temperature
- 1 teaspoon fresh lemon juice
- ¼ teaspoon salt
- ⅛ teaspoon black pepper

SPECIAL EQUIPMENT: **an instant-read thermometer**

MAKE SALMON MOUSSELINE:

▶ Put oven rack in middle position and preheat oven to 400°F.

▶ Remove bones from salmon with needlenose pliers or tweezers, then pat fillet dry and cut into 1-inch pieces. Purée salmon in a food processor, then add egg white, nutmeg, salt, and pepper and purée until smooth. Add cream with motor running and blend, scraping down side of processor bowl if necessary, until combined well. Transfer mousseline to a bowl and chill, covered, 15 minutes.

PREPARE SOLE:

▶ Blanch parsley in a 4- to 5-quart heavy saucepan of boiling salted water (see Tips, page 8) 1 minute.

▶ Drain parsley in a colander and rinse under cold water to stop cooking. Squeeze handfuls of parsley to remove excess water, then transfer parsley to cleaned food processor. Finely chop parsley in processor, then add ½ cup cream and purée (mixture will be fairly dry).

▶ Pat sole fillets dry, then arrange, skinned (smoother) sides up, on a work surface and season with salt and pepper. Divide mousseline evenly among fillets and fold each fillet in half crosswise to enclose mousseline.

▶ Spread butter over bottom of a 13- by 9-inch baking dish, then sprinkle shallot over butter. Arrange folded fillets in baking dish so they are not touching, then pour wine and room-temperature stock around fillets. Bake sole until a thermometer inserted into mousseline registers 110°F, 10 to 12 minutes.

▶ Transfer sole to a platter with a slotted spatula and keep warm, covered. Transfer cooking liquid to a 1- to 2-quart saucepan and boil, uncovered, over high heat until reduced to about ¼ cup, about 5 minutes. Add remaining ¾ cup cream and boil until slightly thickened, about 3 minutes. Add parsley purée and simmer until sauce is slightly thickened, about 2 minutes. Stir in lemon juice, salt, and pepper. Pour sauce through a fine-mesh sieve into a bowl, pressing on and then discarding solids.

▶ Spoon sauce onto 4 plates and top with fish. Garnish with additional parsley. Serve additional sauce on the side.

ABOVE: 1990 Cheddar grits and bacon roulade

WHITE FISH STOCK

MAKES ABOUT 3 CUPS
ACTIVE TIME: 15 MIN   START TO FINISH: 45 MIN

 1 tablespoon unsalted butter, softened
 1 lb mixed bones and heads of white-fleshed fish (such as Pacific cod, porgy, striped bass, turbot, or any combination of these), gills removed and bones and heads rinsed well
 1 small onion, sliced (1 cup)
 12 fresh parsley stems (reserve leaves for another use)
 2 tablespoons fresh lemon juice
 ½ teaspoon salt
 ½ cup dry white wine
 3½ cups cold water

▶ Spread butter over bottom of a 2- to 3-quart heavy saucepan, then add fish bones and heads, onion, parsley stems, lemon juice, and salt. Steam mixture, covered, over moderately high heat, 5 minutes.
▶ Add wine and water and bring to a boil. Skim froth, then reduce heat to moderate and simmer, uncovered, 25 minutes.
▶ Pour stock through a fine-mesh sieve into a large bowl, pressing hard on solids and then discarding them.

COOKS' NOTE: Stock can be made ahead and cooled completely, uncovered, then chilled, covered, 2 days or frozen 1 month.

1990 CHEDDAR GRITS AND BACON ROULADE

SERVES 6
ACTIVE TIME: 45 MIN   START TO FINISH: 1¼ HR

Here, Southern grits are baked into a tender roll that embraces all the elements of a country-style breakfast. Just slice and serve.

 3 tablespoons unsalted butter
 3 tablespoons all-purpose flour plus additional for dusting
 1 cup whole milk
 ⅛ teaspoon freshly grated nutmeg
 ½ teaspoon salt
 ½ teaspoon black pepper
 4 large egg yolks
 2 cups cold water
 ½ cup quick-cooking grits (not instant)
 4½ oz coarsely grated extra-sharp Cheddar (1¾ cups)
 6 large egg whites
 8 bacon slices (7 oz), cooked until crisp, then drained and crumbled (1 cup)
 ⅓ cup finely chopped scallion

SPECIAL EQUIPMENT: a 15- by 10-inch shallow baking pan (see Tips, page 8); parchment paper

▶ Put oven rack in middle position and preheat oven to 350°F. Butter baking pan and line with parchment paper, then butter paper. Dust pan with flour, knocking out excess.
▶ Melt butter (3 tablespoons) in a 1- to 1½-quart heavy saucepan over moderately low heat, then add flour and cook roux, whisking, 3 minutes. Add milk in a slow stream, whisking, then add nutmeg, ¼ teaspoon salt, and ¼ teaspoon pepper. Increase heat to moderate and bring to a boil, whisking constantly, then reduce heat and simmer mixture, whisking occasionally, 5 minutes. Remove from heat and add egg yolks 1 at a time, whisking well after each addition. Transfer to a large bowl and cover surface of mixture with a sheet of buttered parchment (buttered side down, to keep yolk mixture from forming a skin), pressing gently.
▶ Bring 2 cups water to a boil in cleaned saucepan and gradually add grits, whisking constantly. Reduce heat and simmer, uncovered, stirring occasionally, 5 minutes. Remove from heat and whisk in 1 cup cheese, remaining ¼ teaspoon salt, and remaining ¼ teaspoon pepper. Whisk grits into yolk mixture until combined well.
▶ Beat egg whites in another large bowl with an electric mixer at medium-high speed until they just hold stiff peaks, then stir one third of whites into yolk mixture to lighten. Fold in remaining whites gently but thoroughly.
▶ Spread evenly in lined baking pan, then bake until golden and firm to the touch, 25 to 30 minutes.
▶ Toss together bacon, scallion, and remaining ¾ cup cheese in a bowl.
▶ Remove roulade from oven and cover with well-buttered parchment paper (buttered side down) and then a kitchen towel and invert a baking sheet over towel. Invert roulade onto baking sheet. Carefully peel off parchment from top of roulade and discard, then trim ¼ inch from each short side of roulade. Scatter bacon mixture evenly over top of roulade.
▶ Starting with a long side, roll up the roulade jelly-roll style, using towel to help lift and support as you roll and carefully removing parchment as you go. Arrange roulade, seam side down, on baking sheet and bake, uncovered, just until cheese is melted, about 5 minutes.

1991 WARM LENTIL SALAD WITH SAUSAGE

SERVES 4 (MAIN COURSE)
ACTIVE TIME: 35 MIN   START TO FINISH: 50 MIN

This bistro classic is enriched by rounds of smoky, spicy sausage. All you need is a leafy salad and a glass of red wine.

    2   cups French green lentils (13 oz), picked over and rinsed
    6   cups water
    1   California bay leaf or 2 Turkish
    1   teaspoon salt
    1   medium onion, finely chopped (1 cup)
    2   carrots, cut into ¼-inch dice (1 cup)
    2   celery ribs, cut into ¼-inch dice (1 cup)
    1   tablespoon finely chopped garlic
    ½   teaspoon dried thyme, crumbled
    ¼   teaspoon black pepper
    ½   cup plus 2 tablespoons extra-virgin olive oil
    ¼   cup red-wine vinegar
    1   tablespoon Dijon mustard
    ¾   lb smoked kielbasa or other smoked sausage (not low-fat), cut crosswise into ¼-inch-thick slices
    ¼   cup finely chopped fresh flat-leaf parsley

▸Bring lentils, water, and bay leaf to a boil in a 2- to 3-quart heavy saucepan, then reduce heat and simmer, covered, until almost tender, about 15 minutes. Stir in ½ teaspoon salt, then simmer lentils, covered, until tender but not falling apart, 3 to 5 minutes.

▸While lentils simmer, cook onion, carrots, celery, garlic, thyme, ¼ teaspoon salt, and ⅛ teaspoon pepper in 2 tablespoons oil in a 12-inch heavy skillet over moderately low heat, stirring occasionally, until vegetables are just softened, 7 to 9 minutes.

▸Make vinaigrette by whisking together vinegar, mustard, and remaining ¼ teaspoon salt and ⅛ teaspoon pepper in a bowl. Add remaining ½ cup oil in a slow stream, whisking until blended well.

▸Drain lentils in a colander, discarding bay leaf, and return to saucepan along with vegetable mixture and vinaigrette. Cook over low heat, stirring, until heated through. Keep warm, covered.

▸Brown kielbasa in cleaned and dried 12-inch heavy skillet (in 2 batches if necessary), turning over once, about 2 minutes per batch. Stir kielbasa and parsley into lentils.

1992 BLACK-BEAN AND SIRLOIN CHILI

SERVES 8
ACTIVE TIME: 30 MIN   START TO FINISH: 2 HR

Don't wait for the fog to roll in before trying this savory souvenir from Fog City Diner in San Francisco. Embellish with sour cream and cilantro if the spirit moves you.

    2   lb boneless sirloin steak, cut into ½-inch cubes
    ½   teaspoon salt
    ½   teaspoon black pepper
    ⅓   cup olive oil
    2   cups chopped yellow onions (2 medium)
    2   tablespoons finely chopped garlic
    5   fresh jalapeño chiles, seeded and finely chopped (½ cup)
    3   tablespoons chili powder (not pure chile)
    ½   teaspoon cayenne
    ½   teaspoon ground cumin
    ¼   cup masa harina (tortilla flour; see Sources)
    3½ cups beef broth (28 fl oz)
    ½   cup water
    2   cups cooked black beans (drained and rinsed if canned)

ACCOMPANIMENTS: **grated mild Cheddar; finely chopped red onion**

▸Pat sirloin steak dry and season with ½ teaspoon salt and ¼ teaspoon pepper.

▸Heat oil over moderately high heat in a wide 4-quart heavy pot until hot but not smoking, then brown sirloin in 3 batches, transferring as browned with a slotted spoon to a bowl, about 3 minutes per batch.

▸Add onions, garlic, and fresh chiles to fat remaining in pot and cook over moderate heat, stirring occasionally, until softened, about 3 minutes. Add remaining spices and ¼ teaspoon pepper, then cook mixture, stirring, 3 minutes. Add masa harina and cook, stirring, 2 minutes (mixture will be dry).

▸Add broth, water, and sirloin to masa harina mixture and simmer, uncovered, stirring occasionally and scraping with a wooden spoon or spatula (more frequently toward end to prevent scorching), until meat is tender, about 45 minutes. Stir in beans and simmer 10 to 15 minutes to meld flavors.

COOKS' NOTE: Chili can be made 3 days ahead and cooled completely, uncovered, then chilled in an airtight container. Reheat chili slowly (to avoid scorching bottom), thinning with water if necessary.

OPPOSITE: **1991 warm lentil salad with sausage**

1993 THREE-CHEESE PIZZA WITH ONION, SAGE, AND ARUGULA

MAKES 1 (14-INCH) PIZZA
ACTIVE TIME: 45 MIN   START TO FINISH: 2¼ HR

Why a trio of cheeses? Fontina for its melting quality and nutty flavor, Gorgonzola for its biting blue punch, and Parmigiano-Reggiano for its uncanny ability to amplify other cheeses.

FOR DOUGH
  1 (¼-oz) package active dry yeast (2¼ teaspoons)
      About 2 cups unbleached all-purpose flour
  ¾ cup warm water (105–115°F)
1½ teaspoons salt
1½ teaspoons extra-virgin olive oil
  1 to 2 tablespoons cornmeal

FOR TOPPING
  1 tablespoon extra-virgin olive oil
  ¼ lb Italian Fontina cut into ½-inch pieces (⅔ cup)
  2 oz Gorgonzola *dolce*, cut into ¼-inch pieces (see Sources)
  ½ cup thinly sliced red onion (1 medium)

  6 large fresh sage leaves, thinly sliced crosswise
      (1 tablespoon)
  ½ oz finely grated Parmigiano-Reggiano (¼ cup;
      see Tips, page 8)
  ¼ lb loosely packed baby arugula leaves (4 cups)

SPECIAL EQUIPMENT: **a pizza stone**

MAKE DOUGH:
▶ Place pizza stone on floor of gas oven or on lowest rack if using an electric oven and preheat oven to 500°F (allow 1 hour for pizza stone to heat).
▶ Stir together yeast, 1 tablespoon flour, and ¼ cup warm water in a measuring cup and let stand until mixture develops a creamy foam on surface, about 5 minutes. (If mixture doesn't foam, discard and start over with new yeast.)
▶ Stir together 1¼ cups flour with salt in a large bowl. Add yeast mixture, oil, and remaining ½ cup warm water and stir until smooth. Stir in enough flour (about ½ cup) to make dough come away from sides of bowl. (Dough will be wetter than other pizza doughs you may have made.)

54

▸ Knead dough on lightly floured surface with lightly floured hands (reflour hands when dough becomes too sticky) until smooth, soft, and elastic, about 8 minutes. Form dough into a ball, put on a lightly floured surface, and generously dust with flour. Loosely cover with plastic wrap and let rise in a warm draft-free place until doubled in bulk, about 1¼ hours. Dust a wooden peel or a large baking sheet (without sides) with cornmeal.

▸ Do not punch down dough. Carefully dredge dough in a bowl of flour to coat and transfer to a dry work surface. Holding one edge of dough in the air with both hands and letting bottom just touch the work surface, carefully and quickly move hands around edge of dough (like turning a steering wheel), allowing weight of dough to stretch round to roughly 10 inches. Lay dough flat on peel or baking sheet. Continue to work edge of dough with your fingers, stretching it into a 14-inch round.

MAKE TOPPING:

▸ Brush dough with oil, leaving a 1-inch border, then scatter Fontina and Gorgonzola over dough (leaving a 1-inch border). Scatter onion and sage leaves over cheese. Sprinkle pizza with Parmigiano-Reggiano, then line up far edge of peel with far edge of stone in oven and tilt peel, jerking it gently to start pizza moving. When edge of pizza touches stone, quickly pull back peel to transfer pizza to stone (do not pull back pizza). Bake until crust is golden and cheese is bubbling, 10 to 12 minutes. Slide peel under pizza to remove from oven, then top with arugula.

COOKS' NOTE: Dough can rise slowly, covered, in the refrigerator for 1 day. Bring to room temperature before using.

1994 PAN-SEARED FISH FILLETS IN GINGER BROTH

SERVES 4
ACTIVE TIME: 1 HR   START TO FINISH: 1 HR

The stacking and Asian fusion of this dish is very 1990s. But don't worry about its trendiness. Heady wallops of curry and ginger make this preparation timeless.

¼ lb Shanghai bok choy (about 3 small heads; see Sources)
1 medium carrot
2½ tablespoons vegetable oil
1 (1½-inch) piece peeled fresh ginger, cut into very thin matchsticks
¼ cup medium-dry Sherry
2 cups reduced-sodium chicken broth (16 fl oz)
2 teaspoons sugar
3 scallions

4 (4- to 5-oz) sea bass or striped bass fillets with skin, pin bones removed
1 teaspoon salt
½ teaspoon black pepper
1 teaspoon cornstarch
1 teaspoon curry powder
1 teaspoon Asian sesame oil

GARNISH: **fresh cilantro leaves**

▸ Discard any bruised or wilted outer leaves from bok choy, then cut leaves from stalks, keeping leaves and stalks separate. Thinly slice leaves and cut stalks diagonally into ½-inch-wide slices. Halve carrot lengthwise and cut diagonally into ¼-inch-thick slices.

▸ Heat 1 tablespoon vegetable oil in a 4- to 5-quart heavy pot over moderately high heat until hot but not smoking, then stir-fry bok choy stalks, carrot, and ginger 1 minute. Stir in Sherry, broth, and sugar and simmer, covered, 5 minutes.

▸ Meanwhile, cut scallions crosswise into 2-inch pieces, then halve lengthwise and cut into very thin matchsticks.

▸ Add bok choy leaves and scallions to carrot mixture and simmer, covered, until vegetables are tender, 3 to 5 minutes.

▸ While vegetables simmer, pat fish dry and sprinkle with ½ teaspoon salt and ¼ teaspoon pepper. Stir together cornstarch and curry powder, then rub into skin of each fillet. Halve each fillet diagonally with a sharp knife.

▸ Stir sesame oil, remaining ½ teaspoon salt, and remaining ¼ teaspoon pepper into vegetable mixture and keep warm, uncovered, on turned-off burner.

▸ Heat remaining 1½ tablespoons vegetable oil in a 12-inch heavy skillet over moderately high heat until hot but not smoking, then cook fish, skin sides down, gently pressing occasionally with a metal spatula (to keep skin flat), until skin is golden, 2 to 3 minutes. Turn fish over and cook until just cooked through, about 2 minutes more. Remove from heat.

▸ Divide broth and vegetables among 4 shallow bowls and stack 2 fish halves, skin sides up, in center of each bowl.

OPPOSITE: 1995 pho bo

1995 **PHO BO**

Hanoi Beef Noodle Soup

SERVES 6 (MAIN COURSE)

ACTIVE TIME: 1½ HR START TO FINISH: 4½ HR

Vietnam's favorite convenience food is usually purchased at street stands, where the quality of his or her broth can make or break a cook's reputation. The secret ingredients in ours are meaty beef shanks, charred ginger, and onions.

- 2 large onions, halved lengthwise
- 1 (3-inch) piece fresh ginger, left unpeeled
- 4 lb meaty cross-cut beef shanks (sometimes called beef shins; 1½ inches thick)
- 7 qt cold water
- 2 teaspoons star anise pieces
- 1 (3-inch) cinnamon stick
- 3 whole cloves
- 1 tablespoon black peppercorns
- 1 (½-lb) piece boneless beef sirloin steak or tenderloin
- 1 lb dried flat thin or medium rice noodles (*banh pho or pad Thai*)
- ½ cup Asian fish sauce (preferably Vietnamese *nuoc mam*), or to taste
- ½ teaspoon salt, or to taste

SPECIAL EQUIPMENT: **cheesecloth; kitchen string**

ACCOMPANIMENTS: **fresh bean sprouts; very thinly sliced onion (rinsed and drained); fresh cilantro, mint, and basil (preferably Thai) leaves; thinly sliced scallions; lime wedges; thinly sliced fresh Thai or serrano chiles; Asian fish sauce (preferably *nuoc mam*)**

MAKE BROTH:

▶ Roast onions and ginger directly on rack of a gas burner over high heat, turning with tongs, until blistered and blackened, 10 to 15 minutes. (Alternatively, broil onions and ginger on foil-lined rack of a broiler pan about 5 inches from heat, turning occasionally, until charred, 20 to 25 minutes for onions; 25 to 30 minutes for ginger.) Transfer to a bowl and cool. When cool enough to handle, rinse and rub under cold running water to remove any blackened pieces (some areas will remain browned).

▶ While onions and ginger roast, cover shanks with 2 quarts cold water in a 6- to 8-quart pot. Bring to a boil, then drain in a large colander (discard cooking water) and rinse well with cold water. Clean pot.

▶ Wrap star anise, cinnamon stick, cloves, and peppercorns in cheesecloth and tie into a bundle with kitchen string to make a spice bag, then add to cleaned pot along with 4 quarts water, shanks, onions, and ginger. Simmer, uncovered, skimming froth occasionally, 2 hours. Add remaining quart water and return to a boil, then reduce heat and simmer, skimming froth occasionally, until shanks are very tender, about 1 hour more.

PREPARE SIRLOIN AND NOODLES FOR SOUP WHILE BROTH SIMMERS:

▶ Freeze steak until firm but not frozen solid, 30 to 45 minutes, then slice across the grain with a sharp thin knife into less than ⅛-inch-thick slices.

▶ Soak rice noodles in cold water to cover until softened, about 30 minutes, then drain in cleaned large colander. Cook noodles in a 6-quart pot of boiling water, uncovered, stirring, 1 minute, then drain.

FINISH SOUP:

▶ Transfer shanks with tongs to a cutting board. When shanks are cool enough to handle, remove meat from bones and cut into small pieces, discarding bones, fat, and sinew. Set aside 2 cups beef (reserve remainder for another use).

▶ Pour broth through a fine-mesh sieve into a large heatproof bowl, discarding solids. Measure broth: If there is more than 3 quarts (12 cups), boil in cleaned pot until reduced; if there is less, add water. Let stand until fat rises to top, 1 to 2 minutes, then skim off fat if desired.

▶ Combine broth and beef (2 cups) in cleaned 6- to 8-quart pot and bring to a boil, then add fish sauce and salt and return to a boil just before serving.

▶ Divide noodles among 6 large deep bowls. Top noodles with uncooked sliced steak and ladle boiling-hot broth (with pieces of beef shanks) over steak and noodles. (Hot broth will cook steak.)

▶ Serve soup with accompaniments.

COOKS' NOTES: Broth can be made (and strained) 3 days ahead and cooled completely, uncovered, then chilled with 2 cups beef, covered. Bring to a boil just before serving.

• In place of the sliced sirloin steak or tenderloin, you can use beef *shabu-shabu* (paper-thin slices of meat; see Sources) or thinly sliced rare roast beef (from deli counter), torn into pieces.

1996 **STRACCI DI PASTA ALLE MILLE ERBE**

Pasta "Rags" with a Thousand Herbs

SERVES 4

ACTIVE TIME: 1 HR START TO FINISH: 1 HR (NOT INCLUDING MAKING PASTA)

Rags to riches takes on new meaning when such strange bedfellows as basil, tarragon, mint, thyme, marjoram, and rosemary mingle with pasta to create totally new flavors. Every ingredient matters in this recipe from Locanda dell'Amorosa in Sinalunga, Italy, so don't skimp on quality: If you have time, you owe it to yourself to use homemade pasta.

1 lb fresh pasta sheets (recipe follows) or ¾ lb no-boil
   lasagne sheets
   Flour for dusting pasta dough (if using)
¾ lb plum tomatoes (about 4 large)
⅓ cup extra-virgin olive oil
½ cup chopped fresh flat-leaf parsley
½ cup chopped fresh basil
2 tablespoons chopped fresh tarragon
2 tablespoons chopped fresh mint
1½ teaspoons chopped fresh thyme
1 teaspoon chopped fresh sage
1 teaspoon chopped fresh rosemary
½ teaspoon chopped fresh marjoram
¼ teaspoon salt
¼ teaspoon black pepper
1 oz finely grated Pecorino Romano (½ cup; see Tips, page 8)
   plus additional for serving

SPECIAL EQUIPMENT: **a scalloped pastry wheel**
ACCOMPANIMENT: **extra-virgin olive oil for drizzling**

▶ If using fresh pasta, cut sheets into roughly 4- by 1-inch pieces with pastry wheel, then lightly dust with flour and arrange in 1 layer on paper-towel-lined large baking sheets. Let pasta dry until leathery but still pliable, 5 to 30 minutes. If using no-boil lasagne, break sheets into large pieces (about 4 by 1 inch).

▶ Cut an X in bottom of each tomato with a sharp paring knife and blanch tomatoes in a 3-quart saucepan of boiling water 10 seconds. Transfer tomatoes with a slotted spoon to a bowl of ice and cold water and cool. Peel off skin, beginning from scored end, with a paring knife and discard. Halve tomatoes and discard seeds, then cut tomatoes into ¼-inch dice.

▶ Stir together oil and herbs in a large bowl.

▶ Cook pasta in a 6- to 8-quart pot of boiling salted water, uncovered, until al dente, 1 to 2 minutes for fresh pasta (time for dried pasta may vary). Drain, then toss with herb mixture. Add tomatoes, salt, pepper, and cheese and toss again. Season with salt and serve immediately, with additional cheese.

FRESH PASTA SHEETS

MAKES ABOUT 1 POUND
ACTIVE TIME: 1¼ HR   START TO FINISH: 2¼ HR

3 cups unbleached all-purpose flour plus additional
   for dusting
4 large eggs, lightly beaten
1 teaspoon salt
2 to 3 tablespoons water

SPECIAL EQUIPMENT: **a pasta machine**

TO MAKE DOUGH IN A PROCESSOR:

▶ Blend flour, eggs, salt, and 2 tablespoons water in a food processor until mixture just begins to form a ball, adding more water, drop by drop, if dough is too dry (dough should be firm and not sticky). Process dough for 15 seconds more to knead it. Transfer to a floured surface and let stand, covered with an inverted bowl, 1 hour to let the gluten relax and make rolling easier.

TO MAKE DOUGH BY HAND:

▶ Mound flour on a work surface, preferably wooden, and make a well in center. Add eggs, salt, and 2 tablespoons water to well. With a fork, gently beat eggs and water until combined. Gradually stir in enough flour to form a paste, pulling in flour closest to egg mixture and being careful not to make an opening in outer wall of well. Knead remaining flour into mixture with your hands to form a dough, adding more water drop by drop if dough is too dry (dough should be firm and not sticky). Knead dough until smooth and elastic, 8 to 10 minutes. Cover with an inverted bowl and let stand 1 hour to let the gluten relax and make rolling easier.

ROLL PASTA:

▶ Divide dough into 8 pieces, then flatten each piece into a rough rectangle and cover rectangles with an inverted large bowl. Set rollers of pasta machine on widest setting.

▶ Lightly dust 1 rectangle with flour and feed through rollers. (Keep remaining rectangles under bowl.) Fold rectangle in half and feed it, folded end first, through rollers 7 or 8 more times, folding it in half each time and feeding folded end through. Dust with flour if necessary to prevent sticking. Turn dial to next (narrower) setting and feed dough through rollers without folding. Continue to feed dough through rollers once at each setting, without folding, until you reach narrowest setting. Dough will be a smooth sheet (about 36 inches long and 4 inches wide). Cut sheet crosswise in half. Lay sheets of dough on lightly floured baking sheets to dry until leathery but still pliable, about 15 minutes. (Alternatively, lightly dust pasta sheets with flour and hang over the backs of straight-backed chairs to dry.) Roll out remaining pieces of dough in same manner.

COOKS' NOTES: Dough can be made (but not rolled out) 4 hours ahead and chilled, tightly wrapped in plastic wrap.

• Fresh-cut pasta sheets can be chilled in large sealed plastic bags up to 12 hours.

1997 APPLE CHARLOTTES WITH CALVADOS CRÈME ANGLAISE

SERVES 4

ACTIVE TIME: 1 HR   START TO FINISH: 1¾ HR (INCLUDES MAKING SAUCE)

Humble white bread goes haute in this buttery dessert from Quaglino's in London, and captures the very essence of apple.

- ¾ lb Gala apples (about 2)
- ½ cup sugar
- ½ cup Calvados
- ¼ cup golden raisins
- 1 whole clove
- ½ stick (¼ cup) unsalted butter, softened
- 14 slices firm white sandwich bread
      Calvados crème anglaise (recipe follows)

SPECIAL EQUIPMENT: **a 2¼-inch round cookie cutter; 4 deep (6-oz) ramekins (3½ inches across top and 2 inches deep; see Sources)**

▸Peel and core apples, then cut into ½-inch cubes. Boil apples, sugar, Calvados, raisins, and clove in a 2-quart heavy saucepan, stirring, until apples are tender but still hold their shape, 5 to 9 minutes. Pour apples into a medium-mesh sieve set over a bowl, discarding clove. Transfer apples to another bowl and return liquid to saucepan. Boil liquid until syrupy and reduced to about 2 tablespoons, about 3 minutes (mixture will be very bubbly). Stir into apples.

▸Put oven rack in lower third of oven and preheat oven to 375°F.

▸Butter 1 side of each bread slice. Cut out 1 round per slice from 8 slices using cutter (discard scraps). Cut off and discard crusts from remaining 6 slices (forming roughly 3-inch squares). Cut each square into thirds (1 inch wide), then halve crosswise to form 6 (1½- by 1-inch) rectangles. Put 1 round, buttered side down, in bottom of each ramekin. Line side of each ramekin with 9 rectangles, arranging rectangles vertically, with buttered sides against ramekin, and overlapping slightly. Press rectangles gently to help adhere (edges should be flush with rims). Divide apple mixture evenly among ramekins, pressing gently to pack against bread lining. Top with remaining 4 rounds, buttered sides up. Place a sheet of plastic wrap on top of buttered rounds and gently press rounds flush with edges of rectangles.

▸Remove plastic wrap and bake charlottes in ramekins on a baking sheet until golden, about 25 minutes. Wearing an oven mitt, carefully invert hot charlottes onto plates. Spoon chilled crème anglaise over and around them.

COOKS' NOTE: Charlottes can be assembled (but not baked) 4 hours ahead and chilled, ramekins wrapped well in plastic wrap.

CALVADOS CRÈME ANGLAISE

MAKES ABOUT 1⅓ CUPS

ACTIVE TIME: 15 MIN   START TO FINISH: 25 MIN

- ½ vanilla bean
- 1¼ cups whole milk
- 4 large egg yolks
- 3 tablespoons sugar
- 1 tablespoon Calvados

SPECIAL EQUIPMENT: **an instant-read thermometer**

▸Scrape seeds from vanilla bean with tip of a paring knife into a 1- to 2-quart heavy saucepan, then add pod. Add milk and bring just to a boil, then remove from heat.

▸Whisk together yolks and sugar in a bowl. Add hot milk mixture to yolks in a slow stream, whisking, then pour custard into saucepan. Cook over moderately low heat, stirring constantly, until custard is slightly thickened and registers 175°F on thermometer (do not let boil). Remove from heat and stir in Calvados.

▸Pour custard through a fine-mesh sieve into a bowl. Set bowl in a larger bowl of ice water and cool, stirring occasionally, 10 minutes. Remove from ice bath and chill, covered, until ready to use.

COOKS' NOTE: Sauce can be chilled up to 3 days.

1998 MUSTARD CHEDDAR CRACKERS

MAKES 10 TO 12 DOZEN
ACTIVE TIME: 35 MIN START TO FINISH: 5½ HR (INCLUDES CHILLING)

These deliciously tangy nibbles are not only easy to prepare, but the dough can be frozen and kept for when guests drop by unexpectedly.

- 2 sticks (1 cup) unsalted butter, softened
- 1 lb sharp Cheddar, coarsely grated (preferably in a food processor; 5 cups)
- 1 large egg yolk
- ¼ teaspoon Dijon mustard
- 2 tablespoons dry mustard
- ¼ cup brown or yellow mustard seeds
- 2 teaspoons salt
- 2 cups all-purpose flour plus additional for dusting

SPECIAL EQUIPMENT: **parchment paper**

▶ Blend together butter, cheese, and yolk in a food processor until smooth. Add remaining ingredients and pulse until just combined. (If you have a small processor, divide butter mixture after blending and pulse with remaining ingredients in 2 batches.) Transfer dough (it will be very soft) to a bowl and chill, covered, 15 minutes.

▶ Halve dough, then shape each half into a 12-inch log on a lightly floured surface. Wrap logs in wax paper and foil, then chill until firm, at least 4 hours.

▶ Put oven racks in upper and lower thirds of oven and preheat oven to 350°F. Line 2 large baking sheets with parchment paper.

▶ Unwrap logs and cut into ⅛-inch-thick slices with a sharp thin knife, then arrange slices about 1 inch apart on baking sheets. Bake in batches, switching position of sheets halfway through baking, until pale golden, 12 to 15 minutes. Transfer crackers to racks to cool, about 5 minutes. Line sheets with clean parchment between batches.

COOKS' NOTES: Dough, once formed into logs, can be chilled up to 1 week or frozen 2 months.
• Crackers, cooled completely, keep in an airtight container at room temperature 1 week.

1999 POZOLE ROJO

Pork and Hominy Stew with Red Chiles
SERVES 8 TO 10
ACTIVE TIME: 1½ HR   START TO FINISH: 2½ HR

Who said you can only enjoy a good rich stew in the depths of winter? Born in the hot climate of Mexico, this melt-in-your-mouth pork and red-chile dish also makes a satisfying but not-too-filling end to a warm summer day.

- 1 large head garlic
- 4 lb country-style pork ribs (not lean)
- 12 cups cold water
- 4 cups reduced-sodium chicken broth (32 fl oz)
- 1 teaspoon dried oregano (preferably Mexican), crumbled
- 6 dried New Mexico or guajillo red chiles (2 oz; see Sources)
- 1½ cups boiling-hot water
- 1 cup coarsely chopped white onion (1 large)
- 1 tablespoon salt
- 4 (15-oz) cans white hominy (also called *pozole*), drained and rinsed

ACCOMPANIMENTS: **fried tortilla strips (see cooks' note, below); ½-inch cubes of California avocado; thinly sliced cabbage or lettuce; chopped white onion; chopped radishes; lime wedges; crumbled dried oregano (preferably Mexican); dried hot red pepper flakes**

▸Peel garlic and reserve 2 whole cloves, then slice remaining cloves. Combine sliced garlic, pork, water, and broth in a 7- to 8-quart heavy pot and bring to a boil, skimming froth. Add oregano, then reduce heat and simmer, uncovered, skimming occasionally, until pork is very tender, about 1½ hours.
▸Meanwhile, discard stems from chiles (do not seed), then soak in boiling-hot water (1½ cups) in a bowl, turning occasionally, until softened, about 30 minutes (do not drain). Purée chiles with soaking water, onion, 2 teaspoons salt, and reserved garlic cloves in a blender until smooth, about 1 minute.
▸Transfer pork with tongs to a large bowl, reserving broth in pot. Shred pork, using 2 forks (discard bones). Return pork to broth, then add hominy, chile purée, and remaining teaspoon salt and simmer, uncovered, skimming froth and stirring occasionally, 30 minutes. Season with salt.
▸Serve *pozole* in shallow bowls with accompaniments.

COOKS' NOTES: *Pozole* can be made 3 days ahead and cooled completely, uncovered, then chilled, covered. Reheat over moderately high heat, stirring occasionally, until stew comes to a boil.

• To make fried tortilla strips, halve 8 (6-inch) soft corn tortillas and cut crosswise into ¼-inch-thick strips. Fry in 3 batches in ½ inch of hot oil in a 12-inch heavy skillet over moderately high heat, stirring occasionally with a slotted spoon, until golden, 2 to 4 minutes per batch. Transfer with slotted spoon to paper towels to drain. Tortilla strips can be made 1 day ahead and cooled completely, then kept in an airtight container at room temperature.

2000 BAKED SHRIMP IN CHIPOTLE SAUCE

SERVES 4
ACTIVE TIME: 10 MIN   START TO FINISH: 25 MIN

Peeling these shrimp (a spin on New Orleans's classic barbecue shrimp), slurping their shells, and scooping up the hot, buttery sauce with crusty bread makes for nothing less than a feast. Best of all, it's ready in a flash.

- ½ stick (¼ cup) unsalted butter
- ¼ cup dry red wine
- 1½ tablespoons Worcestershire sauce
- 1 to 2 canned chipotle chiles in *adobo*, minced, plus 2 to 3 teaspoons *adobo* sauce
- 1 large garlic clove, minced
- 1½ teaspoons salt
- 1½ lb medium shrimp in shell (31 to 35 per pound)

SPECIAL EQUIPMENT: **a 2- to 3-qt ceramic or glass shallow baking dish**
ACCOMPANIMENT: **baguette**

▸Put oven rack in middle position and preheat oven to 400°F.
▸Melt butter in a saucepan and stir in wine, Worcestershire sauce, chipotles with *adobo* sauce (to taste), garlic, and salt. Toss shrimp with sauce in baking dish and bake until shrimp are just cooked through, 10 to 12 minutes. Sauce can be briefly simmered (with shrimp removed) to reduce it as needed.

COOKS' NOTE: Shrimp with heads on can be used; you'll need 1¾ pounds.

2001 CHOCOLATE SOUFFLÉ CAKE WITH ORANGE CARAMEL SAUCE

SERVES 8 TO 10
ACTIVE TIME: 1 HR   START TO FINISH: 2½ HR

You won't believe such a sophisticated dessert can result from just six ingredients. Citrusy caramel sauce teases out the deep flavors of the cake, which has a crisp crust and an unctuous chocolate center.

2	sticks (1 cup) unsalted butter, cut into pieces, plus additional for greasing pan
9	oz fine-quality bittersweet chocolate (not more than 60% cacao if marked), chopped
6	large eggs, separated
⅔	cup plus ½ cup superfine granulated sugar
½	teaspoon salt
3	navel or Valencia oranges

SPECIAL EQUIPMENT: a 10-inch springform pan

MAKE SOUFFLÉ CAKE:

▸ Put a small roasting pan filled halfway with hot water in bottom third of oven (to provide moisture during baking). Position another oven rack in middle of oven, then preheat oven to 325°F. Butter springform pan and line bottom with a round of parchment or wax paper. Butter paper.

▸ Melt butter (2 sticks) and chocolate together in a 2-quart heavy saucepan over low heat, stirring, then remove from heat. Beat together yolks, ⅓ cup sugar, and salt in a large bowl with an electric mixer at medium-high speed until thick enough to form a ribbon that takes 2 seconds to dissolve into mixture when beater is lifted, 6 to 8 minutes in a stand mixer or 10 to 14 minutes with a handheld. Stir warm chocolate mixture into yolk mixture until combined well.

▸ Beat whites in another large bowl with cleaned beaters at medium speed until they just hold soft peaks. Gradually add ⅓ cup sugar, beating until whites just hold stiff peaks. Stir one fourth of whites into chocolate mixture to lighten, then fold in remaining whites gently but thoroughly.

▸ Pour batter into springform pan and bake in middle of oven (do not place springform pan in hot water) until a wooden pick or skewer inserted in center comes out with crumbs adhering, about 1 hour (a crust will form and crack on top of cake as it bakes). Transfer to a rack and cool 10 minutes (cake will "deflate" as it cools).

▸ Run a thin knife carefully around edge of cake, then remove side of pan. Cool cake on bottom of pan 30 minutes. Invert a rack over cake and invert cake onto rack, then remove bottom of pan and carefully peel off paper. Invert a serving plate over cake, then invert cake onto plate.

MAKE SAUCE WHILE CAKE BAKES:

▸ Remove zest from 2 oranges (see Tips, page 8) and trim any white pith from zest with a paring knife. Cut enough very thin strips of zest to measure ¼ cup. Squeeze juice from all 3 oranges and pour through a fine-mesh sieve into a bowl. Measure out 1 cup juice and reserve remainder for another use.

▸ Cook remaining ½ cup sugar in a dry 1- to 2-quart heavy saucepan over moderate heat, undisturbed, until it begins to melt. Continue to cook, stirring occasionally with a fork, until sugar is melted into a deep golden caramel. Add zest and cook, stirring, until fragrant, about 15 seconds. Tilt pan and carefully pour in juice (caramel will harden and steam vigorously). Cook over moderately low heat, stirring, until caramel is dissolved, then cool sauce.

▸ Serve cake with orange caramel sauce.

COOKS' NOTE: We recommend making this cake, without sauce, 1 day ahead to allow flavors to develop. Cool completely, then chill, covered with plastic wrap. Bring to room temperature before serving.

2002 CAULIFLOWER CHEDDAR GRATIN WITH HORSERADISH CRUMBS

SERVES 8

ACTIVE TIME: 45 MIN   START TO FINISH: 55 MIN

The nutty, sweet undertones of cauliflower are particularly suited to meld with the tangy, salty Cheddar and the spicy horseradish.

    3 lb cauliflower (1 large head), cut into
         1½- to 2-inch florets
    ½ stick (¼ cup) unsalted butter
    2 tablespoons all-purpose flour
  1½ cups whole milk
    6 oz sharp Cheddar, coarsely grated (2 cups)
    ½ cup finely chopped scallion greens
    ½ teaspoon salt
    ½ teaspoon black pepper
  20 (2-inch) square saltine crackers
    2 tablespoons drained bottled horseradish

▶ Preheat oven to 450°F. Butter a 2-quart shallow baking dish.
▶ Cook cauliflower in a 5- to 6-quart pot of boiling salted water (see Tips, page 8) until just tender, 6 to 8 minutes. Drain cauliflower well in a colander and transfer to baking dish.
▶ While cauliflower cooks, melt 2 tablespoons butter in a 3- to 4-quart heavy saucepan over moderately low heat and whisk in flour. Cook roux, whisking, 3 minutes. Add milk in a slow stream, whisking, and bring to a boil, whisking frequently. Reduce heat and simmer sauce, whisking occasionally, 8 minutes. Remove from heat and add cheese, scallion greens, salt, and pepper, whisking until cheese is melted. Pour cheese sauce over cauliflower and stir gently to combine.
▶ Coarsely crumble crackers into a bowl. Melt remaining 2 tablespoons butter in a small saucepan, then remove from heat and stir in horseradish. Pour over crumbs and toss to coat.
▶ Sprinkle crumb topping evenly over cauliflower.
▶ Bake gratin until topping is golden brown, about 10 minutes.

2003 SHORT RIBS BRAISED IN COFFEE ANCHO CHILE SAUCE

SERVES 6

ACTIVE TIME: 40 MIN   START TO FINISH: 4½ HR

Inspired by chef Robert Del Grande of Cafe Annie, in Houston, we combine succulent short ribs with bitter undertones of coffee and mellow heat of chiles, then add maple syrup and lime juice to cut the spiciness. We recommend serving these ribs over soft polenta.

    4 dried ancho chiles, stemmed, seeded, and ribs discarded
    2 cups boiling-hot water
    1 medium onion, quartered
    3 garlic cloves, coarsely chopped
    2 tablespoons finely chopped canned chipotle chiles
         in *adobo* plus 2 teaspoons *adobo* sauce
    2 tablespoons pure maple syrup
    1 tablespoon fresh lime juice
    1 tablespoon salt
    6 lb beef short ribs or flanken
    1 teaspoon black pepper
    1 tablespoon vegetable oil
    ½ cup brewed coffee

▶ Preheat oven to 350°F.
▶ Soak ancho chiles in boiling-hot water until softened, about 20 minutes, then drain in a colander set over a bowl. Taste soaking liquid: It will be a little bitter, but if unpleasantly so, discard it; otherwise, reserve for braising. Transfer ancho chiles to a blender and purée with onion, garlic, chipotles with sauce, maple syrup, lime juice, and 1 teaspoon salt.
▶ Pat ribs dry and sprinkle with pepper and remaining 2 teaspoons salt. Heat oil in a 12-inch heavy skillet over moderately high heat until hot but not smoking, then brown ribs in 3 batches, turning occasionally, about 5 minutes per batch. Transfer as browned to a roasting pan just large enough to hold ribs in 1 layer.
▶ Carefully add chile purée to fat remaining in skillet (it will spatter and steam) and cook over moderately low heat, stirring frequently, 5 minutes. Add reserved chile soaking liquid (or 1½ cups water) and coffee and bring to a boil, then pour over ribs (liquid should reach about halfway up sides of meat).
▶ Cover roasting pan tightly with foil and braise ribs until very tender, 3 to 3½ hours. Skim fat from pan juices. Serve ribs with pan juices.

COOKS' NOTE: Ribs improve in flavor if braised 2 days ahead. Cool completely, uncovered, then chill, ribs covered directly with parchment or wax paper and roasting pan covered with foil. Remove any solidified fat before reheating.

2004 COWBOY CHRISTMAS BREAKFAST

SERVES 12 (OR 8 COWBOYS)
ACTIVE TIME: 30 MIN   START TO FINISH: 1½ HR

Sausage, egg, scallion, and cheese are layered over garlicky "Texas toast" in the heartiest take on savory bread pudding we've ever come across. This stick-to-your-ribs breakfast for a crowd can be completely assembled the night before.

½ stick (¼ cup) unsalted butter, softened, plus additional for greasing baking dish
1 (1-lb) package bulk breakfast sausage (not links)
1 (15-inch-long) loaf Italian bread (about 4 inches wide)
1 garlic clove, chopped
2 dozen large eggs
1 cup whole milk
2 teaspoons salt
1 teaspoon black pepper
1 large bunch scallions, chopped (1¼ cups)
¼ lb sharp Cheddar, coarsely grated (1 cup)

▸ Put oven rack in middle position and preheat oven to 375°F. Generously butter bottom and sides of a 13- by 9-inch baking dish.

▸ Cook sausage in a 12-inch heavy skillet over moderately high heat, stirring frequently and breaking up any large lumps with a fork, until browned, about 10 minutes. Pour off fat from skillet, then cool sausage to room temperature.

▸ Cut half of bread into 1-inch-thick slices and reserve remaining half for another use. Pulse butter (½ stick) and garlic in a food processor until smooth. Spread a thin layer of garlic butter on both sides of each bread slice, arranging bread in 1 layer in bottom of baking dish. Sprinkle sausage on top.

▸ Whisk together eggs, milk, salt, and pepper in a large bowl until frothy, then whisk in scallions and half of cheese. Pour egg mixture over sausage (bread will float to the top), pushing down on bread with a spatula to help it absorb liquid. Sprinkle with remaining cheese.

▸ Bake, tightly covered with a large sheet of buttered foil (buttered side down), 30 minutes, then carefully remove foil and bake until top is slightly puffed and custard is set in center, about 20 minutes more. Transfer baking dish to a rack and let stand 10 minutes. Cut into 12 squares and serve immediately.

COOKS' NOTE: Dish can be assembled (but not baked) 12 hours ahead and chilled, tightly covered with buttered foil. Bake as directed above.

2005 CAESAR SALAD

SERVES 6
ACTIVE TIME: 25 MIN   START TO FINISH: 25 MIN

We've run recipes for this classic salad in various incarnations every few years since the 1940s—with and without raw egg, with and without anchovies, changing up the cheese and even mixing in pasta or shellfish. This version is simply the best.

1 large garlic clove, halved lengthwise
¾ to 1 cup extra-virgin olive oil
1 (3-oz) Portuguese roll or a 7-inch piece of baguette, cut into ¾-inch cubes
8 anchovy fillets packed in oil, drained
1 large egg
2 tablespoons fresh lemon juice
3 hearts of romaine (an 18-oz package), leaves separated but left whole
1 oz finely grated Parmigiano-Reggiano (½ cup; see Tips, page 8)

SPECIAL EQUIPMENT: **a very large salad bowl (preferably wooden)**

▸ Season salad bowl by rubbing a cut half of garlic followed by 1 teaspoon oil onto bottom and side of bowl (reserve garlic).

▸ Heat ¾ cup oil with both halves of reserved garlic in an 8-inch heavy skillet over moderately high heat, turning garlic occasionally, until golden, 1 to 2 minutes, then discard garlic. Add bread cubes to oil and fry, turning occasionally, until golden on all sides, about 2 minutes. Transfer croutons to paper towels to drain. Pour oil through a small fine-mesh sieve into a heatproof measuring cup and add enough additional olive oil to bring total to 6 tablespoons.

▸ Put anchovies in salad bowl and mash to a paste using 2 forks. Whisk in egg and lemon juice, then add reserved oil (warm or at room temperature) in a slow stream, whisking until emulsified. Season with salt to taste.

▸ Add romaine leaves to dressing and toss to coat. Add croutons and toss briefly.

▸ Divide salad among 6 large plates, then sprinkle with cheese and pepper to taste. Serve immediately.

COOKS' NOTES: The egg in this recipe is not cooked, which may be of concern if salmonella is a problem in your area.
• Dressing and tossing the lettuce leaves whole will result in an overall crisper salad.
• Although the croutons are best warm, they can be fried 1 hour ahead.

THE MENU COLLECTION

There are so many ways to entertain—cocktail parties, impromptu cookouts, open-house potlucks, holiday meals steeped in tradition, elegant dinner parties—and we support them all. In fact, we think nothing beats gathering friends and family to share home-cooked food. The catch is finding time to plan such get-togethers. Here, then, are eighteen seasonal menus guaranteed to inspire, whether you're hosting a formal dinner or a picnic that includes every cousin.

Gourmet has always been known for extravagant menus, and we still believe it's worth pulling out all the stops every now and then. Christmas is a natural time to entertain lavishly, and *Crimson Tidings* reflects the warmth and elegance of the season. To start, lobster gelées sit pretty on plates drizzled with fresh tarragon oil, while tiny dumplings stuffed with chicken liver and mushrooms add a rich accent to ruby-red beet consommé (pictured opposite). The theme continues with a majestic prime rib roast with red wine sauce, glazed red pearl onions, and a salad of red-leaf lettuces before ending on a rosy note, with tender quince apple strudels.

Merry and Bright is a festive, very grown-up cocktail party that reconfigures comforting classics into sophisticated new guises. Everyone will love nibbling on tiny grilled cheese sandwiches with mushrooms and truffle oil, pork cornets filled with sour cherry sauce, and crisp chocolate marshmallow squares.

And who says grand entertaining can only happen after dark? *A Huntin' We Will Go* proves that breakfast can be the most important meal of the day—especially when it includes delectables like duck confit hash, baked eggs with Cantal cheese, and brown sugar and cayenne-glazed bacon. Your guests will happily raise their glasses—filled with piquant aquavit bloody marys—to this merry meal.

But for every over-the-top menu, we offer others that are a breeze to pull together. Take *South by Southwest*: Much of this three-course affair, including the hearty lamb chili, cool coffee flan, and chocolate almond shortbread, can be made at least one day ahead. The same goes for *Just the Four of Us*, which boasts a juicy turkey roulade and individual chocolate cranberry cakes topped with bourbon-spiked whipped cream. It's a tempting alternative to a traditional Thanksgiving feast (though we have one of those, too, in *The Generous Table*).

When the great outdoors beckons, we have plenty of meals best enjoyed alfresco. Although some menus are set in fantasy fields of lavender (*A Day in the Country*) or on a picturesque beach along the Grecian coast (*Edible Odyssey*), these meals will taste just as good served in your own backyard. A summertime reunion (*We Are Family*) calls for fresh spins on old favorites, like sugar snap pea and cabbage slaw and chicken salad with fennel. No one will be able to keep their hands off dessert: gooey praline ice cream sandwiches and nectarine raspberry pies that practically shout, "Summer is here!"

There's no secret to great entertaining—delicious food combined with good company creates its own wonderful alchemy. These are the meals that will be remembered forever. All you need to add are your guests.

SOUTH BY SOUTHWEST

SUPPER IN NEW MEXICO

SERVES 6 TO 8

**CACTUS, CHAYOTE, AND
GREEN-APPLE SALAD**

**LAMB CHILI WITH MASA
HARINA DUMPLINGS**

BOEGER EL DORADO BARBERA '03

COFFEE FLAN

**CHOCOLATE ALMOND
SHORTBREAD**

CACTUS, CHAYOTE, AND GREEN-APPLE SALAD

SERVES 6 TO 8 (FIRST COURSE)

ACTIVE TIME: 45 MIN   START TO FINISH: 1¼ HR

This refreshing salad is a delicious balance of savory and sweet with the bonus of a little heat.

  1 lb fresh nopales (prickly pear cactus paddles; about 5;
      see cooks' note, below)
  2 chayotes (1 lb total), peeled, halved lengthwise, and
      seeds discarded, then cut into ¼-inch-thick sticks (3 to
      4 inches long)
  1 Granny Smith apple, left unpeeled, halved, cored, and thinly
      sliced lengthwise

  2 scallions, trimmed and thinly sliced
  4 navel oranges
  3 tablespoons fresh lime juice
  ¼ teaspoon salt
  ⅛ teaspoon black pepper
  ⅓ cup raw (green) hulled pumpkin seeds
  5 tablespoons olive oil
      Rounded ⅛ teaspoon cayenne

▶ Put 1 cactus paddle, flat side down, on a work surface. Scrape horizontally from narrow base of paddle toward wider end with a vegetable peeler or knife to cut off thorns and brown spots. Dethorn paddle on other side in same manner, then trim all around edge. Repeat with remaining paddles, then cut paddles crosswise into ¼-inch-thick slices.

▶ Blanch cactus in a 6- to 8-quart pot of boiling salted water (see Tips, page 8) until just softened, about 1 minute. Immediately transfer with a slotted spoon to a bowl of ice and cold water to stop cooking. Drain in a colander and rinse under cold water. Pat dry, then transfer to a large bowl along with chayotes, apple, and scallions.

▶ Cut peel and all white pith from 3 oranges with a sharp knife. Working over bowl containing cactus mixture, cut segments free from membranes, letting segments fall into bowl. Squeeze juice from membranes and remaining orange into bowl, then add lime juice, salt, and pepper and toss. Let stand until chayotes are wilted, about 30 minutes.

▶ While salad stands, toast pumpkin seeds in 2 tablespoons oil in a 10-inch heavy skillet over moderately low heat, stirring frequently, until puffed and pale golden, 3 to 4 minutes. Remove from heat and stir in cayenne. Cool seeds in oil in skillet.

▶ Drain salad in a colander set over a bowl, then transfer juice to a 1-quart saucepan and boil until syrupy and reduced to about ⅓ cup, 4 to 5 minutes. Remove from heat and whisk in remaining 3 tablespoons oil. Return salad to bowl and toss with dressing, pumpkin seeds with oil from skillet, and salt to taste.

COOKS' NOTE: If you can't find fresh nopales, use blanched thin green beans.

LAMB CHILI WITH MASA HARINA DUMPLINGS

SERVES 6 TO 8

ACTIVE TIME: 1¼ HR   START TO FINISH: 4¼ HR

No one is going to ask "Where's the beef?" when confronted with this chili. Slowly cooking the meat with lard, peppers, and spices creates a wonderfully complex sauce that's topped off with tender corn-flavored dumplings.

FOR CHILI

- 10 dried mild New Mexico chiles (2½ to 3 oz)
- 5 cups water
- 3¼ lb boneless lamb shoulder, trimmed and cut into 1½-inch pieces
- ½ teaspoon black pepper
- 1¼ teaspoons salt
- 3 tablespoons lard or vegetable oil
- 1 large onion, chopped (2 cups)
- 4 garlic cloves, minced
- 2 Turkish bay leaves or 1 California
- 2 teaspoons ground cumin
- 1½ teaspoons dried oregano, crumbled
- 3 tablespoons finely chopped canned chipotle chiles in *adobo*

FOR DUMPLINGS

- ¾ cup masa harina (corn tortilla mix)
- ¼ cup all-purpose flour
- 1 teaspoon baking powder
- ¼ teaspoon baking soda
- ¼ teaspoon salt
- ¼ cup chilled lard or unsalted butter, cut into small pieces
- ¾ cup well-shaken buttermilk
- 2 tablespoons chopped fresh cilantro

MAKE CHILI:

▶ Simmer dried chiles in 2 cups water, covered, in a 2-quart heavy saucepan until very soft, about 20 minutes. Reserve ¾ cup cooking liquid, then drain in a colander. Stem chiles (do not remove seeds), then purée in a blender with reserved cooking liquid until smooth (use caution when blending hot liquids). Force purée through a fine-mesh sieve into a bowl. Reserve purée.

▶ Pat lamb dry, then sprinkle with pepper and 1 teaspoon salt. Heat 2 tablespoons lard in a 6-quart wide heavy pot or a 3-inch-deep straight-sided skillet over moderately high heat until hot but not smoking, then brown lamb in 4 batches (without crowding), turning occasionally, about 5 minutes per batch. Transfer to a bowl.

▶ Add remaining tablespoon lard to pot, then cook onion, garlic, bay leaves, and remaining ¼ teaspoon salt over moderate heat, stirring occasionally, until softened, 4 to 5 minutes. Add cumin and oregano and cook, stirring frequently, 1 minute. Stir in reserved chile purée and chipotles and simmer, stirring frequently and scraping up brown bits from bottom of pot, 5 minutes. Add lamb along with any juices accumulated in bowl and remaining 3 cups water, then bring to a boil. Reduce heat and simmer, covered, until lamb is tender, about 2½ hours.

MAKE DUMPLINGS:

▶ Stir together masa harina, flour, baking powder, baking soda, and salt in a bowl. Blend in lard pieces with a pastry blender or your fingertips until mixture resembles coarse meal. Add buttermilk, stirring just until dough is moistened (do not overmix).

▶ Skim fat off chili and discard bay leaves, then drop 8 or 9 heaping tablespoons of dough onto simmering chili, about 2 inches apart. Reduce heat to low and gently simmer, covered, until tops of dumplings are dry to the touch, 15 to 20 minutes. Sprinkle with cilantro.

COOKS' NOTE: Chili is best when made at least 1 day ahead, without dumplings and cilantro, and can be made 2 days ahead and cooled completely, uncovered, then chilled, covered. Discard fat from surface and reheat stew before adding dumplings and sprinkling with cilantro.

▶ Blend remaining ingredients in a blender, in 2 batches if your blender is small, until smooth. Pour custard through a fine-mesh sieve over caramel in dish, then transfer dish to a 17- by 11-inch roasting pan lined with a kitchen towel. Cover dish loosely with a piece of foil, then pour enough boiling-hot water into roasting pan to reach 1 inch up side of dish. Bake until custard is set but still wobbly in center when gently shaken and a knife inserted in center comes out clean, 1 to 1¼ hours. Transfer dish to a rack to cool completely, about 40 minutes. Chill flan, covered, until cold, at least 8 hours and up to 1 day.

▶ To unmold flan, run a thin knife around edge of dish to loosen flan. Invert a large platter with a lip over dish. Holding dish and platter securely together, quickly invert and turn out flan onto platter. Caramel will pour out over and around flan.

CHOCOLATE ALMOND SHORTBREAD

MAKES 32 COOKIES

ACTIVE TIME: 15 MIN   START TO FINISH: 1 HR (INCLUDES COOLING)

These crumbly cookies are extremely easy to make, and they improve with time. We recommend baking them a couple of days ahead.

- ½   cup blanched whole almonds (3 oz)
- 1   cup all-purpose flour
- 5   tablespoons superfine granulated sugar
- 2   tablespoons unsweetened cocoa powder (preferably Dutch-process)
- ½   teaspoon cinnamon
- ¼   teaspoon salt
- 1   stick (½ cup) unsalted butter, cut into small pieces
  Confectioners sugar for dusting

▶ Put oven rack in middle position and preheat oven to 375°F.

▶ Pulse almonds with flour, granulated sugar, cocoa, cinnamon, and salt in a food processor until very finely chopped. Add butter and pulse just until a dough forms.

▶ Press dough evenly into an ungreased 9-inch square baking pan with your fingers. Cut dough into 16 squares with a sharp knife, then cut squares diagonally to make a total of 32 triangles.

▶ Bake until cookies are dry to the touch, 15 to 17 minutes. Transfer pan to a rack and run a thin knife around edge of pan to loosen cookies while hot. Recut hot cookies into triangles, then cool completely in pan. Dust with confectioners sugar just before serving.

COOKS' NOTE: Cookies can be made 5 days ahead and kept in an airtight container at room temperature.

COFFEE FLAN

SERVES 6 TO 8

ACTIVE TIME: 30 MIN   START TO FINISH: 10½ HR (INCLUDES CHILLING)

Condensed milk gives this Spanish dessert its silky texture.

- ¾   cup sugar
- 1   (14-oz) can sweetened condensed milk (1¼ cups)
- 3¾   cups whole milk
- 5   large eggs
- 4½   teaspoons instant-coffee granules dissolved in 4 teaspoons hot water
- 1   teaspoon vanilla
- ⅛   teaspoon salt

▶ Put oven rack in middle position and preheat oven to 350°F.

▶ Cook sugar in a dry small heavy saucepan over moderate heat, undisturbed, until it begins to melt. Continue to cook, stirring occasionally with a fork, until sugar melts into a deep golden caramel. Immediately pour into a 9-inch round ceramic or glass baking dish or metal cake pan (2 inches deep) and tilt dish to coat bottom (use caution, dish will be hot). Cool until hardened, 10 to 15 minutes.

MEAL OF FORTUNE

A LUNAR NEW YEAR BANQUET

SERVES 8

SHRIMP AND PORK POT STICKERS

WINTER MELON SOUP

WHITE-CUT CHICKEN

WHOLE BLACK BASS WITH GINGER AND SCALLIONS

BUDDHA'S DELIGHT

BLACK-BEAN SHRIMP WITH CHINESE BROCCOLI

STEAMED WHITE RICE

CLOS FLORIDÈNE GRAVES BLANC '03

EIGHT-TREASURE PUDDINGS

FOR HELP IN FINDING THE ASIAN INGREDIENTS
IN THIS MENU, SEE SOURCES.

SHRIMP AND PORK POT STICKERS

MAKES 24 DUMPLINGS
ACTIVE TIME: 1½ HR   START TO FINISH: 1½ HR

FOR DUMPLINGS
1½ to 1¾ cups all-purpose flour plus additional for dusting
½ cup lukewarm water
3 fresh or 4 rinsed canned water chestnuts (3 oz)
½ lb shrimp in shell, peeled, deveined, and coarsely chopped
   (1 cup)
¼ lb ground fatty pork (from shoulder)
¾ cup chopped scallions (from 1 bunch)
1½ tablespoons soy sauce
2 teaspoons minced peeled fresh ginger
1 teaspoon Asian sesame oil
1 tablespoon peanut or vegetable oil

FOR SAUCE
⅓ cup soy sauce
2 tablespoons Chinese black vinegar (preferably Chinkiang)
2 tablespoons water
1 teaspoon Asian chile oil, or to taste

SPECIAL EQUIPMENT: a 3½-inch round biscuit or cookie cutter

MAKE DUMPLINGS:
▶ Stir together 1½ cups flour and lukewarm water (½ cup) in a bowl until a shaggy dough forms. Knead on a lightly floured surface, adding more flour as needed if dough is sticky, until smooth, about 1 to 2 minutes. Dust dough lightly with flour and cover with an inverted bowl, then let stand at room temperature at least 10 minutes and up to 1 hour (to let gluten relax).
▶ If using fresh water chestnuts, scrub very well, then peel with a sharp paring knife and rinse. Cover fresh water chestnuts with 1½ cups water in a 1-quart saucepan and bring to a boil, then boil until crisp-tender and slightly translucent, about 5 minutes. Drain in a colander and rinse under cold water to cool.
▶ Cut fresh or canned water chestnuts into ¼-inch dice and put in a medium bowl along with shrimp, pork, scallions, soy sauce, ginger, and sesame oil. Knead mixture with your hands until just combined, then chill, covered, 10 minutes.
▶ While shrimp mixture chills, line a large baking sheet with paper towels and dust lightly with flour, then lightly dust work surface with flour. Halve dough and cover 1 half with inverted bowl. Pat remaining half into a flat square, then roll out into a 13-inch square (less than ⅛ inch thick) with a lightly floured

rolling pin, dusting work surface with additional flour as needed. Cut out 12 rounds, very close together, using cutter. (If dough sticks to cutter, lightly dip cutter in flour and shake off excess). Reroll scraps if necessary.
▶ Transfer rounds to lined baking sheet and cover loosely with another layer of paper towels lightly dusted (on top) with flour. Roll out remaining half of dough and cut out 12 more rounds in same manner, then transfer rounds to top layer of paper towels.
▶ Line another large baking sheet with paper towels and dust lightly with flour. With your hand palm-up, put 1 dough round on fingers near palm, then put 1 tablespoon pork mixture in center of round and fold it over filling to form an open half-moon shape. With a wet finger, moisten border along lower inner edge of round. Using thumb and forefinger of one hand, form 10 to 12 tiny pleats along unmoistened edge of dumpling skin, pressing pleats against moistened border to enclose filling. The moistened border will stay smooth and will automatically curve in a semicircle. Stand dumpling on a baking sheet and form 23 more dumplings in same manner (you may have some filling left over), arranging them in 1 layer, about ½ inch apart. Cover loosely with paper towels.
MAKE SAUCE:
▶ Stir together soy sauce, vinegar, water, and chile oil in a small bowl. Restir just before serving.
COOK DUMPLINGS:
▶ Heat vegetable oil in a 10-inch nonstick skillet over moderately high heat until hot but not smoking, then arrange 7 dumplings, seam sides up, in a tight spiral pattern in center of skillet. Arrange remaining 17 dumplings along outer edge (they should touch one another; if you have trouble fitting them, angle one a little more sharply than the others and reposition others to fall into place). Fry dumplings until bottoms are pale golden, 2 to 3 minutes. Add ½ cup water, tilting skillet to distribute, then cover tightly with a lid and cook until liquid is evaporated and bottoms of dumplings are crisp and golden, 7 to 10 minutes. (Use a spatula to loosen and lift edges to check bottoms; replace lid and continue cooking if necessary, checking after 1 to 2 minutes.) Remove lid and invert a large plate with a rim over skillet. Using pot holders and holding plate and skillet tightly together, invert dumplings onto plate. Serve immediately, with dipping sauce.

COOKS' NOTE: Dumplings can be formed (but not cooked) 1 day ahead. Chill in 1 layer on lightly floured paper towels, not touching and loosely covered with more paper towels, in an airtight container.

OPPOSITE (CLOCKWISE FROM UPPER LEFT): white-cut chicken; black-bean shrimp with Chinese broccoli; shrimp and pork pot stickers; and whole black bass with ginger and scallions

WINTER MELON SOUP

SERVES 8 (FIRST COURSE)
ACTIVE TIME: 45 MIN START TO FINISH: 4¾ HR

From the rich broth to the velvety cubes of winter melon—a gourd commonly used in Chinese cuisine for the wonderfully soft texture it takes on during cooking—this wholesome soup is immensely satisfying.

FOR BROTH

- 1 (3- to 3½-lb) whole chicken, preferably organic free-range
- 1 bunch scallions, halved crosswise
- 2 oz Smithfield or other cured ham (1 piece or sliced), trimmed of any spice coating
- 1 (1-inch) piece peeled fresh ginger, smashed
- 14 cups water
- 1 tablespoon salt

FOR SOUP

- 5 (1-inch-wide) large dried scallops
- 1 (2-lb) wedge winter melon
- 2 oz Smithfield or other cured ham (1 piece or sliced), trimmed of any spice coating and cut into very thin matchsticks (½ cup)
- 1 (2-inch) piece fresh ginger, peeled and cut into very thin matchsticks (2 tablespoons)
- 3 scallions, thinly sliced (½ cup)

MAKE BROTH:

▶ Rinse chicken inside and out, then stuff cavity with scallions, ham, and ginger. Bring water with chicken and salt to a boil in a deep 7- to 8-quart stockpot or pasta pot, then reduce heat and cook at a bare simmer, uncovered, skimming off froth occasionally, 3 hours.

▶ Remove and discard chicken, then pour broth through a fine-mesh sieve into a large bowl. Let stand 5 minutes. Skim off fat. (You will have about 10 to 12 cups broth and need only 9 cups for this soup; reserve remainder for the black-bean shrimp with Chinese broccoli, page 81, or for another use.)

MAKE SOUP:

▶ Bring 2 cups broth to a boil in a 1-quart heavy saucepan, then add scallops and remove from heat. Soak, covered, 15 minutes.

▶ Return scallop mixture to low heat and simmer, uncovered, until scallops are soft and pale, about 15 minutes. Remove from heat and cool in cooking liquid. Transfer scallops with a slotted spoon to a bowl, reserving cooking liquid. Shred scallops into "threads" with a fork or your fingers, discarding tough ligament from side of each scallop if attached. Bring remaining 7 cups broth to a simmer in cleaned 7- to 8-quart pot with scallops and reserved cooking liquid.

▶ Cut off and discard rind from winter melon. Remove and discard seeds, then cut melon into ⅓-inch cubes (about 5 cups). Add to broth and gently simmer, uncovered, until melon is transparent, 20 to 30 minutes.

▶ Stir in ham, ginger, scallions, and salt to taste just before serving.

COOKS' NOTES: Broth can be made 5 days ahead and cooled completely, uncovered, then chilled, covered. Remove any solidified fat before using.

• Soup, without final addition of ham, ginger, and scallions, can be made 3 days ahead and cooled completely, uncovered, then chilled, covered.

WHITE-CUT CHICKEN

SERVES 8 (AS PART OF A CHINESE MEAL)
ACTIVE TIME: 30 MIN START TO FINISH: 1½ HR

It's traditional to serve a whole chicken, including the head and feet, for Chinese New Year. The white meat symbolizes purity, and serving the entire bird represents unity. Plunging the chicken into ice water after poaching ensures that the meat is perfectly juicy and tender. A very simple but powerful dipping sauce tops it off. Use only a tiny amount—it's quite strong.

FOR CHICKEN

- 1 (3- to 3½-lb) whole chicken (with head and feet if desired), neck (if without head) and giblets reserved for another use if desired
- 1 bunch scallions, halved crosswise
- 2 oz Smithfield or other cured ham (1 piece or sliced), trimmed of any spice coating
- 6 (¼-inch-thick) round slices peeled fresh ginger
- 14 cups water
- 1 teaspoon salt
- 1 teaspoon Asian sesame oil
- ½ cup fresh cilantro leaves

FOR DIPPING SAUCE

- 1 bunch scallions (white and pale green parts only), cut into very thin 2-inch strips
- 3 tablespoons light soy sauce (preferably Pearl River Bridge brand)
- 3 tablespoons peanut or vegetable oil
- 1 tablespoon finely grated (with a rasp) peeled fresh ginger

SPECIAL EQUIPMENT: a rasp grater; a well-seasoned 14-inch flat-bottomed wok; a heavy cleaver

MAKE CHICKEN:

▶ Rinse chicken inside and out, then bend legs to tuck feet (if still attached) inside cavity. Stuff cavity with scallions, ham, and ginger.

▶ Bring water with salt to a boil in a deep 7- to 8-quart stockpot or pasta pot. Add chicken, breast side down (chicken may not be completely covered with liquid), then reduce heat and simmer, covered, 20 minutes.

▶ Remove from heat and let stand, covered, 30 minutes. Turn chicken over and let stand, covered, 15 minutes more (chicken will be cooked through).

▶ While chicken stands, fill a large bowl three-fourths full with ice and cold water. Carefully remove chicken from pot with a large slotted spoon and plunge into ice water to stop cooking. Let stand, gently turning over once (be careful not to tear skin), until cool, about 10 minutes total. Carefully transfer to a cutting board and discard scallions, ham, and ginger from cavity. Pat dry. Rub skin with sesame oil.

MAKE DIPPING SAUCE:

▶ Stir together scallions and soy sauce in a small heatproof bowl.

▶ Heat wok over high heat until a drop of water vaporizes instantly. Pour oil around side of wok, then tilt wok to swirl oil, coating sides. When oil just begins to smoke, carefully add ginger (oil will spatter) and stir-fry 30 seconds. Immediately remove from heat and pour over scallion mixture, stirring to combine (scallions will wilt).

▶ To cut chicken so that it can be easily eaten with chopsticks, cut off the head and neck (if attached) with a cleaver. Cut off the feet. (These parts, along with the back, are not always eaten.) Cut off the drumsticks and thighs, then cut crosswise through the bone into 1-inch pieces. Cut off the wings, separating them at the joints. Cut through the ribs separating breast from back, then cut backbone crosswise into 3 pieces. (Striking the cleaver with a rubber mallet makes the cuts clean.) Cut the breast crosswise through the bone into 1-inch pieces. Recompose bird on a platter or mound all pieces in a bowl.

▶ Drizzle 2 tablespoons dipping sauce over chicken and sprinkle with cilantro leaves. Serve warm or at room temperature, with remaining dipping sauce on the side.

COOKS' NOTES: Chicken can be cooked and rubbed with sesame oil (but not cut) 1 day ahead and chilled, covered.

• Chicken can be cut up and arranged on platter 4 hours ahead and chilled, covered. Bring to room temperature 1 hour before serving. Drizzle with dipping sauce just before serving.

• Dipping sauce can be made 4 hours ahead and kept, covered, at room temperature.

WHOLE BLACK BASS WITH GINGER AND SCALLIONS

SERVES 8 (AS PART OF A CHINESE MEAL)
ACTIVE TIME: 20 MIN   START TO FINISH: 50 MIN

A whole fish, representing abundance, is almost always included on the celebratory Chinese table. Ours is flavored lightly with ginger and scallions, so as not to overpower the fresh taste of the fish.

  1   (3-lb) whole black bass or sea bass (not Chilean), cleaned, leaving head and tail intact
 ½   teaspoon salt
  1   bunch scallions, white and pale green parts cut into very thin 2-inch strips and greens reserved separately
  1   (1-inch) piece fresh ginger, peeled and cut into very thin matchsticks
  3   tablespoons light soy sauce (preferably Pearl River Bridge brand)
 ¼   teaspoon sugar
  1   tablespoon peanut or vegetable oil

SPECIAL EQUIPMENT: a large shallow baking dish (about 15 by 10 inches) to fit inside a 17- by 12- by 2½-inch roasting pan; heavy-duty foil; a well-seasoned 14-inch flat-bottomed wok

▶ Put oven rack in middle position and preheat oven to 400°F. Put baking dish in roasting pan.

▶ Rinse fish and pat dry, then rub inside and out with salt. Transfer to baking dish and sprinkle with scallion strips (white and pale green) and ginger.

▶ Stir together soy sauce and sugar until sugar is dissolved, then pour over fish. Add enough boiling-hot water to roasting pan to reach halfway up side of baking dish. Oil a large sheet of heavy-duty foil, then tent foil (oiled side down) over fish and tightly seal around roasting pan. Carefully transfer roasting pan to oven and bake until fish is just cooked through, 30 to 35 minutes.

▶ While fish bakes, cut enough scallion greens diagonally into very thin slices to measure ½ cup (reserve remaining scallion greens for another use).

▶ Just before serving, remove foil from fish and sprinkle with scallion greens. Heat wok over high heat until a bead of water vaporizes instantly. Pour oil around side of wok, then tilt wok to swirl oil, coating side, and heat until smoking. Remove from heat and immediately pour oil over scallion greens and fish.

COOKS' NOTE: Fish can be prepared (but not steamed) 6 hours ahead and chilled, covered.

BUDDHA'S DELIGHT

SERVES 8 (AS PART OF A CHINESE MEAL)
ACTIVE TIME: 45 MIN   START TO FINISH: 1½ HR

*Subtle and delicate, this dish, called Buddha's Delight because
it's completely vegetarian, is all about texture. Prepared with
fresh vegetables, it's sublime. If you can't find fresh, don't use
canned (frozen bamboo shoots and ginkgo nuts are acceptable,
however). Traditional Buddha's Delight doesn't call for garlic, but
we find it makes all the difference.*

12 large dried black mushrooms (3 oz)
 5 cups boiling-hot water plus additional for soaking bean
      curd skins
 2 dried bean curd skins (2 oz total)
½ lb fresh or thawed frozen large bamboo shoots
 2 to 3 oz very thin bean thread noodles (2 small skeins; also
      known as cellophane, glass, or mung bean noodles)
 1 (½-lb) firm fresh tofu cake, or ½ cake from a 14- to
      16-oz package, rinsed and drained
 2 tablespoons peanut or vegetable oil
 1 (½-inch) piece fresh ginger, peeled and very thinly sliced
 2 garlic cloves, chopped
½ cup peeled shelled fresh or frozen ginkgo nuts

⅓ cup vegetarian oyster sauce
¼ cup light soy sauce (preferably Pearl River Bridge brand)
¼ cup Chinese rice wine (preferably Shaoxing) or
      medium-dry Sherry
¾ teaspoon sugar
 2 cups fresh soybean sprouts (¼ lb)
 2 romaine hearts, trimmed and quartered lengthwise,
      then cut into 2-inch pieces (6 cups)

▸Soak mushrooms in 5 cups boiling-hot water in a bowl, keeping
them submerged with a small plate and turning mushrooms over
occasionally, until softened and cool enough to handle, about
30 minutes. Squeeze excess liquid from caps back into bowl and
reserve liquid, then cut out and discard stems from mushrooms.
Cut caps into 1-inch wedges.

▸While mushrooms soak, carefully break bean curd skins in half
crosswise, then halve each portion crosswise again. Transfer to
a bowl, then add enough boiling-hot water to cover and soak,
turning occasionally, until softened, about 30 minutes.

▸If using fresh bamboo, trim bottoms of shoots, then halve
shoots lengthwise with a sharp heavy knife. Pull off and discard
leaves from shoots, then remove any blemishes with a sharp
paring knife (don't worry about natural dotted pattern along base
of shoots).

▶ Cover fresh or frozen bamboo with cold water by 1 inch in a 2-quart saucepan and bring to a boil. Boil 2 minutes, then drain in a colander and rinse under cold water. Repeat boiling and rinsing, then arrange bamboo halves, cut sides down, on a cutting board and cut lengthwise into ¼-inch-thick slices.

▶ Soak noodles in cold water to cover until softened, about 5 minutes, then drain in colander and transfer to a bowl.

▶ Drain bean curd skins in colander. When cool enough to handle, squeeze dry and cut crosswise into 1-inch pieces.

▶ Halve tofu lengthwise, then cut each half crosswise into ½-inch-thick slices.

▶ Heat oil in a 5- to 6-quart wide heavy pot over moderate heat until hot but not smoking. Add ginger and garlic and cook, stirring, 30 seconds. Add mushrooms, bean curd skins, bamboo, and ginkgo nuts and cook, stirring, 2 minutes. Stir in oyster sauce, soy sauce, rice wine, and sugar and simmer 1 minute. Add reserved mushroom-soaking liquid and bring to a boil. Gently stir in tofu and soybean sprouts, then reduce heat to low and simmer, covered, 15 minutes. Gently stir in noodles and simmer, covered, 5 minutes. Add romaine hearts (pot will be full) and turn to coat, then simmer, covered, until romaine is tender, about 5 minutes.

COOKS' NOTES: Mushrooms, bean curd skins, and noodles can be soaked (but not drained) 1 day ahead and chilled in their soaking liquid separately, covered. Drain (reserve mushroom-soaking liquid) before using.

• Bamboo shoots can be cooked 1 day ahead and cooled completely, then cut and chilled in cold water, covered. Drain before using.

• Buddha's Delight, without romaine, can be made 2 hours ahead and kept at room temperature, uncovered. Bring to a boil and proceed with recipe.

BLACK-BEAN SHRIMP WITH CHINESE BROCCOLI

SERVES 8 (AS PART OF A CHINESE MEAL)
ACTIVE TIME: 50 MIN START TO FINISH: 50 MIN (DOES NOT INCLUDE MAKING BROTH)

A Chinese meal is incomplete without something leafy, and this dish features gai lan*, or Chinese broccoli.*

¾ cup homemade chicken broth (reserved from winter melon soup, page 78) or store-bought chicken broth (reduced-sodium if canned)

3 tablespoons Chinese rice wine (preferably Shaoxing) or medium-dry Sherry

3 teaspoons light soy sauce (preferably Pearl River Bridge brand)

2 teaspoons cornstarch

1 teaspoon sugar

¼ teaspoon salt

1½ lb gai lan (Chinese broccoli)

1½ lb large shrimp in shell (21 to 25 per lb), peeled and deveined

1 tablespoon peanut or vegetable oil

1 (1-inch) piece fresh ginger, peeled and cut into very thin matchsticks

2 tablespoons fermented black beans, rinsed and chopped

2 garlic cloves, minced

½ fresh jalapeño chile (including seeds), or to taste, cut crosswise into ⅛-inch-thick slices

1 teaspoon Asian sesame oil

SPECIAL EQUIPMENT: **a well-seasoned 14-inch flat-bottomed wok**

▶ Stir together broth, rice wine, soy sauce, cornstarch, sugar, and salt in a small bowl until cornstarch is dissolved.

▶ Remove any bruised or withered outer leaves from *gai lan*, then trim and peel stalks, halving thick ones lengthwise. Cut crosswise into 2½-inch pieces, separating leafy parts from thick stems.

▶ Cook stems in a 6- to 8-quart pot of boiling salted water, uncovered, until crisp-tender, about 3 minutes. Add leafy parts and cook until all of *gai lan* is just tender, 3 to 5 minutes. Drain well, then transfer to a clean kitchen towel and pat dry. Transfer to a large dish and keep warm, loosely covered with foil.

▶ Pat shrimp dry. Heat wok over high heat until a drop of water vaporizes instantly. Pour peanut oil around side of wok, then tilt wok to swirl oil, coating side. When oil just begins to smoke, add ginger and stir-fry 5 seconds. Add black beans, garlic, and jalapeño and stir-fry 1 minute. Working quickly, add shrimp, spreading in 1 layer on bottom and side of wok. Cook, undisturbed, 3 minutes, then stir-fry until shrimp are just pink on both sides, about 1 minute more. Stir broth mixture, then add to shrimp and bring to a boil. Boil, stirring, 2 minutes. Remove from heat and drizzle with sesame oil, then stir to combine.

▶ Pour shrimp and sauce over *gai lan*.

COOKS' NOTE: *Gai lan* can be trimmed and cut 1 day ahead and chilled in sealed plastic bags lined with paper towels. Bring to room temperature before using.

OPPOSITE: black-bean shrimp with Chinese broccoli (left); winter melon soup (right)

EIGHT-TREASURE PUDDINGS

SERVES 8 (DESSERT)

ACTIVE TIME: 1 HR   START TO FINISH: 3½ HR

*Unlike most Western rice puddings, these desserts are chewy
rather than creamy, with a delightful surprise inside.*

2¼ cups Chinese or Japanese short-grain sticky ("sweet") rice
 1 teaspoon peanut or vegetable oil plus additional for greasing
3½ cups cold water
 ½ cup Chinese rock sugar pieces
 ⅓ cup dried pitted Chinese jujubes, cut lengthwise into
      ¼-inch-thick strips
 8 pitted prunes, quartered (⅓ cup)
 8 large dried apricots, cut into ¼-inch-thick strips (⅓ cup)
 3 tablespoons dried sour cherries
 3 tablespoons diced (¼ inch) candied orange peel
 8 walnut halves
 8 teaspoons canned sweet red beans or sweet red-bean paste
      (from a 14- to 16-oz can)

SPECIAL EQUIPMENT: **a 9-inch round cake pan (2 inches deep);
8 (6- to 8-oz) custard cups or heatproof bowls; a 17- by 12- by
2½-inch roasting pan; heavy-duty foil**

▶Rinse rice in a large sieve under cold running water until water
runs clear, then drain. Combine rice, oil, and 2 cups cold water
in cake pan.

▶Put ½ inch of water in a 12-inch-wide pot or deep skillet. Set
a metal rack (or a few metal cookie cutters) in bottom of pot,
then set cake pan (with rice) on rack and bring water to a
boil. Cover pot and steam over high heat, checking water level
occasionally and adding more water if necessary, until rice is
cooked, about 40 minutes. Carefully remove pan and cool to
room temperature.

▶Meanwhile, bring remaining 1½ cups cold water to a boil in
a 2-quart heavy saucepan with rock sugar, jujubes, prunes,
apricots, cherries, and orange peel, then reduce heat and
simmer, covered, until fruit is very soft and liquid is reduced to
¾ cup, about 45 minutes. Stir in walnuts and simmer 1 minute.
Immediately drain in a medium-mesh sieve set over a bowl,
reserving syrup and fruit separately. Remove walnuts from fruit
and set aside.

▶Put oven rack in middle position and preheat oven to 350°F.

▶Lightly oil custard cups and a ⅓-cup measure. Put 1 walnut
half in bottom of each cup, then spoon 2 tablespoons mixed fruit
(per cup) on top, spreading evenly around bottom of each cup.
Drizzle 1 teaspoon reserved fruit syrup over fruit in each cup,
then press ⅓ cup rice (per cup) on top of fruit with dampened
fingertips. Using your fingertips or back of a small spoon, make
a small indentation in rice and fill with 1 teaspoon red beans
(per cup), leaving at least a ½-inch border of rice. Drizzle
1 teaspoon fruit syrup over each rice pudding, then cover with
2 tablespoons rice (dip measuring spoon in water before
measuring rice to prevent sticking). Using a small piece of
plastic wrap, press rice in cups to flatten surface. Discard wrap.

▶Arrange cups in roasting pan. Oil a sheet of heavy-duty foil,
then cover pan with foil (oiled side down) and seal tightly.
Bake in a water bath (see Tips, page 8) 1 hour, then let stand,
covered, 5 minutes. Run a knife around edge of each cup to
loosen rice, then invert each pudding onto a dish. Drizzle with
remaining fruit syrup.

COOKS' NOTE: Puddings can be cooked (but not unmolded)
3 days ahead and cooled completely, uncovered, then chilled
(chill remaining fruit syrup separately), covered with plastic
wrap. Reheat puddings in a shallow roasting pan, covered with
foil, in a preheated 400°F oven until centers are warm, about
15 minutes (or reheat in a microwave instead). Bring remaining
fruit syrup to room temperature before serving.

ABOVE: Buddha's delight; OPPOSITE: eight-treasure pudding

CIRCLE OF FRIENDS

A SOUL-SATISFYING DINNER

SERVES 4

**CELERY-ROOT SOUP
WITH BACON AND
GREEN APPLE**

RAMOS PINTO WHITE PORT

**DUCK WITH WALNUT
SHERRY VINAIGRETTE**

**BRAISED ENDIVES WITH
HARICOTS VERTS**

CHÂTEAU LA COUSTARELLE
GRANDE CUVÉE PRESTIGE
CAHORS '01

**QUINCE CALVADOS CRÊPE
SOUFFLÉS**

SPECIAL EQUIPMENT: **an adjustable-blade slicer**

▸ Halve leeks lengthwise, then coarsely chop. Wash leeks in a bowl of cold water, agitating them, then lift out onto paper towels and pat dry.

▸ Cook bacon slices in a 4-quart heavy pot over moderate heat, turning occasionally, until crisp, 6 to 8 minutes. Transfer to paper towels.

▸ Pour off all but 2 teaspoons fat from pot, then add oil and cook leeks over moderate heat, stirring occasionally, until softened, about 6 minutes. Add celery root and cook, stirring, 2 minutes. Add water and broth and bring to a boil, then reduce heat and simmer, uncovered, until celery root is very tender, 35 to 40 minutes.

▸ While soup simmers, thinly slice apple lengthwise into ⅛-inch-thick slices with slicer, working around core, then cut slices into ⅛-inch matchsticks with a knife. Gently toss with celery and celery leaves.

▸ Purée soup in batches in a blender until smooth (use caution when blending hot liquids), transferring to a bowl. Return soup to cleaned pot. (If soup is too thick, thin with ½ to ¾ cup water.) Stir in salt, pepper, and half-and-half and cook over moderately low heat, stirring occasionally, until warm. Season with salt, then divide among 4 bowls and top with apple-celery mixture and coarsely crumbled bacon.

CELERY-ROOT SOUP WITH BACON AND GREEN APPLE

SERVES 4

ACTIVE TIME: 30 MIN   START TO FINISH: 1¼ HR

Silky smooth and with a crunchy topping, this seductive soup packs a range of flavors—earthy, smoky, and tart-sweet. If you decide to omit the bacon, substitute 1 tablespoon butter when you cook your vegetables.

3	medium leeks (¾ lb), white and pale green parts only
3	bacon slices (2 oz)
1	tablespoon olive oil
1½	lb celery root, peeled with a knife and cut into ½-inch pieces
3	cups water
1¾	cups reduced-sodium chicken broth
1	Granny Smith apple
¾	celery rib, very thinly sliced on a long diagonal (½ cup)
⅓	cup inner celery leaves
1	teaspoon salt
¼	teaspoon black pepper
½	cup half-and-half

COOKS' NOTE: Soup, without half-and-half, can be made 1 day ahead and cooled completely, uncovered, then chilled, covered. Reheat over moderately low heat, then add half-and-half and cook until heated through. Cool bacon completely, then chill, wrapped in paper towels in a sealed plastic bag. Recrisp in a preheated 300°F oven 6 to 8 minutes, or wrap in a paper towel and recrisp in a microwave 30 seconds to 1 minute. Prepare apple-celery mixture while reheating soup and recrisping bacon.

DUCK WITH WALNUT SHERRY VINAIGRETTE

SERVES 4

ACTIVE TIME: 20 MIN START TO FINISH: 50 MIN

You'd never guess such a sensational main course was so easy to prepare. Roasting and then quickly broiling the duck results in tender meat with crisp, golden-brown skin—and no messy stovetop to clean.

> 2 lb boneless Moulard duck breast halves with skin (about 2)
> ¾ teaspoon salt
> ½ teaspoon black pepper
> ⅓ cup finely chopped shallots
> 2 teaspoons sugar
> 3½ tablespoons Sherry vinegar
> ⅓ cup walnut oil (see Sources)
> ½ cup walnut halves, toasted (see Tips, page 8) and chopped

SPECIAL EQUIPMENT: **an instant-read thermometer**

▸ Put a 13- by 9-inch shallow flameproof roasting pan (not glass) in middle of oven and preheat oven to 375°F.

▸ Pat duck dry and trim off any excess fat. Score duck skin in a crosshatch pattern at ½-inch intervals with a sharp knife, then sprinkle with ½ teaspoon salt and ¼ teaspoon pepper. Place duck, skin sides down, in roasting pan and roast until thermometer inserted diagonally into center registers 135°F, 25 to 30 minutes for medium-rare.

▸ Preheat broiler. Turn duck over and broil (skin sides up) 6 inches from heat until fat is golden, 1 to 2 minutes. Transfer to a cutting board and let stand, loosely covered with foil, 10 minutes. (Internal temperature will rise to at least 145°F.)

▸ While duck stands, pour off all but 2 teaspoons fat from pan, then add shallots and sauté over moderately high heat, stirring, until golden brown, about 2 minutes. Add sugar and cook, stirring, until sugar is dissolved. Add vinegar, along with remaining ¼ teaspoon each of salt and pepper, and cook, stirring and scraping up brown bits, 30 seconds. Transfer to a bowl, then whisk in oil until combined. Stir in walnuts.

▸ Thinly slice duck and serve with walnut Sherry vinaigrette drizzled around plates.

BRAISED ENDIVES WITH HARICOTS VERTS

SERVES 4

ACTIVE TIME: 15 MIN START TO FINISH: 40 MIN

A mix of pleasantly bitter and crisp-tender vegetables perfectly complements the duck with walnut Sherry vinaigrette (recipe precedes). Some of the nutty, sweet vinaigrette will inevitably end up on the vegetables, enhancing their flavor.

> 1½ tablespoons unsalted butter, cut into bits, plus additional for greasing wax paper
> ½ lb haricots verts or other thin green beans, trimmed
> 4 Belgian endives (1 lb), trimmed, leaving leaves attached, and halved lengthwise
> ½ cup reduced-sodium chicken broth
> 1 tablespoon fresh lemon juice
> 1 teaspoon sugar
> ¼ teaspoon salt

▸ Cut out a round of wax paper to fit just inside a 12-inch heavy skillet, then butter 1 side of round.

▸ Fit endives, cut sides down, snugly in skillet. Add broth, lemon juice, butter bits, sugar, and salt, then cover endives with wax-paper round, buttered side down, and simmer until endives are tender and liquid is thickened and reduced to about a quarter of its original volume, 20 to 25 minutes.

▸ Meanwhile, cook beans in a 4-quart pot of boiling salted water, uncovered, until just tender, about 5 minutes. Drain and rinse under cold water to stop cooking, then drain again.

▸ Remove wax paper from endives, then gently stir in beans and cook until beans are just heated through, about 1 minute.

COOKS' NOTE: Beans can be cooked 1 day ahead and chilled in a sealed plastic bag lined with dampened paper towels.

QUINCE CALVADOS CRÊPE SOUFFLÉS

SERVES 4

ACTIVE TIME: 1 HR   START TO FINISH: 2½ HR

Light and fluffy, these impressive desserts look, smell, and taste extraordinary—meringue gives them a cloudlike texture, while quince adds a delicious fragrance and beautiful pink hue. And they're very manageable for a small dinner party if you make your crêpes and prepare the quince ahead (see cooks' note, below). Bring them both to room temperature when you sit down to dinner; when it's time for dessert, you'll only need to beat your egg whites and assemble the soufflés for baking.

FOR CRÊPES

- ⅔ cup whole milk
- ¼ cup plus 1 tablespoon all-purpose flour
- 1 large egg
- 1½ tablespoons unsalted butter, melted, plus additional for brushing skillet
- 1 teaspoon sugar
- ¼ teaspoon salt

FOR QUINCE PURÉE

- 3 cups water
- ⅔ cup sugar
- 4 (3-inch-long) strips of fresh lemon zest (½ inch wide)
- 1½ lb quince (2 medium), peeled and halved, then each half cut into 6 wedges and cored
- ½ teaspoon vanilla
- 2 tablespoons Calvados
- 2 teaspoons fresh lemon juice

FOR SOUFFLÉS

- 2 large egg whites
- 1½ tablespoons granulated sugar
- 1½ tablespoons unsalted butter, melted
- Confectioners sugar for dusting

MAKE CRÊPE BATTER:

▸ Whisk together all crêpe ingredients until smooth, then chill, covered, 30 minutes.

POACH QUINCE:

▸ Combine water, sugar, zest, and a pinch of salt in a 3-quart heavy saucepan and cook over moderate heat, stirring, until sugar is dissolved. Add quince and simmer, covered, until fruit is very tender but not falling apart, 1 to 1¼ hours. Discard zest.

COOK CRÊPES WHILE FRUIT POACHES:

▸ Lightly brush an 8- to 9-inch nonstick skillet with butter, then heat over moderately high heat until hot but not smoking. Holding skillet off heat, pour in a scant ¼ cup batter, immediately tilting and rotating skillet to coat bottom. (If batter sets before

skillet is coated, reduce heat slightly.) Return skillet to heat and cook crêpe until just set and golden around edges, 10 to 15 seconds. Loosen edge of crêpe with a heatproof rubber spatula, then transfer crêpe to a plate. Brush skillet with more butter and make 3 more crêpes in same manner, stacking crêpes on plate.

FINISH PREPARING QUINCE:

▸ Measure out ¾ cup poached fruit with a slotted spoon and 3 tablespoons cooking syrup (reserve remainder in saucepan), then purée in a food processor with vanilla and 1 tablespoon Calvados until smooth.

▸ Transfer remaining fruit from reserved syrup with a slotted spoon to a bowl. Pour syrup through a fine-mesh sieve into another bowl, then return to saucepan and boil until reduced to about ½ cup, 8 to 12 minutes. Stir in lemon juice and remaining tablespoon Calvados and cool.

▸ Measure out ¾ cup reserved fruit, then chop and set aside. Stir remaining fruit into reduced syrup and set aside separately.

MAKE SOUFFLÉS:

▸ Put oven rack in middle position and preheat oven to 400°F.

▸ Beat whites with a pinch of salt using an electric mixer at medium-high speed until they just hold soft peaks. Add granulated sugar in a slow stream, beating, and beat at medium-high speed until whites just hold stiff peaks. Fold one third of whites into quince purée, then fold in remaining whites gently but thoroughly. Gently fold in chopped fruit.

▸ Brush bottom sides of crêpes with some melted butter and put in a 15- by 10-inch shallow baking pan (about half of each crêpe will hang over). Divide soufflé mixture among crêpes, spooning it in center and spreading it over half of each crêpe. Gently fold other half of each crêpe over filling to rest on top. Bake until filling is puffed, set, and pale golden in spots, 10 to 12 minutes.

▸ Dust crêpes with confectioners sugar and serve immediately with reserved quince and syrup.

COOKS' NOTES: Crêpes can be made 1 day ahead and cooled completely, uncovered, then chilled, covered.

• Poached quince in syrup and quince purée will improve in color if made at least 1 day ahead and can be made 5 days ahead. Cool poached quince in syrup completely, uncovered, then chill, covered. If possible, make quince purée at least 1 day after poaching (to allow color of quince to improve) and chill, covered.

LET IT SNOW

DINNER BY THE FIRE

SERVES 8

CHICKEN LIVER MOUSSE

MISSION HILL FAMILY ESTATE
OKANAGAN VALLEY
S.L.C. CHARDONNAY '04

CASSOULET

MISSION HILL FAMILY ESTATE
OKANAGAN VALLEY OCULUS '02

**ENDIVE AND CHICORY
SALAD WITH GRAINY
MUSTARD VINAIGRETTE**

ASSORTED CHEESES

**BROWN-SUGAR SPICE
CAKE WITH CREAM AND
CARAMELIZED APPLES**

JACKSON-TRIGGS
PROPRIETORS' RESERVE
NIAGARA PENINSULA
VIDAL ICE WINE '04

CALVADOS TODDIES

OFF-TO-BED BUTTER COOKIES

CHICKEN LIVER MOUSSE

SERVES 8 (HORS D'OEUVRE)
ACTIVE TIME: 20 MIN   START TO FINISH: 6¼ HR (INCLUDES CHILLING)

If you like chicken liver mousse, you'll definitely want to try this recipe, which uses a completely different method than most. Puréeing the chicken livers and then baking them in a hot water bath results in an extremely tender spread.

 2 tablespoons finely chopped shallot
 1 teaspoon olive oil
 1 garlic clove, minced
 ⅓ cup Cognac or other brandy
 6 oz chicken livers, trimmed (¾ cup)
 5 large egg yolks
 1 cup whole milk
 ¼ cup all-purpose flour
1¼ teaspoons salt
 ½ teaspoon black pepper
 ¼ teaspoon freshly grated nutmeg
 ¼ teaspoon ground allspice
 ¾ stick (6 tablespoons) unsalted butter
    Several bay leaves (preferably fresh; see cooks' note, below)

SPECIAL EQUIPMENT: a 2½- to 3-cup ovenproof crock or terrine
ACCOMPANIMENTS: crackers or toasted baguette slices; flaky sea salt; cornichons

▶Put oven rack in middle position and preheat oven to 350°F.
▶Cook shallot in oil in a 10-inch heavy skillet over moderate heat, stirring occasionally, until softened, about 4 minutes. Add garlic and cook, stirring, 1 minute. Remove from heat and carefully add Cognac (use caution; if Cognac ignites, shake skillet), then boil until reduced to about 2 tablespoons, 1 to 2 minutes.
▶Transfer to a blender and add livers and yolks, then purée until smooth. Add milk, flour, salt, pepper, nutmeg, and allspice and blend until combined. Pour into crock, skimming off any foam.
▶Put crock in a larger baking pan and bake in a water bath (see Tips, page 8) until mousse is just set and a small sharp knife inserted in center comes out clean, about 55 minutes.
▶Melt butter in a small saucepan over low heat, then remove from heat and let stand 3 minutes.
▶Arrange bay leaves decoratively on top of mousse. Skim froth from butter, then spoon enough clarified butter over mousse to cover its surface, leaving milky solids in bottom of saucepan.
▶Chill mousse completely, uncovered, about 4 hours. Bring to room temperature about 1 hour before serving.

COOKS' NOTES: Mousse can be made 5 days ahead and chilled, covered after 4 hours.
• The bay leaves in this recipe are decorative. If fresh leaves are unavailable, use only 2 or 3 dried ones. Otherwise, the flavor they impart will be too strong. Don't eat them (fresh or dried), because they can be hard and sharp.

CASSOULET

SERVES 8
ACTIVE TIME: 45 MIN   START TO FINISH: 4½ HR (IF QUICK-SOAKING
BEANS)

*In this version of cassoulet, garlic-crumb topping is served on
the side. Rather than acting as a thickener, the crumbs give our
brothy version of the dish a crisp layer of texture.*

FOR CASSOULET

1½ lb dried white beans such as Great Northern or cannellini
    (3⅔ cups), picked over and rinsed
2 sprigs fresh parsley
1 Turkish or ½ California bay leaf
2 whole cloves
½ teaspoon black peppercorns
5 sprigs fresh thyme
1½ lb boneless pork shoulder, cut into ½-inch-thick slices
4 qt water
2 onions, chopped
1 carrot, cut into ½-inch pieces
2 tablespoons finely chopped garlic plus 2 cloves, halved
2 tablespoons olive oil
8 confit duck legs
1 tablespoon salt
¾ teaspoon black pepper
1 lb *saucisson à l'ail* or other fully cooked garlic pork sausage
    (not cured or dried), casing removed

FOR GARLIC-CRUMB TOPPING

1 tablespoon minced garlic
2 tablespoons olive oil
1½ cups coarse fresh bread crumbs (from a baguette)
½ teaspoon salt
⅛ teaspoon black pepper
2 tablespoons chopped fresh flat-leaf parsley

SPECIAL EQUIPMENT: **cheesecloth; kitchen string; a 17- by
11-inch heavy roasting pan or 7-qt shallow flameproof
casserole dish**

MAKE CASSOULET:

▶ Cover beans with cold water by 2 inches in a bowl and soak at
room temperature at least 8 and up to 24 hours, or quick-soak
(see cooks' note, below). Drain well in a colander.
▶ Make a bouquet garni by wrapping parsley, bay leaf, cloves,
peppercorns, and 2 sprigs thyme in cheesecloth and tying
with kitchen string, then put in a 5- to 6-quart heavy pot along
with pork shoulder and water (4 quarts). Simmer, uncovered,
skimming froth occasionally, 1¼ hours.

▶ Add beans, onions, carrot, and chopped garlic and simmer,
uncovered, stirring occasionally, until beans are just tender,
about 45 minutes.
▶ While beans simmer, put oven rack in middle position and
preheat oven to 375°F. Straddle roasting pan across 2 burners
and heat 1 tablespoon oil in roasting pan over moderately high
heat until hot but not smoking, then brown duck legs, turning
occasionally to brown skin and meat all over, about 10 minutes.
Transfer duck legs with tongs to a platter as browned.
▶ Pour off all but 2 tablespoons fat from roasting pan, then
reduce heat to moderately low and cook halved garlic cloves,
stirring, until fragrant, about 1 minute. Remove from heat.
▶ Drain bean and pork mixture in a colander set over a large bowl
(discard bouquet garni). Stir salt and pepper into broth in bowl
and reserve.
▶ Spread bean and pork mixture in roasting pan (with garlic
halves), then nestle duck legs, skin sides up, in mixture. Add
remaining 3 sprigs thyme and 6 cups reserved broth (liquid
should come up around base of duck legs; reserve remaining
broth, covered and chilled, for reheating if making dish ahead,
or for another use). Bake, uncovered, 30 minutes.
▶ While cassoulet bakes, heat remaining tablespoon oil in a
10-inch heavy skillet over moderately high heat until hot but not
smoking. If necessary, halve sausage crosswise to fit in skillet,
then brown, turning occasionally, about 3 minutes. Transfer to
a cutting board and cool slightly. When sausage is cool enough
to handle, halve pieces lengthwise, then cut crosswise into
½-inch-thick slices.
▶ Nestle sausage slices into cassoulet and bake, uncovered,
30 minutes more. Let cassoulet stand 10 minutes. Gently
stir beans, mashing some with back of spoon, to thicken broth
before serving.

PREPARE GARLIC-CRUMB TOPPING WHILE CASSOULET
FINISHES BAKING:

▶ Cook garlic in oil in cleaned 10-inch skillet over moderate heat,
stirring, until fragrant, about 1 minute. Add bread crumbs, salt,
and pepper and cook, stirring, until crumbs are crisp and golden,
about 3 minutes. Transfer to a small bowl and stir in parsley.
▶ Serve cassoulet with crumb topping.

COOKS' NOTES: To quick-soak beans, cover dried beans with cold
water by 2 inches in a 4- to 5-quart pot. Bring to a boil and cook,
uncovered, over moderate heat 2 minutes. Remove from heat and
soak beans, uncovered, 1 hour.
• Cassoulet can be made 3 days ahead and cooled completely,
uncovered, then chilled, covered. Reheat, covered, in a preheated
350°F oven 30 minutes. If beans have soaked up the liquid, add
some of reserved broth before reheating.

ENDIVE AND CHICORY SALAD WITH GRAINY MUSTARD VINAIGRETTE

SERVES 8

ACTIVE TIME: 15 MIN   START TO FINISH: 15 MIN

We like to serve these bitter greens with an assortment of cheeses, such as Bouc Émissaire, Brick Chaput, and Chaput Pont Couvert (see Sources).

- ½ garlic clove
- ½ teaspoon salt
- 1 tablespoon coarse-grain mustard
- 1 tablespoon red-wine vinegar
- ¼ teaspoon black pepper
- ¼ cup extra-virgin olive oil
- 2 medium Belgian endives (10 oz), sliced crosswise ½ inch thick
- ½ lb chicory (French curly endive; 1 head), tough outer leaves discarded and remaining leaves torn into 2-inch pieces (about 9 cups)

▶ Mince garlic with a large heavy knife, then mash to a paste with salt using flat side of knife.
▶ Whisk together garlic paste, mustard, vinegar, and pepper, then add oil in a slow stream, whisking until emulsified.
▶ Just before serving, toss greens with vinaigrette.

BROWN-SUGAR SPICE CAKE WITH CREAM AND CARAMELIZED APPLES

MAKES 9 PIECES

ACTIVE TIME: 45 MIN   START TO FINISH: 1¾ HR

In this recipe, simple pantry ingredients come together to make a homey cake that's so tender and moist, you'll be fighting over the last piece.

FOR CARAMELIZED APPLES
- 8 Gala apples (3½ lb)
- ¾ stick (6 tablespoons) unsalted butter, softened
- ¾ cup packed light brown sugar

FOR CAKE
- 1½ cups all-purpose flour
- 1½ teaspoons baking powder
- ½ teaspoon baking soda
- ½ teaspoon salt
- ½ teaspoon ground allspice
- ½ teaspoon freshly grated nutmeg
- ⅛ teaspoon ground cloves
- 1 stick (½ cup) unsalted butter, softened
- ⅓ cup packed light brown sugar
- 1 large egg
- ½ cup dark amber or Grade B maple syrup
- ½ cup sour cream
- 1 teaspoon vanilla

FOR CREAM
- 1¼ cups chilled heavy cream
- ½ cup sour cream
- 2 tablespoons sugar

SPECIAL EQUIPMENT: **an 8-inch square nonstick cake pan (2 inches deep)**

▶ Put oven rack in middle position and preheat oven to 350°F. Lightly butter and flour cake pan, knocking out excess flour.

MAKE CARAMELIZED APPLES:
▶ Peel and core apples, then cut into ½-inch-thick wedges.
▶ Spread softened butter in an even layer over bottom of a 12-inch heavy skillet and sprinkle with brown sugar. Add apple wedges and cook over moderate heat, without stirring, until sugar is melted and apples start to give off liquid, about 10 minutes. Cook, stirring occasionally, until apples are just tender and juices become syrupy, about 30 minutes more.
▶ Pour syrup from skillet into a small heatproof bowl, then sauté apples, stirring occasionally, until caramelized and very tender, about 30 minutes more. Return syrup to apples and cook until heated through, about 2 minutes.

MAKE CAKE WHILE APPLES COOK:

▶ Whisk together flour, baking powder, baking soda, salt, and spices in a bowl.

▶ Beat together butter and brown sugar in a large bowl with an electric mixer at medium speed until pale and fluffy. Beat in egg until combined. Add maple syrup, sour cream, and vanilla and beat until combined well. Reduce speed to low and add flour mixture, then mix until just incorporated.

▶ Spread batter in cake pan and bake until cake is golden brown and a wooden pick or skewer inserted in center comes out clean, 35 to 40 minutes. Cool in pan on a rack 10 minutes.

MAKE CREAM JUST BEFORE SERVING:

▶ Beat cream with sour cream and sugar using cleaned beaters at high speed until it just holds soft peaks.

TO SERVE:

▶ Run a thin knife around edge of pan, then invert cake onto a plate and cut into squares. Serve warm or at room temperature, topped with warm apple mixture and cream.

COOKS' NOTES: Caramelized apples can be made 1 day ahead and cooled completely, uncovered, then chilled, covered. Reheat over low heat.

• Cake can be made 1 day ahead and cooled completely, uncovered, then kept, loosely covered with plastic wrap, at room temperature.

CALVADOS TODDIES

MAKES 8 DRINKS

ACTIVE TIME: 15 MIN   START TO FINISH: 1 HR

These warm little drinks are delicious—you may want to make a double batch.

  2 qt filtered apple juice
1½ cups brewed black tea such as English Breakfast
1½ cups Calvados
  8 cinnamon sticks

▶ Boil apple juice in a 4- to 5-quart wide heavy pot over high heat until syrupy and reduced to about 1½ cups, about 50 minutes.

▶ Combine apple syrup, tea, and Calvados in a 1½- to 2-quart saucepan and heat over moderate heat until hot (do not boil). Divide toddy among 8 small cups and serve with a cinnamon stick in each.

COOKS' NOTE: Apple syrup can be made 1 week ahead and cooled completely, uncovered, then chilled, covered.

OFF-TO-BED BUTTER COOKIES

MAKES ABOUT 4 DOZEN

ACTIVE TIME: 20 MIN   START TO FINISH: 1½ HR (INCLUDES CHILLING DOUGH)

Crumbly, delicate, and glistening with golden sugar, these easy slice-and-bake cookies are the ideal complement to the Calvados toddies (recipe precedes). Perfect as an after-dinner nibble or an everyday treat, they will quickly become one of your favorite standbys.

1½ cups all-purpose flour
¼ teaspoon salt
1½ sticks (¾ cup) unsalted butter, softened
¼ cup plus 2 tablespoons granulated sugar
  2 teaspoons heavy cream
  3 tablespoons turbinado sugar such as Sugar in the Raw

SPECIAL EQUIPMENT: **parchment paper**

▶ Stir together flour and salt in a bowl.

▶ Beat together butter and granulated sugar with an electric mixer at medium-high speed in a large bowl until pale and fluffy. Reduce speed to low, then add flour mixture in 3 batches, mixing, and continue to mix until batter just comes together in clumps. Gather clumps to form a dough, then press dough with lightly floured hands into a smooth 1¼-inch-thick log on a very lightly floured work surface. Chill, wrapped in plastic wrap, at least 1 hour.

▶ Put oven racks in upper and lower thirds of oven and preheat oven to 350°F. Line 2 large baking sheets with parchment paper.

▶ Cut chilled log crosswise into ¼-inch-thick slices and arrange slices about ½ inch apart on baking sheets. Brush tops of cookies lightly with cream, then sprinkle generously with turbinado sugar.

▶ Bake cookies, switching position of sheets halfway through baking, until edges are pale golden, 12 to 15 minutes total. Cool on sheets on racks.

COOKS' NOTES: Dough log can be chilled, wrapped well in plastic wrap, up to 3 days or frozen, wrapped in plastic and foil, 1 month (thaw in refrigerator just until dough can be sliced).

• Cookies keep 4 days in an airtight container at room temperature.

IT STARTED IN NAPLES

MICHELE SCICOLONE'S FAMILY FAVORITES

SERVES 8

BROCCOLI RABE CROSTINI

BENITO FERRARA VIGNA
CICOGNA GRECO DI TUFO '04

**RIGATONI WITH TOMATO SAUCE
AND RICOTTA**

MEATLOAF, OLD NAPLES STYLE

**SWEET PEAS WITH LETTUCE
AND MINT**

NEAPOLITAN POTATO PIE

MASTROBERARDINO
RADICI TAURASI AGLIANICO '00

EASTER WHEAT-BERRY CAKE

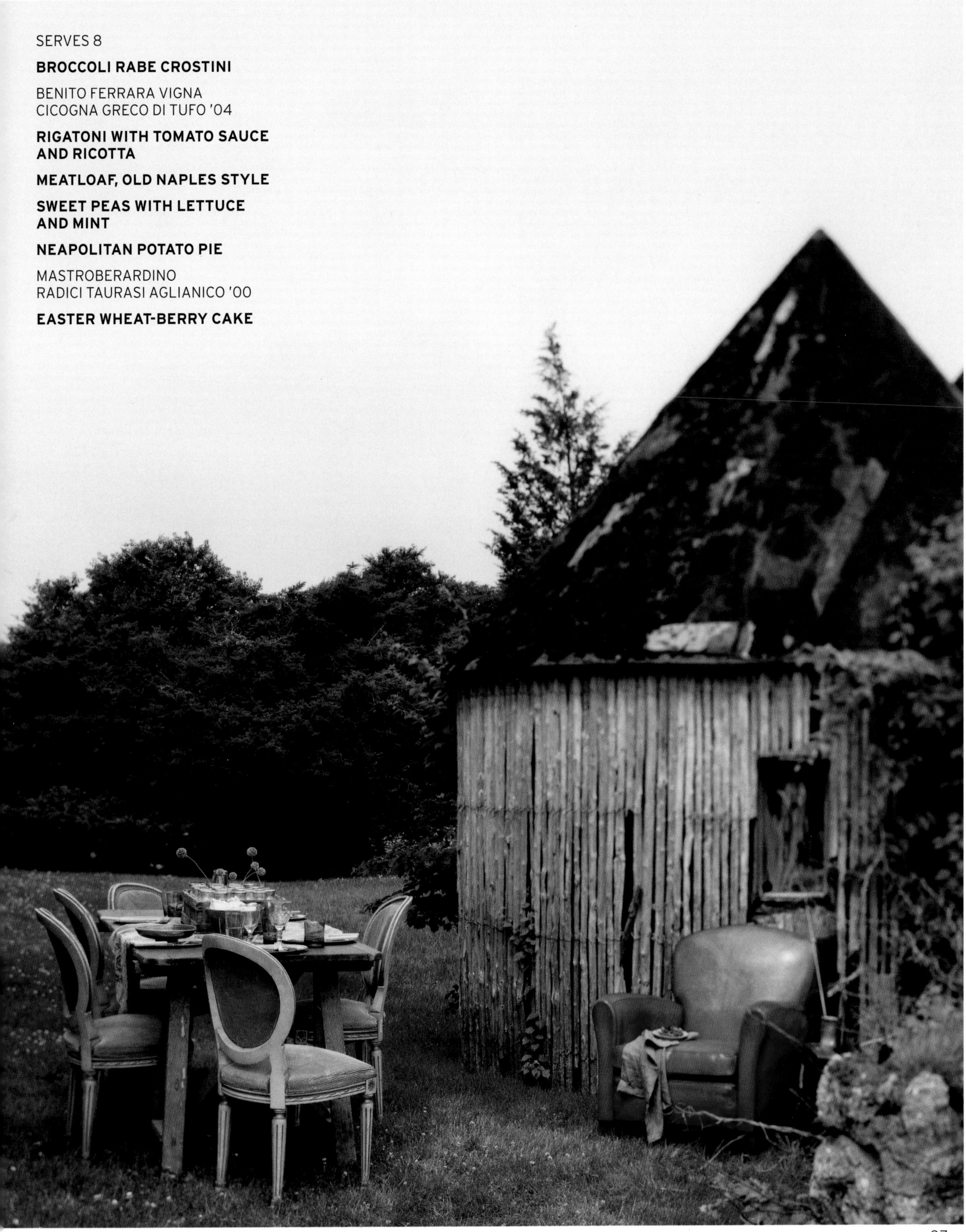

BROCCOLI RABE CROSTINI

MAKES 16 HORS D'OEUVRES
ACTIVE TIME: 30 MIN   START TO FINISH: 30 MIN

A popular side dish, emerald-green broccoli rabe tastes even better as an hors d'oeuvre served on crusty bread. After blanching and a quick sauté, the beautifully wilted stems—still dripping with olive oil and garlic—are piled on little toasts.

FOR TOASTS

16 (⅓-inch-thick) slices from a 10-inch-long Italian loaf
 2 tablespoons olive oil
 1 garlic clove, halved crosswise

FOR BROCCOLI RABE TOPPING

 1 lb broccoli rabe, tough ends discarded and remainder chopped
 2 large garlic cloves, thinly sliced
⅛ teaspoon dried hot red-pepper flakes
¼ cup olive oil
 3 tablespoons water
½ teaspoon salt

MAKE TOASTS:

▶ Preheat broiler. Put bread slices in a large shallow baking pan. Brush both sides of slices with oil, then lightly season with salt and pepper. Broil 4 inches from heat, turning over halfway through broiling, until golden, about 4 minutes total. Rub both sides of toasts with cut sides of garlic (discard garlic).

MAKE BROCCOLI RABE TOPPING:

▶ Cook broccoli rabe in a 6-quart wide heavy pot of boiling salted water (see Tips, page 8), uncovered, until tender, 5 to 6 minutes. Drain well in a colander, gently pressing out excess water. Wipe pot clean.

▶ Cook garlic slices and red-pepper flakes in oil in pot over moderate heat, stirring occasionally, until garlic is golden, about 2 minutes. Add broccoli rabe, water, and salt and cook, covered, stirring occasionally, 2 minutes.

ASSEMBLE CROSTINI:

▶ Spoon a heaping tablespoon of warm broccoli rabe topping onto each toast.

COOKS' NOTES: Toasts can be made 1 day ahead and cooled completely, then kept in an airtight container at room temperature.

• Broccoli rabe topping can be made 1 day ahead and cooled completely, uncovered, then chilled, covered. Reheat before assembling crostini.

RIGATONI WITH TOMATO SAUCE AND RICOTTA

SERVES 8 (FIRST COURSE)
ACTIVE TIME: 1 HR   START TO FINISH: 1 HR (INCLUDES MAKING SAUCE)

Pasta, lush tomatoes, and a pool of ricotta lend this dish all the flavor of a lasagne—without the heaviness. We served the ricotta on the side for a more attractive presentation, but you could also stir it into the cooked pasta.

 1 lb rigatoni
2½ cups marinara sauce (recipe follows) or other tomato sauce, heated through
 1 cup ricotta (½ lb; preferably fresh)

ACCOMPANIMENT: finely grated Pecorino Romano

▶ Cook pasta in a 6-quart pot of boiling salted water (see Tips, page 8), uncovered, until al dente, then drain in a colander.
▶ Toss pasta with warm marinara sauce in a large bowl. Serve with ricotta and grated Pecorino Romano.

MARINARA SAUCE

MAKES ABOUT 2½ CUPS
ACTIVE TIME: 40 MIN   START TO FINISH: 40 MIN

This robust sauce tastes best when made with fresh tomatoes, but canned tomatoes work just fine (see cooks' note, below).

  3   lb fresh plum tomatoes or 1 (28-oz) can whole tomatoes
        in juice
  2   large garlic cloves, crushed with side of a large heavy knife
        Pinch of dried hot red-pepper flakes
  ¼   cup olive oil
1¼   teaspoons salt
  4   fresh basil leaves, torn into bits

▸ If using fresh tomatoes, cut a shallow X in bottom of each tomato with a paring knife and blanch tomatoes in 3 batches in a 5- to 6-quart pot of boiling water, 1 minute per batch. Transfer blanched tomatoes with a slotted spoon to a cutting board and, when cool enough to handle, peel, beginning from scored end, with knife, then halve lengthwise and seed. Chop tomatoes (fresh or canned), reserving juice (from cutting board or can).
▸ Cook garlic and red-pepper flakes in oil in a 4-quart heavy pot over moderate heat, stirring, until garlic is golden, about 5 minutes. Discard garlic, then add tomatoes with their juice and salt and simmer, uncovered, until sauce is thickened, about 20 minutes. Remove from heat and stir in basil and salt to taste.

COOKS' NOTES: Sauce can be made ahead and cooled completely, uncovered, then chilled, covered, up to 5 days or frozen in an airtight container 2 months.
• If using canned tomatoes, whose sodium content varies, use only ¼ teaspoon salt, then season your finished sauce with additional salt if desired.

MEATLOAF, OLD NAPLES STYLE

SERVES 8
ACTIVE TIME: 30 MIN   START TO FINISH: 1¾ HR

Ideal for a Sunday supper, this is the kind of substantial centerpiece Italian grandmothers have been making for years.

  ⅔   cup torn (½-inch) pieces crustless day-old Italian bread
  ⅓   cup milk
  1   lb ground beef chuck (not lean)
  2   large eggs, lightly beaten
  1   teaspoon salt
  ¼   teaspoon black pepper

  ¼   lb baked ham, finely chopped (1 cup)
  2   oz sliced provolone, finely chopped (½ cup)
  ¼   cup fine dry bread crumbs (not seasoned)
  3   hard-boiled large eggs, peeled

SPECIAL EQUIPMENT: **an instant-read thermometer**

▸ Put oven rack in middle position and preheat oven to 350°F. Oil a 9-inch square baking pan.
▸ Stir together bread and milk in a large bowl and let stand 10 minutes.
▸ Add beef, lightly beaten eggs, salt, and pepper to bread mixture and mix with your hands until combined, then mix in ham and cheese.
▸ Scatter 2 tablespoons bread crumbs in an 8- by 4-inch rectangle on a 16-inch-long sheet of wax paper. Spread half of meat mixture into an 8- by 4-inch rectangle over crumbs, then arrange hard-boiled eggs lengthwise, about ½ inch apart, in a row down middle of meat mixture. Cover eggs with remaining meat mixture, pressing it to form a single 8- by 4-inch loaf. Transfer with a spatula from wax paper to baking pan and sprinkle top and sides with remaining 2 tablespoons crumbs.
▸ Bake until thermometer inserted near center of loaf (but avoiding eggs) registers 155°F, 50 to 60 minutes. Let stand 10 minutes before serving. (Internal temperature will rise to 165°F while loaf stands.)

SWEET PEAS WITH LETTUCE AND MINT

SERVES 8
ACTIVE TIME: 20 MIN   START TO FINISH: 20 MIN

In this recipe, frozen peas taste as good as fresh, thanks to the addition of bright mint and crunchy lettuce.

  1   medium onion, finely chopped
  5   tablespoons unsalted butter
  1   (1-lb) bag frozen peas (5 cups; not thawed)
  2   tablespoons water
2½   cups thinly sliced lettuce leaves such as romaine (3 oz)
  ¾   cup loosely packed fresh mint leaves, torn into small pieces
  ½   teaspoon salt
  ¼   teaspoon black pepper

▸ Cook onion in butter in a 4-quart heavy pot over moderate heat, stirring, until softened, about 6 minutes. Stir in peas and water and cook, covered, stirring occasionally, until peas are tender, about 5 minutes. Remove from heat and stir in lettuce, mint, salt, and pepper.

NEAPOLITAN POTATO PIE

SERVES 8
ACTIVE TIME: 45 MIN   START TO FINISH: 1¾ HR

From the comfort of buttery mashed potatoes to the bold flavors of salami and cheese—this savory pie has so much going on, it could be a meal in itself. If you're making this entire menu, bake the potato pie before the meatloaf, then reheat the pie in the oven for 10 minutes while the meatloaf stands.

2½ lb yellow-fleshed potatoes such as Yukon Gold (3 or
    4 large), scrubbed
1 cup milk
½ stick (¼ cup) unsalted butter, softened, plus additional
    for buttering pan
¼ cup fine dry bread crumbs (not seasoned)
½ teaspoon salt
¼ teaspoon black pepper
¼ teaspoon freshly grated nutmeg
1 large egg, lightly beaten
½ lb mozzarella (preferably fresh), chopped
¼ lb salami or prosciutto, chopped
2½ oz finely grated Parmigiano-Reggiano (1 cup plus
    2 tablespoons; see Tips, page 8)

▶ Cover potatoes with salted cold water (see Tips, page 8) by 2 inches in a 5-quart pot. Bring to a boil, then reduce heat and simmer, uncovered, until potatoes are tender, 18 to 20 minutes.
▶ Shortly before potatoes are done, bring milk just to a simmer in a small saucepan over moderate heat, then remove from heat.
▶ Put oven rack in middle position and preheat oven to 400°F. Butter a 2- to 2½-quart shallow baking dish and sprinkle with bread crumbs.
▶ Drain potatoes well in a colander. When cool enough to handle, peel potatoes and return to pot along with hot milk, salt, pepper, nutmeg, and 3 tablespoons butter. Mash with a potato masher until combined well and almost smooth. Stir in egg, mozzarella, salami, and 1 cup Parmigiano-Reggiano.
▶ Spread potato mixture evenly in baking dish. Sprinkle with remaining 2 tablespoons Parmigiano-Reggiano and dot with remaining tablespoon butter. Bake until top is browned, 35 to 45 minutes. Let potato pie stand 5 minutes before serving.

COOKS' NOTE: Potato pie can be assembled 1 day ahead and chilled, covered. Bring to room temperature before baking.

EASTER WHEAT-BERRY CAKE

SERVES 8 TO 10 (DESSERT)

ACTIVE TIME: 1¼ HR START TO FINISH: 13½ HR (INCLUDES SOAKING AND CHILLING)

Referred to in Italy as pastiera napoletana, *this lattice-crusted dessert is like a cheesecake, with chewy wheat berries suspended inside. A delicate whiff of orange-flower water lends it a subtle hint of spring.*

FOR FILLING

- ½ cup hulled soft wheat berries (¼ lb; see Sources)
- 1 stick (½ cup) unsalted butter, cut into ½-inch cubes
- 1 teaspoon finely grated fresh orange zest (see Tips, page 8)
- 1 lb ricotta (preferably fresh; 2 cups)
- 4 large eggs at room temperature, lightly beaten
- ⅔ cup granulated sugar
- 2 tablespoons orange-flower water (see Sources)
- ¾ teaspoon cinnamon
- ½ cup finely chopped candied citron (3 oz; see Sources)
- ½ cup finely chopped candied orange peel (3 oz)

FOR PASTRY DOUGH

- 3 cups all-purpose flour
- ½ teaspoon cinnamon
- ½ teaspoon salt
- 1½ sticks (¾ cup) unsalted butter, softened
- 1 cup confectioners sugar
- 1 whole large egg
- 2 large egg yolks
- 2 teaspoons orange-flower water

SPECIAL EQUIPMENT: **a 9- to 9½-inch (24-cm) springform pan**
GARNISH: **confectioners sugar**

SOAK WHEAT BERRIES FOR FILLING:

‣ Cover wheat berries with cold water in a bowl, then soak, covered and chilled, at least 8 hours. Drain in a sieve and rinse.

MAKE DOUGH WHILE WHEAT BERRIES SOAK:

‣ Whisk together flour, cinnamon, and salt in a bowl. Beat together butter and confectioners sugar in a large bowl with an electric mixer at medium speed until light and fluffy, about 3 minutes. Beat in whole egg, yolks, and orange-flower water until smooth. Reduce speed to low, then add flour mixture and mix until incorporated. Gather dough into a ball (it will be soft) and quarter. Form one quarter of dough into a 3-inch disk, then form remaining three quarters of dough into a 6-inch disk. Chill disks, wrapped in plastic wrap, until firm, at least 1 hour.

FINISH MAKING FILLING:

‣ Cover soaked wheat berries with cold water by 2 inches in a 2-quart saucepan and simmer, covered, until wheat berries are tender, about 30 minutes. Drain in sieve, then transfer to a bowl and stir in butter and zest. Cool completely, about 15 minutes.

‣ Stir together ricotta, eggs, sugar, orange-flower water, cinnamon, candied citron, and candied orange peel in a large bowl, then stir in wheat-berry mixture.

ASSEMBLE AND BAKE CAKE:

‣ Put oven rack in lower third of oven and preheat oven to 350°F.

‣ Roll out larger disk of dough into a 14-inch round on a well-floured surface with a floured rolling pin. Fit dough into ungreased springform pan, pressing dough all the way up side to rim of pan (dough is very tender and will crack; patch any cracks). Chill until cold, about 20 minutes.

‣ Roll out remaining dough into a 10-inch round on well-floured surface with floured rolling pin and transfer to a baking sheet. Cut dough into ½-inch-wide strips with a fluted pastry wheel or a sharp knife.

‣ Spoon filling into chilled piecrust (filling will not reach top).

‣ Arrange 5 dough strips parallel to each other on filling (1 inch apart), pressing ends of strips into crust. (Patch together any cracks in strips; if dough becomes too soft to handle, chill until firmer.) Arrange another 5 strips diagonally over them to form a lattice. Fold edge of crust over ends of lattice strips, pressing to seal.

‣ Bake until pastry is golden and filling is puffed and set, about 1 to 1¼ hours. Transfer in pan to a rack and cool 10 minutes. Run a thin knife around edge of cake and remove side of pan. Cool cake completely on rack, about 2 hours.

COOKS' NOTES: Dough can be chilled up to 1 day. Bring to room temperature before rolling out.

• Cake can be baked 1 day ahead and cooled completely, uncovered, then chilled, covered. Bring to room temperature before serving if desired.

EDIBLE ODYSSEY

SEASIDE PICNIC IN GREECE

SERVES 8

**EGGPLANT-AND-BULGUR-
STUFFED VEGETABLES**

HERB AND CHEESE PIE

MERCOURI FOLOÏ RODITIS '04

**GRILLED MARINATED
LEG OF LAMB**

PANFRIED ROMAINE

DOMAINE SPIROPOULOS
RED STAG AGIORGITIKO '02

**YOGURT MOUSSE WITH
APRICOT SAUCE**

EGGPLANT-AND-BULGUR-STUFFED VEGETABLES

SERVES 8 (FIRST COURSE)

ACTIVE TIME: 1 HR   START TO FINISH: 2½ HR

Slow-cooking these colorful vegetables renders them soft and silky. And serving them Mediterranean-style—at room temperature—makes entertaining easy, especially when dining alfresco.

  1 (1½-lb) eggplant
  8 small round tomatoes (about 2½ inches in diameter; 2½ lb total)
1¾ teaspoons salt
  4 small zucchini (1½ lb), halved lengthwise
  1 large onion, chopped (2 cups)
  6 tablespoons extra-virgin olive oil plus additional for brushing vegetables
  ⅔ cup medium bulgur
  ½ teaspoon sugar
  ½ teaspoon ground allspice
  ¾ teaspoon black pepper
  ⅓ cup dried currants
  4 small (not baby) yellow or orange bell peppers with stems (2 lb total), halved lengthwise through stem, then ribs and seeds discarded
  ¼ cup chopped fresh flat-leaf parsley

SPECIAL EQUIPMENT: **a well-seasoned 12-inch cast-iron skillet**

▸ Heat skillet over moderate heat until hot, then cook eggplant, turning occasionally with tongs, until blackened on all sides and tender, 35 to 45 minutes. Transfer to a cutting board. When cool enough to handle, peel eggplant, then cut flesh into ½-inch pieces.

▸ While eggplant cooks, core tomatoes and cut off top ½ inch from each. Cut tops into ¼-inch dice and set aside. Scoop out insides of tomatoes with a melon-ball cutter or a spoon into a medium-mesh sieve set over a bowl, leaving shells intact. Force pulp and juice through sieve, discarding seeds. Add enough water to juice to total 2 cups and set aside. Sprinkle tomato shells with ¼ teaspoon salt, then invert onto a rack set in a shallow baking pan and drain 20 minutes.

▸ Scoop flesh from zucchini halves into a bowl using a melon-ball cutter or spoon, leaving ¼-inch-thick shells. Coarsely chop flesh and set aside.

▸ Cook chopped zucchini and onion in ¼ cup oil in a 12-inch heavy skillet over moderate heat, stirring occasionally, until softened and beginning to brown, 5 to 7 minutes. Add bulgur, sugar, allspice, 1 teaspoon salt, and ¼ teaspoon pepper and

cook, stirring, until bulgur is coated, about 1 minute. Add juice mixture, diced tomatoes, and currants and bring to a boil. Remove from heat and cover skillet, then let stand until liquid is absorbed and bulgur is tender, about 10 minutes.

▸ While bulgur stands, put oven racks in upper and lower thirds of oven and preheat oven to 400°F.

▸ Arrange tomato and zucchini shells, cut sides up, in an oiled 15- by 10-inch shallow baking pan. Brush insides of shells with oil and sprinkle with ¼ teaspoon pepper (total), then sprinkle zucchini only with ¼ teaspoon salt. Put bell pepper halves in an oiled 13- by 9-inch baking pan, then brush insides with some oil and sprinkle with remaining ¼ teaspoon salt and ¼ teaspoon pepper.

▸ Stir eggplant pieces, 2 tablespoons parsley, and salt and pepper to taste into bulgur mixture. Spoon stuffing into vegetable shells, then drizzle stuffing with remaining 2 tablespoons oil and cover pans loosely with foil.

▸ Bake, switching position of pans halfway through baking, until vegetable shells are just tender but not falling apart, 20 to 30 minutes for tomatoes and zucchini and 30 to 40 minutes for bell peppers. Cool vegetables to room temperature, about 30 minutes. Sprinkle with remaining 2 tablespoons parsley just before serving.

COOKS' NOTES: Stuffed vegetables can be baked 1 day ahead and cooled completely, uncovered, then chilled, covered. Bring to room temperature before serving (this will take about 1 hour).
• Eggplant can be broiled 4 to 6 inches from heat in a preheated broiler, turning occasionally, until it collapses, 15 to 20 minutes.

HERB AND CHEESE PIE

SERVES 8 (FIRST COURSE)

ACTIVE TIME: 40 MIN   START TO FINISH: 2½ HR (INCLUDES COOLING)

This fennel-and-scallion-enriched version of tyropita *(Greek cheese pie) uses feta and cottage cheese to create a filling that's mildly tangy yet mellow.*

  1 medium fennel bulb (sometimes labeled "anise"; 1 lb) with fronds
  6 scallions (1 bunch), chopped
  ½ teaspoon salt
  1 stick (½ cup) unsalted butter
  1 lb 4% cottage cheese (3 cups)
  ½ lb feta, crumbled (2 cups)
  4 large eggs, lightly beaten
  2 tablespoons semolina (sometimes labeled "semolina flour"; see Sources)
  ¼ cup chopped fresh dill

¼ teaspoon black pepper
2 tablespoons fine dry bread crumbs (not seasoned)
8 (17- by 12-inch) phyllo sheets, thawed if frozen

SPECIAL EQUIPMENT: a 9- to 9½-inch (24-cm) springform pan

▶ Put oven rack in lower third of oven and preheat oven to 400°F.
▶ Cut off stalks from fennel bulb. Chop enough fronds to measure ¼ cup and discard stalks. Cut fennel bulb (including core) into ¼-inch dice.
▶ Cook fennel bulb, chopped scallions, and ¼ teaspoon salt in 2 tablespoons butter in a 10-inch heavy skillet, covered, over moderate heat, stirring occasionally, until tender, about 10 minutes. Remove lid and cook until any liquid is evaporated, 1 to 2 minutes more. Transfer to a large bowl and stir in cheeses, eggs, semolina, fennel fronds, dill, pepper, and remaining ¼ teaspoon salt until combined.
▶ Melt remaining 6 tablespoons butter and brush springform pan with some of butter, then sprinkle bottom with 1 tablespoon bread crumbs. Unroll phyllo and cover stack with plastic wrap and a dampened kitchen towel. Working quickly, brush 1 phyllo sheet with some butter (keep remaining sheets covered) and gently fit it into springform pan, allowing ends to hang over. Rotate pan slightly, then butter another phyllo sheet and place on top (sheets should not align). Sprinkle with remaining tablespoon bread crumbs. Butter and fit 4 more phyllo sheets into pan, rotating pan for each sheet (overhang should cover entire rim).
▶ Spread cheese mixture in phyllo shell.
▶ Butter another phyllo sheet, then fold in half crosswise and butter again. Fold again (to quarter) and brush with butter, then lay over center of filling. Repeat with remaining phyllo sheet, laying it over folded sheet in opposite direction. Fold overhang toward center to enclose filling and folded phyllo, then brush top with butter.
▶ Bake until puffed and deep golden brown, 40 to 50 minutes. Once pie is golden brown, loosely cover pan with a sheet of foil to prevent overbrowning. Cool in pan on a rack 5 minutes. Remove side of pan and continue to cool pie on rack.
▶ Cut into wedges (leave bottom of pan under pie). Serve warm or at room temperature.

COOKS' NOTE: Pie can be baked 6 hours ahead and kept, uncovered, at room temperature.

GRILLED MARINATED LEG OF LAMB
SERVES 8
ACTIVE TIME: 30 MIN   START TO FINISH: 10 HR (INCLUDES MARINATING)

The uniform thickness of a butterflied boneless leg of lamb makes it extremely simple to cook and serve. This cut of meat shouldn't be hard to find, but if you get one that is boned and tied, ask your butcher to butterfly it.

½ cup extra-virgin olive oil
¼ cup fresh lemon juice
4 garlic cloves, minced
1 tablespoon dried oregano (preferably Greek), crumbled
2 teaspoons salt
1 teaspoon black pepper
1 (4½- to 5-lb) butterflied boneless leg of lamb, trimmed of fat

SPECIAL EQUIPMENT: a large (2-gallon) heavy-duty sealable plastic bag; 3 or 4 (10- to 12-inch) metal skewers

▶ Combine oil, lemon juice, garlic, oregano, salt, and pepper in sealable plastic bag. Add lamb and seal bag, pressing out air. Turn bag to coat lamb, then put bag in a shallow baking pan and marinate, chilled, turning bag over occasionally, at least 8 hours.
▶ Bring lamb to room temperature, about 1 hour, before grilling.
▶ Prepare grill for cooking over direct heat with medium-hot charcoal (moderate heat for gas); see Tips, page 8.
▶ Remove lamb from marinade (discard marinade) and run 3 or 4 skewers lengthwise through lamb about 2 inches apart. Grill on a lightly oiled grill rack, covered only if using gas grill, turning over occasionally and, if necessary, moving around on grill to avoid flare-ups, until thermometer registers 125 to 128°F, 8 to 14 minutes total for medium-rare.
▶ Transfer lamb to a cutting board and remove skewers. Let lamb stand, loosely covered with foil, 20 minutes. (Internal temperature will rise to 135°F while meat stands.) Cut across the grain into slices.

COOKS' NOTES: If you aren't able to grill outdoors, lamb can be cooked in a hot lightly oiled well-seasoned large (2-burner) ridged grill pan, uncovered, turning over once, 12 to 14 minutes per side.
• Lamb can marinate up to 24 hours.

PANFRIED ROMAINE

SERVES 8

ACTIVE TIME: 20 MIN   START TO FINISH: 1 HR (INCLUDES COOLING)

Cooking romaine in olive oil brings out its sweetness while preserving its crunch.

6 romaine hearts (two 18-oz packages), trimmed and halved lengthwise
¼ cup extra-virgin olive oil
About 1¼ teaspoons fine sea salt

▶ Rinse romaine halves, then shake off water and pat dry.
▶ Heat 1 tablespoon oil in a 12-inch heavy skillet over moderate heat until hot but not smoking, then add 3 romaine halves, cut sides down, and sprinkle with a rounded ¼ teaspoon sea salt.
▶ Cook, turning over once with tongs, until browned, about 2 minutes total, then cover and cook until just crisp-tender, 2 to 3 minutes more. Transfer to a platter.
▶ Cook remaining romaine halves in oil in 3 batches in same manner, transferring to platter. Cool to room temperature before serving.

COOKS' NOTE: Romaine can be made 2 hours ahead and kept, loosely covered, at room temperature.

YOGURT MOUSSE WITH APRICOT SAUCE

SERVES 8

ACTIVE TIME: 45 MIN   START TO FINISH: 10¼ HR (INCLUDES DRAINING YOGURT)

The sweet and tangy apricot sauce that anchors this refreshing dessert is a nod to the spoon sweets—fruit preserves that are eaten from small spoons—traditionally served in Greece to arriving guests.

FOR MOUSSE

1 (32-oz) container well-stirred whole-milk yogurt
1½ teaspoons unflavored gelatin (from 1 envelope)
1 cup whole milk
½ vanilla bean, halved lengthwise
½ cup sugar
1 (4- by 1-inch) strip fresh lemon zest (see Tips, page 8)
¾ cup chilled heavy cream

FOR SAUCE

½ vanilla bean, halved lengthwise
½ cup sugar
¼ cup water
1 lb fresh apricots, quartered and pitted
1 teaspoon fresh lemon juice, or to taste

MAKE MOUSSE:

▶ Drain yogurt in a paper-towel-lined sieve set into a bowl in refrigerator, pouring off and discarding liquid occasionally, 8 hours, then transfer to a clean bowl. Sprinkle gelatin over ¼ cup milk in a small bowl and let stand 1 minute to soften.
▶ Scrape seeds from vanilla bean pod into remaining ¾ cup milk in a 1-quart heavy saucepan, then add pod, sugar, and zest and bring to a simmer over moderate heat, stirring until sugar is dissolved. Stir in gelatin mixture until dissolved. Pour through a fine-mesh sieve set into a metal bowl, discarding solids, then set bowl in a larger bowl half-filled with ice and cold water and let stand, stirring frequently, until cool, about 10 minutes.
▶ Add milk mixture gradually to yogurt, whisking. Beat cream with an electric mixer at high speed until it just holds soft peaks, then fold into yogurt mixture gently but thoroughly. Chill mousse, covered, folding twice in first 20 minutes, until set, about 2 hours.

MAKE SAUCE WHILE MOUSSE CHILLS:

▶ Scrape seeds from vanilla bean pod into a 2-quart heavy saucepan, then add pod, sugar, water, apricots, and 1 teaspoon lemon juice and cook, uncovered, over moderate heat, stirring frequently and skimming off any foam, until fruit is tender, 8 to 12 minutes. Cool to room temperature, about 30 minutes. Add lemon juice to taste and discard pod. Serve sauce topped with mousse.

COOKS' NOTES: You can substitute 1½ cups Greek yogurt for the whole-milk yogurt. (Do not drain Greek yogurt.)
• Mousse can be made 1 day ahead and chilled, covered.
• Sauce can be made 3 days ahead and cooled completely, uncovered, then chilled, covered. Bring to room temperature before serving.

OPPOSITE: grilled marinated leg of lamb; panfried romaine

WE ARE FAMILY

A SUMMER REUNION TO REMEMBER

SERVES 12

BLACKBERRY LIMEADE

RHUBARB GINGER COOLER

**WATERMELON WITH PARMESAN
AND MINT**

**CHICKEN AND FENNEL SALAD
SANDWICHES**

SHRIMP SALAD ROLLS

**SUGAR SNAP PEA AND
CABBAGE SLAW**

SALT AND VINEGAR POTATO SALAD

HERBED CORN ON THE COB

ROBERT SINSKEY PINOT BLANC '04

**PRALINE ICE CREAM
SANDWICHES**

**DOUBLE-CRUST NECTARINE
RASPBERRY PIES**

RENWOOD ORANGE MUSCAT '05

RHUBARB GINGER COOLER

MAKES 12 DRINKS

ACTIVE TIME: 15 MIN START TO FINISH: 2 HR (INCLUDES CHILLING)

To call this bracing pink drink a rhubarb-infused ginger ale doesn't do it justice; it's much less syrupy-sweet and more cooling. The slightly tart flavor of rhubarb pairs well with lush picnic dishes.

3½ lb fresh rhubarb stalks, cut into ½-inch pieces (10 cups)
2½ cups cold water
1¾ cups sugar
  3 tablespoons coarsely chopped peeled fresh ginger
     About 2 cups sparkling water

▶ Bring rhubarb, cold water, sugar, and ginger to a simmer in a 4- to 5-quart pot over moderate heat, uncovered, stirring once or twice, then simmer 1 minute. Remove from heat and let steep, uncovered, 1 hour.
▶ Pour mixture through a large fine-mesh sieve into a large bowl, gently stirring but not pressing on solids (discard solids; you will have about 6 cups syrup). Chill syrup completely, about 45 minutes.
▶ Serve syrup in glasses over ice with a splash of sparkling water.

COOKS' NOTES: Syrup can be made 3 days ahead and chilled, covered. Add sparkling water just before serving.
• Syrup keeps, frozen, 3 months.

BLACKBERRY LIMEADE

MAKES 12 DRINKS

ACTIVE TIME: 15 MIN START TO FINISH: 15 MIN

A sweet blackberry syrup mellows mouth-puckering limes in an intensely fruity (and kid-friendly) drink.

  2 cups fresh lime juice (from 8 to 12 limes)
1⅔ cups superfine granulated sugar
  1 qt cold water
  2 tablespoons blackberry syrup, store-bought (see Sources) or homemade (see cooks' note, below)

GARNISH: thin lime slices

▶ Stir together all ingredients in a pitcher until sugar is dissolved. Serve over ice.

COOKS' NOTE: To make blackberry syrup, heat ¼ cup blackberry jam with 1 tablespoon water in a small saucepan over moderately low heat, stirring, until jam is dissolved. Pour mixture through a fine-mesh sieve into a small bowl, pressing on and then discarding solids. Syrup keeps, covered and chilled, 1 week.

WATERMELON WITH PARMESAN AND MINT

SERVES 12 (HORS D'OEUVRE)

ACTIVE TIME: 20 MIN START TO FINISH: 20 MIN

Watermelon chunks in savory salads have been all the rage in the past few years, but we wanted a way to retain the fruit's best trait: how enjoyable it is to eat out of hand on a hot day. These wedges, sprinkled with salt, pepper, cheese, and heady fresh mint, are a light, refreshing start to a warm-weather meal. And they leave your other hand free to hold a drink or chase after the kids.

  1 (4-lb) piece watermelon
½ teaspoon black pepper
¼ teaspoon salt
½ oz Parmigiano-Reggiano, grated with a rasp (¾ cup)
1½ tablespoons chopped fresh mint

▶ Cut piece of watermelon lengthwise into narrow wedges about 1½ inches wide, then cut wedges crosswise into ¾-inch-thick slices (they will be tall and pointed). Trim rind to enable slices to stand upright.

▶ Just before serving, stir together pepper and salt and sprinkle over slices. Stir together cheese and chopped mint and sprinkle slices again.

CHICKEN AND FENNEL SALAD SANDWICHES

SERVES 12

ACTIVE TIME: 45 MIN   START TO FINISH: 2¾ HR

Roasting the chickens and using both dark and white meat results in chicken salad with deep flavor. (Buying rotisserie chickens will save time, but be sure to choose minimally seasoned birds.) Fennel, standing in for the usual celery, along with fennel seed and fresh basil, adds an unexpected note of sophistication.

FOR CHICKENS

- 3 (3- to 3½-lb) whole chickens
- 4 teaspoons salt
- ¾ teaspoon black pepper
- ½ stick (¼ cup) unsalted butter, softened

FOR DRESSING AND SANDWICHES

- 1¼ cups mayonnaise
- ½ cup plain yogurt
- 1 teaspoon finely grated fresh lemon zest (see Tips, page 8)
- ¼ cup fresh lemon juice
- 1½ teaspoons fennel seeds, toasted (see Tips, page 8) and cooled, then lightly crushed
- 1½ teaspoons salt
- 1 teaspoon black pepper
- 1 cup chopped fresh basil
- 3 cups chopped fennel bulb (sometimes called anise; from 2 to 3 medium bulbs, stalks discarded)
- 12 rolls or buns

SPECIAL EQUIPMENT: **an instant-read thermometer**

ROAST CHICKENS:

▶ Put oven rack in middle position and preheat oven to 425°F.

▶ Rinse chickens inside and out and pat dry. Stir together salt and pepper, then sprinkle over chickens inside and out. Put 1 tablespoon softened butter evenly under skin of each breast, then rub remaining tablespoon butter over skin of each. Arrange chickens in a 17- by 12-inch shallow heavy baking pan and roast, switching position of chickens and rotating pan halfway through roasting to help cook evenly, until thermometer inserted into fleshy part of each thigh (do not touch bone) registers 170°F, about 1 hour. Cool completely, about 1 hour.

▶ Discard skin and bones from chickens, then coarsely shred meat and transfer to a large bowl.

MAKE DRESSING AND ASSEMBLE SANDWICHES:

▶ Stir together mayonnaise, yogurt, zest, lemon juice, fennel seeds, salt, pepper, and basil, then pour over chicken in bowl. Add chopped fennel and stir to combine. Season with salt and pepper.

▶ Serve chicken salad in rolls.

COOKS' NOTE: Chicken salad, without basil, can be made 1 day ahead and chilled, covered. Stir in basil before serving.

SHRIMP SALAD ROLLS

SERVES 12

ACTIVE TIME: 45 MIN   START TO FINISH: 2 HR

They're inspired by lobster rolls, but we think you'll find these sandwiches more popular with a crowd of all ages—not to mention more affordable and easier on the cook.

- 4 lb large shrimp in shell (21 to 25 per lb)
- 1½ cups mayonnaise
- 3 tablespoons fresh lemon juice
- 3 tablespoons chopped fresh tarragon, or to taste
- ¾ teaspoon salt
- ¾ teaspoon black pepper
- 2 cups chopped celery
- 12 hot dog rolls (preferably top-split)

▶ Cook half of shrimp in a 5- to 6-quart pot of generously salted (2 tablespoons) boiling water, stirring occasionally, until shrimp are just cooked through, 3 to 4 minutes. Transfer shrimp with a slotted spoon to a platter and return water to a boil. Cook remaining shrimp in same manner (then discard water), transferring to platter. When shrimp are cool enough to handle, peel, then chill, covered, until completely cold, about 1 hour.

▶ Whisk together mayonnaise, lemon juice, tarragon, salt, and pepper in a large bowl and chill until ready to use.

▶ Devein shrimp and cut into ½-inch pieces. Season with salt and pepper, then add to dressing along with celery, and toss to combine. Serve salad in rolls.

COOKS' NOTES: Shrimp can be cooked 1 day ahead and chilled, covered.

• Though best eaten the same day, shrimp salad can be made 1 day ahead and chilled, covered.

SUGAR SNAP PEA AND CABBAGE SLAW

SERVES 12

ACTIVE TIME: 45 MIN   START TO FINISH: 2¾ HR (INCLUDES CHILLING)

Sugar snap peas add a fresh crispness to this slaw; buttermilk dressing keeps it tangy and light and contrasts nicely with the other dishes on this menu. And it's so easy to make. We bet that, after a taste, you'll never rely on that mayonnaisey deli slaw again.

2½ lb green cabbage (preferably Savoy), quartered,
     cored, and thinly sliced (14 cups)
 ¾ lb sugar snap peas, trimmed and thinly sliced
     diagonally (4 cups)
 ¾ cup well-shaken buttermilk
 ½ cup sour cream
 ¼ cup chopped fresh dill
  2 garlic cloves, minced
1¾ teaspoons salt
 ½ teaspoon black pepper
  1 tablespoon white distilled vinegar

▶Toss together cabbage and peas in a large bowl. Whisk together remaining ingredients and pour over slaw, stirring to combine well. Add salt to taste, then chill, covered, at least 2 hours.

COOKS' NOTE: Slaw can be chilled, covered, up to 1 day.

SALT AND VINEGAR POTATO SALAD

SERVES 12

ACTIVE TIME: 20 MIN   START TO FINISH: 45 MIN

If your pulse quickens at the suggestion of salt and vinegar potato chips, you'll be hooked on this warm potato salad after one bite. A little Old Bay seasoning gives it a modest kick.

  1 large red onion, cut lengthwise into ⅓-inch-wide wedges
     and layers separated
 ½ cup plus 2 tablespoons cider vinegar
  2 teaspoons salt
  5 lb medium yellow-fleshed potatoes such as Yukon Gold
  2 to 2½ teaspoons Old Bay seasoning
1¼ teaspoons sugar
 ¾ cup extra-virgin olive oil

▶Toss together onion, 2 tablespoons vinegar, and ½ teaspoon salt in a bowl. Marinate at room temperature, tossing occasionally, until slightly softened and pink, about 45 minutes.
▶Cover potatoes with salted cold water (see Tips, page 8) in a 5- to 6-quart pot, then simmer, uncovered, until just tender, 15 to 20 minutes.
▶While potatoes cook, whisk together 2 teaspoons Old Bay seasoning with sugar, remaining 1½ teaspoons salt, and remaining ½ cup vinegar in a small bowl.
▶Drain potatoes in a colander, and when cool enough to handle but still warm, peel and cut into ½-inch-wide wedges. Toss warm potatoes with vinegar mixture in a large bowl. Add onion mixture and oil, tossing to combine. Add more Old Bay seasoning (to taste) if desired. Serve warm or at room temperature.

COOKS' NOTE: Onion can be marinated, covered and chilled, up to 1 day.

HERBED CORN ON THE COB

SERVES 12

ACTIVE TIME: 25 MIN   START TO FINISH: 1½ HR

Lemon thyme, available at farmers markets and specialty produce markets, lends this corn a delicate lemony-herbal flavor, but feel free to use regular fresh thyme instead. Steaming the corn in the husks allows you to cook it in butter, and you can pull back the husks and use them as a handle while eating.

 12 ears of corn in the husk, stem ends trimmed
  1 stick (½ cup) plus 1 tablespoon unsalted butter,
     softened, plus additional for serving
 36 sprigs fresh lemon thyme

SPECIAL EQUIPMENT: an 8- to 12-qt stockpot with a tight-fitting lid

▶ Shuck corn, leaving husks attached at base. Discard corn silk. Spread about ¾ tablespoon butter over each cob, then lay 3 thyme sprigs against each cob, pressing them gently into butter. Pull husks back up over corn. Remove 3 pieces of husk and tear into 12 strips total. Tie top of each husk closed with a strip, then let stand 1 hour (for flavors to develop).
▶ Bring 1 inch of water to a boil in pot (see cooks' note, below), then stand 4 to 6 ears of corn in pot (depending on size of pot), tied ends up, and steam, covered, moving outer ears to inside once with tongs, until crisp-tender, about 6 minutes. Steam remaining ears of corn, in batches if necessary, in same manner, adding water as necessary. Serve with salt and additional butter on the side.

COOKS' NOTES: If you don't have a pot deep enough to stand corn in, use a large roasting pan with a rack. Straddle pan across 2 burners and add just enough water to reach rack. Bring to a boil, then arrange half of corn in 1 layer on rack. Cover pan tightly with foil and steam about 6 minutes. Repeat with remaining corn.
• Corn can be husked and reassembled with butter and thyme (but not cooked) 1 day ahead and chilled, covered.

PRALINE ICE CREAM SANDWICHES

MAKES 24 SANDWICHES
ACTIVE TIME: 45 MIN   START TO FINISH: 3 HR (INCLUDES FREEZING)

This recipe is delightfully devoid of fuss; you simply make one big sandwich and then cut it into small pieces.

FOR PRALINE
  1 cup pecans (3½ oz), coarsely chopped
1½ teaspoons salt
  1 cup sugar

FOR SANDWICH LAYERS
1½ sticks (¾ cup) unsalted butter at room temperature
      plus additional for greasing pan
1½ cups all-purpose flour
  1 teaspoon baking powder
  ¼ teaspoon baking soda
  ½ teaspoon salt
1¼ cups packed dark brown sugar
  2 large eggs
  1 teaspoon vanilla

FOR FILLING
  2 pt store-bought premium vanilla ice cream, softened

SPECIAL EQUIPMENT: 2 (15½- by 10½-inch) baking pans (¾ inch deep; also called jelly roll pans); parchment paper; an offset metal spatula

MAKE PRALINE:
▶ Stir together pecans and salt in a small bowl. Put a large sheet of foil on a work surface.
▶ Cook sugar in a 10-inch heavy skillet over moderate heat, undisturbed, until it begins to melt. Continue to cook, stirring occasionally, until sugar melts into a golden caramel. Add salted pecans, stirring until coated well, then spread on foil and cool completely, about 15 minutes. Peel praline off foil and finely chop with a large heavy knife.

MAKE SANDWICH LAYERS:
▶ Put oven racks in upper and lower thirds of oven and preheat oven to 375°F. Draw a large X with butter from corner to corner in each baking pan, then line bottom of each pan with parchment paper, leaving a 1-inch overhang on each side, pressing to help parchment adhere to X.
▶ Whisk together flour, baking powder, baking soda, and salt in a small bowl. Beat together butter and brown sugar in another bowl with an electric mixer at medium-high speed until pale and fluffy, about 3 minutes. Add eggs 1 at a time, beating well after each addition, then beat in vanilla. Reduce speed to low and add flour mixture in 2 batches, mixing until just combined.
▶ Divide batter between baking pans (about 1½ cups each) and spread into thin, even layers with offset spatula. Sprinkle with praline and bake, switching position of pans halfway through baking, until sandwich layers are golden brown but still tender, about 10 minutes. Cool in pans 10 minutes, then transfer with parchment to racks and cool completely, about 30 minutes. Clean 1 baking pan.
▶ Line cleaned baking pan with fresh parchment, leaving a 1-inch overhang on each side. Invert sandwich layers onto work surface and carefully peel off and discard parchment, then trim edges.

ASSEMBLE SANDWICHES:
▶ Transfer 1 sandwich layer, praline side down, to baking pan and spread evenly with ice cream. Top ice cream with second sandwich layer, praline side up, pressing gently to form an even sandwich. Wrap baking pan in plastic wrap and freeze ice cream sandwich at least 1 hour.
▶ Cut into 24 sandwiches before serving.

COOKS' NOTE: Ice cream sandwich, wrapped in plastic wrap and then foil, can be frozen up to 1 week. Cut before serving.

OPPOSITE: praline ice cream sandwiches

DOUBLE-CRUST NECTARINE RASPBERRY PIES

MAKES 2 (9-INCH) PIES
ACTIVE TIME: 1½ HR START TO FINISH: 6 HR
(INCLUDES MAKING AND CHILLING PASTRY AND COOLING PIES)

Nestled in a flaky crust, nectarines and raspberries seem to tease the best out of each other—these pies are fragrant and floral, sweet and tart. Even if you've never had the combination of fruits before, it instantly tastes like an American classic.

FOR PASTRY

- 5 cups all-purpose flour
- 3 sticks (1½ cups) cold unsalted butter, cut into ½-inch cubes but left in sticks
- ½ cup cold vegetable shortening (preferably trans-fat-free)
- 1 teaspoon salt
  About ¾ cup ice water
- 1 tablespoon milk
- 2 tablespoons sugar

FOR FILLING

- 6 lb nectarines
- 3 cups raspberries (¾ lb)
- 3 tablespoons fresh lemon juice
- ¼ cup quick-cooking tapioca
- ¼ cup cornstarch
- ¼ teaspoon salt
- 1½ cups sugar

SPECIAL EQUIPMENT: **a pastry or bench scraper; an electric coffee/spice grinder; 2 (9-inch) glass or metal pie plates (5-cup capacity)**

MAKE PASTRY:

▶ Blend together 2½ cups flour, 1½ sticks butter, ¼ cup shortening, and ½ teaspoon salt in a bowl with your fingertips or a pastry blender (or pulse in a food processor) until mixture resembles coarse meal with some roughly pea-size butter lumps. Drizzle evenly with 5 tablespoons ice water and gently stir with a fork (or pulse) until incorporated.

▶ Squeeze a small handful: If it doesn't hold together, add more ice water to dough, 1 tablespoon at a time, stirring (or pulsing) until just combined. (Do not overwork, or pastry will be tough.)

▶ Turn out dough onto a work surface and divide into 6 portions. With heel of your hand, smear each portion once or twice in a forward motion to help distribute fat. Gather all of dough together with scraper and press into 2 balls, then flatten each into a 5-inch disk. Make 2 more disks in same manner with remaining 2½ cups flour, 1½ sticks butter, ¼ cup shortening, and ½ teaspoon salt. Chill dough, each disk wrapped tightly in plastic wrap, until firm, at least 1 hour.

PREPARE FILLING WHILE DOUGH CHILLS:

▶ Cut nectarines into ½-inch-wide wedges, then toss with raspberries and lemon juice in a large bowl.

▶ Grind tapioca to a powder in grinder, then whisk together with cornstarch, salt, and sugar in a small bowl (do not toss with fruit until dough is rolled out).

ROLL OUT PASTRY AND PREPARE PIES:

▶ Put oven rack in lower third of oven and put a large sheet of foil on rack. Preheat oven to 425°F.

▶ Roll out 2 disks of dough, 1 at a time (keep remaining disks chilled), on a lightly floured surface with a lightly floured rolling pin, into 13-inch rounds, then fit into pie plates (do not trim) and chill until ready to use.

▶ Roll out remaining 2 disks (for top crusts) in same manner and set aside (keep flat).

▶ Gently toss sugar mixture with fruit and divide between pie shells.

▶ Cover pies with pastry rounds and trim edges with kitchen shears, leaving a ½-inch overhang. Press edges together, then crimp decoratively. Brush pastry tops with milk and sprinkle all over with sugar (2 tablespoons total). Cut several steam vents in top of each pie with a small sharp knife.

▶ Bake pies on foil 20 minutes. Reduce oven temperature to 375°F and continue to bake, checking frequently and covering edge of each pie with a strip of foil or pie shield if crusts are browning too fast, until crusts are golden brown and filling is bubbling, about 40 minutes more.

▶ Cool pies to room temperature on racks, at least 2 hours.

COOKS' NOTES: Dough (in disks) can be chilled up to 1 day.
• Pie shells can be made 1 day ahead and chilled, loosely covered. Pastry rounds for top crusts can be rolled out and chilled, layered between sheets of plastic wrap. Bring pastry rounds to cool room temperature before assembling pies.

TAKE YOUR PICK

A BOUNTIFUL DINNER FROM THE GARDEN

SERVES 8

HERBED GOAT-CHEESE TOASTS

SUMMER VEGETABLE TERRINE

GUENOC LAKE COUNTY SAUVIGNON BLANC '05

RACK OF LAMB WITH GARLIC AND HERBS

**GLAZED FINGERLING POTATOES AND
BABY VEGETABLES**

STAG'S LEAP WINE CELLARS S.L.V. CABERNET
SAUVIGNON '02

FRUIT IN LEMON-VERBENA SYRUP

CASSIS SORBET

HERBED GOAT-CHEESE TOASTS

MAKES 40 HORS D'OEUVRES
ACTIVE TIME: 15 MIN   START TO FINISH: 20 MIN

*In this spread, goat cheese tastes particularly mild because of
the little bit of whipped cream folded in. Take the cheese out to
soften before heading for the farmers market, and by the time you
get back, it will be ready to mix with whatever herbs you've found.*

40 (¼-inch-thick) slices from 1 baguette
3 tablespoons olive oil
6 oz mild soft goat cheese at room temperature
¼ cup chopped mixed tender fresh herbs such as
      basil, chives, chervil, dill, parsley, and tarragon; or
      1 tablespoon chopped mixed strong fresh herbs such
      as rosemary and thyme
1½ tablespoons minced shallot
¼ teaspoon black pepper, or to taste
⅓ cup well-chilled heavy cream

▶ Put oven racks in upper and lower thirds of oven and preheat
oven to 350°F.
▶ Divide baguette slices between 2 shallow baking pans. Lightly
brush tops of slices with oil, then lightly season with salt and
pepper. Bake, switching position of pans halfway through
baking, until toasts are crisp but not hard, about 10 minutes.
▶ Stir together goat cheese, herbs, shallot, and pepper. Season
with salt.
▶ Beat cream with a whisk until it just holds soft peaks, then fold
into cheese mixture. Serve with toasts.

COOKS' NOTES: Toasts can be baked 1 day ahead and cooled
completely, uncovered, then kept in an airtight container at
room temperature.
• Cheese mixture can be made 1 day ahead and chilled, covered.
Bring to room temperature before serving.

SUMMER VEGETABLE TERRINE

SERVES 8 (FIRST COURSE)
ACTIVE TIME: 2 HR   START TO FINISH: 7 HR (INCLUDES CHILLING)

*This dramatic terrine isn't just visually arresting; it's also
delicious—and a sophisticated change of pace from a salad to
start the meal. We used beets, haricots verts, and wax beans
here, but feel free to improvise if other vegetables look tempting
at your farmers market; you'll need a total of 6 cups of cooked
vegetables. Since the vegetables are cooked until very tender,
the terrine slices beautifully.*

2½ lb mixed baby (1-inch) or medium (2-inch) Chioggia and
      golden beets with greens (about 16 baby or 6 medium;
      see cooks' note, below)
2 large leeks, trimmed of any discolored leaves or ends,
      leaving green parts attached
2 medium carrots, thinly sliced crosswise
2 celery ribs, sliced, reserving leaves
2 shallots, thinly sliced crosswise
2 cups dry white wine
1 teaspoon salt
10 black peppercorns
3¼ cups cold water
½ cup chopped mixed tender fresh herbs, stems reserved
      for stock
1 (½-oz) bunch fresh chives, coarser bottom third cut off
      and reserved and remainder chopped
4½ teaspoons gelatin (from two ¼-oz envelopes)
⅓ lb haricots verts, trimmed
⅓ lb wax beans, trimmed
¼ cup extra-virgin olive oil, plus additional for oiling terrine
      Fleur de sel for sprinkling
      Coarsely ground black pepper for sprinkling

SPECIAL EQUIPMENT: heavy-duty foil; a nonreactive (6-cup
capacity) rectangular terrine or loaf pan (see cooks' note, below)
GARNISH: fresh herb sprigs

ROAST BEETS:
▶ Put oven rack in middle position and preheat oven to 450°F.
▶ Trim beets, leaving ½ inch of stems intact. Divide between
2 sheets of heavy-duty foil and wrap foil to enclose beets. Roast
in a shallow baking pan until very tender, 1 to 1½ hours. Let
steam in foil 15 minutes, then peel beets and cut into 1-inch-
wide wedges if large. Season with salt and pepper.
MAKE GELATIN MIXTURE WHILE BEETS ROAST:
▶ Halve leeks lengthwise, then coarsely chop. Wash leeks in a
bowl of water, agitating them, then lift out with a slotted spoon
and transfer to a 3-quart saucepan. Add carrots to leeks along
with sliced celery, shallots, wine, salt, peppercorns, and 3 cups
cold water and bring to a boil, then reduce heat and simmer,
uncovered, 30 minutes.
▶ Add celery leaves, herb stems, and coarse parts of chives and
simmer 10 minutes. Pour stock through a fine-mesh sieve into
a 1-quart glass measure or heatproof bowl, discarding solids. If
stock measures more than 2½ cups, return to saucepan and boil
until reduced to 2½ cups, about 10 to 15 minutes. If there is
less, add water. Season with salt and pepper.
▶ Stir gelatin into remaining ¼ cup cold water and let stand
1 minute to soften, then add to hot stock, stirring until dissolved.
Set aside.

PREPARE BEANS:

▸Boil haricots verts and wax beans in separate batches in a 5- to 6-quart pot of boiling salted water (see Tips, page 8), uncovered, until very tender, 6 to 7 minutes per batch, transferring with a slotted spoon to a bowl of ice and cold water to stop cooking. Drain in a colander and pat dry. Transfer to a large bowl and season with salt and pepper.

ASSEMBLE TERRINE:

▸Very lightly oil terrine, then line long sides and bottom with a sheet of plastic wrap, smoothing out any wrinkles and allowing at least 2 inches of overhang on each side. Pour about ½ cup gelatin mixture into terrine and quick-chill in freezer until just set, about 10 minutes.

▸Lay one third of beans lengthwise over set gelatin layer. Sprinkle with one third of chopped herbs (including chives), then loosely top with half of beets, leaving some space between them (for gelatin to fill and hold vegetables together). Repeat layering with half of remaining beans and herbs and all of beets, then end with a third layer of beans and herbs. Stir remaining gelatin mixture again, then slowly pour in all but ½ cup (reserve remainder at room temperature), pushing down vegetables if necessary to just cover with gelatin mixture. Chill, uncovered, until top is set, 1½ to 2 hours.

▸If reserved ½ cup gelatin mixture has begun to set, heat until just liquefied but not hot, then pour over set terrine. Chill until firm, about 2 hours.

TO SERVE:

▸Run a thin knife along short sides (ends) of terrine, then invert terrine onto a cutting board, gently pulling on plastic overhang to help unmold (discard plastic wrap). Carefully cut terrine with a very sharp knife into 8 slices, transferring each slice to a plate as cut, using a metal spatula to hold outside of each slice steady. Drizzle oil (¼ cup) around plates and sprinkle *fleur de sel* and pepper over oil and terrine.

COOKS' NOTES: Do not use red beets in place of the Chioggia or golden beets, as they will dye all the vegetables red.

• Stainless steel, glass, and enameled cast iron are nonreactive; avoid pure aluminum and uncoated iron, which can impart an unpleasant taste and color to recipes with acidic ingredients in them.

• Terrine can be chilled in pan, covered with plastic wrap after 2 hours up to 2 days.

RACK OF LAMB WITH GARLIC AND HERBS

SERVES 8

ACTIVE TIME: 20 MIN   START TO FINISH: 1 HR

Herb-and-bread-crumb coatings are classic on rack of lamb, but leaving out the crumbs lightens the dish (and the juicy chops taste more summery as a result). This recipe is best made with new garlic—garlic that has not been aged. It is covered with a moist membrane rather than papery skin and is often sold with greens attached. If you're lucky enough to find some, substitute ¼ cup chopped garlic greens for half of the parsley in the herb mixture.

FOR LAMB

  2 (8-rib) frenched racks of lamb (each rack 1½ lb), trimmed of all but a thin layer of fat

1½ teaspoons salt

 ¾ teaspoon black pepper

  1 teaspoon vegetable oil

FOR HERB COATING

 ½ head new garlic or 3 large regular garlic cloves, minced

 ¼ cup finely chopped fresh flat-leaf parsley

  1 tablespoon finely chopped fresh thyme

  2 teaspoons finely chopped fresh rosemary

 ½ teaspoon salt

 ¼ teaspoon black pepper

1½ tablespoons extra-virgin olive oil

SPECIAL EQUIPMENT: **an instant-read thermometer**

BROWN LAMB:

▸Heat a dry 12-inch heavy skillet over high heat until hot, at least 2 minutes. Meanwhile, pat lamb dry and rub meat all over with salt and pepper. Add vegetable oil to hot skillet, then brown racks, in 2 batches if necessary, on all sides (not ends), about 10 minutes per batch.

▸Transfer racks to a small (13- by 9-inch) roasting pan.

COAT AND ROAST LAMB:

▸Put oven rack in middle position and preheat oven to 350°F.

▸Stir together garlic, herbs, salt, pepper, and oil. Coat meaty parts of lamb with herb mixture, pressing to help adhere. Roast 15 minutes, then cover lamb loosely with foil and roast until thermometer inserted diagonally into center of meat registers 120°F, 5 to 10 minutes more. Let stand, covered, 10 minutes. (Internal temperature will rise to 125 to 130°F for medium-rare while lamb stands.)

▸Cut each rack into 4 double chops.

GLAZED FINGERLING POTATOES AND BABY VEGETABLES

SERVES 8

ACTIVE TIME: 30 MIN   START TO FINISH: 45 MIN

- 1 lb fingerling or other new potatoes, halved lengthwise
- 1½ lb baby carrots with greens, peeled if desired and greens trimmed to ½ inch
- 1½ lb baby turnips (about 1 inch) with greens, greens trimmed to ½ inch
- ½ head new garlic or 3 large regular garlic cloves, thinly sliced
- 8 sprigs fresh thyme
- 1½ teaspoons salt
- ½ teaspoon black pepper
- ½ cup olive oil
- 1½ cups water
- 2 tablespoons unsalted butter

GARNISH: **fresh thyme sprigs**

▶ Combine all ingredients except water and butter in a deep 12-inch heavy skillet or wide 3- to 6-quart heavy pot and toss to coat with oil. Add water to skillet and bring to a boil. Cover skillet tightly and simmer vigorously over moderate heat, shaking skillet occasionally, until vegetables are tender, about 10 minutes.

▶ Transfer vegetables with a slotted spoon to a platter, discarding thyme sprigs, then boil cooking liquid 1 minute to emulsify oil. Remove from heat and add butter, swirling skillet until butter is incorporated. Pour sauce over vegetables.

FRUIT IN LEMON-VERBENA SYRUP

SERVES 8

ACTIVE TIME: 15 MIN   START TO FINISH: 1 HR

A lemony-floral syrup and a scoop of cassis sorbet (recipe follows) amplify the sweet-tart tug-of-war in a bowl of summer fruits.

- 5 cups mixed fresh fruit such as raspberries, blackberries, red or white currants (left on stems if desired), pink gooseberries (see cooks' note), blueberries, strawberries, and cherries (pitted or halved if large)
- 1¼ cups sugar
- 8 (6-inch) sprigs fresh lemon verbena (see Sources)
- 1¼ cups water
- 2 tablespoons fresh lemon juice, or to taste

ACCOMPANIMENT: **cassis sorbet (recipe follows)**

▶ Put fruit in a large bowl and gently toss with ½ cup sugar, then let stand 20 minutes.

▶ Rub verbena sprigs in your hands to bruise leaves and stems, then combine with water and remaining ¾ cup sugar in a 2-quart heavy saucepan. Bring to a boil, stirring until sugar is dissolved. Simmer 1 minute, then remove from heat and let steep, covered, 5 minutes.

▶ Stir lemon juice into warm syrup and pour through a medium-mesh sieve over fruit. Discard verbena sprigs and gently stir fruit. Let macerate at room temperature 30 minutes to 1 hour.

▶ Divide among 8 soup plates.

COOKS' NOTES: Do not use black currants or green gooseberries for this recipe because they are too tart to eat raw.
• Fruit can be macerated, covered and chilled, up to 6 hours.

CASSIS SORBET

SERVES 8

ACTIVE TIME: 5 MIN   START TO FINISH: 2 HR

Cassis, also known as black currant, has a deep, velvety, ripe-berry flavor, along with a slight sourness; this sorbet plays up those qualities.

- ¼ cup sugar
- 2 tablespoons light corn syrup
- 3 cups black-currant nectar (preferably Looza brand; see cooks' note)
- ¼ cup crème de cassis

SPECIAL EQUIPMENT: **an ice cream maker**

▶ Bring sugar, corn syrup, and ½ cup nectar to a boil, stirring until sugar is dissolved, then boil 1 minute. Transfer to a metal bowl and stir in crème de cassis and remaining 2½ cups nectar. Set bowl in a larger bowl of ice and cold water and let mixture stand, stirring occasionally, until cold, about 10 minutes. Freeze in ice cream maker, then transfer to an airtight container and put in freezer to harden, at least 1 hour.

COOKS' NOTES: We prefer Looza brand black-currant nectar, but if you can find only black-currant syrup or concentrated juice drink, which are much sweeter, omit the sugar in this recipe and use 1 cup of syrup or juice drink diluted with 2 cups water.
• Sorbet can be made 2 days ahead.

FRESH FROM THE FARM

AN IMPROMPTU SUMMER GATHERING

SERVES 6

**ANGEL-HAIR PASTA WITH
FRESH TOMATO SAUCE**

**GRILLED SALMON WITH
LIME BUTTER SAUCE**

GRILLED CORN WITH HERBS

GREEN BEANS AND ARUGULA

ROBERT MONDAVI STAGS LEAP DISTRICT
CABERNET SAUVIGNON '01

ZUCCHINI GINGER CUPCAKES

ANGEL-HAIR PASTA WITH FRESH TOMATO SAUCE

SERVES 6 (FIRST COURSE)

ACTIVE TIME: 20 MIN START TO FINISH: 25 MIN

This dish focuses on the goodness of ripe tomatoes, letting them be just what they're meant to be—wonderful.

> 1   small garlic clove
> 3   lb tomatoes
> 2   tablespoons fresh lemon juice
> 1   teaspoon salt
> 1   teaspoon sugar (optional)
> ½   teaspoon black pepper
> 1   lb dried *capellini* (angel-hair pasta)
> ½   cup chopped fresh basil

ACCOMPANIMENTS: **finely grated Parmigiano-Reggiano; extra-virgin olive oil for drizzling (optional)**

▸ Mince garlic and mash to a paste with a pinch of salt using a large heavy knife.

▸ Core and coarsely chop two thirds of tomatoes. Halve remaining tomatoes crosswise, then rub cut sides of tomatoes against large holes of a box grater set in a large bowl, reserving pulp and discarding skin. Toss pulp with chopped tomatoes, garlic paste, lemon juice, salt, sugar (if using), and pepper. Let stand until ready to use, at least 10 minutes.

▸ While tomatoes stand, cook pasta in a 6- to 8-quart pot of boiling salted water (see Tips, page 8), uncovered, until al dente, about 2 minutes. Drain in a colander and immediately add to tomato mixture, tossing to combine. Sprinkle with basil.

COOKS' NOTE: Tomato mixture can stand at room temperature up to 2 hours.

GRILLED SALMON WITH LIME BUTTER SAUCE

SERVES 6

ACTIVE TIME: 15 MIN START TO FINISH: 45 MIN

Just a sprinkle of zest and a dab of lime butter sauce (recipe follows) beautifully highlight the flavor of grilled salmon.

> 6   (6-oz) pieces center-cut salmon fillet (about 1 inch thick) with skin
> 1½ teaspoons finely grated fresh lime zest (see Tips, page 8)
> 6   tablespoons lime butter sauce (recipe follows)

▸ Prepare grill for cooking over medium-hot charcoal (moderate heat for gas); see Tips, page 8.

▸ Season salmon all over with salt and pepper, then grill, flesh sides down, on lightly oiled grill rack (covered only if using gas grill) 4 minutes. Turn fillets over and grill (covered only if using gas grill) until just cooked through, 4 to 6 minutes more. Sprinkle fillets with zest and top each with 1 tablespoon lime butter sauce.

COOKS' NOTE: If you aren't able to grill outdoors, salmon can be cooked in a hot lightly oiled well-seasoned large (2-burner) ridged grill pan over moderately high heat.

LIME BUTTER SAUCE

MAKES ABOUT ¾ CUP

ACTIVE TIME: 5 MIN START TO FINISH: 5 MIN

Once you see how versatile this sauce is—it works perfectly with the grilled salmon and the corn—you'll want to make it for a host of your summer favorites.

> 1   large garlic clove, chopped
> ¼   cup fresh lime juice
> 1   teaspoon salt
> ½   teaspoon black pepper
> 1   stick (½ cup) unsalted butter, melted

▸ Purée garlic with lime juice, salt, and pepper in a blender until smooth. With motor running, add melted butter and blend until emulsified, about 30 seconds.

COOKS' NOTE: Lime butter sauce can be made 1 day ahead and chilled, covered. Stir before using.

GRILLED CORN WITH HERBS

SERVES 6

ACTIVE TIME: 15 MIN START TO FINISH: 1 HR

Corn grilled in its husk isn't just easy—the silk adds sweetness and provides an extra layer of moisture so the kernels stay tender.

> 8   ears of corn in the husk
> ¼   cup chopped mixed fresh herbs such as chives, parsley, basil, sage, and tarragon
> 6   tablespoons lime butter sauce (recipe precedes)

► Prepare grill for cooking over medium-hot charcoal (moderate heat for gas); see Tips, page 8.

► Grill corn (in husks) on lightly oiled grill rack, turning, covered, until kernels are tender, 20 to 30 minutes. Remove corn from grill and let stand until cool enough to handle but still warm, about 10 minutes.

► Discard husks and stem ends from corn. Cut kernels off cobs with a large knife and toss with herbs and lime butter sauce.

COOKS' NOTE: If you aren't able to grill outdoors, corn (in husks) can be roasted directly on middle rack of a preheated 450°F oven 30 minutes.

GREEN BEANS AND ARUGULA

SERVES 6

ACTIVE TIME: 15 MIN   START TO FINISH: 25 MIN

This dish is a welcome departure from run-of-the-mill sides. Lemon zest and golden garlic give wilted arugula and tender green beans multidimensional flavor.

1½ lb green beans, trimmed
 2 tablespoons extra-virgin olive oil
 3 large garlic cloves, thinly sliced lengthwise
½ lb arugula, tough stems discarded and leaves chopped (6 cups)
 1 teaspoon finely grated fresh lemon zest (see Tips, page 8)
¾ teaspoon salt
¼ teaspoon black pepper

► Cook green beans in a 6-quart pot of boiling salted water (see Tips, page 8), uncovered, until tender, 4 to 6 minutes. Drain in a colander.

► Heat oil in a 12-inch heavy skillet over moderately high heat until hot but not smoking, then sauté garlic, stirring, until golden, about 1 minute. Add green beans, arugula, zest, salt, and pepper and cook, tossing, until arugula is wilted, about 2 minutes.

FOLLOWING PAGES: angel-hair pasta with fresh tomato sauce, grilled salmon with lime butter, and green beans and arugula; zucchini ginger cupcakes

ZUCCHINI GINGER CUPCAKES

MAKES 12 CUPCAKES

ACTIVE TIME: 30 MIN   START TO FINISH: 1¾ HR (INCLUDES COOLING)

FOR CUPCAKES

⅓ cup crystallized ginger (1¾ oz), coarsely chopped
 2 cups all-purpose flour
 1 teaspoon ground ginger
 1 teaspoon ground cinnamon
 1 teaspoon finely grated fresh orange zest (see Tips, page 8)
 1 teaspoon salt
 1 teaspoon baking soda
½ teaspoon baking powder
 2 cups coarsely grated zucchini (2 medium)
¾ cup mild olive oil
¾ cup mild honey
 2 large eggs, lightly beaten
 1 teaspoon vanilla

FOR FROSTING

 8 oz cream cheese, softened
 2 tablespoons unsalted butter, softened
½ cup confectioners sugar
 1 teaspoon vanilla
½ teaspoon ground ginger
½ teaspoon ground cinnamon
½ teaspoon finely grated fresh orange zest (see Tips, page 8)

SPECIAL EQUIPMENT: a muffin pan with 12 (½-cup) cups; 12 paper liners

BAKE CUPCAKES:

► Put oven rack in middle position and preheat oven to 350°F. Line muffin cups with liners.

► Pulse crystallized ginger in food processor until finely ground, then add flour, ground ginger, cinnamon, zest, salt, baking soda, and baking powder and pulse until combined.

► Whisk together zucchini, oil, honey, eggs, and vanilla in a medium bowl, then stir in flour mixture until just combined.

► Divide batter among muffin cups and bake until golden and a wooden pick or skewer inserted in center of a cupcake comes out clean, 20 to 24 minutes.

► Cool in pan on a rack 10 minutes. Remove cupcakes from pan and cool completely, 1 hour.

MAKE FROSTING:

► Beat together frosting ingredients with an electric mixer at high speed until combined well and fluffy, 3 to 5 minutes.

► Frost tops of cooled cupcakes.

COOKS' NOTE: Cupcakes can be made 1 day ahead and kept in 1 layer in an airtight container at room temperature.

A DAY IN THE COUNTRY

A MIDDAY MEAL IN PROVENCE

SERVES 6

**ANCHOVY FENNEL TOASTS WITH
ROASTED RED PEPPERS**

L'ALYCASTRE CÔTES DE PROVENCE
BLANC '05

**GRILLED POUSSINS WITH LEMON
HERB BUTTER**

GRILLED BABY POTATOES

**HARICOT VERT AND RED-ONION
SALAD WITH PISTOU**

**MESCLUN SALAD WITH BANON
CHEESE**

MONTIRIUS VACQUEYRAS PROVENCE
ROUGE '03

**RASPBERRY CRÈME FRAÎCHE
TART WITH LAVENDER HONEY**

ANCHOVY FENNEL TOASTS WITH ROASTED RED PEPPERS

MAKES 24 HORS D'OEUVRES

ACTIVE TIME: 30 MIN   START TO FINISH: 45 MIN

Straight anchovy butter can be intense (indeed, we've given a range on the anchovies, so salt fiends can indulge), but the toasted, ground fennel seeds make these crunchy hors d'oeuvres taste clean, not heavy. Roasted red peppers add a burst of juicy sweetness and a hint of smokiness.

  2 **small red bell peppers (¾ lb total)**

2½ **teaspoons fennel seeds**

  1 **stick (½ cup) unsalted butter, softened**

  6 **to 9 flat anchovy fillets (from a 2-oz can), patted dry and minced**

  1 **teaspoon fresh lemon juice**

 ½ **teaspoon black pepper**

24 **(¼-inch-thick) diagonal slices of baguette**

SPECIAL EQUIPMENT: **an electric coffee/spice grinder or a mortar and pestle**

▸Roast bell peppers on racks of gas burners (or see cooks' note, below) over high heat, turning with tongs, until skins are blackened, 10 to 12 minutes. Transfer to a large bowl and cover tightly with plastic wrap, then let steam, covered, about 20 minutes.

▸When peppers are cool enough to handle, peel, then halve lengthwise, discarding stems and seeds. Cut peppers lengthwise into ⅛-inch-wide strips.

▸Toast fennel seeds in a dry small heavy skillet over moderately low heat, shaking skillet frequently, until lightly browned, 3 to 4 minutes, then transfer to a bowl and cool. Finely grind fennel seeds in grinder, then stir into butter along with anchovies, lemon juice, and pepper until combined well.

▸Preheat broiler.

▸Broil baguette slices in a large shallow baking pan (18 by 12 inches) 3 to 4 inches from heat until golden, about 1 minute. Turn slices over and spread generously with anchovy butter. Broil toasts until butter is golden and bubbling, about 1 minute, then transfer to a platter. Top with bell pepper strips.

COOKS' NOTES: Bell peppers can be roasted by broiling in a shallow baking pan 5 inches from heat, turning occasionally, about 15 minutes.
• Anchovy butter can be made 1 day ahead and chilled, covered. Soften butter before using, about 1 hour.
• Toasts, without bell peppers, can be made 2 hours ahead. Reheat, buttered sides up, under preheated broiler until hot, about 30 seconds, then top with bell peppers.

GRILLED POUSSINS WITH LEMON HERB BUTTER

SERVES 6
ACTIVE TIME: 50 MIN   START TO FINISH: 1¾ HR

This is the ideal way to prepare young chickens, since there are two safeguards against their drying out (always a risk with small birds). The herbed butter slipped beneath the skin melts, basting and flavoring the meat as it cooks; the gentle, indirect heat lightly chars the skin without toughening the meat. As a result, every bite is juicy and perfectly seasoned.

1½   sticks (¾ cup) unsalted butter (1 stick softened and ½ stick melted and cooled)
 2   tablespoons chopped fresh thyme leaves
 1   tablespoon finely chopped fresh rosemary
1½   tablespoons loosely packed finely grated fresh lemon zest (see Tips, page 8)
3½   teaspoons fine sea salt
1¼   teaspoons black pepper
 6   (1¼- to 1½-lb) poussins or small Cornish hens
 1   lemon, cut lengthwise into 6 wedges
18   sprigs fresh thyme

SPECIAL EQUIPMENT: **kitchen string; a large chimney starter (if using charcoal); an instant-read thermometer**
GARNISH: **fresh thyme and rosemary sprigs**

▶ Stir together 1 stick softened butter, thyme, rosemary, zest, 1 teaspoon sea salt, and ¾ teaspoon pepper in a bowl until combined well.
▶ Trim necks of poussins flush with bodies if necessary. Rinse poussins inside and out and pat dry. Discard any excess fat from opening of cavities, then sprinkle cavities with a total of 1½ teaspoons sea salt and remaining ½ teaspoon pepper. Starting at cavity end of each bird, gently slide an index finger

between skin and flesh of breasts and legs to loosen skin (be careful not to tear skin). Using a teaspoon measure or small spoon, slide 1 teaspoon herb butter under skin of each breast half and each drumstick (4 teaspoons per poussin), using your finger on outside of skin to push butter out of spoon.
▶ Put 1 lemon wedge and 3 thyme sprigs into cavity of each poussin, then tie legs together with kitchen string and tuck wing tips under body. Arrange in a large pan. Pat poussins dry, then brush with melted butter and sprinkle with remaining teaspoon salt.
TO COOK POUSSINS USING A CHARCOAL GRILL:
▶ Open vents on bottom of grill and on lid. Light charcoal (80 to 100 briquettes) in chimney starter and pour evenly over 2 opposite sides of bottom rack, leaving about an 8-inch-wide space in center of bottom rack free of coals. When charcoal fire is medium-hot (you can hold your hand 5 inches above grill rack for 3 to 4 seconds), remove poussins from pan and arrange in center of lightly oiled grill rack with no coals underneath and cook, covered with lid, until thermometer inserted in fleshy part of a thigh registers 170°F, 35 to 50 minutes. (Add more briquettes if necessary during grilling to maintain heat.)
TO COOK POUSSINS USING A GAS GRILL:
▶ Preheat all burners on high, covered, 10 minutes, then reduce to moderately high. Turn off 1 burner (middle burner if there are 3) and put poussins on lightly oiled rack above shut-off burner. Remove poussins from pan, then grill, covered with lid, until thermometer inserted in fleshy part of a thigh registers 170°F, 35 to 45 minutes.

COOKS' NOTES: If you aren't able to grill outdoors, poussins can be roasted (at least 2 inches apart) in a lightly oiled large shallow baking pan in a preheated 475°F oven, 35 to 45 minutes.
• If you're also making the grilled baby potatoes (page 134), grill the poussins first, over indirect heat, then transfer them to a platter and keep them warm, loosely covered with foil. Spread the coals out onto the rack. Add 15 briquettes evenly to coals and wait until they just light, about 5 minutes, then grill the baby potatoes over direct heat.
• Poussins can be prepared (but not grilled) 1 day ahead and chilled, covered with plastic wrap. Let stand at cool room temperature 30 minutes before grilling.

GRILLED BABY POTATOES

SERVES 6

ACTIVE TIME: 20 MIN   START TO FINISH: 1 HR

Boiled first to ensure tenderness all the way through, these spuds gain a smoky flavor and crackly roasted skin from a brief stint on the grill. If you have fresh rosemary left over from the poussins, strip off all but the top 1 inch of leaves and skewer the potatoes on the woody stems—it looks beautiful on the serving plate and gives the potatoes a lovely perfume.

30 baby potatoes (1 to 1½ inches in diameter; 1¾ lb total)
 1 tablespoon plus 1 teaspoon coarse kosher salt
 3 tablespoons extra-virgin olive oil

SPECIAL EQUIPMENT: **12 (6- to 8-inch) woody rosemary stems or bamboo skewers, soaked in water 30 minutes**

▶ Cover potatoes by 1 inch in cold water in a 4-quart pot, then add 1 tablespoon kosher salt and bring to a boil over high heat. Reduce heat and simmer until potatoes are just tender, 12 to 15 minutes.
▶ Drain potatoes in a colander and transfer to a large shallow pan to cool quickly.
▶ If using a charcoal grill, open vents on bottom of grill, then light charcoal. Charcoal fire is hot when you can hold your hand 5 inches above rack for 1 to 2 seconds. If using a gas grill, preheat burners on high, covered, 10 minutes, then reduce heat to moderately high.
▶ Meanwhile, toss potatoes with 1 tablespoon oil and remaining teaspoon kosher salt, then push 2 or 3 potatoes onto each rosemary stem.
▶ Grill potato skewers directly over coals, turning over occasionally with tongs, until grill marks appear, 3 to 4 minutes total.
▶ Transfer potatoes to a platter and drizzle with remaining 2 tablespoons oil.

COOKS' NOTES: Potatoes can be boiled 1 day ahead and chilled, covered. Bring to room temperature before grilling.
• If you aren't able to grill outdoors, potatoes can be broiled in a shallow baking pan 3 to 4 inches from heat, turning over once, until lightly browned, 2 to 3 minutes.

HARICOT VERT AND RED-ONION SALAD WITH PISTOU

SERVES 6 (SIDE DISH)

ACTIVE TIME: 35 MIN   START TO FINISH: 45 MIN

This is an unusual use for pistou, *a Provençal variant of pesto made of basil, garlic, olive oil, and salt. It's normally stirred into simple vegetable soups to give them some oomph, but it brings the same lively savoriness to green beans, contrasting nicely with their buttery quality. Don't worry about being knocked over by raw onions on top of all the other strong flavors—soaking them in cold water for 15 minutes removes some of their pungency while preserving their crunch.*

FOR *PISTOU*
 2 cups loosely packed fresh basil leaves
 6 garlic cloves, minced (1½ tablespoons)
¼ cup plus 2 tablespoons extra-virgin olive oil
½ teaspoon fine sea salt
FOR SALAD
 1 medium red onion, halved lengthwise, then thinly
      sliced crosswise
1½ lb haricots verts or other thin green beans, trimmed

MAKE *PISTOU*:
▶ Purée all *pistou* ingredients in a food processor until basil is finely chopped.
MAKE SALAD:
▶ Soak onion in cold water 15 minutes, then drain in a colander and pat dry.
▶ While onion soaks, cook beans in a 6- to 8-quart pot of boiling salted water (see Tips, page 8), uncovered, stirring occasionally, until just tender, 3 to 6 minutes, then drain in a large colander. Transfer to a large bowl of ice and cold water to stop cooking, then drain again and pat dry.
▶ Toss beans and onion with *pistou*. Season with salt and pepper.

COOKS' NOTES: *Pistou* can be made 6 hours ahead and transferred to a small bowl, then chilled, covered.
• Beans can be cooked 1 day ahead and chilled in a sealed large plastic bag lined with paper towels.

OPPOSITE: grilled poussins with lemon herb butter; grilled baby potatoes

MESCLUN SALAD WITH BANON CHEESE

SERVES 6

ACTIVE TIME: 15 MIN   START TO FINISH: 15 MIN

Traditionally made from cow's or goat's milk and wrapped in chestnut leaves, Banon cheese is named after the town in northern Provence from which it hails. When the leaves are green, the cheese is fresh, mild, and sweet; when the leaves are brown, it is ripe and soft. Either way, it's a great complement to classic mesclun greens. In the spirit of Provence, we encourage you to bypass the ready-made mesclun mix and create your own blend of peppery, sweet, and tender baby lettuces from the array that you can find at the farmers market.

1	tablespoon white-wine vinegar
¼	teaspoon salt
¼	teaspoon black pepper
¼	cup olive oil
¾	lb loosely packed mixed baby lettuces such as lolla rossa, oak-leaf, or Bibb (16 cups)
3	individual Banon cheeses (9 oz total) or soft goat cheese, at room temperature

ACCOMPANIMENT: *fougasse* or baguette

▶ Whisk together vinegar, salt, and pepper in a bowl until salt is dissolved, then add oil, whisking until emulsified.
▶ Just before serving, toss lettuces with just enough vinaigrette to coat, then divide among plates. Halve cheeses and serve 1 half with each salad.

RASPBERRY CRÈME FRAÎCHE TART WITH LAVENDER HONEY

SERVES 6

ACTIVE TIME: 30 MIN   START TO FINISH: 1¾ HR

Here, lush summer raspberries are framed by a rich crust and a cool, creamy layer that underlines their tart juiciness. A drizzling of warm lavender honey draws out a luxurious floral sweetness—put out the extra honey in a crock so everyone can add as much or as little as they like.

FOR CRUST

1¼	cups all-purpose flour
¼	cup sugar
½	teaspoon salt
7	tablespoons cold unsalted butter, cut into ½-inch cubes
1	large egg

FOR FILLING

4	oz cream cheese, softened
¼	cup crème fraîche
3½	tablespoons lavender honey
4	cups raspberries (18 oz)

SPECIAL EQUIPMENT: **a 9-inch fluted round tart pan (1 inch deep) with a removable bottom; heavy-duty foil; pie weights or raw rice**
ACCOMPANIMENT: **warm lavender honey**

MAKE CRUST:

▶ Pulse together all crust ingredients in a food processor just until mixture resembles coarse crumbs. Put tart pan on a baking sheet and press dough evenly onto bottom and up side of tart pan with your fingertips. Chill shell, covered, on baking sheet until firm, about 30 minutes.
▶ Put oven rack in middle position and preheat oven to 350°F. Line shell with a buttered sheet of heavy-duty foil (buttered side down) and fill shell one third of the way up with pie weights.
▶ Bake (on sheet) until edge is pale golden, 20 to 25 minutes. Carefully remove pie weights and foil, then bake until edge and bottom are golden, about 20 minutes more. Cool completely in pan on a rack.

MAKE FILLING:

▶ Beat cream cheese in a bowl with a handheld electric mixer at high speed until smooth, then add crème fraîche and 1½ tablespoons honey and beat until combined well. Spread filling evenly in shell, then top with raspberries. Heat remaining 2 tablespoons honey in a very small saucepan over moderately low heat, stirring constantly, until liquefied, then drizzle over raspberries. Serve with additional melted honey on the side.

COOKS' NOTES: Tart shell can be made 1 day ahead and cooled completely, uncovered, then kept (in pan), wrapped in plastic wrap, at cool room temperature.
• Filling can be made 1 day ahead and chilled, covered. Bring to cool room temperature before assembling tart, 1 hour.

INTO THE BLUE

WEEKEND BARBECUE

SERVES 8

**GRILLED BREADED
PORK CHOPS**

**QUINOA WITH CORN,
SCALLIONS, AND MINT**

VEGETABLE KEBABS

LITTORAI SAVOY VINEYARD
ANDERSON VALLEY PINOT NOIR '04

**RASPBERRY-BLUEBERRY
SNOW CONES**

**FROZEN STRAWBERRY
MARGARITA PIE**

GRILLED BREADED PORK CHOPS

SERVES 8
ACTIVE TIME: 30 MIN   START TO FINISH: 45 MIN

Fruity olive oil and rich parmesan cheese add flavor to these hearty grilled chops. Coating the pork with fresh bread crumbs, as we do here, creates a light and crunchy crust, which seals in all the meaty juices and keeps the chops moist.

   4   cups fine fresh bread crumbs (from 10 slices firm white
         sandwich bread)
  ¾   oz finely grated Parmigiano-Reggiano (⅔ cup; see Tips,
         page 8)
         Rounded ½ teaspoon salt
  ¼   teaspoon black pepper
   8   (¾- to 1-inch-thick) bone-in center-cut pork chops (4½ lb)
   1   cup olive oil

▶ Put oven rack in middle position and preheat oven to 350°F. Spread bread crumbs in a shallow baking pan and toast in oven, stirring once or twice, until dry but not golden, 7 to 10 minutes.

Cool bread crumbs completely, then stir together with cheese, salt, and pepper in a shallow bowl or a 9-inch pie plate. Lightly season chops with additional salt and pepper.
▶ Line a baking sheet with wax paper. Put olive oil in another shallow bowl or 9-inch pie plate. Dip each chop in oil, letting excess drip off, then dredge both sides of chop in bread-crumb mixture, pressing gently to help crumbs adhere, and transfer to baking sheet.
▶ Prepare grill for cooking over medium-hot charcoal (moderate heat for gas); see Tips, page 8. Grill chops on well-oiled grill rack, covered only if using gas grill, turning over once or twice, until pork is cooked through and crumbs are golden brown, about 10 minutes total.

COOKS' NOTES: Pork chops can be breaded 2 hours ahead and chilled, loosely covered.
• If you aren't able to grill outdoors, you can broil pork chops on the lightly oiled rack of a broiler pan in 2 batches, 4 to 6 inches from preheated broiler, turning over once, until golden brown, about 6 minutes per batch.

QUINOA WITH CORN, SCALLIONS, AND MINT

SERVES 8

ACTIVE TIME: 30 MIN   START TO FINISH: 30 MIN

    4 ears corn, shucked
    1 tablespoon finely grated fresh lemon zest (from 2 lemons;
          see Tips, page 8)
    2 tablespoons fresh lemon juice
  ½ stick (¼ cup) unsalted butter, melted
    1 tablespoon mild honey
  ½ teaspoon salt
  ¼ teaspoon black pepper
    2 cups quinoa (about 10 oz)
    4 scallions, chopped
  ½ cup chopped fresh mint

▶ Put corn in a 5- to 6-quart wide pot, then add water to cover and bring to a boil, covered. Remove from heat and let stand, covered, 5 minutes. Transfer corn with tongs to a cutting board. When cool enough to handle, cut kernels off cobs with a large heavy knife.

▶ Meanwhile, whisk together lemon zest and juice, butter, honey, salt, and pepper in a large bowl until combined.

▶ Wash quinoa in 3 changes of cold water in a bowl, draining in a large sieve each time.

▶ Cook quinoa in a 4- to 5-quart pot of boiling salted water (see Tips, page 8), uncovered, until almost tender, about 10 minutes. Drain in sieve, then set sieve over same pot with 1 inch of simmering water (water should not touch bottom of sieve). Cover quinoa with a folded kitchen towel, then cover sieve with a lid (don't worry if lid doesn't fit tightly) and steam until quinoa is tender, fluffy, and dry, about 5 minutes. Remove from heat and let stand (still covered) 5 minutes.

▶ Add quinoa to dressing and toss until dressing is absorbed, then stir in corn, scallions, mint, and salt and pepper to taste.

VEGETABLE KEBABS

SERVES 8

ACTIVE TIME: 1¼ HR   START TO FINISH: 1¾ HR

FOR VINAIGRETTE

  ½ cup white-wine vinegar
    1 tablespoon balsamic vinegar (preferably white)
    1 large garlic clove, minced
1¼ teaspoons sugar
  ½ teaspoon salt
  ¼ teaspoon black pepper
    1 cup olive oil

FOR VEGETABLES

    1 lb small zucchini, cut crosswise into
          ¾-inch-thick slices
  ¼ cup olive oil
1½ teaspoons salt
  ¾ teaspoon black pepper
  ¾ lb cherry tomatoes
    1 lb baby eggplant (about 4 inches long),
          cut crosswise into ¾-inch-thick slices
  10 oz cremini mushrooms, trimmed
    2 yellow bell peppers, cut into 1½-inch pieces
    1 large red onion, cut into 1½-inch pieces

SPECIAL EQUIPMENT: 18 (12-inch) metal or wooden skewers (soaked in warm water 30 minutes if wooden)

MAKE VINAIGRETTE:

▶ Whisk together all vinaigrette ingredients in a glass measure until combined.

SKEWER AND GRILL VEGETABLES:

▶ Toss zucchini in a large bowl with 2 teaspoons oil, ¼ teaspoon salt, and ⅛ teaspoon black pepper. Repeat with remaining vegetables, working with 1 type at a time and keeping each batch separate. Thread vegetables onto skewers (thread zucchini and eggplant horizontally through slices so cut sides will lie flat on grill; leave about ⅛ inch between tomatoes, mushrooms, bell peppers, and onions), using 3 skewers per type of vegetable and not mixing vegetables on any skewer.

▶ Prepare grill for cooking over medium-hot charcoal (moderate heat for gas); see Tips, page 8. Grill kebabs in 2 batches on lightly oiled grill rack, covered only if using gas grill, turning over once, until vegetables are tender (vegetables, except tomatoes, should be lightly browned; tomatoes should be blistered and shriveled), 6 to 10 minutes (timing will vary among vegetables).

▶ Transfer skewers as cooked to a platter and, if desired, remove vegetables from skewers. Drizzle with some of vinaigrette and serve remaining vinaigrette on the side.

COOKS' NOTES: Vegetables can be threaded onto skewers 1 day ahead and chilled, covered.

• If you aren't able to grill outdoors, you can broil vegetable skewers in 2 batches on oiled rack of a broiler pan 4 to 6 inches from preheated broiler, turning over once, until golden, about 6 minutes per batch.

OPPOSITE: grilled breaded pork chops; vegetable kebabs; and quinoa with corn, scallions, and mint (left); raspberry-blueberry snow cones (right)

RASPBERRY-BLUEBERRY SNOW CONES

SERVES 8

ACTIVE TIME: 15 MIN   START TO FINISH: 1¼ HR

You don't have to feel guilty about giving these to the kids—they're made with real fruit syrup and are bursting with sweet berry flavor.

2½ cups raspberries (6 oz)
 3 cups blueberries (10 oz)
 ½ cup sugar
 ½ cup water
 8 cups lightly packed shaved ice (made with
      an ice shaver, preferably manual)

SPECIAL EQUIPMENT: **an ice shaver, preferably manual**

▶ Coarsely mash 1½ cups raspberries and 2 cups blueberries with sugar and water in a 2- to 3-quart heavy saucepan using a potato masher. Bring to a boil, stirring, then boil, uncovered, stirring occasionally, 3 minutes. Transfer to a blender and purée until almost smooth, about 1 minute (use caution when blending hot liquids). Pour berry mixture through a fine-mesh sieve into a bowl, pressing lightly on and then discarding solids. Cool syrup, uncovered, then chill, its surface loosely covered with plastic wrap, until cold, about 1 hour.
▶ For each serving, spoon 3 tablespoons syrup over 1 cup lightly packed shaved ice and top with ¼ cup of remaining mixed berries. Serve immediately.

COOKS' NOTE: Syrup can be chilled in an airtight container up to 1 week.

FROZEN STRAWBERRY MARGARITA PIE

SERVES 8

ACTIVE TIME: 40 MIN   START TO FINISH: 5½ HR (INCLUDES FREEZING)

FOR CRUST
1¼ cups graham cracker crumbs from 9 (2¼- by 4¾-inch)
      crackers
 2 tablespoons sugar
 5 tablespoons unsalted butter, melted
FOR FILLING
 1 lb strawberries, halved (3½ cups)
 1 tablespoon finely grated fresh lime zest (from 3 limes;
      see Tips, page 8)
 ¼ cup fresh lime juice (from 2 limes)
 1 (14-oz) can sweetened condensed milk
 2 tablespoons tequila
 2 tablespoons triple sec, Cointreau, or other
      orange-flavored liqueur
1½ cups chilled heavy cream

GARNISH: **small strawberries**

MAKE CRUST:
▶ Put oven rack in middle position and preheat oven to 350°F.
▶ Stir together graham cracker crumbs, sugar, and butter in a bowl with a fork until combined well, then press mixture evenly onto bottom and up side of a buttered 9-inch metal or glass pie plate (4-cup capacity).
▶ Bake 10 minutes, then cool in pie plate on a rack, about 30 minutes.
MAKE FILLING:
▶ Purée strawberries, zest, lime juice, condensed milk, tequila, and liqueur in a blender until just smooth, then transfer to a large bowl.
▶ Beat cream in another bowl with an electric mixer at medium speed until it just holds stiff peaks. Fold one third of cream into strawberry mixture gently but thoroughly to lighten, then fold in remainder in 2 batches.
▶ Pour filling into crust, mounding it slightly, and freeze, uncovered, until firm, about 4 hours. Remove from freezer and let soften in refrigerator, about 40 minutes, before serving (pie should be semisoft).

COOKS' NOTES: Pie can be frozen up to 3 days, covered with plastic wrap after 4 hours and then wrapped in heavy-duty foil.
• Pie can also be made in a 9-inch (24-cm) springform pan. Press crumb mixture onto bottom and 1 inch up side of pan.

A HUNTIN' WE WILL GO

A HEARTY BREAKFAST AFTER THE CHASE

AQUAVIT BLOODY MARYS

MAKES 6 DRINKS
ACTIVE TIME: 15 MIN   START TO FINISH: 15 MIN

*This classic tomato juice cocktail gets extra flavor from aquavit,
a distilled spirit infused with fragrant herbs and spices.*

- 1   cup aquavit, chilled
- 1   qt tomato or tomato-vegetable juice such as V8, chilled
- 3   tablespoons fresh lemon juice
- 2   tablespoons Worcestershire sauce
- 2   tablespoons drained bottled horseradish
- ½   teaspoon hot sauce such as Tabasco
- ¼   teaspoon black pepper

GARNISH: **lemon slices; small celery ribs**

▶ Stir together all ingredients with salt to taste in a pitcher. Serve
over ice in 6 (12-ounce) highball glasses.

DUCK CONFIT HASH

SERVES 6 (MAIN COURSE)
ACTIVE TIME: 1¾ HR   START TO FINISH: 1¾ HR

*Hash has never been so decadent. Pieces of duck confit, tender
vegetables, and golden-brown potatoes meld with a lavish drizzle
of heavy cream and Madeira to create a breakfast centerpiece.*

- 3   (6-oz) confit duck legs (see Sources)
- 1   large onion, chopped (2 cups)
- ¾   lb carrots (3 large), cut into ⅓-inch dice
- 1½ lb yellow-fleshed potatoes such as Yukon Gold (3 large),
      peeled and cut into ⅓-inch dice
- 1¼ teaspoons salt
- ¾   teaspoon black pepper
- ¾   cup heavy cream
- ¼   cup Madeira
- ¼   cup chopped fresh flat-leaf parsley

▶ Cook duck legs, skin sides down, in a 12-inch cast-iron or
heavy nonstick skillet over moderate heat, turning over once,

until skin is golden and some of fat is rendered, about 8 minutes total. Transfer duck to a cutting board, reserving fat in skillet. When duck legs are cool enough to handle, remove skin with any visible fat, then chop skin and fat into ½-inch pieces and return to skillet (reserve meat). Cook over moderate heat, stirring occasionally and pressing down on larger pieces, until fat is rendered and skin is deep golden and crisp all over, about 5 minutes. Remove skin with a slotted spoon and drain on paper towels.

▸ Pour off all but 3 tablespoons fat from skillet, then add onion and cook over moderate heat, stirring occasionally, until golden brown, about 15 minutes. Add carrots, potatoes, ½ teaspoon salt, and ¼ teaspoon pepper and cook, stirring frequently, until vegetables are browned, 20 to 30 minutes.

▸ Meanwhile, coarsely shred duck meat, discarding bones and any gristle.

▸ Stir duck into vegetables along with cream, Madeira, parsley, fried duck skin, and remaining ¾ teaspoon salt and ½ teaspoon pepper, and stir until combined. Reduce heat to moderately low, then smooth top of mixture and cook, undisturbed, until bottom of hash is golden when lifted with a spatula, 4 to 8 minutes.

SCANDINAVIAN RYE MUFFINS

MAKES 24 SMALL MUFFINS
ACTIVE TIME: 25 MIN   START TO FINISH: 3¼ HR

Lightly spiced and flavored with caraway seeds and crystals of sea salt, these yeast-bread muffins are satisfying without being heavy.

1½	teaspoons active dry yeast (from a ¼-oz package)
1½	teaspoons packed light brown sugar
1	cup warm water (105–115°F)
⅔	cup rye flour
1¾	cups plus 1 tablespoon all-purpose flour
1½	teaspoons finely grated fresh orange zest (see Tips, page 8)
¾	teaspoon salt
¼	teaspoon anise seeds
¼	teaspoon ground cumin
¾	teaspoon caraway seeds
2	tablespoons unsalted butter, melted and cooled, plus additional for greasing
2	tablespoons molasses (not blackstrap)
	Vegetable oil for greasing
1	large egg, lightly beaten, for egg wash
½	teaspoon flaky sea salt such as Maldon

SPECIAL EQUIPMENT: an instant-read thermometer; 2 nonstick mini-muffin pans with 12 (1¾-inch-wide) muffin cups

▸ Stir together yeast, brown sugar, and ¼ cup warm water in a large bowl until yeast is dissolved. Let stand until foamy, about 15 minutes. (If mixture doesn't foam, discard and start over with new yeast.)

▸ Whisk together rye flour, 1 cup all-purpose flour, zest, salt, anise seeds, cumin, and ½ teaspoon caraway seeds. Add flour mixture along with melted butter, molasses, and remaining ¾ cup warm water to yeast mixture and beat with an electric mixer at medium speed 5 minutes. Reduce speed to low and add ½ cup all-purpose flour, beating until combined. Add remaining ¼ cup plus 1 tablespoon all-purpose flour and beat until incorporated. (Dough will be very sticky.) Scrape down dough from side of bowl with a rubber spatula and let rise, bowl covered tightly with plastic wrap, in a draft-free place at warm room temperature until doubled in bulk, about 1½ hours.

▸ Put oven rack in middle position and preheat oven to 350°F. Butter muffin pans.

▸ Stir down dough (it will be too sticky to punch down). Divide dough evenly among 24 muffin cups, about a rounded tablespoon per cup. (Grease tablespoon with oil as necessary to prevent sticking.) Let dough rest, uncovered, in a draft-free place at warm room temperature 30 minutes. Gently brush tops of muffins with some of egg wash, then sprinkle with sea salt and remaining ¼ teaspoon caraway seeds.

▸ Bake until muffins are puffed and a wooden pick or skewer inserted into center comes out clean, 25 to 35 minutes. Turn out muffins onto a rack and cool to warm or room temperature.

COOKS' NOTES: Dough can be made (but not allowed to rise) 1 day ahead and chilled, bowl wrapped tightly in plastic wrap. Put chilled dough in muffin pan as directed and let rise 1 hour, then proceed with recipe.

• Muffins can be made 2 days ahead and cooled completely, uncovered, then kept in an airtight container at room temperature.

• Muffins keep, frozen in sealed plastic bags, 2 weeks. Reheat on a baking sheet in a preheated 350°F oven until muffins are heated through, 8 to 10 minutes for frozen.

BAKED EGGS WITH CANTAL CHEESE

SERVES 6

ACTIVE TIME: 25 MIN   START TO FINISH: 40 MIN

Made with airy whipped egg whites and strategically placed yolks, this dish has the soft, yolky flavor of eggs Benedict but without all the hassle. Plus it looks so gorgeous, your guests will feel extra special when it arrives at the table.

	Butter for greasing ramekins
6	large eggs
¼	teaspoon salt
¼	teaspoon black pepper
⅛	teaspoon freshly grated nutmeg
⅛	teaspoon cream of tartar
3	oz coarsely grated Cantal cheese (1 cup)
6	tablespoons crème fraîche
1	tablespoon chopped fresh chives

SPECIAL EQUIPMENT: **6 (8-oz) ramekins or a 13- by 9- by 2-inch baking dish**

▶ Put oven rack in middle position and preheat oven to 350°F. Butter ramekins or baking dish.

▶ Separate eggs, putting whites in a large bowl and carefully sliding whole, unbroken yolks into a small bowl of cold water.

▶ Beat whites with salt, pepper, nutmeg, and cream of tartar using an electric mixer at medium-high speed until they just hold stiff peaks. Fold in ½ cup cheese gently but thoroughly, then divide mixture among ramekins or transfer to baking dish, smoothing top slightly (whites will stand above rims of ramekins). Make an indentation in center of whites in each ramekin or make 6 evenly spaced indentations if using baking dish. Carefully remove yolks from water 1 at a time with your fingers and put 1 yolk in each indentation.

▶ Stir crème fraîche and spoon 1 tablespoon on top of each yolk, then sprinkle eggs with remaining cheese. Transfer ramekins (if using) to a large shallow baking pan.

▶ Bake until whites are puffed and pale golden (yolks will jiggle slightly), 10 to 14 minutes. Sprinkle with chives and serve immediately.

COOKS' NOTE: The egg yolks in this recipe are not fully cooked, which may be of concern if salmonella is a problem in your area. If desired, continue baking eggs until yolks are set.

ROASTED TOMATOES

SERVES 6

ACTIVE TIME: 5 MIN   START TO FINISH: 1¼ HR

A long turn in the oven gives these juicy plum tomatoes good caramelization, lending sweetness to their robust flavor.

	Olive oil for greasing pan plus additional for drizzling (optional)
6	large plum tomatoes (1½ lb), halved lengthwise
¾	teaspoon salt
½	teaspoon black pepper

▶ Put oven rack in middle position and preheat oven to 350°F. Oil a shallow baking pan.

▶ Arrange tomatoes, cut sides up, in 1 layer in pan and sprinkle with salt and pepper.

▶ Roast tomatoes until skins are wrinkled and beginning to brown on bottom, about 1 hour. Transfer to a serving dish and keep warm, covered with tented foil (do not let foil touch tomatoes), until ready to serve. Serve warm or at room temperature.

COOKS' NOTE: Tomatoes can be roasted 2 hours ahead and cooled completely, then kept, covered with plastic wrap, at room temperature. Reheat in shallow baking pan in a preheated 350°F oven until tomatoes are heated through, about 10 minutes.

SWEET-AND-SPICY BACON

SERVES 6

ACTIVE TIME: 10 MIN   START TO FINISH: 45 MIN

It's difficult to improve on the rich, smoky flavor of bacon, but we've done it: As this bacon sizzles in the oven, the brown sugar and hint of cayenne create an addictive sweet-hot glaze.

1½	tablespoons packed light brown sugar
	Rounded ¼ teaspoon cayenne
	Rounded ¼ teaspoon black pepper
1	lb thick-cut bacon (about 12 slices)

▶ Put oven rack in middle position and preheat oven to 350°F.

▶ Stir together brown sugar, cayenne, and black pepper in a small bowl.

▶ Arrange bacon slices in 1 layer (not overlapping) on rack of a large broiler pan. Bake 20 minutes. Turn slices over and sprinkle evenly with spiced sugar. Continue baking until bacon is crisp and deep golden, 20 to 35 minutes more (check bacon every 5 minutes). Transfer to paper towels to drain.

ENGLISH MUFFIN TOASTS

MAKES 4 TO 5 DOZEN SMALL TOASTS
ACTIVE TIME: 15 MIN   START TO FINISH: 45 MIN

It's amazing how much buttery goodness is packed into the craggy holes of these little nibbles. Their crunchy texture makes them ideal for dipping into soft-cooked egg yolks.

  6   **English muffins, left unsplit (see cooks' note, below)**
  ¾   **stick (6 tablespoons) unsalted butter, melted**
      Rounded ¼ teaspoon salt

▶ Put oven rack in middle position and preheat oven to 375°F.
▶ Cut muffins crosswise (not horizontally) into ⅓-inch-thick strips. Arrange muffin strips, cut sides down, in 1 layer on a large baking sheet, then brush strips evenly with all of butter. Bake, moving darker toasts to center and paler toasts to edges of sheet, until tops are pale golden, 10 to 15 minutes. Turn slices over and bake until toasts are golden on both sides, about 10 minutes more. Sprinkle buttered sides of toasts with salt, then serve warm or at room temperature.

COOKS' NOTES: This recipe works only with unsplit English muffins, so avoid ones that have been precut. However, muffins labeled "fork split" can be used.
• Toasts can be made 1 day ahead and cooled completely, uncovered, then kept in an airtight container at room temperature.

ROASTED PEARS WITH ALMOND CRUNCH

SERVES 6
ACTIVE TIME: 20 MIN   START TO FINISH: 1¼ HR

The heady flavor of almond is threaded through this lovely dessert. The combination of Amaretto and warm pear juices creates a fragrant syrup, and a crisp, nutty topping adds welcome contrast to the tender roasted fruit.

FOR ALMOND CRUNCH
  1   **large egg white**
  3   **tablespoons sugar**
  ⅛   **teaspoon salt**
  ¾   **cup sliced almonds (preferably with skins; 2¾ oz)**
FOR PEARS
  3   **firm Bosc pears (1½ lb total)**
  2   **tablespoons unsalted butter, softened**
  ¼   **cup plus 1 tablespoon sugar**
  3   **tablespoons Amaretto or other almond-flavored liqueur**
  ½   **cup water**

SPECIAL EQUIPMENT: **parchment paper; a melon-ball cutter (optional)**
ACCOMPANIMENT: **mascarpone cheese (optional)**

MAKE ALMOND CRUNCH:
▶ Put oven rack in middle position and preheat oven to 350°F.
▶ Line a baking sheet with parchment.
▶ Whisk together egg white, sugar, and salt until sugar is completely dissolved, then add almonds, stirring until coated. Spread mixture in a very thin layer on parchment-lined sheet, spreading almonds away from center of pan.
▶ Bake until deep golden, 15 to 25 minutes. Cool on baking sheet on a rack, then break into pieces.
ROAST PEARS:
▶ Increase oven temperature to 425°F.
▶ Halve pears lengthwise and core with melon-ball cutter or a paring knife.
▶ Spread 1 tablespoon butter on bottom of an 8-inch square glass baking dish and sprinkle with ¼ cup sugar.
▶ Arrange pears, cut sides up, on sugar, then dot pears with remaining tablespoon butter. Sprinkle remaining tablespoon sugar over pears, then drizzle with 1 tablespoon Amaretto.
▶ Roast pears, uncovered, until barely tender, about 25 minutes (sugar will harden on bottom).
▶ Add water, a pinch of salt, and remaining 2 tablespoons Amaretto to baking dish and stir (around pears) until sugar is dissolved, then baste pears with pan juices.
▶ Roast pears, basting twice with pan juices, until tender, about 15 minutes more.
▶ Serve pears, warm or at room temperature, drizzled with pan juices and topped with almond crunch.

COOKS' NOTES: Pears, without almond crunch, can be roasted 1 day ahead and cooled completely, then chilled, covered (pears may discolor slightly). Reheat in a preheated 350°F oven, basting once with pan juices, 10 minutes.
• Almond crunch can be made 4 days ahead and kept in an airtight container at room temperature.

GATHERING HOME

AN EARLY FALL HARVEST LUNCH

SERVES 8

GIARDINIERA

HEIRLOOM TOMATO SALAD WITH MOZZARELLA AND BASIL

BLACK-OLIVE GRISSINI

SUMMER-SQUASH SOUP WITH PARSLEY MINT PISTOU

JULIUSSPITAL IPHÖFER JULIUS-ECHTER-BERG SILVANER KABINETT TROCKEN '05

ROAST CAPON WITH LEMON, THYME, AND ONIONS

GRILLED MUSHROOM SALAD WITH ARUGULA

POTATO AND KALE GALETTE

SWEET-POTATO, APPLE, AND FONTINA GALETTE

ROBERT WEIL KIEDRICHER GRÄFENBERG RIESLING ERSTES GEWÄCHS '05

BLACKBERRY BROWN-SUGAR CAKE

NECTARINE ALMOND FRANGIPANE TART

SEEBRICH NIERSTEINER HIPPING RIESLING AUSLESE '04

GIARDINIERA
Pickled Vegetables
MAKES ABOUT 10 CUPS
ACTIVE TIME: 1 HR   START TO FINISH: 1 DAY (INCLUDES CHILLING)

These vegetables pick up a little spice and sourness from the pickling, but they stay crisp and retain their individual flavors.

FOR PICKLING LIQUID
2½ cups distilled white vinegar
3   cups water
¾   cup sugar
5   tablespoons kosher salt
1   teaspoon yellow mustard seeds
½   teaspoon dried hot red-pepper flakes

FOR VEGETABLES
1   head cauliflower (2 lb), trimmed and broken into
    1- to 1½-inch florets (6 cups)
1   red bell pepper, cut into 1-inch pieces
1   yellow bell pepper, cut into 1-inch pieces
4   carrots, cut diagonally into ½-inch-thick slices (2 cups)
4   celery ribs, cut into 1-inch-thick slices (3 cups)
1   cup drained bottled whole *peperoncini* (4 oz)
1   cup large brine-cured green olives (preferably Sicilian; 6 oz)
½   cup oil-cured black olives (6 oz)

MAKE PICKLING LIQUID:
▶ Bring pickling-liquid ingredients to a boil in a 3-quart nonreactive saucepan (see cooks' note, below) over moderate heat, stirring until sugar is dissolved. Transfer to a 4-quart nonreactive bowl and cool about 30 minutes.

COOK VEGETABLES:
▶ Bring about 6 quarts unsalted water to a boil in an 8-quart pot. Have ready a large bowl of ice and cold water. Add cauliflower to pot and boil until crisp-tender, about 4 minutes, then transfer with a slotted spoon to ice bath to stop cooking. Cook remaining vegetables separately in same manner, allowing 4 minutes each for bell peppers and carrots and 2 minutes for celery. Drain vegetables in a colander and spread out on 2 large kitchen towels to dry.

▶ Add cooked vegetables, *peperoncini*, and olives to pickling liquid. Weight vegetables with a plate to keep them submerged, then chill, covered, at least 1 day.

COOKS' NOTES: Stainless steel, glass, and enameled cast iron are nonreactive; avoid pure aluminum and uncoated iron, which can impart an unpleasant taste to recipes with acidic ingredients.
• Pickled vegetables keep, covered and chilled, 1 week.

HEIRLOOM TOMATO SALAD WITH MOZZARELLA AND BASIL
SERVES 8 TO 10
ACTIVE TIME: 30 MIN   START TO FINISH: 30 MIN

Allow this salad to sit a few minutes after tossing; the mozzarella milk and tomato juices emerge and add flavor to the dressing.

2   tablespoons red-wine vinegar
1   teaspoon Dijon mustard
1   teaspoon salt
½   teaspoon sugar
½   teaspoon black pepper
½   cup extra-virgin olive oil
4   lb mixed heirloom tomatoes, quartered if small or cut
     into ¼-inch-wide wedges if larger
1   lb cherry tomatoes
1   lb very small mozzarella balls (¼ inch; sometimes
     called *perlini*) or 1 lb lightly salted mozzarella, cut into
     ¼-inch pieces
1½   cups loosely packed small basil leaves or torn large leaves

▶ Whisk together vinegar, mustard, salt, sugar, and pepper in a large bowl. Add oil in a slow stream, whisking constantly until dressing is emulsified. Add tomatoes, mozzarella, and basil and toss well. Season with salt and pepper.

COOKS' NOTES: Salad, without vinaigrette, can be assembled 2 hours ahead and kept at room temperature. Salad can be dressed 1 hour ahead and kept at room temperature, covered.
• Vinaigrette keeps, covered and chilled, 1 week.

OPPOSITE (clockwise from lower left): *giardiniera*; black-olive *grissini*; summer squash soup with parsley mint *pistou*; heirloom tomato salad with mozzarella and basil

BLACK-OLIVE GRISSINI

MAKES 32 BREADSTICKS

ACTIVE TIME: 1 HR   START TO FINISH: 1½ HR

This play of bitter, sweet, and crunchy goes beautifully with an aperitif or a cold glass of beer or white wine.

- ½ cup rye flour
- ¾ cup all-purpose flour
- 1 teaspoon baking powder
- ½ teaspoon baking soda
- 1 teaspoon sugar
- ¼ teaspoon salt
- ¼ cup Kalamata or other brine-cured black olives (3 oz), pitted and finely chopped
- ½ cup well-shaken buttermilk
- 2 tablespoons unsalted butter, melted and cooled to room temperature
- 1 large egg beaten with 1 tablespoon water to make egg wash

SPECIAL EQUIPMENT: **parchment paper**

▶ Put oven racks in upper and lower thirds of oven and preheat oven to 350°F. Line 2 large baking sheets with parchment.

▶ Whisk together flours, baking powder, baking soda, sugar, and salt in a large bowl, then stir in olives, buttermilk, and butter until a dough forms. Turn out onto a lightly floured surface and knead 5 or 6 times.

▶ Halve dough and form each half into a 12-inch log. Cut each log into 16 pieces. Roll each piece into a 10-inch-long rope and arrange ½ inch apart on lined baking sheets.

▶ Brush breadsticks lightly with some of egg wash. Bake, switching position of sheets halfway through baking, until golden and crisp, 25 to 30 minutes total. Cool on sheets on a rack 30 minutes.

COOKS' NOTE: *Grissini* can be baked and cooled 1 week ahead and kept in an airtight container at room temperature.

SUMMER-SQUASH SOUP WITH PARSLEY MINT PISTOU

SERVES 8

ACTIVE TIME: 1½ HR   START TO FINISH: 1½ HR

It's hard to believe there's no cream in this soup, it's so velvety. Minty pistou, *added at the last minute, provides complexity.*

FOR SQUASH SOUP
- ¾ stick (6 tablespoons) unsalted butter, cut into pieces
- 1 medium onion, halved lengthwise and thinly sliced crosswise
- ½ teaspoon salt
- 2 lb yellow summer squash, halved and thinly sliced
- 2 carrots, thinly sliced
- 1 yellow-fleshed potato (½ lb), peeled, halved, and thinly sliced
- 4 cups chicken stock or reduced-sodium chicken broth

FOR PISTOU
- ¾ cup loosely packed fresh mint leaves
- ½ cup loosely packed fresh flat-leaf parsley sprigs
- 1 large scallion, chopped (½ cup)
- ¼ cup extra-virgin olive oil
- 2 tablespoons water
- ¼ teaspoon salt

MAKE SOUP:

▶ Melt butter in a 6- to 8-quart wide heavy pot over moderate heat, then cook onion with salt, stirring, until softened, about 8 minutes. Add squash, carrots, potato, and stock and bring to a boil. Reduce heat, then simmer, partially covered, until vegetables are very tender, about 20 minutes. Remove from heat and cool soup, uncovered, 10 minutes.

▶ Working in batches, purée soup in a blender until smooth (use caution when blending hot liquids) and transfer to a bowl. Return purée to cleaned pot and thin with water if desired; simmer 3 minutes. Season with salt.

MAKE *PISTOU* WHILE VEGETABLES SIMMER:

▶ Pulse mint, parsley, and scallion in a food processor until finely chopped. With motor running, add oil in a stream, then add water and salt, blending until incorporated.

▶ Swirl 1 tablespoon *pistou* into each bowl of soup.

COOKS' NOTES: Soup (without *pistou*) can be made 2 days ahead and cooled, uncovered, then chilled, covered. Reheat before serving, thinning with additional water if desired.

• *Pistou* keeps, its surface covered with plastic wrap, chilled, 3 days. Bring to room temperature before using.

ROAST CAPON WITH LEMON, THYME, AND ONIONS

SERVES 8 TO 10

ACTIVE TIME: 1½ HR   START TO FINISH: 3½ HR

Capon's richness is perfectly complemented by mellow roasted onions and shallots. Though you can find frozen capons in almost every supermarket, we recommend ordering a fresh one from the butcher—the meat will be silkier and more delicious.

1	(8- to 9-lb) capon or oven stuffer; preferably not frozen
2¾	teaspoons salt
1¾	teaspoons black pepper
1	stick (½ cup) unsalted butter, softened
1½	tablespoons finely grated fresh lemon zest (see Tips, page 8)
4	teaspoons chopped fresh thyme plus 10 sprigs fresh thyme
2	lemons, halved
¼	cup fresh lemon juice
6	shallots, trimmed, leaving root ends intact, and halved lengthwise
4	medium red onions, trimmed, leaving root ends intact, and cut lengthwise into 1-inch-wide wedges
4	medium yellow onions, trimmed, leaving root ends intact, and cut lengthwise into 1-inch-wide wedges
2	cups chicken stock or reduced-sodium chicken broth
2	tablespoons all-purpose flour

SPECIAL EQUIPMENT: **kitchen string; an instant-read thermometer**
GARNISH: **lemon wedges and fresh thyme sprigs**

▶ Rinse capon inside and out and discard any excess fat from cavity. Pat capon dry inside and out, then sprinkle cavity with ½ teaspoon salt and ½ teaspoon pepper. Put capon in a large flameproof roasting pan (17 by 12 by 3 inches) and let stand at room temperature 30 minutes.

▶ Put oven rack in middle position and preheat oven to 425°F.

▶ While capon is standing, stir together butter, zest, 1 tablespoon chopped thyme, 1 teaspoon salt, and ½ teaspoon pepper in a small bowl.

▶ Starting at neck cavity, gently slide an index finger between skin and flesh of breast to loosen skin (be careful not to tear skin). Push butter mixture evenly under skin on both sides of breast, then rub outside of capon to distribute butter evenly. Tuck wings under.

▶ Put thyme sprigs and lemon halves in large cavity and tie legs together with string. Pour lemon juice all over capon and sprinkle with 1 teaspoon salt and ½ teaspoon pepper.

▶ Roast capon 30 minutes. Reduce oven temperature to 375°F and add shallots and onions to pan, tossing with pan juices. Continue roasting capon, basting with pan juices and stirring shallots and onions every 30 minutes, until thermometer inserted 2 inches into fleshy part of a thigh (do not touch bone) registers 170°F, about 1½ hours more.

▶ Tilt capon so juices in large cavity run into roasting pan, then transfer capon to a cutting board (do not clean roasting pan) and let stand, uncovered, 20 to 30 minutes. Transfer shallots and onions to a sieve held over roasting pan to drain any pan juices. Transfer shallots and onions to a bowl and stir in remaining ¼ teaspoon salt and ¼ teaspoon pepper.

▶ Pour pan juices into a 1-quart glass measure, then skim off fat and reserve fat and juices separately.

▶ Straddle roasting pan across 2 burners. Add 1 cup chicken stock to pan and deglaze pan by boiling over high heat, scraping up brown bits, about 1 minute. Add to glass measure with pan juices.

▶ Cook flour and 2 tablespoons reserved fat in a 3-quart heavy saucepan over moderately high heat, whisking, until smooth, then add remaining cup chicken stock in a stream, whisking constantly to prevent lumps. Whisk in reserved pan juices and cook, whisking occasionally, until sauce is reduced to about 1½ cups, 10 to 15 minutes. Pour through a fine-mesh sieve into a bowl and stir in remaining teaspoon chopped fresh thyme and salt and pepper to taste.

▶ Carve capon and serve with shallots, onions, and sauce.

GRILLED MUSHROOM SALAD WITH ARUGULA

SERVES 8

ACTIVE TIME: 45 MIN   START TO FINISH: 1 HR

It might look like a lot of mushrooms when you're putting the salad together, but it allows everyone to have a generous helping.

½   cup Champagne vinegar
2   teaspoons sugar
1½   teaspoons salt
1   teaspoon black pepper
½   cup finely chopped shallots (4 small)
1   cup extra-virgin olive oil
½   lb whole fresh portabella mushrooms, stems discarded
½   lb fresh shiitake mushrooms, stems discarded
½   lb fresh cremini mushrooms, trimmed
¾   lb fresh chanterelle mushrooms, trimmed
½   lb baby arugula, or regular arugula torn into bite-size
    pieces (16 cups)
⅔   cup Parmigiano-Reggiano shavings (made with a
    vegetable peeler from a 2-oz piece)

SPECIAL EQUIPMENT: **a well-seasoned large (2-burner) ridged grill pan (preferably cast-iron)**

▶ Whisk together vinegar, sugar, salt, pepper, and shallots in a large bowl. Add oil in a slow stream, whisking constantly until combined. Reserve half of vinaigrette in another large bowl and add mushrooms to remaining vinaigrette. Toss to coat and marinate 5 minutes.
▶ Transfer mushrooms to another bowl with a slotted spoon, discarding marinade.
▶ Heat lightly oiled grill pan over moderately high heat until hot but not smoking, then grill mushrooms in 3 batches, turning frequently, until golden brown, about 5 minutes per batch. Transfer as grilled to a cutting board and cool to room temperature.
▶ Cut portabellas into ½-inch-wide wedges, then halve shiitake and cremini mushrooms and cut chanterelles (if large) lengthwise into ½-inch pieces.
▶ Transfer mushrooms to reserved vinaigrette, tossing to coat, then add arugula, cheese, and salt and pepper to taste and toss again.

COOKS' NOTES: Mushrooms (marinated but without additional vinaigrette) can be grilled and cut 4 hours ahead and cooled, uncovered, then kept, loosely covered, at room temperature. Pour off any juices before adding to vinaigrette.
• Vinaigrette keeps, covered and chilled, 1 day.

POTATO AND KALE GALETTE

SERVES 8 TO 10

ACTIVE TIME: 45 MIN   START TO FINISH: 1 HR

A crisp potato cake would be tempting enough—even without the surprise of garlicky kale sandwiched between its layers.

1   lb kale, tough stems and center ribs discarded
1   stick (½ cup) butter, 6 of the tablespoons melted
    and cooled
4   garlic cloves, finely chopped
¾   teaspoon salt
¾   teaspoon black pepper
2   lb russet (baking) potatoes (4 medium)

SPECIAL EQUIPMENT: **a 12-inch heavy nonstick skillet; an adjustable-blade slicer**

▶ Cook kale in a 4- to 6-quart pot of boiling salted water (see Tips, page 8), uncovered, until just tender, 4 to 6 minutes. Drain in a colander and rinse under cold water to stop cooking. Drain well, squeezing handfuls of kale to extract excess moisture, then coarsely chop.
▶ Heat 2 tablespoons (unmelted) butter in skillet over moderately high heat until foam subsides, then add garlic and cook, stirring occasionally, until golden, about 1 minute. Add kale, ¼ teaspoon salt, and ¼ teaspoon pepper and sauté, stirring, until kale is tender, about 4 minutes. Transfer to a bowl and clean skillet.
▶ Peel potatoes and thinly slice crosswise (1⁄16 inch thick) with slicer. Working quickly to prevent potatoes from discoloring, generously brush bottom of skillet with some of melted butter and cover with one third of potato slices, overlapping slightly. Dab potatoes with some of melted butter.
▶ Spread half of kale over potatoes and sprinkle with ⅛ teaspoon salt and ⅛ teaspoon pepper.
▶ Cover with half of remaining potato slices and dab with butter, then top with remaining kale. Sprinkle with ⅛ teaspoon salt and ⅛ teaspoon pepper. Top with remaining potatoes and sprinkle with remaining ¼ teaspoon salt and ¼ teaspoon pepper.
▶ Brush a sheet of foil with melted butter, then brush galette with any remaining butter and place foil, buttered side down, on top. Place a 10-inch heavy skillet on top of foil to weight galette.
▶ Cook galette over moderate heat until underside is golden brown, 12 to 15 minutes. Remove top skillet and foil. Wearing oven mitts, carefully slide galette onto a baking sheet and invert skillet over it. Holding them together, invert galette, browned side up, back into skillet. Cook, uncovered, over moderate heat until underside is golden brown and potatoes are tender, 12 to 15 minutes. Slide onto a serving plate.

SWEET-POTATO, APPLE, AND FONTINA GALETTE

SERVES 8
ACTIVE TIME: 45 MIN   START TO FINISH: 1½ HR

Amaretti may seem odd in a vegetable galette, but Italians use them to enhance squash—and they work with sweet potatoes, too. Whereas the potato and kale galette (page 156) is savory, this is a little sweet, so it's worth making both.

  8 *amaretti* (Italian almond macaroons; from 4 paper-wrapped
        bundles), finely ground in a food processor (⅓ cup)
1½ oz Italian Fontina, coarsely grated (½ cup)
  1 cup finely grated Parmigiano-Reggiano
  ⅞ teaspoon black pepper
1½ lb sweet potatoes (2 medium)
  ¾ stick (6 tablespoons) unsalted butter, melted and cooled
  1 lb Gala apples (3 medium)
  ½ teaspoon salt

SPECIAL EQUIPMENT: **an adjustable-blade slicer; a 12-inch ovenproof heavy skillet; an apple corer**

▶ Stir together *amaretti* crumbs, cheeses, and ½ teaspoon pepper in a small bowl.

▶ Peel sweet potatoes and thinly slice crosswise (1/16 inch thick) with slicer, then generously brush bottom of skillet with some melted butter and cover with one third of sweet-potato slices, overlapping slightly. Dab potatoes with butter, then sprinkle evenly with half of *amaretti* mixture.

▶ Core and peel apples, then thinly slice crosswise (into 1/16-inch-thick rings) with slicer. Working quickly to prevent discoloring, add half of apples to skillet, overlapping slices slightly, and sprinkle with ⅛ teaspoon salt and ⅛ teaspoon pepper. Top with half of remaining sweet-potato slices and dab with butter, then sprinkle with remaining *amaretti* mixture. Cover with remaining apples in an even layer. Sprinkle with ⅛ teaspoon salt and ⅛ teaspoon pepper and cover with remaining sweet potatoes. Sprinkle with remaining ¼ teaspoon salt and ⅛ teaspoon pepper. Brush a sheet of foil with butter, then brush galette with any remaining butter and place foil, buttered side down, on top. Place a 10-inch heavy skillet on top of foil to weight galette.

▶ Put oven rack in middle position and preheat oven to 375°F.

▶ Cook galette on top of stove over moderate heat until underside is golden, about 10 minutes. Remove top skillet and foil.

▶ Wearing oven mitts, carefully slide galette onto a baking sheet and invert skillet over it. Holding them together, invert galette, browned side up, back into skillet. Cook, uncovered, over moderately high heat until underside is pale golden, about 10 minutes. Transfer skillet to oven and bake galette until a knife inserted in center cuts through easily, about 20 minutes. Slide onto a serving plate.

COOKS' NOTES: If you are also making roast capon (page 155), galette can be baked at the same time in upper third of oven.
• Galette can be made 2 days ahead and cooled, uncovered, then chilled, wrapped in foil. Unwrap and transfer to a baking sheet, then reheat in a 375°F oven until heated through, about 15 minutes.

OPPOSITE: nectarine almond frangipane tart; blackberry brown-sugar cake

BLACKBERRY BROWN-SUGAR CAKE

SERVES 10

ACTIVE TIME: 1¼ HR   START TO FINISH: 2¾ HR

Marshmallowy buttercream tops the crunchy crust and tender interior of this rich cake. Fresh, juicy blackberries add a lush fruitiness and tame the cake's sweetness with their slightly tart flavor.

FOR BLACKBERRY JAM

- 1 lb blackberries (about 3½ cups)
- ½ cup sugar
- 1 teaspoon fresh lemon juice

FOR CAKE

- ⅔ cup walnuts (2 oz)
- 1 cup granulated sugar
- 2 sticks (1 cup) unsalted butter, softened, plus additional for greasing pans
- 2 cups all-purpose flour
- 1¼ teaspoons baking soda
- ¾ teaspoon salt
- 1 cup well-shaken buttermilk
- 1 teaspoon finely grated fresh orange zest (see Tips, page 8)
- 2 tablespoons fresh orange juice
- 1½ teaspoons vanilla
- 1 cup packed light brown sugar
- 2 large eggs

FOR BUTTERCREAM

- 3 large egg whites at room temperature
- ¼ teaspoon salt
- ¾ cup packed dark brown sugar
- ⅓ cup water
- 3 sticks (1½ cups) unsalted butter, cut into pieces and softened
- 1½ teaspoons vanilla

FOR ASSEMBLING CAKE

- 1 lb blackberries (about 3½ cups)

SPECIAL EQUIPMENT: **a heavy-duty stand mixer with whisk and paddle attachments; 3 (8-inch) round cake pans; 3 cooling racks; a candy thermometer**

MAKE BLACKBERRY JAM:

▸ Mash blackberries with sugar using a potato masher or fork in a 3- to 4-quart heavy saucepan. Cook over moderately high heat, stirring occasionally, until slightly thickened, about 7 minutes. Stir in lemon juice, then force through a sieve into a bowl, discarding seeds. Chill jam, its surface covered with wax paper, until softly set, at least 15 minutes.

MAKE CAKE:

▸ Put oven racks in upper and lower thirds of oven and preheat oven to 350°F.

▸ Pulse walnuts with ½ cup granulated sugar in a food processor until finely ground.

▸ Generously butter cake pans and put a rounded ⅓ cup nut mixture into each pan. Tilt each pan to coat bottom and sides with nut mixture, letting excess remain in bottom of pan.

▸ Sift together flour, baking soda, and salt in a bowl. Stir together buttermilk, orange zest and juice, and vanilla in a small bowl.

▸ Beat together butter (2 sticks), brown sugar, and remaining ½ cup granulated sugar in bowl of mixer with paddle attachment at medium-high speed until pale and fluffy, about 5 minutes. Add eggs, 1 at a time, beating well after each addition. Reduce speed to low and add flour and buttermilk mixtures alternately in batches, beginning and ending with flour mixture and mixing just until batter is smooth. Divide batter among cake pans.

▸ Bake, switching position of pans halfway through baking, until a wooden pick or skewer inserted in centers of cakes comes out clean and edges begin to pull away from sides of pans, about 30 minutes. Cool in pans on racks 15 minutes, then run a thin knife around edge of each pan. Invert racks over pans, then flip cakes onto racks to cool completely, about 1 hour.

MAKE BUTTERCREAM:

▸ Put egg whites and salt in cleaned bowl of mixer.

▸ Bring brown sugar and water to a boil in a 1-quart heavy saucepan over moderately high heat, stirring until sugar is dissolved, and washing down side of pan occasionally with a pastry brush dipped in water. When sugar syrup reaches a boil, start beating egg whites with whisk attachment at medium-high speed until whites just hold soft peaks. (Do not beat again until sugar syrup is ready.)

▸ Meanwhile, put thermometer into sugar syrup and continue boiling until syrup reaches 238 to 242°F (soft ball stage). Immediately remove from heat and, with mixer at high speed, slowly pour hot syrup down side of bowl into egg whites (avoid beaters), beating constantly.

▸ Continue to beat meringue, scraping down bowl once or twice with a rubber spatula, until meringue is cool to the touch, about 10 minutes. (It is important that meringue is properly cooled before proceeding.)

▸ With mixer at medium speed, gradually add butter to meringue 1 piece at a time, beating well after each addition and until incorporated. (If meringue is too warm and buttercream looks soupy after some of butter is added, briefly chill bottom of bowl in a large bowl filled with ice water for a few seconds before continuing to beat in remaining butter.) Continue beating until buttercream is smooth. (Mixture may look curdled before all of butter is added, but will come back together as beating continues.) Add vanilla and beat 1 minute more.

ASSEMBLE CAKE:

▶ Put 1 cake layer, nut side up, on a cake plate or platter. Spread 1½ cups buttercream on top but not side, then top with another cake layer, nut side up. Spread top with 1½ cups buttercream, then top with remaining layer, nut side up.

▶ Gently toss whole blackberries with jam in a large bowl. Arrange blackberries, stemmed sides down, on top of cake.

COOKS' NOTES: Jam keeps, chilled in an airtight container, 2 weeks. Bring to room temperature before using.

• Cake layers can be baked 2 days ahead and kept, wrapped in plastic, at room temperature.

• Buttercream can be made ahead and chilled, covered, 1 week or frozen 1 month. Bring to room temperature (do not use a microwave) and beat with electric mixer until smooth before using.

• Assembled cake keeps, loosely covered, at room temperature 1 day.

NECTARINE ALMOND FRANGIPANE TART

SERVES 8

ACTIVE TIME: 1 HR START TO FINISH: 5½ HR

With its juicy fruit, creamy filling, and intense glaze, all nestled into a crunchy crust, this dessert would please any tart lover.

FOR PASTRY DOUGH
- 1 cup all-purpose flour
- 3 tablespoons sugar
- ½ teaspoon salt
- ¾ stick (6 tablespoons) cold unsalted butter, cut into ½-inch pieces
- ½ teaspoon finely grated fresh lemon zest (see Tips, page 8)
- 2 large egg yolks
- ½ teaspoon vanilla
- 1½ teaspoons water

FOR FRANGIPANE FILLING
- 7 to 8 oz almond paste (not marzipan or almond filling)
- ½ stick (¼ cup) unsalted butter, softened
- 3 tablespoons sugar
- ⅛ teaspoon almond extract
- 2 large eggs
- 3 tablespoons all-purpose flour
- ½ teaspoon salt
- 1¼ lb firm-ripe nectarines

FOR GLAZE
- ⅓ cup peach preserves
- 2 tablespoons water
- 1 tablespoon Disaronno Amaretto (optional)

SPECIAL EQUIPMENT: a pastry or bench scraper; an 11- by 8- by 1-inch rectangular or 11-inch round fluted tart pan with a removable bottom; pie weights or raw rice

MAKE DOUGH:

▶ Put oven rack in middle position and preheat to 375°F.

▶ Pulse flour, sugar, and salt in a food processor until combined. Add butter and zest and pulse until mixture resembles coarse meal with some small (roughly pea-size) butter lumps. Add yolks, vanilla, and water and pulse just until incorporated and dough begins to form large clumps.

▶ Turn dough out onto a work surface and divide into 4 portions. Smear each portion once with heel of your hand in a forward motion to help distribute fat. Gather dough together using scraper and form into a ball, then flatten into a rectangle.

▶ Put dough in tart pan and pat out with well-floured fingers into an even layer over bottom and up sides so it extends about ¼ inch above rim. Chill 30 minutes.

▶ Lightly prick tart shell all over with a fork, then line with foil and fill with pie weights. Bake shell until golden around edge, about 15 minutes. Carefully remove foil and weights and bake until shell is golden all over, about 15 minutes more. Cool shell completely in pan on a rack. Leave oven on.

MAKE FILLING:

▶ Beat together almond paste, butter, sugar, and almond extract in a bowl with an electric mixer at medium-high speed until creamy, about 3 minutes. Reduce speed to low and add eggs, 1 at a time, beating well after each addition, then mix in flour and salt.

▶ Halve nectarines, discarding pits, then cut into ¼-inch-wide wedges.

▶ Spread frangipane filling evenly in tart shell. Stand nectarine wedges, skin sides down, decoratively in filling, being careful not to push too far into filling.

▶ Bake tart until frangipane is puffed and golden and edges of nectarines are golden brown, about 1¼ hours.

MAKE GLAZE:

▶ Heat peach preserves and water in a 1-quart saucepan over moderately high heat, stirring, until preserves are melted. Remove from heat and force through a fine-mesh sieve into a small bowl, discarding solids. Stir in Amaretto (if using).

▶ Brush top of hot tart generously with glaze and cool in pan on rack 15 minutes. Remove side of pan and cool tart completely, about 2 hours.

COOKS' NOTES: Pastry dough, formed into a rectangle and wrapped in plastic, can be chilled 3 days.

• Tart can be baked and cooled 1 day ahead and kept, covered, at room temperature.

JUST THE FOUR OF US

THANKSGIVING WITH FRIENDS

SERVES 4

IRON HORSE CLASSIC
VINTAGE BRUT '01

**CARROT SOUP WITH
TOASTED ALMONDS**

**TURKEY ROULADE WITH
CIDER SAUCE**

CREAMED LEEKS

**ROASTED KOHLRABI AND
BUTTERNUT SQUASH**

FARIÑA GRAN COLEGIATA
CAMPUS TORO '02

**CHOCOLATE CRANBERRY CAKES
WITH BOURBON WHIPPED CREAM**

QUADY ELYSIUM CALIFORNIA
BLACK MUSCAT '05

CARROT SOUP WITH TOASTED ALMONDS

SERVES 4 (FIRST COURSE)
ACTIVE TIME: 25 MIN START TO FINISH: 45 MIN

The secret to this simple recipe is using sweet, flavorful carrots.

- 1 cup sliced shallots (about 4 large)
- 1 Turkish or ½ California bay leaf
- ¼ teaspoon ground ginger
  Rounded ⅛ teaspoon curry powder
- 1 teaspoon chopped fresh thyme
- ½ stick (¼ cup) unsalted butter
- 1 small boiling potato (3 oz)
- 1½ lb carrots, peeled and cut crosswise into
  ¼-inch-thick pieces
- 1¾ cups reduced-sodium chicken broth (14 fl oz)
- 1 cup apple cider (preferably unfiltered)
- 1¼ cups water
- ¾ teaspoon salt
- ¼ teaspoon black pepper
- ¼ cup sliced almonds, toasted (see Tips, page 8)

▶ Cook shallots, bay leaf, ginger, curry powder, and thyme in butter in a 2- to 3-quart heavy saucepan over moderately low heat, stirring occasionally, until shallots are softened and pale golden, 6 to 8 minutes.

▶ Meanwhile, peel potato and cut into ½-inch cubes.

▶ Add potato to shallot mixture along with carrots, broth, cider, water, salt, and pepper and bring to a boil. Reduce heat and simmer, covered, until carrots are tender, 20 to 25 minutes. Discard bay leaf.

▶ Purée soup in 2 batches in a blender until smooth, transferring as blended to a large bowl (use caution when blending hot liquids). Return to saucepan to reheat if necessary. Serve soup sprinkled with almonds.

COOKS' NOTES: Soup can be made 2 days ahead and cooled completely, uncovered, then chilled, covered. Reheat over low heat. Thin with additional water if necessary.

• Almonds can be toasted 2 days ahead and cooled completely, uncovered, then kept in an airtight container at room temperature.

TURKEY ROULADE WITH CIDER SAUCE

SERVES 4 (WITH LEFTOVERS)
ACTIVE TIME: 1¼ HR   START TO FINISH: 3 HR

Even if you love dark meat, you won't be disappointed with this easy alternative to serving a whole turkey. Roasting the turkey breast at high heat for a short time locks in tons of meaty juice, and the filling combines stuffing and cranberry sauce in one dish. Pan juices, whisked together with apple cider, top it all off.

2	cups diced (¼ inch) firm white sandwich bread (from 4 slices)
1	cup dried cranberries
½	cup water
½	cup diced (¼ inch) celery
½	cup finely chopped onion
1	teaspoon finely chopped garlic
2	teaspoons finely chopped fresh sage
1½	teaspoons salt
¾	teaspoon black pepper
½	stick (¼ cup) unsalted butter at room temperature plus 1 tablespoon melted
½	lb chicken livers (see cooks' note, below), trimmed
1	large egg
¼	cup whole milk
1	(4½- to 5-lb) boneless turkey breast half with skin
½	cup medium-dry Sherry
⅓	cup soy sauce
2	whole cloves
1	Turkish or ½ California bay leaf
1¼	cups apple cider (preferably unfiltered)
1	tablespoon cornstarch

SPECIAL EQUIPMENT: kitchen string; heavy-duty foil; an instant-read thermometer

MAKE STUFFING:

▶ Put oven rack in middle position and preheat oven to 350°F.
▶ Toast bread cubes on a baking sheet until dry and just beginning to brown around edges, 12 to 15 minutes.
▶ Simmer cranberries in water (½ cup) in a small heavy saucepan over low heat, uncovered, stirring once or twice, until cranberries are tender and all of water is absorbed, about 8 minutes. Remove from heat.
▶ Cook celery, onion, garlic, 1 teaspoon sage, ¼ teaspoon salt, and ⅛ teaspoon pepper in 2 tablespoons butter in a 12-inch heavy skillet over moderate heat, stirring occasionally, until vegetables are softened, about 3 minutes. Transfer to a small bowl. Wipe skillet clean.
▶ Pat chicken livers dry and sprinkle with ¼ teaspoon salt and

⅛ teaspoon pepper. Heat 2 tablespoons butter in cleaned skillet over high heat until foam subsides, then sauté livers until edges are browned but livers are still pink inside, about 3 minutes. Transfer with a slotted spoon to a cutting board, reserving pan juices, and cool completely, then cut into ¼-inch dice.
▶ Whisk together egg and milk in a large bowl, then stir in toasted bread cubes, cranberries, onion mixture, livers, reserved pan juices, ¼ teaspoon salt, and ⅛ teaspoon pepper. Let stand at room temperature until bread has absorbed all of liquid and stuffing is completely cool, about 10 minutes.

PREPARE TURKEY:

▶ Leave oven rack in middle position and preheat oven to 450°F.
▶ Arrange turkey, skin side up, on a work surface with narrower, pointed end nearest you. Determine which long side of the breast is thickest, then, starting from that side and holding knife parallel to work surface, cut breast horizontally almost in half, stopping 1 inch from other side. Open breast like a book and put between 2 sheets of plastic wrap.
▶ Pound turkey to 1-inch thickness with flat side of a meat pounder or with a rolling pin. Discard top sheet of plastic wrap and pat turkey dry. Arrange with a short side nearest you and sprinkle with ¼ teaspoon salt and ⅛ teaspoon pepper.
▶ Spread stuffing evenly over turkey, leaving a 1-inch border on all sides. Fold short end nearest you over stuffing to enclose, gently pressing on stuffing, then roll up breast tightly. Arrange rolled turkey breast seam side down, then tie crosswise at 1-inch intervals with string. Brush turkey with melted butter (1 tablespoon), then sprinkle with remaining ½ teaspoon salt and ¼ teaspoon pepper.
▶ Roast turkey, seam side down, in a 13- by 9- by 2-inch roasting pan, uncovered, until golden brown, about 30 minutes.
▶ Add Sherry, soy sauce, cloves, bay leaf, 1 cup cider, and remaining teaspoon sage to roasting pan. Cover roasting pan with heavy-duty foil and continue roasting until thermometer inserted diagonally 2 inches into center of roulade registers 170°F, 35 to 45 minutes more. Transfer turkey to a cutting board and let stand, loosely covered with foil, 15 minutes before slicing. (Internal temperature will rise to 180°F.)

MAKE SAUCE WHILE TURKEY STANDS:

▶ Pour juices from roasting pan through a fine-mesh sieve into a small heavy saucepan. Skim off fat and bring to a boil.
▶ Whisk together cornstarch and remaining ¼ cup cider, then whisk into boiling sauce and boil, whisking, until slightly thickened, 1 to 2 minutes.
▶ Slice turkey and serve with sauce.

COOKS' NOTES: For the chicken livers, you can substitute 1 cup bottled peeled cooked chestnuts, rinsed, drained, and chopped.
• Stuffing can be made 1 day ahead and cooled completely, uncovered, then chilled, covered.

CREAMED LEEKS

SERVES 4

ACTIVE TIME: 35 MIN   START TO FINISH: 1 HR

Put a spin on creamed onions this holiday by using an ingredient from the same family instead. Not only do these leeks bake into something extraordinary, they get you out of the time-consuming task of peeling all those tiny pearl onions.

3½ lb leeks, root ends trimmed
 2 cups coarse fresh bread crumbs (from a country loaf, crusts discarded)
 ¾ teaspoon salt
 ⅜ teaspoon black pepper
 ¾ stick (6 tablespoons) unsalted butter
 1 cup heavy cream

SPECIAL EQUIPMENT: **a 1½-qt gratin or other shallow baking dish (10 by 8 inches)**

▸Put oven rack in middle position and preheat oven to 450°F.
▸Cut each leek into an 8-inch length, measuring from root end, and halve lengthwise, then cut crosswise into roughly 1½-inch pieces. (You should have about 8 cups.) Wash leek pieces in a large bowl of cold water, agitating them, then lift out and transfer to another bowl. Repeat with clean water, then drain leeks well.
▸Cook bread crumbs with ¼ teaspoon salt and ⅛ teaspoon pepper in 3 tablespoons butter in a 10-inch heavy skillet over moderate heat, stirring, until crisp and pale golden, 3 to 4 minutes. Remove from heat.
▸Cut out a round from parchment or wax paper to fit just inside a 12-inch heavy skillet.
▸Cook leeks with remaining ½ teaspoon salt and ¼ teaspoon pepper in remaining 3 tablespoons butter in a 12-inch heavy skillet over moderately low heat, leeks covered directly with parchment, stirring occasionally, until tender, about 12 minutes.
▸Discard parchment and transfer leeks with a slotted spoon to gratin dish. Pour cream slowly over leeks, then scatter bread crumbs on top. Bake until cream is bubbling and slightly thickened and crumbs are golden brown, about 15 minutes.

COOKS' NOTES: Bread crumbs can be cooked 1 day ahead and cooled completely, uncovered, then kept in an airtight container at room temperature. Scatter cooked bread crumbs over leeks just before baking.
• Leeks can be cooked and assembled in dish with cream (but not sprinkled with crumbs and baked) 1 day ahead and cooled completely, uncovered, then chilled, covered.

ROASTED KOHLRABI AND BUTTERNUT SQUASH

SERVES 4

ACTIVE TIME: 20 MIN   START TO FINISH: 1 HR

We love the contrasts at play in this dish—from its earthy, sweet flavors to its velvety, crisp textures. The convenience of being able to roast these vegetables along with the stuffed turkey roulade (page 165) is just another reason to make them.

 4 medium kohlrabi (2¼ lb with greens or 1¾ lb without)
 2 tablespoons extra-virgin olive oil
 2 teaspoons finely chopped fresh thyme
 ½ teaspoon salt
 ¼ teaspoon black pepper
2½ lb butternut squash

SPECIAL EQUIPMENT: **a 17- by 12- by 1-inch shallow heavy baking pan**

▸Put oven rack just below middle position and put baking pan on rack, then preheat oven to 450°F.
▸Trim and peel kohlrabi, then cut into ¾-inch pieces. Toss kohlrabi with 1 tablespoon oil, 1 teaspoon thyme, ¼ teaspoon salt, and ⅛ teaspoon pepper in a bowl. Transfer kohlrabi to preheated pan in oven and roast 15 minutes.
▸Meanwhile, peel butternut squash, then quarter lengthwise, seed, and cut into ¾-inch pieces. Toss squash with remaining 1 tablespoon oil, 1 teaspoon thyme, ¼ teaspoon salt, and ⅛ teaspoon pepper in same bowl.
▸Stir kohlrabi, turning it, then push it to one side of pan. Add squash to opposite side of pan and roast, stirring and turning squash over halfway through roasting, until vegetables are tender and lightly browned, about 30 minutes total (after squash is added).
▸Toss vegetables to combine and transfer to a dish.

COOKS' NOTES: Kohlrabi and butternut squash can be cut 1 day ahead and chilled in separate sealed plastic bags.
• If roasting vegetables along with turkey, preheat pan for 15 minutes while turkey roasts, then roast vegetables underneath turkey.

CHOCOLATE CRANBERRY CAKES WITH BOURBON WHIPPED CREAM

SERVES 4
ACTIVE TIME: 1 HR   START TO FINISH: 2¼ HR (INCLUDES COOLING)

These luscious cranberry-studded cakes enriched with bourbon and pecans break away from traditional pumpkin pie without eliminating all those beloved ingredients that say Thanksgiving.

1¼ sticks (10 tablespoons) unsalted butter
 2   tablespoons all-purpose flour plus additional for dusting molds
 1   cup dried cranberries (4½ oz)
 ¼   cup plus 2 teaspoons bourbon
 7   oz fine-quality bittersweet chocolate (not more than 60% cacao if marked), chopped
 ¼   cup pecans, toasted (see Tips, page 8) and cooled
 3   large eggs, separated
 ½   cup packed light brown sugar
 ½   cup chilled heavy cream
 1   teaspoon confectioners sugar plus additional for dusting

SPECIAL EQUIPMENT: **parchment paper; 4 (4- by 1¼-inch) tartlet molds with removable bottoms (see Sources) or 4 (8-oz) ramekins (4 inches across and 1¼ inches deep; see cooks' note, below)**

▶ Put oven rack in middle position and preheat oven to 350°F.
▶ Cut out 4 rounds of parchment paper to fit just inside bottom of each mold, then set rounds aside. Melt 2 tablespoons butter, then brush molds with some of it. Line bottom of each mold with a round of parchment and brush parchment with some melted butter. Chill molds 5 minutes (to set butter), then brush parchment and side of each mold with more melted butter. Chill molds 5 minutes more. Dust molds with flour, knocking out excess, and set aside.
▶ Simmer cranberries and ¼ cup bourbon in a small saucepan over low heat until cranberries are tender and bourbon is absorbed, about 5 minutes. Remove from heat.
▶ Melt chocolate and remaining stick butter in a small heavy saucepan over low heat, stirring constantly, until smooth. Remove from heat and cool 10 minutes.
▶ Pulse pecans with flour (2 tablespoons) in a food processor until finely ground, being careful not to process to a paste.
▶ Beat together yolks and brown sugar in a large bowl with an electric mixer at medium speed until thick and pale, about 2 minutes. Add chocolate mixture and beat until just combined, then stir in pecan mixture and cranberries.
▶ Beat whites with a pinch of salt in another bowl using cleaned beaters until they just hold stiff peaks. Fold one third of whites into chocolate mixture to lighten, then fold in remaining whites gently but thoroughly.
▶ Divide batter among molds (they will be very full), then put molds in a shallow baking pan and bake until a wooden pick or skewer inserted into center of a cake comes out with tip wet and remainder of pick dry, about 25 minutes. (Batter will rise above rims but will not spill over.) Transfer cakes to a rack and cool in molds 30 minutes. (Cakes will continue to set as they cool.)
▶ Beat heavy cream with confectioners sugar and remaining 2 teaspoons bourbon in a small bowl using cleaned beaters until it just holds soft peaks.
▶ Remove side from each mold, then slide each cake from bottom onto a dessert plate, discarding parchment. Lightly dust each cake with confectioners sugar and serve with a dollop of bourbon whipped cream.

COOKS' NOTES: Cakes are best eaten the day they're made but can be baked (but not unmolded) 1 day ahead (texture will become more dense). Cool completely, uncovered, then keep in a sealed large plastic bag at room temperature.
• To make a single, larger cake, the batter can be baked in a 9½-inch round tart pan with a removable bottom, about 25 minutes.

GAME PLAN

2 DAYS AHEAD
-Make soup
-Toast almonds for soup

1 DAY AHEAD
-Make stuffing and butterfly (but do not stuff) turkey breast
-Cut kohlrabi and butternut squash
-Cook bread crumbs for leeks
-Cook leeks and assemble with cream (but not crumbs)
-Bake cakes

THANKSGIVING DAY
-Stuff and roast turkey
-After turkey has roasted 15 minutes, finish preparing kohlrabi and butternut squash, then roast underneath turkey in oven
-While turkey stands, sprinkle leeks with bread crumbs and bake

JUST BEFORE SERVING
-Reheat soup, then sprinkle with almonds
-Whip cream for cakes

THE
GENEROUS TABLE

A HOMESPUN THANKSGIVING

SERVES 12

MIXED NUTS IN SHELLS

ASSORTED CHEDDAR CRISPS

LEACOCK'S SERCIAL MADEIRA,
5 YEARS OLD

**SIMPLE ROAST TURKEY WITH
RICH TURKEY GRAVY**

**CHESTNUT, PRUNE, AND
PANCETTA STUFFING**

**CRANBERRY, APPLE, AND
WALNUT CONSERVE**

**BRUSSELS SPROUTS
WITH SHALLOTS AND
WILD MUSHROOMS**

ROOT VEGETABLE GRATIN

**ESCAROLE, FENNEL, AND
OAK-LEAF SALAD**

DOMAINE DROUHIN LAURÈNE
PINOT NOIR '03

**SMALL PEAR AND
ALMOND CAKES**

CARAMEL PUMPKIN PIE

FICKLIN OLD VINE TINTA PORT

ASSORTED CHEDDAR CRISPS

MAKES ABOUT 100 THIN CRACKERS

ACTIVE TIME: 1¼ HR   START TO FINISH: 3 HR (INCLUDES CHILLING)

One dough yields three kinds of thin, buttery Cheddar crackers. While it's a good idea to keep appetizers to a minimum on Thanksgiving, these (along with purchased mixed nuts in the shell) will pique everyone's appetite just enough. Make sure you sample one of each—there won't be any leftovers.

- 1 stick (½ cup) unsalted butter, softened
- ¾ lb sharp Cheddar, coarsely grated (preferably in a food processor)
- 1 large egg yolk
- 1 cup all-purpose flour
- 1 teaspoon dried mustard
- ¾ teaspoon salt
- 1 teaspoon cracked black pepper
- 1 teaspoon caraway seeds
- 1 teaspoon nigella seeds

SPECIAL EQUIPMENT: **parchment paper**

▶ Blend together butter, cheese, and yolk in food processor until smooth. Add flour, dried mustard, and salt and pulse until just combined. Transfer dough to a sheet of wax paper and divide into 3 portions (do not clean processor).

▶ Return 1 portion to processor, add pepper, and pulse until combined well, then transfer to another sheet of wax paper. Shape into a 7-inch-long log (1½ inches thick), using paper as an aid, then roll up log in paper and twist ends of paper to close. Make 2 more logs on separate sheets of wax paper in same manner, using caraway seeds for second log and nigella seeds for third log (instead of pepper) and cleaning processor in between batches. Chill logs until firm, about 2 hours.

▶ Put oven rack in middle position and preheat oven to 350°F. Line a large baking sheet with parchment paper.

▶ Unwrap 1 log and cut enough thin slices (about ⅛ inch thick) from it to fill baking sheet, arranging slices 1 inch apart. Bake until edges of crackers are golden, 10 to 12 minutes. Transfer on parchment to a rack and cool slightly, about 15 minutes. Make more crackers in batches with remaining dough.

▶ Serve crackers warm or at room temperature.

COOKS' NOTES: **Dough can be chilled, wrapped additionally in foil or in a sealed plastic bag, 1 week or frozen 2 months.**
• **Crackers can be baked 1 week ahead and cooled completely, uncovered, then kept in an airtight container at room temperature. If desired, reheat on 2 baking sheets in a preheated 350°F oven about 5 minutes.**

SIMPLE ROAST TURKEY WITH RICH TURKEY GRAVY

SERVES 12 (WITH LEFTOVERS)

ACTIVE TIME: 30 MIN   START TO FINISH: 3¾ HR (DOES NOT INCLUDE MAKING STOCK)

This is the ultimate turkey lover's turkey—no bells and whistles, just a succulent bird with crispy skin and lots of delicious gravy.

- 1 (16-lb) turkey at room temperature 1 hour, any feathers and quills removed with tweezers or needlenose pliers, and neck and giblets removed and reserved for another use if desired
- 1 tablespoon salt
- 1¾ teaspoons black pepper
- 2 cups water
- 7 to 8 cups turkey stock (recipe follows)
- 1 stick (½ cup) unsalted butter
- ¾ cup all-purpose flour
- 1½ to 2 tablespoons cider vinegar

SPECIAL EQUIPMENT: 2 small metal skewers; kitchen string; a 17- by 14-inch flameproof roasting pan with a flat rack; an instant-read thermometer; a 2-qt glass measuring cup

MAKE TURKEY:

▸ Put oven rack in lowest position and preheat oven to 450°F.

▸ Rinse turkey inside and out, then pat dry. Sprinkle turkey cavities and skin with salt and pepper. Fold neck skin under body and secure with metal skewers, then tie drumsticks together with kitchen string and tuck wings under body.

▸ Put turkey on rack in roasting pan. Add 1 cup water to pan and roast without basting, rotating pan halfway through roasting, until thermometer inserted into fleshy part of thighs (test both thighs; do not touch bones) registers 170°F, 2¼ to 2¾ hours.

▸ Carefully tilt turkey so any juices from inside large cavity run into roasting pan, then transfer turkey to a platter, reserving juices in roasting pan. Let turkey stand, uncovered, 30 minutes (temperature of thigh meat will rise to 180°F).

MAKE GRAVY WHILE TURKEY STANDS:

▸ Pour pan juices through a fine-mesh sieve into measuring cup (do not clean roasting pan), then skim off and discard fat. (If using a fat separator, pour pan juices through sieve into separator and let stand until fat rises to top, 1 to 2 minutes. Carefully pour pan juices from separator into measure, discarding fat.)

▸ Straddle roasting pan across 2 burners, then add remaining cup water and deglaze roasting pan by boiling over high heat, stirring and scraping up brown bits, 1 minute. Pour through sieve into measuring cup containing pan juices.

▸ Add enough turkey stock to pan juices to bring total to 8 cups (if stock is congealed, heat to liquefy).

▸ Melt butter in a 4-quart heavy pot and stir in flour. Cook roux over moderate heat, whisking, 5 minutes. Add stock mixture in a stream, whisking constantly to prevent lumps, then bring to a boil, whisking occasionally. Stir in any turkey juices accumulated on platter and simmer 5 minutes. Season gravy with salt and pepper, then stir in cider vinegar (to taste).

TURKEY STOCK

MAKES ABOUT 13 CUPS
ACTIVE TIME: 20 MIN   START TO FINISH: 4½ HR

This recipe yields enough rich, dark stock for the gravy and the chestnut, prune, and pancetta stuffing (page 172).

  6 lb turkey parts such as wings, drumsticks, and thighs
  3 medium yellow onions, left unpeeled, trimmed and halved
  3 celery ribs, cut into 2-inch lengths
  3 carrots, quartered
  5 qt cold water
  6 fresh parsley stems (without leaves)
  1 Turkish or ½ California bay leaf
10 black peppercorns
1½ teaspoons salt

SPECIAL EQUIPMENT: a 17- by 14-inch flameproof roasting pan

▸ If using turkey wings, halve at joints with a cleaver or large knife, then crack wing bones in several places with back of cleaver or knife. (Do not crack bones if using other parts.) Pat turkey dry.

▸ Put oven rack in lowest position of oven and preheat oven to 500°F. Roast turkey parts, skin sides down, in dry roasting pan, turning over once, until browned well, about 45 minutes. Transfer to an 8- to 10-quart stockpot with tongs, reserving fat in roasting pan.

▸ Add onions (cut sides down), celery, and carrots to fat in pan and roast, stirring halfway through roasting, until golden, about 20 minutes total. Add vegetables to turkey in stockpot.

▸ Straddle pan across 2 burners, then add 2 cups water and deglaze by boiling, stirring and scraping up brown bits, 1 minute. Add deglazing liquid to turkey and vegetables in stockpot, then add parsley stems, bay leaf, peppercorns, salt, and remaining 4½ quarts water. Reduce heat and gently simmer, partially covered, 3 hours.

▸ Pour stock through a large fine-mesh sieve into a large bowl, discarding solids. Measure stock: If there is more than 13 cups, boil in cleaned pot until reduced to 13 cups. If there is less, add enough water to bring total to 13 cups. If using immediately, let stand until fat rises to top, 1 to 2 minutes, then skim off and discard fat. If not, cool completely, uncovered, then chill, covered, before skimming fat (it will be easier to remove when cool or cold).

COOKS' NOTE: Stock can be chilled in an airtight container 1 week or frozen 3 months.

CHESTNUT, PRUNE, AND PANCETTA STUFFING

SERVES 12

ACTIVE TIME: 45 MIN   START TO FINISH: 2 HR (DOES NOT INCLUDE MAKING STOCK)

There's lots of bold flavor in this hearty stuffing, which, though inspired by a classic Italian combination, happens to work in perfect concert with everything on the American holiday table. Baking it in a wide dish ensures plenty of crusty topping for everyone.

 1 (1½-lb) sourdough loaf, cut into ⅓-inch dice
    (18 cups)
 1 lb coarsely chopped pancetta slices (about 3 cups)
 1 stick (½ cup) unsalted butter, cut into tablespoons
 3 cups chopped celery (5 to 6 ribs)
 4 cups chopped onions (2 large)
 2 tablespoons chopped fresh sage
1½ teaspoons salt
 ½ teaspoon black pepper
 3 (7- to 8-oz) jars peeled cooked whole chestnuts, halved
    (4 cups)
 ¾ lb pitted prunes (2 cups), quartered
 5 cups turkey stock (page 171), heated to liquefy, or
    reduced-sodium chicken broth (40 fl oz)
 4 large eggs, lightly beaten

SPECIAL EQUIPMENT: **a 4-quart shallow ovenproof baking dish (15 by 10 by 2 inches)**

▶Put oven rack in upper third of oven and preheat oven to 400°F.

▶Scatter bread in a single layer in 2 large shallow baking pans (17 by 12 inches) and toast, stirring once or twice and switching position of pans halfway through baking, until golden and dry, about 15 minutes. Transfer to a very large bowl.

▶Cook pancetta in a 12-inch heavy skillet over moderate heat, stirring occasionally, until browned, 12 to 15 minutes. Add butter and heat until melted, then add celery and onions and cook, stirring occasionally, until softened, about 12 minutes. Stir in sage, salt, and pepper and cook 1 minute. Add pancetta mixture along with chestnuts and prunes to bowl containing bread. Whisk together stock and eggs, then stir into bread mixture until combined well. Transfer to baking dish (stuffing will mound above dish).

▶Bake, loosely covered with a buttered sheet of foil (buttered side down) 30 minutes, then remove foil and bake until top is browned, 10 to 15 minutes more.

COOKS' NOTES: Stuffing, without stock-and-egg mixture, can be assembled (but not baked) 1 day ahead and chilled, covered. Stir in stock mixture, then proceed with recipe.

• Stuffing can be baked 6 hours ahead and cooled completely, uncovered, then chilled, loosely covered. Reheat, covered, in a preheated 400°F oven until hot, about 30 minutes.

CRANBERRY, APPLE, AND WALNUT CONSERVE

MAKES ABOUT 12 CUPS

ACTIVE TIME: 15 MIN   START TO FINISH: 25 MIN

Adding the cranberries in three stages, along with crumbled nuts, results in a wonderful conserve with layers of texture and flavor. The turbinado sugar imparts subtle caramel undertones.

1½ cups water
 3 cups turbinado sugar such as Sugar in the Raw
 1 (3-inch) cinnamon stick
 ¼ teaspoon ground allspice
 3 (12-oz) bags fresh cranberries (2¼ lb; about 11 cups)
 3 Gala or Pink Lady apples
 2 cups walnuts (6 oz), toasted (see Tips, page 8), cooled,
    and broken into small pieces
 2 tablespoons Calvados or brandy

▶Simmer water, sugar, cinnamon stick, allspice, and half of cranberries (about 5½ cups) in a 4- to 5-quart heavy pot over moderate heat, stirring occasionally, until cranberries just start to pop, about 5 minutes. Add half of remaining cranberries (about 3 cups) and simmer, stirring occasionally, 5 minutes.

▶Meanwhile, peel and core apples, then cut into ¼-inch dice. Add to cranberry mixture along with walnuts and remaining cranberries, then simmer, stirring occasionally, 5 minutes. Stir in Calvados and simmer 1 minute. Remove from heat and cool to warm or room temperature. Discard cinnamon stick.

COOKS' NOTE: Conserve can be made 1 week ahead and cooled completely, uncovered, then chilled, covered. Bring to room temperature or warm if desired.

OPPOSITE: chestnut, prune, and pancetta stuffing; cranberry, apple, and walnut conserve; rich turkey gravy

BRUSSELS SPROUTS WITH SHALLOTS AND WILD MUSHROOMS

SERVES 12

ACTIVE TIME: 45 MIN   START TO FINISH: 1¼ HR

FOR BRUSSELS SPROUTS

  3 lb Brussels sprouts, trimmed and halved lengthwise
  ¼ cup olive oil
  ½ tablespoon minced garlic
  1 teaspoon salt
  ¼ teaspoon black pepper

FOR SHALLOTS

  1 cup vegetable oil
  ½ lb large shallots (about 6), cut crosswise into ⅛-inch-thick
      slices and separated into rings (2½ cups)

FOR MUSHROOMS

  ¾ stick (6 tablespoons) unsalted butter
  1¼ lb mixed fresh wild mushrooms such as chanterelle and
      oyster, trimmed, quartered if large
  ¼ cup dry white wine
  1 tablespoon chopped fresh thyme
  ½ teaspoon salt
  ¼ teaspoon black pepper
  ½ cup water

SPECIAL EQUIPMENT: **a deep-fat thermometer**

ROAST BRUSSELS SPROUTS:

▶ Put oven rack in upper third of oven and preheat oven to 450°F.

▶ Toss Brussels sprouts with oil, garlic, salt, and pepper, then spread out in 1 layer in 2 large shallow baking pans (17 by 12 inches). Roast, stirring occasionally and switching position of pans halfway through roasting, until tender and browned, 25 to 35 minutes.

FRY SHALLOTS WHILE BRUSSELS SPROUTS ROAST:

▶ Heat oil in a 10-inch heavy skillet over moderate heat until temperature measures 250°F (see cooks' note, below), then fry shallots in 3 batches, stirring occasionally, until golden brown, 3 to 5 minutes per batch (watch closely, as shallots can burn easily). Quickly transfer with a slotted spoon to paper towels to drain, spreading in a single layer. (Shallots will crisp as they cool.) Pour off oil from skillet (do not clean).

SAUTÉ MUSHROOMS AND ASSEMBLE DISH:

▶ Heat 5 tablespoons butter in skillet over moderately high heat until foam subsides, then sauté mushrooms, stirring occasionally, until golden brown and tender, about 7 minutes.

▶ Add wine, thyme, salt, and pepper and boil, uncovered, stirring occasionally, until liquid is reduced to a glaze, about 2 minutes. Add water (½ cup) and remaining tablespoon butter and simmer, swirling skillet, until butter is melted. Transfer to a serving dish and stir in Brussels sprouts. Sprinkle with some of shallots and serve with remaining shallots on the side.

COOKS' NOTES: To take the temperature of a shallow amount of oil, put bulb in skillet and turn thermometer facedown, resting other end against rim of skillet. Check temperature frequently.

• Shallots can be fried 1 day ahead and cooled completely, uncovered, then kept in an airtight container lined with paper towels at room temperature.

• Brussels sprouts can be roasted 5 hours ahead and cooled completely, uncovered, then kept, loosely covered, at room temperature.

• Mushrooms can be sautéed 1 hour ahead and kept in skillet, partially covered. Reheat Brussels sprouts in a preheated 400°F oven and proceed with recipe.

ROOT VEGETABLE GRATIN

SERVES 12

ACTIVE TIME: 20 MIN   START TO FINISH: 1¼ HR

This unfussy gratin requires no "arranging"—you just spread the root vegetables in the baking dish.

1	lb parsnips (about 4 medium)
1	medium celery root (sometimes called celeriac; ¾ lb total)
1	lb sweet potatoes
1½	lb russet (baking) potatoes
2	teaspoons salt
1	teaspoon finely chopped garlic
½	teaspoon black pepper
¼	teaspoon freshly grated nutmeg
½	cup reduced-sodium chicken broth
1¾	cups plus 2 tablespoons heavy cream

SPECIAL EQUIPMENT: **an adjustable-blade slicer; a 3-quart gratin or other shallow flameproof baking dish (not glass; 13 by 9 inches)**

▶ Put oven rack in upper third of oven and preheat oven to 400°F.

▶ Peel parsnips and cut crosswise into 3-inch lengths with a knife, then cut lengthwise around core into ⅛-inch-thick slices with slicer (discard core). Transfer to a large bowl.

▶ Peel celery root and all potatoes (prepare russet potatoes last to avoid discoloration) and halve lengthwise, then cut crosswise into ⅛-inch-thick slices with slicer. Add to parsnips along with salt, garlic, pepper, nutmeg, broth, and 1¾ cups cream, tossing to combine. Transfer to gratin dish, spreading evenly.

▶ Cut out a piece of parchment or wax paper to fit just inside gratin dish, then butter 1 side of parchment. Cover vegetables directly with parchment, buttered side down, then put dish in a shallow baking pan (to catch any drips). Bake until gratin is bubbling all over and vegetables are tender when pierced with a knife, about 50 minutes. Discard parchment.

▶ Just before serving, preheat broiler. Drizzle top of gratin with remaining 2 tablespoons cream and broil 4 to 6 inches from heat until browned, 2 to 3 minutes.

COOKS' NOTES: Gratin, without final 2 tablespoons of cream, can be baked (but not broiled) 6 hours ahead and cooled completely, uncovered, then chilled, loosely covered. Reheat, covered, in a preheated 400°F oven until hot, about 30 minutes. Drizzle with cream and broil just before serving.

• If you're also making the stuffing (page 172), bake this gratin in lower third of oven while stuffing bakes in upper third.

ESCAROLE, FENNEL, AND OAK-LEAF SALAD

SERVES 12

ACTIVE TIME: 30 MIN   START TO FINISH: 30 MIN

Soft and crisp, bitter and sweet—this simple salad is a clean, bright counterpoint to the rest of the meal.

¾	cup apple cider (preferably unfiltered)
1	(¾-lb) fennel bulb (sometimes labeled "anise"), stalks discarded and bulb quartered lengthwise
2½	tablespoons cider vinegar
1	teaspoon finely chopped shallot
¾	teaspoon salt
¼	teaspoon black pepper
¼	cup extra-virgin olive oil
12	cups loosely packed small or torn tender pale escarole leaves (from hearts of 2 heads)
6	oz small oak-leaf lettuce leaves or other tender lettuce such as Boston (12 cups loosely packed)

SPECIAL EQUIPMENT: **an adjustable-blade slicer**

▶ Boil apple cider in a small saucepan or skillet over moderate heat until reduced to about 2 tablespoons, 5 to 8 minutes. Cool to room temperature.

▶ Shave fennel into ⅛-inch-thick slices with slicer.

▶ Whisk together reduced cider syrup, vinegar, shallot, salt, and pepper in a small bowl, then add oil, whisking to combine. Toss dressing with fennel, escarole, and lettuce in a large bowl just before serving.

COOKS' NOTES: Fennel can be shaved and greens can be washed and dried 1 day ahead and chilled separately, wrapped well in dampened paper towels, in sealed plastic bags.

• Dressing can be made 2 days ahead and chilled, covered.

SMALL PEAR AND ALMOND CAKES

SERVES 12

ACTIVE TIME: 45 MIN   START TO FINISH: 1½ HR

Muscat-poached Seckel pears are tucked into moist almond cakes for a charming dessert. Besides being cute, these tiny cakes leave guests room for pumpkin pie.

FOR POACHED PEARS
- 12   firm small Seckel pears (2 to 3 inches long; see cooks' note, below)
- 1   tablespoon fresh lemon juice
- 2   cups Essencia or other Muscat wine
- ½   tablespoon unsalted butter

FOR CAKES
- 1½   cups whole blanched almonds (½ lb)
- 1   cup plus 1 tablespoon sugar
- 2   sticks (1 cup) unsalted butter, softened, plus additional for greasing ramekins
- 1   teaspoon pure vanilla extract
- 4   large eggs
- ⅔   cup all-purpose flour plus additional for dusting
- ⅜   teaspoon salt

SPECIAL EQUIPMENT: **a small melon-ball cutter; 12 (4-oz) ramekins or 2 muffin pans with 6 large (1-cup) muffin cups**

POACH PEARS:

▶ Peel pears, leaving stems intact, then core from bottom with melon-ball cutter. Toss pears with lemon juice in a bowl as peeled, then arrange on their sides in a 10-inch heavy skillet. Add wine, butter, and lemon juice from bowl (liquid will not cover pears) and bring to a boil. Reduce heat and simmer, covered, until pears are just tender, 10 to 20 minutes. Transfer pears with a slotted spoon to a dish. Boil poaching liquid, uncovered, until just syrupy and reduced to about ¼ cup, 12 to 15 minutes. Spoon syrup over pears and cool to room temperature, stirring occasionally, about 10 minutes.

PREPARE CAKES:

▶ Put oven rack in middle position and preheat oven to 400°F.

▶ Pulse almonds with ½ cup sugar in a food processor until finely ground, then transfer to a bowl (do not clean processor).

▶ Process butter with ½ cup sugar in processor until pale and creamy, then pulse in vanilla. Add eggs 1 at a time, blending well after each addition, then pulse in almond mixture, flour, and salt until just combined.

▶ Lightly butter and flour ramekins, knocking out excess flour, then arrange in a baking pan. Divide batter among ramekins (about a slightly rounded ¼ cup per ramekin), then gently nestle a pear, leaning it slightly and pressing it very lightly, into batter

in center of each cake. (Cakes will rise around pears as they bake.) Reserve reduced poaching liquid for another use. Sprinkle pears and tops of cakes with remaining tablespoon sugar.

▶ Bake, rotating pan halfway through baking, until cakes are just firm and pale golden with slightly darker edges, about 20 minutes.

▶ Transfer ramekins to a rack and cool 10 minutes, then run a thin knife around edge of each cake and invert onto a plate. Turn cakes right side up and serve warm or at room temperature.

COOKS' NOTES: **If you can only find Forelle pears, which are slightly larger than Seckels, use 6, peeled, cored, and halved lengthwise.**

• Pears can be poached 2 days ahead and chilled, covered.

• Cakes can be baked 8 hours ahead and cooled completely, uncovered, then kept, loosely covered with plastic wrap, at room temperature.

GAME PLAN

1 WEEK AHEAD
- Make crackers
- Make turkey stock
- Make conserve
- Make pie dough and freeze

2 DAYS AHEAD
- Make dressing for salad
- Poach pears for cakes

1 DAY AHEAD
- Assemble stuffing (without stock-and-egg mixture)
- Fry shallots for Brussels sprouts dish
- Wash and dry escarole and lettuce and shave fennel for salad
- Thaw pie dough and bake pie shell

THANKSGIVING MORNING
- Bake pie
- Bake cakes

6 HOURS AHEAD
- Assemble gratin and bake (but do not broil)
- Stir stock-and-egg mixture into stuffing and bake

5 HOURS AHEAD
- Roast Brussels sprouts

4 HOURS AHEAD
- Roast turkey

1 HOUR AHEAD
- Sauté mushrooms

30 MINUTES AHEAD
- Reheat stuffing and gratin
- Make gravy while turkey stands
- Reheat Brussels sprouts, then mushrooms, and finish dish

JUST BEFORE SERVING
- Reheat crackers (if desired)
- Make salad
- Broil gratin

CARAMEL PUMPKIN PIE

SERVES 12

ACTIVE TIME: 45 MIN   START TO FINISH: 6 HR (INCLUDES COOLING)

Caramelized sugar laces this classic with a sensuous richness, extraordinary in the context of this unbelievably light and delicately spiced pie. And since it's cooked in a deep quiche pan, a single pie will serve 12 guests.

FOR PASTRY

- 1½   cups all-purpose flour
- 1¼   sticks (10 tablespoons) cold unsalted butter, cut into ½-inch cubes
- ¼   teaspoon salt
- 4   to 5 tablespoons ice water

FOR FILLING

- 1   cup sugar
- ⅓   cup water
- 2   cups heavy cream
- 1   (15-oz) can solid-pack pumpkin (not pie filling; a scant 2 cups)
- 1¼   teaspoons ground ginger
- 1¼   teaspoons ground cinnamon
- ¼   teaspoon freshly grated nutmeg
      Pinch of ground cloves
      Scant ½ teaspoon salt
- 4   large eggs, lightly beaten

SPECIAL EQUIPMENT: **a pastry or bench scraper; a 10-inch fluted metal quiche pan (2 inches deep) with a removable bottom; pie weights or raw rice**
ACCOMPANIMENT: **lightly sweetened whipped cream**

MAKE DOUGH:

▸ Blend together flour, butter, and salt in a bowl with your fingertips or a pastry blender (or pulse in a food processor) until most of mixture resembles coarse meal with some small (roughly pea-size) butter lumps. Drizzle evenly with 4 tablespoons ice water and gently stir with a fork (or pulse in processor) until incorporated.

▸ Squeeze a small handful of dough: If it doesn't hold together, add more ice water, ½ tablespoon at a time, stirring (or pulsing) until incorporated, then test again. (Do not overwork dough or pastry will be tough.)

▸ Turn mixture out onto a lightly floured surface and divide into 4 portions. With heel of your hand, smear each portion once or twice in a forward motion to help distribute fat. Gather all of dough together with scraper and press into a ball, then flatten into a 5-inch disk. Chill dough, wrapped tightly in plastic wrap, until firm, at least 1 hour.

▸ Put oven rack in middle position and preheat oven to 375°F.

▸ Roll out dough on a lightly floured surface with a lightly floured rolling pin into a 14-inch round, then fit into quiche pan and trim excess dough flush with rim of pan. Chill until firm, about 30 minutes.

BAKE PIE SHELL:

▸ Lightly prick bottom of shell all over with a fork, then line with foil and fill with pie weights. Put quiche pan on a baking sheet and bake pie shell until side is set and edge is pale golden, 18 to 20 minutes. Carefully remove weights and foil and bake shell until bottom is golden, about 10 minutes more. Cool completely in pan on a rack, about 30 minutes.

MAKE FILLING WHILE SHELL COOLS:

▸ Bring sugar and water to a boil in a 3- to 3½-quart heavy saucepan, stirring until sugar is dissolved. Boil syrup, washing down side of pan occasionally with a pastry brush dipped in cold water and gently swirling pan (do not stir), until mixture is a deep golden caramel, about 10 minutes.

▸ Reduce heat to moderate and carefully add 1 cup cream (mixture will bubble vigorously), stirring until caramel is dissolved. Stir in remaining cup cream and bring just to a simmer.

▸ Whisk together pumpkin purée, spices, and salt in a large bowl. Whisk in hot cream mixture, then add eggs, whisking until combined well. Pour filling into cooled crust and bake until puffed 1½ inches from edge and center is just set, 55 to 60 minutes. Cool in pan on a rack, about 2 hours. (Pie will continue to set as it cools.) Remove side of pan before serving.

COOKS' NOTES: **Dough can be chilled up to 1 day or frozen, wrapped well in foil, 1 month.**
• **Pie shell can be baked 1 day ahead and kept, wrapped in plastic wrap, at room temperature.**
• **Pie is best eaten the same day but can be baked 1 day ahead and cooled completely, then chilled, covered. Bring to room temperature before serving.**

MORNING LIGHT

HANUKKAH BRUNCH

SERVES 8

BLOOD-ORANGE MIMOSAS

PARMESAN PUFFS

EGG NOODLE, CHARD, AND FONTINA TORTE

FRISÉE AND CELERY SALAD WITH TOASTED FENNEL-SEED DRESSING

FRIED BITTERSWEET CHOCOLATE BREAD

PARMESAN PUFFS

MAKES ABOUT 32 HORS D'OEUVRES
ACTIVE TIME: 25 MIN   START TO FINISH: 25 MIN

> About 6 cups vegetable oil
> ¼ lb finely grated Parmigiano-Reggiano
>   (not pregrated; see Tips, page 8)
> ¼ cup all-purpose flour
> ½ teaspoon black pepper
> ¼ teaspoon salt
> 4 large egg whites at room temperature

SPECIAL EQUIPMENT: a deep-fat thermometer

▶ Heat 2 inches oil in a deep 3-quart heavy saucepan over moderate heat until it registers 360°F on thermometer.
▶ While oil heats, mix together cheese, flour, pepper, and salt in a bowl until combined well. Beat whites in another bowl with an electric mixer until they just hold stiff peaks. Fold in ½ cup cheese mixture to lighten, then fold in remaining cheese mixture gently but thoroughly.
▶ Drop about 8 teaspoons of batter, 1 teaspoon at a time, into oil and fry, turning occasionally, until balls of batter are puffed, crisp, and golden, about 2 minutes. Transfer with a slotted spoon to paper towels to drain briefly. Make 3 more batches in same manner, returning oil to 360°F between batches. Serve immediately.

BLOOD-ORANGE MIMOSAS

MAKES 8 DRINKS
ACTIVE TIME: 15 MIN   START TO FINISH: 1¼ HR (INCLUDES CHILLING)

You'll want to mix up a pitcher of this bubbly drink for its gorgeous ruby hue alone. It's a refreshing prelude to any holiday meal, and it goes so well with the parmesan puffs (recipe follows).

> 3 cups fresh blood-orange juice (from about
>   10 oranges)
> ⅓ cup Grand Marnier or other orange-flavored liqueur
> 1 tablespoon plus 1 teaspoon sugar
> 1 (750-ml) bottle Prosecco, chilled well

▶ Stir together juice, liqueur, and sugar in a 2-quart pitcher until sugar is dissolved. Chill until cold, about 1 hour. Slowly pour in Prosecco, stirring to combine. Serve immediately.

COOKS' NOTE: Juice mixture, without Prosecco, can be chilled, covered, up to 1 day. Stir in Prosecco just before serving.

EGG NOODLE, CHARD, AND FONTINA TORTE

SERVES 8
ACTIVE TIME: 30 MIN   START TO FINISH: 2 HR

> ¼ cup olive oil
> 2 lb green Swiss chard, stems and center ribs discarded
> 1 large onion, halved lengthwise, then cut lengthwise into
>   ¼-inch-thick slices
> 2 garlic cloves, finely chopped
> 1¼ teaspoons salt
> ½ teaspoon black pepper
> ¼ lb dried egg fettuccine
> 8 large eggs
> 1 cup whole milk
> ⅔ cup mascarpone (5 oz)
> ½ lb Italian Fontina, rind discarded and cheese cut into
>   ½-inch cubes

SPECIAL EQUIPMENT: a 9- to 9½-inch (24-cm) springform pan

▶Put oven rack in middle position and preheat oven to 375°F. Grease pan with 2 teaspoons oil and wrap outside with foil.

▶Cook chard in a 5- to 6-quart pot of boiling salted water (see Tips, page 8), uncovered, until just tender, about 3 minutes. Transfer with a slotted spoon to a sieve set over a bowl. Reserve cooking water in pot. Press hard on chard to extract as much water as possible, then transfer to a cutting board and chop.

▶Cook onion in 3 tablespoons oil in a 12-inch heavy skillet over moderate heat, stirring occasionally, until softened and golden brown, about 15 minutes. Add garlic and cook, stirring, 1 minute. Stir in chard, ½ teaspoon salt, and ¼ teaspoon pepper and remove from heat. Cool chard mixture to warm.

▶While chard cools, return cooking water to a boil and cook fettuccine, uncovered, until al dente. Drain fettuccine in a colander, then transfer to a large bowl and toss with remaining teaspoon oil. Blend together eggs, milk, mascarpone, and remaining ¾ teaspoon salt and ¼ teaspoon pepper in a blender until smooth.

▶Stir chard and Fontina into pasta mixture, then stir in egg mixture. Pour into greased springform pan set in a large shallow baking pan (to catch any drips). Pat down chard to make surface even if necessary.

▶Bake until just set and top is golden brown, 50 minutes to 1 hour. Cool in springform pan on a rack 10 minutes, then run a small sharp knife around inside edge of pan to loosen torte. Remove side of pan and serve torte hot or warm.

COOKS' NOTES: Chard can be trimmed, washed, and dried 1 day ahead and chilled in a sealed plastic bag.
• Cheese can be cut 1 day ahead and chilled in a sealed bag.

FRISÉE AND CELERY SALAD WITH TOASTED FENNEL-SEED DRESSING

SERVES 8
ACTIVE TIME: 30 MIN   START TO FINISH: 30 MIN

2   teaspoons fennel seeds, toasted (see Tips, page 8)
¼   cup olive oil
3   tablespoons fresh lemon juice
3   tablespoons finely chopped shallot (1 large)
1   teaspoon salt
½   teaspoon sugar
½   lb frisée (French curly endive), torn into bite-size pieces (10 cups)
3   Belgian endives, cut crosswise into ½-inch-wide slices
3   celery ribs, thinly sliced crosswise (2 cups)

SPECIAL EQUIPMENT: an electric coffee/spice grinder

▶Grind fennel seeds in grinder until ground but not powdery. Transfer to a small bowl or cup, then stir in oil until combined. Let stand 15 minutes.

▶Whisk together lemon juice, shallot, salt, and sugar in another small bowl or cup until salt and sugar are dissolved. Stir fennel oil, then add to shallot mixture in a slow stream, whisking until combined.

▶Toss frisée, endives, and celery in a large bowl with just enough vinaigrette to coat.

COOKS' NOTES: Fennel oil can be made 1 day ahead and chilled, covered. Bring to room temperature before adding to shallot mixture.
• Frisée and celery can be washed and dried 1 day ahead and chilled in a sealed plastic bag lined with dampened paper towels.

FRIED BITTERSWEET CHOCOLATE BREAD

SERVES 8
ACTIVE TIME: 15 MIN   START TO FINISH: 15 MIN

Buttery and crunchy, with a rich, oozy center, these little sandwiches (a cross between panini and chocolate croissants) provide a sweet ending that can be prepared in just minutes.

½   stick (¼ cup) unsalted butter, softened
16   (½-inch-thick) baguette slices, cut on a long diagonal
1   (3- to 4-oz) fine-quality bittersweet chocolate bar (no more than 70% cacao if marked), broken into ½-inch pieces

▶Generously butter 1 side of each baguette slice. Place 8 slices, buttered sides down, on a work surface and cover each slice with chocolate, leaving a ¼-inch border around edge. Top with remaining 8 slices, buttered sides up, to make 8 sandwiches.

▶Heat a dry 12-inch heavy skillet (not nonstick) over moderate heat until hot but not smoking, then fry 4 sandwiches, turning over once, until golden, 3 to 4 minutes total. Transfer sandwiches to a plate and wipe skillet clean. Fry remaining sandwiches in same manner. Serve warm.

COOKS' NOTE: Sandwiches can be assembled 2 hours ahead and kept, covered with plastic wrap, at room temperature. Fry just before serving.

FOLLOWING PAGES: frisée and celery salad with toasted fennel-seed dressing; blood-orange mimosas; and egg noodle, chard, and Fontina torte (left); fried bittersweet chocolate bread (right)

MERRY
AND BRIGHT

A COCKTAIL PARTY FOR THE HOLIDAYS

SERVES 10 TO 12

**CRANBERRY GIN
AND TONICS**

**RED-LENTIL AND
RED-PEPPER PÂTÉ**

**CHORIZO AND POTATO
SPANISH TORTILLA BITES**

**PORK CORNETS WITH
SOUR-CHERRY SAUCE**

**GRILLED CHEESE WITH
SAUTÉED MUSHROOMS**

**CRISP CHOCOLATE
MARSHMALLOW SQUARES**

SCHRAMSBERG BRUT ROSÉ '03

CRANBERRY GIN AND TONICS

MAKES 10 DRINKS
ACTIVE TIME: 15 MIN   START TO FINISH: 2¼ HR (INCLUDES CHILLING)

Festive and beautiful, this cocktail is packed with real cranberry flavor. Forcing some of the berries through a sieve into the syrup intensifies the drink's fruitiness.

  2 (12-oz) bags fresh cranberries
  1 cup sugar
  ½ cup water
3⅓ cups chilled tonic water
1¼ cups gin
  3 tablespoons plus 1 teaspoon fresh lime juice

▶ Bring cranberries, sugar, and water to a simmer in a 3- to 3½-quart saucepan, then simmer, uncovered, stirring occasionally, until berries just begin to pop, about 2 minutes. Drain cranberries in a fine-mesh sieve set over a 1-quart glass measuring cup, then reserve 2 cups cranberries and force remaining berries through sieve into syrup. Discard solids remaining in sieve, then add reserved cranberries to syrup. Cool to room temperature. Transfer to a pitcher and chill until cold, about 2 hours.

▶ Add remaining ingredients to syrup, stirring gently to combine. Serve drinks over ice in 8- to 10-ounce glasses.

COOKS' NOTE: Cranberry syrup can be made 1 day ahead and chilled, covered. Add remaining ingredients just before serving.

RED-LENTIL AND RED-PEPPER PÂTÉ

SERVES 12

ACTIVE TIME: 1¼ HR   START TO FINISH: 10½ HR (INCLUDES CHILLING)

This vegetarian pâté, satisfyingly rich with a silky texture, will entice even the most die-hard carnivores. If you're not worried about keeping it vegetarian, you can substitute an equal amount of unflavored gelatin for the agar flakes.

FOR PÂTÉ

- ¾ stick (6 tablespoons) unsalted butter, softened
- 1 cup thinly sliced onions (2 medium)
- 3 large garlic cloves, chopped
- 1 Turkish or ½ California bay leaf
- 1¼ teaspoons salt
- 1½ teaspoons ground coriander
- 1 teaspoon paprika (not hot)
- 1 teaspoon smoked paprika (sweet or hot)
- ½ teaspoon black pepper
- ¼ teaspoon cayenne
- 1 cup dry white wine
- 1½ cups red lentils (10 oz), picked over and rinsed
- 2 cups water
- 1 tablespoon agar flakes (see Sources)
- 1 teaspoon balsamic vinegar
- 8 oz cream cheese, softened
- ¾ cup chopped bottled roasted red peppers (6 oz), patted dry
- 1 teaspoon finely chopped fresh oregano or marjoram

FOR TOPPING

- 1 tablespoon extra-virgin olive oil
- ¼ cup chopped bottled roasted red and/or yellow peppers (2 oz), patted dry
- 1 teaspoon balsamic vinegar
- 1 teaspoon finely chopped fresh oregano or marjoram

SPECIAL EQUIPMENT: **a 1-qt rectangular ceramic terrine; parchment paper**

ACCOMPANIMENT: **lightly toasted baguette slices**

MAKE PÂTÉ:

▶ Lightly oil terrine, then line bottom and ends with a strip of parchment paper, allowing at least 2 inches of overhang on each end of terrine.

▶ Heat 2 tablespoons butter in a 2- to 3-quart heavy saucepan over moderately high heat until foam subsides, then cook onions, garlic, bay leaf, and ½ teaspoon salt, stirring occasionally, until onions are golden brown, about 12 minutes.

▶ Meanwhile, stir together coriander, paprikas, black pepper, cayenne, and ½ teaspoon salt in a small bowl.

▶ Add spice mixture to onion mixture in saucepan and cook, stirring constantly, until very fragrant, about 1 minute. Add wine and bring to a simmer, uncovered, then reduce heat to low and add lentils, water, and agar flakes. Cover saucepan and simmer, stirring occasionally, 20 minutes. Remove lid and continue to cook, stirring occasionally, until lentils have fallen apart and mixture is thickened, about 20 minutes more. Stir in vinegar and discard bay leaf.

▶ Purée cream cheese, ½ cup red peppers, and remaining 4 tablespoons butter in a food processor until smooth. Add lentil mixture and remaining ¼ teaspoon salt and purée until smooth.

▶ Force mixture through a fine-mesh sieve into a bowl with a large rubber spatula, scraping sieve. Discard lentil skins. Stir in oregano and remaining ¼ cup red peppers. Pour mixture into terrine, smoothing top, and chill, loosely covered, at least 8 hours.

▶ Run a sharp paring knife along long sides of terrine, then invert a platter over terrine and invert pâté onto platter. Holding 1 end of parchment overhang against platter, lift off terrine. Discard parchment paper. Let pâté stand at room temperature 1 hour before serving.

MAKE TOPPING:

▶ Stir together oil, red and/or yellow peppers, vinegar, oregano, and salt and pepper to taste.

▶ Serve pâté topped with pepper mixture.

COOKS' NOTES: Pâté, without topping, can be chilled in terrine up to 2 days.

• Topping can be made 1 day ahead and chilled, covered.

PAGE 191, FROM TOP: chorizo and potato Spanish tortilla bites; pork cornets with sour-cherry sauce; grilled cheese with sautéed mushrooms; red-lentil and red-pepper pâté; and crisp chocolate marshmallow squares

CHORIZO AND POTATO SPANISH TORTILLA BITES

MAKES 64 HORS D'OEUVRES
ACTIVE TIME: 30 MIN   START TO FINISH: 1½ HR

Rest assured that your guests won't leave your party feeling hungry—these omeletlike hors d'oeuvres, not to be confused with Mexican flour tortillas, are as hearty as they are delicious.

- 1   bunch scallions
- 2   tablespoons extra-virgin olive oil
- 2   medium onions, chopped (1½ cups)
- 4   garlic cloves, finely chopped
- 1¼   teaspoons salt
- ½   teaspoon black pepper
- 6   oz Spanish chorizo (cured spiced pork sausage), cut into ¼-inch dice
- 1½   lb yellow-fleshed potatoes such as Yukon Gold (about 4 medium), peeled and cut into ¼-inch dice
- 9   large eggs
- ¾   cup sour cream
- 5   oz Manchego or white Cheddar, coarsely grated (2 cups)

▶ Put oven rack in middle position and preheat oven to 400°F. Lightly oil a 13- by 9-inch baking pan or dish.
▶ Finely chop white and green parts of scallions and reserve separately.
▶ Heat oil in a 12-inch heavy skillet over moderately high heat until hot but not smoking, then cook onions, garlic, white parts of scallions, ¾ teaspoon salt, and ¼ teaspoon pepper, stirring occasionally, until onions are golden, about 6 minutes. Add chorizo and cook, stirring occasionally, until just beginning to brown and release oil, about 4 minutes. Reduce heat to moderate, then stir in potatoes and cover skillet. Cook, stirring occasionally, until potatoes are tender, about 10 minutes. Transfer mixture to a large bowl and cool slightly.
▶ Whisk together eggs, sour cream, cheese, scallion greens, and remaining ½ teaspoon salt and ¼ teaspoon pepper in a bowl, then pour into baking pan. Sprinkle potato mixture over eggs (some potatoes will stick out). Bake until custard is set, about 20 minutes. Cool in pan on a rack to warm or room temperature. Trim ½ inch off each side, then cut tortilla into 1½- by 1-inch rectangles.

COOKS' NOTE: Tortilla can be baked 1 day ahead and cooled completely, uncovered, then chilled, covered. Cut into squares, then bring to room temperature before serving or reheat to warm in a preheated 325°F oven.

PORK CORNETS WITH SOUR-CHERRY SAUCE

MAKES ABOUT 40 HORS D'OEUVRES
ACTIVE TIME: 35 MIN   START TO FINISH: 4 HR (INCLUDES CHILLING)

- 2   teaspoons fennel seeds
- 2   teaspoons salt
- ½   teaspoon whole black peppercorns
- 2   (1-lb) pork tenderloins
- ½   lb shallots (about 7), peeled and halved lengthwise
- 2   tablespoons olive oil
- 2   cups dry red wine
- 1   cup dried sour cherries (5 oz)
- ½   cup sugar
- 2   (5-inch) sprigs fresh rosemary

SPECIAL EQUIPMENT: **an electric coffee/spice grinder; an instant-read thermometer**
GARNISH: **40 (1-inch) sprigs fresh rosemary or wooden picks**

▶ Put oven rack in middle position and preheat oven to 400°F.
▶ Very finely grind fennel seeds, salt, and peppercorns in grinder, then rub all over pork.
▶ Toss shallots with oil in a 13- by 9-inch flameproof roasting pan, then nestle tenderloins among shallots (without crowding) and roast until thermometer inserted into thickest end of pork registers 155°F, about 30 to 35 minutes. Put 2 layers of foil on a work surface and transfer pork to foil. Cool to room temperature, about 1 hour, then wrap in foil and chill until cold, about 2 hours.
▶ While pork cools, put roasting pan with shallots over a burner, then add wine and deglaze pan by boiling, stirring and scraping up any brown bits with a wooden spoon, 1 minute. Transfer mixture to a 2- to 2½-quart heavy saucepan. Add cherries, sugar, and rosemary and boil until liquid is reduced to about 2 cups, 15 to 20 minutes. Discard rosemary sprigs (do not discard any leaves that have fallen off stems). Transfer mixture to a food processor and pulse until coarsely chopped. Transfer to a bowl and chill, uncovered, until cold, about 1½ hours.
▶ Cut chilled pork with a carving knife or an electric meat slicer diagonally into ⅛-inch-thick slices. Roll up each slice into a cornet (cone) shape and pierce in center with a rosemary sprig to secure. Fill opening of each cornet with about ½ teaspoon cherry sauce. Discard rosemary sprigs when eating.

COOKS' NOTES: Pork and cherry sauce can be chilled separately up to 1 day. Cover cherry sauce after 1½ hours of chilling.
• For a more casual presentation, serve the pork slices on a platter with the sauce on the side.

GRILLED CHEESE WITH SAUTÉED MUSHROOMS

MAKES 32 HORS D'OEUVRES
ACTIVE TIME: 45 MIN   START TO FINISH: 1¼ HR

1¼ sticks (10 tablespoons) unsalted butter
1 lb cremini mushrooms, trimmed and chopped
½ teaspoon salt
¼ teaspoon black pepper
⅓ cup dry white wine
½ lb chilled Italian Fontina, rind discarded and cheese
   coarsely grated (2 cups)
2 tablespoons finely chopped fresh flat-leaf parsley
16 very thin slices firm white sandwich bread
   About ½ teaspoon white-truffle oil (optional)

▸ Heat 2 tablespoons butter in a 12-inch heavy nonstick skillet over moderately high heat until foam subsides, then cook mushrooms with salt and pepper, stirring occasionally, until liquid mushrooms give off is evaporated, about 8 minutes. Add wine and boil, stirring occasionally, until liquid is evaporated, about 5 minutes. Cool mushrooms to room temperature, about 10 minutes.
▸ Toss mushrooms with cheese and parsley in a bowl.
▸ Divide cheese mixture among 8 slices of bread (a scant ½ cup per slice), spreading evenly, then top with remaining 8 slices.
▸ Heat 1 tablespoon butter in cleaned skillet over moderate heat until foam subsides, then cook 2 sandwiches, without turning over, until undersides are browned, about 3 minutes. Transfer sandwiches to a cutting board. Heat 1 tablespoon butter in skillet until foam subsides, then return sandwiches, browned sides up, to skillet and cook until undersides are browned, about 3 minutes more, transferring back to cutting board as cooked. Make 3 more batches in same manner.
▸ Trim off crusts and cut each sandwich into 4 triangles. Top each triangle with a drop of truffle oil (if using).

COOKS' NOTE: Sandwiches can be assembled (but not cooked) 3 hours ahead and chilled, stacked and wrapped in plastic wrap.

CRISP CHOCOLATE MARSHMALLOW SQUARES

MAKES ABOUT 60 SQUARES
ACTIVE TIME: 30 MIN   START TO FINISH: 3 HR (INCLUDES COOLING)

FOR GANACHE
5 oz fine-quality bittersweet chocolate (no more than 60% cacao if marked), chopped
3 oz fine-quality bittersweet chocolate (70% cacao), chopped
¾ cup heavy cream
2 tablespoons Tía Maria, Kahlúa, or other coffee-flavored liqueur
1 tablespoon instant-espresso powder or instant-coffee granules

FOR MARSHMALLOW SQUARES
¼ lb marshmallows (15 individual large marshmallows or 2 cups small)
2 tablespoons unsalted butter
2 tablespoons sugar
2 tablespoons unsweetened cocoa powder
⅛ teaspoon salt
3 cups puffed-rice cereal such as Rice Krispies

MAKE GANACHE:
▸ Melt chocolates with cream, liqueur, and espresso powder in a metal bowl set over a saucepan of barely simmering water or in top of a double boiler, whisking occasionally, until smooth, 6 to 8 minutes. Remove from heat and let stand at room temperature until thickened, about 2 hours.

MAKE MARSHMALLOW SQUARES:
▸ Line a 13- by 9-inch baking pan with a long sheet of foil, leaving a 1-inch overhang on each end.
▸ Melt marshmallows and butter with sugar, cocoa powder, and salt in a 2½- to 3-quart heavy saucepan over low heat, stirring frequently, until smooth, 3 to 5 minutes.
▸ Remove from heat and gently stir in puffed-rice cereal. Transfer to lined baking pan, pressing mixture evenly onto bottom with dampened fingertips. Cool to room temperature, about 20 minutes, then carefully lift from pan by grasping both ends of foil. Peel off and discard foil, then cut into 1-inch squares.
▸ Spread some of ganache on half of squares, using about ½ teaspoon ganache each, then top with remaining squares. Reheat remaining ganache in metal bowl over barely simmering water, whisking occasionally, until loosened, then drizzle over tops of squares (you will have some ganache left over).
▸ Let squares stand until set, about 15 minutes.

COOKS' NOTE: Marshmallow squares with ganache can be made 1 day ahead and chilled, covered with plastic wrap after ganache is set. Bring to room temperature, uncovered, before serving.

CRIMSON TIDINGS

A LAVISH CHRISTMAS FEAST

SERVES 8

VEUVE CLICQUOT-PONSARDIN '99

**LOBSTER GELÉES WITH
FRESH TARRAGON OIL**

LOBSTER CLAW TOASTS

PARAISO EAGLE'S PERCH
CHARDONNAY '03

BEET CONSOMMÉ

LIVER AND MUSHROOM PIROZHKI

**PRIME RIB ROAST WITH
RED-WINE SAUCE**

POMMES DUCHESSE GRATIN

GLAZED RED PEARL ONIONS

**RED SALAD WITH CHAMPAGNE
VINAIGRETTE**

MARSTON FAMILY VINEYARD
SPRING MOUNTAIN CABERNET
SAUVIGNON '02

**QUINCE APPLE STRUDELS
WITH QUINCE SYRUP**

STAR-FRUIT CHIPS

LOLONIS CUVÉE EUGENIA LATE
HARVEST SAUVIGNON BLANC

LOBSTER GELÉES WITH FRESH TARRAGON OIL

SERVES 8

ACTIVE TIME: 1¾ HR   START TO FINISH: 5¼ HR (INCLUDES MAKING
TARRAGON OIL)

*This dramatic first course won't soon be forgotten. Chunks of
sweet lobster meat bound by a shimmering jelly of fennel-
and-tarragon-scented lobster stock promises the most pristine
lobster salad you'll ever taste.*

8   qt water
4   (1¼-lb) live lobsters
1   cup dry white wine
3   carrots, chopped
2   celery ribs, chopped
1   fennel bulb (sometimes labeled "anise") with fronds,
     stalks, and bulb chopped and fronds reserved for
     fresh tarragon oil (recipe follows)
1   medium onion, finely chopped
3   large garlic cloves, minced
3   (6-inch) plus 8 (1-inch) sprigs fresh tarragon
1   teaspoon salt
¼   teaspoon fennel seeds, slightly crushed
¼   teaspoon dried hot red-pepper flakes
2½ teaspoons unflavored gelatin (from two ¼-oz envelopes)
1½ teaspoons tarragon white-wine vinegar
⅓   cup fresh tarragon oil (recipe follows)

SPECIAL EQUIPMENT: a 10- to 12-qt pot; heavy-duty (sometimes
labeled "fine") cheesecloth; 8 (5- to 6-oz) baba au rhum molds
or ramekins
ACCOMPANIMENT: lobster claw toasts (page 197)

COOK LOBSTERS AND MAKE STOCK:

▶ Bring 6 quarts water to a boil in pot, then plunge 2 lobsters
headfirst into water and cook, covered, 8 minutes from time
they enter water. Transfer with tongs to a shallow baking pan
to cool. Return water to a boil and cook remaining 2 lobsters
in same manner.

▶ When lobsters are cool enough to handle, remove meat from
tail and claws and set aside. Cut tail shells and lobster bodies
(not including claws) into 1-inch pieces with kitchen shears,
then rinse well, discarding gills, eye sacs, tomalley, any roe, and
claw shells. Transfer to a 6- to 8-quart heavy pot, then add wine,
carrots, celery, fennel, onion, garlic, large tarragon sprigs, salt,
fennel seeds, red-pepper flakes, and remaining 2 quarts water
and bring to a boil. Reduce heat and simmer, uncovered, until
liquid is reduced to about 6 cups, about 1½ hours.

▶ While stock reduces, scrape any coagulated white albumin
from lobster meat with a knife and cut meat into ½-inch pieces,
then chill, covered.

MAKE GELÉES:

▶ Pour stock through a dampened cheesecloth-lined large
sieve into a large bowl, pressing on and then discarding solids.
Transfer 2¾ cups stock to a bowl. (Cool remaining stock
completely, uncovered, then freeze in an airtight container for
another use.) Sprinkle gelatin evenly over ¼ cup stock in a
1-quart saucepan, then let stand 1 minute to soften. Heat over
moderately low heat, stirring, just until gelatin is dissolved, then
stir in vinegar and remaining 2½ cups stock.

▶ Put molds in a baking pan. Add 2 teaspoons gelatin mixture to
each mold and freeze until set, about 10 minutes. Put 1 small
sprig of tarragon and a tip of claw meat in bottom of each mold,
then divide lobster meat among molds. Fill with remaining
gelatin mixture and chill, covered with plastic wrap, until set,
at least 2 hours.

▶ To unmold, dip 1 mold in a pan of hot water 3 to 5 seconds to
loosen. Run a thin knife around edge of mold and invert gelée
out onto a plate. Repeat with remaining molds. Drizzle plates
with fresh tarragon oil.

COOKS' NOTE: Gelées can be chilled in molds up to 2 days.

FRESH TARRAGON OIL

MAKES ABOUT ⅓ CUP

ACTIVE TIME: 10 MIN   START TO FINISH: 10 MIN

Beautifully bright green, this herbaceous oil really enhances the anise flavor in the lobster gelées (recipe precedes).

½ cup chopped fresh tarragon
½ cup chopped fennel fronds
½ cup mild olive oil
¼ teaspoon salt

▶ Purée herbs, oil, and salt in a blender until smooth, then pour through a fine-mesh sieve into a bowl, pressing hard on and then discarding solids. Chill if not using immediately.

COOKS' NOTE: Oil can be made 2 days ahead and chilled, covered. Bring to room temperature before using.

LOBSTER CLAW TOASTS

MAKES ABOUT 16

ACTIVE TIME: 5 MIN   START TO FINISH: 20 MIN

Salty, crunchy bites, tasting of the sea, complement the lobster gelées' delicate, melting texture.

1 (12-inch) length thin baguette (about 2 inches in diameter)
2½ tablespoons extra-virgin olive oil
1 scant tablespoon coarse sea salt (preferably flaky)

▶ Put oven rack in middle position and preheat oven to 350°F.
▶ Cut baguette with a serrated knife on a long diagonal into ⅛-inch-thick slices (about 5 to 6 inches long). Cut a lengthwise slit about 3 inches long from center through edge of a slice, then cross ends, overlapping them, to form a "claw." Repeat with remaining slices. Brush both sides of slices with oil and arrange in 1 layer on a large baking sheet, then sprinkle with sea salt.
▶ Bake until crisp and golden, about 15 minutes. Cool on a rack.

COOKS' NOTES: If sea salt is very coarse, crush it lightly.
• Toasts can be made 3 days ahead and kept in an airtight container at room temperature.

OPPOSITE: red salad with Champagne vinaigrette

BEET CONSOMMÉ

SERVES 8

ACTIVE TIME: 30 MIN   START TO FINISH: 3¼ HR

This is a more refined version of borscht, the Slavic classic. Often, borscht's underlying flavor comes from using ham or a beef broth, but here smoked turkey becomes the secret ingredient, imparting a smoky depth that's not too heavy.

3 lb medium beets without greens (8 medium; about 4 lb with greens), scrubbed well and trimmed, leaving 1 inch of stems attached
4 qt water
1¼ to 1½ lb smoked turkey legs or wings
2 carrots, cut into ½-inch pieces
2 celery ribs, cut into ½-inch pieces
1 large onion, cut into ½-inch pieces
1 garlic clove, smashed
4 sprigs fresh dill plus 2 tablespoons chopped fresh dill
1 Turkish or ½ California bay leaf
1 teaspoon salt
¼ teaspoon whole black peppercorns
2 teaspoons fresh lemon juice
2 teaspoons sugar

SPECIAL EQUIPMENT: heavy-duty (sometimes labeled "fine") cheesecloth
ACCOMPANIMENT: liver and mushroom *pirozhki* (page 198)

▶ Boil beets, covered, in water (4 quarts) in a 6- to 8-quart pot over moderate heat until tender, about 40 minutes. Transfer beets with a slotted spoon to a plate to cool slightly, reserving cooking water. When beets are cool enough to handle, slip off skins. Cut 1 beet into ¼-inch dice and reserve for garnish. Cut remaining beets into ½-inch pieces and return to cooking liquid in pot. Add turkey, carrots, celery, onion, garlic, dill sprigs, bay leaf, salt, and peppercorns and simmer, partially covered, 1½ to 2 hours. Pour soup through a dampened cheesecloth-lined sieve set into a 3-quart heavy saucepan, discarding solids. Measure soup: If there is more than 6 cups, boil in cleaned pot until reduced; if there is less, add enough water to total 6 cups.
▶ Skim fat from consommé, then add lemon juice and sugar and heat until hot.
▶ Divide diced beet and chopped dill among 8 shallow soup plates and ladle consommé on top.

COOKS' NOTE: Consommé, without diced beet and chopped dill, can be made 1 week ahead and cooled completely, uncovered, then chilled, covered.

LIVER AND MUSHROOM PIROZHKI

MAKES 32

ACTIVE TIME: 1 HR   START TO FINISH: 3 HR

The Russian version of pierogies, pirozhki *are small turnovers that are baked rather than boiled. Their savory, rich mushroom-and-liver filling packs a big punch within a crisp little pastry.*

FOR DOUGH

1½   cups all-purpose flour plus additional for rolling out dough
  1   stick (½ cup) cold unsalted butter, cut into ½-inch cubes
  1   teaspoon salt
      Pinch of sugar
  7   tablespoons sour cream
  1   large egg beaten with 1 tablespoon water for egg wash

FOR FILLING

  ½   small onion, finely chopped
  ½   lb cremini mushrooms, finely chopped (1¼ cups)
  3   tablespoons unsalted butter
  ¼   lb chicken livers, rinsed, trimmed, and finely chopped
  ¼   teaspoon salt
  ⅛   teaspoon black pepper

SPECIAL EQUIPMENT: **a (2½-inch) round cookie or biscuit cutter**

MAKE DOUGH:

▶ Blend together flour, butter, salt, and sugar in a bowl with your fingertips or a pastry blender (or pulse in a food processor) just until mixture resembles coarse meal with some roughly pea-size butter lumps. Stir in sour cream with a fork just until a dough forms. Turn out dough on a lightly floured work surface and roll out with a lightly floured rolling pin into a 6- by 4-inch rectangle. Fold into thirds like a letter, then roll out and fold in same manner 2 more times. Chill dough, wrapped in plastic wrap, until firm, at least 1 hour.

MAKE FILLING:

▶ Cook onion and mushrooms in butter in a 10-inch heavy skillet over moderate heat, stirring occasionally, until browned well and mushrooms are completely dry, about 15 minutes. Add livers and cook, stirring frequently, until just browned, 2 to 3 minutes. Cool slightly, then pulse in food processor just until mixture holds together. Stir in salt and pepper and cool completely, uncovered, about 20 minutes.

ASSEMBLE AND BAKE *PIROZHKI:*

▶ Put oven rack in middle position and preheat oven to 375°F.
▶ Roll out dough on a lightly floured work surface with a lightly floured rolling pin into a roughly 13-inch round (⅛ inch thick). Cut out rounds with cutter. Put 1 level teaspoon filling in center of 1 round, then fold round over filling to form a half moon, pressing edges with your fingers to seal. Repeat with remaining

rounds and filling in same manner, rerolling and cutting scraps once. Arrange ½ inch apart on an ungreased baking sheet, then brush tops of dough lightly with egg wash. Bake until *pirozhki* are golden, about 25 minutes (edges will open slightly during baking). Cool on a rack to warm, about 15 minutes.

COOKS' NOTES: Dough can be chilled up to 2 days.
• Filling can be made 2 days ahead and cooled completely, uncovered, then chilled, covered.
• *Pirozhki* can be assembled (but not baked) and chilled on a baking sheet, covered, up to 1 day or frozen on baking sheet until frozen hard, then gently transferred to a sealed plastic bag and kept, frozen, up to 1 week. Thaw on baking sheet 30 minutes before baking.

PRIME RIB ROAST WITH RED-WINE SAUCE

SERVES 8
ACTIVE TIME: 1 HR   START TO FINISH: 3¾ HR

This luscious cut of meat definitely has a celebratory presence. For the best flavor, look for well-marbled meat.

FOR ROAST
1   (4-rib) prime rib roast with ribs (sometimes called standing rib roast; 9 to 10 lb)
½   oz (2 tablespoons) dried porcini mushrooms, ground to a powder in a blender
1   tablespoon kosher salt
¾   teaspoon black pepper

FOR SAUCE
2   small onions (1 left unpeeled and halved lengthwise, and 1 peeled and chopped)
¾   stick (6 tablespoons) unsalted butter
⅔   cup chopped shallots (about 3 large)
1   carrot, finely chopped
1   celery rib, finely chopped
2   garlic cloves, smashed
1   tablespoon tomato paste
2   sprigs fresh flat-leaf parsley
1   sprig fresh thyme
1   Turkish or ½ California bay leaf
4   black peppercorns
1   (750-ml) bottle dry red wine such as a good-quality Côtes du Rhône
½   oz dried porcini mushrooms
2   cups boiling-hot water
⅔   cup veal demi-glace
½   teaspoon salt

SPECIAL EQUIPMENT: **an instant-read thermometer**

COOK ROAST:
▶ Let roast stand at room temperature 1 hour.
▶ Put oven rack in middle position and preheat oven to 450°F. Trim all but a thin layer of fat from roast, then rub roast all over with porcini powder, salt, and pepper. Transfer to a rack set in a 13- by 9-inch roasting pan. Roast beef 20 minutes, then reduce temperature to 350°F and roast until thermometer inserted into center of meat registers 110°F, 1½ to 2 hours more. Transfer to a large platter and let stand, uncovered, 30 minutes. (Internal temperature of meat will rise to 130°F for medium-rare.)

PREPARE SAUCE WHILE MEAT COMES TO ROOM TEMPERATURE AND ROASTS:
▶ Cook halved onion, cut sides down, undisturbed, in 1 tablespoon butter in a 2-quart heavy nonreactive saucepan (see cooks' note, below) over moderate heat until browned well, about 4 minutes. Add chopped onion, shallots, carrot, celery, garlic, and 2 tablespoons butter and reduce heat to moderately low, then cook, covered, stirring occasionally, until chopped vegetables are softened, 8 to 10 minutes. Add tomato paste, herbs, bay leaf, peppercorns, and 2 cups wine and boil, uncovered, over moderately high heat until liquid is reduced to about ¼ cup, 25 to 30 minutes. Pour through a fine-mesh sieve set into another 2-quart heavy saucepan, pressing on and then discarding solids.
▶ While wine reduces, soak porcini in boiling-hot water (2 cups) in a bowl until softened, about 20 minutes. Drain porcini in a paper-towel-lined sieve set over a bowl and reserve soaking liquid. Rinse porcini and pat dry, then finely chop. Set aside.
▶ Add porcini-soaking liquid, demi-glace, and remaining 1¾ cups wine to reduced liquid in saucepan and boil, uncovered, over moderately high heat, skimming off froth occasionally, until reduced to about 2 cups, 20 to 35 minutes. Stir in reserved porcini, then reduce heat to low and whisk in ½ teaspoon salt, any juices from meat accumulated on platter, and remaining 3 tablespoons butter until incorporated.
▶ Slice roast across the grain and serve with sauce on the side.

COOKS' NOTES: Red-wine sauce can be made 2 days ahead and cooled completely, uncovered, then chilled, covered. Reheat before using.
• Stainless steel, glass, and enameled cast iron are nonreactive; avoid pure aluminum and uncoated iron, which can impart an unpleasant taste and color to recipes with acidic ingredients.

POMMES DUCHESSE GRATIN

Creamy Mashed Potato Gratin

SERVES 8

ACTIVE TIME: 25 MIN   START TO FINISH: 2 HR

  3   lb russet (baking) potatoes
  1   cup heavy cream
  5   tablespoons unsalted butter
  1   garlic clove, minced
  3   large eggs
1¼   teaspoons salt
  ¼   teaspoon white pepper
  ⅛   teaspoon freshly grated nutmeg

SPECIAL EQUIPMENT: **a potato ricer or a food mill fitted with medium disk**

▸ Put oven rack in middle position and preheat oven to 400°F.
▸ Prick each potato a few times, then bake in a shallow baking pan until tender, about 1 hour.
▸ When potatoes are just cool enough to handle, halve and scoop out flesh. Force flesh through ricer or food mill into a bowl.
▸ Heat cream with butter and garlic in a 3-quart heavy saucepan over moderately low heat until hot, then stir into potatoes. Beat in eggs 1 at a time with a fork until blended, then stir in salt, white pepper, and nutmeg. Spoon mixture into a buttered 2-quart (10-inch) round or oval shallow gratin or casserole dish. Bake until top is puffed and golden, 30 to 40 minutes.

COOKS' NOTES: Gratin can be prepared (but not baked) 1 day ahead and cooled completely, uncovered, then chilled, its surface covered with buttered wax paper and dish wrapped in plastic wrap. Bring to room temperature, about 1 hour, before baking.
• If you have only one oven, bake gratin while rib roast stands.

GLAZED RED PEARL ONIONS

SERVES 8 (MAKES ABOUT 4 CUPS)

ACTIVE TIME: 1½ HR   START TO FINISH: 2½ HR

2½   lb fresh red pearl onions
  ¾   cup apple juice
  ¾   cup reduced-sodium chicken broth
  2   tablespoons unsalted butter
  2   (4-inch) sprigs fresh thyme
  ½   teaspoon salt
  ¼   teaspoon black pepper

GARNISH: **fresh thyme leaves for sprinkling**

▸ Blanch pearl onions in a 6- to 8-quart pot of boiling water 1 minute, then drain in a colander. When onions are cool enough to handle, peel.
▸ Cook onions with remaining ingredients, covered, in a 12-inch heavy skillet over moderately low heat, shaking pan occasionally, until onions are tender and glazed and most of liquid is evaporated, about 45 minutes. Discard thyme.

COOKS' NOTES: Onions can be blanched and peeled (but not cooked) 2 days ahead and chilled, covered.
• Onions can be cooked 1 day ahead and cooled completely, uncovered, then chilled, covered. Reheat over low heat, about 10 minutes, before serving.

RED SALAD WITH CHAMPAGNE VINAIGRETTE

SERVES 8 TO 10

ACTIVE TIME: 20 MIN   START TO FINISH: 20 MIN

We were surprised at how many different varieties of gorgeous red lettuces and red greens we were able to find to create this visually stunning salad. Tossed with a simple vinaigrette, it is a lovely counterpoint to the richness of the meat and potatoes.

  2   tablespoons Champagne vinegar
  ½   teaspoon salt
  ¼   teaspoon black pepper
  ¼   cup plus 1 tablespoon mild olive oil (preferably French)
  8   cups loosely packed mixed young red lettuces such as red leaf, lolla rossa, red oak, and red romaine, torn into bite-size pieces if large
  4   cups loosely packed mixed young red greens such as red endive, baby kale and chard, radicchio di Treviso, and red mustard, torn into bite-size pieces if large

▸ Whisk together vinegar, salt, and pepper in a large bowl, then add oil in a slow stream, whisking until emulsified. Add lettuces and greens and toss to coat. Serve immediately.

COOKS' NOTE: Lettuces and greens can be washed and dried 1 day ahead and chilled in sealed plastic bags lined with paper towels.

OPPOSITE: quince apple strudel with quince syrup and star chips

QUINCE APPLE STRUDELS WITH QUINCE SYRUP

MAKES 2 (10-INCH) STRUDELS
ACTIVE TIME: 1¾ HR   START TO FINISH: 5½ HR

Served with small scoops of ice cream and a pink-hued syrup, this fruit-filled dessert delivers a glorious finale to a special dinner. Strudel dough looks more difficult to make than it really is. The secret is using bread flour, a high-gluten flour, which allows you to stretch a small amount of dough over a large surface.

FOR QUINCE SYRUP AND FILLING

- 2   lb quinces (4 or 5), peeled, quartered, cored, and cut into ¾-inch pieces
- Reserved syrup from star-fruit chips (recipe follows; see cooks' note, below, if not making)
- ½   vanilla bean, halved lengthwise
- 1   (4- by 1-inch) strip fresh lemon zest plus 1 teaspoon finely grated (see Tips, page 8)
- 2   lb Gala apples (4 or 5), peeled, cored, and cut into ¾-inch pieces
- ½   stick (¼ cup) unsalted butter, melted
- ¼   teaspoon salt
- ½   cup sugar
- 1   cup soft dried tart cherries (6 oz)
- 1   tablespoon fresh lemon juice
- 1   slice firm white sandwich bread
- ½   cup slivered almonds (2 oz), lightly toasted (see Tips, page 8)

FOR DOUGH

- 2   cups bread flour
- 1   tablespoon granulated sugar
- ½   teaspoon salt
- 1   large egg yolk
- ¾   cup lukewarm water
- 1¼   sticks (10 tablespoons) unsalted butter, melted and cooled slightly
- About ½ cup all-purpose flour for rubbing into cloth
- ¼   cup confectioners sugar

SPECIAL EQUIPMENT: a stand mixer fitted with paddle attachment; parchment paper; a (36-inch) round or square work table; a cotton sheet or smooth, lint-free tablecloth large enough to hang over edge of table; a small blowtorch (optional)
ACCOMPANIMENT: 1 qt store-bought premium vanilla ice cream; star-fruit chips (recipe follows)

MAKE QUINCE SYRUP AND FILLING:

▶ Combine quince with reserved star-fruit syrup in a 3-quart heavy saucepan and bring to a boil, stirring until sugar is dissolved. Scrape seeds from vanilla bean into mixture, then add pod and strip of zest. Reduce heat and simmer, partially covered, until quince is very tender and begins to turn pinkish, 50 to 60 minutes.

▶ While quince is simmering, put oven rack in middle position and preheat oven to 400°F.

▶ Meanwhile, toss apples with butter, finely grated zest, salt, and ¼ cup sugar in a large shallow baking pan until coated well, spreading in an even layer. Roast, stirring occasionally, until apples are very tender and any liquid they release is evaporated, 45 minutes to 1 hour.

▶ Pour quince mixture into a large sieve set over a bowl, discarding pod and zest, and reserve syrup. If syrup measures more than 1 cup, return to saucepan and boil until reduced to about 1 cup; if less, add enough water to total 1 cup. Cool syrup completely.

▶ Stir together quince and cherries in a large bowl. Fold roasted apples and lemon juice into quince mixture and cool to room temperature, stirring occasionally, about 30 minutes.

▶ Pulse bread in a blender or food processor to fine crumbs, then add nuts and remaining ¼ cup sugar and pulse just until nuts are finely chopped. Set aside.

MAKE DOUGH WHILE APPLES ROAST:

▶ Stir together bread flour, granulated sugar, and salt in bowl of mixer, then make a well in center and add yolk, lukewarm water, and 2 tablespoons melted butter. Beat at medium speed until dough becomes silky and elastic, and then forms a soft sticky ball that comes away from side of bowl, 8 to 10 minutes.

▶ Turn dough out onto a lightly floured surface and form into a ball. Lightly brush with some melted butter, then cover with a warmed inverted bowl (rinse bowl with hot water to warm and dry) and let stand 1 to 1¼ hours to let the gluten relax and make stretching easier.

STRETCH DOUGH:

▶ Put oven rack in middle position and preheat oven to 375°F. Line a large baking sheet (17 by 13 inches) with parchment paper. In a draft-free room, cover work table with sheet, then rub all-purpose flour into sheet all over, except overhang.

▶ Put dough in center of table and stretch it into a 12-inch round with your fingers. Using floured backs of hands (remove all rings, bracelets, and watches), reach under dough and begin gently stretching and thinning dough from center out to edges, moving around table as you work and intermittently stretching and thinning thicker edges slightly. Gradually stretch dough paper-thin into at least a 36-inch square (square will hang over edge of table), letting it rest for a few minutes whenever it resists stretching and occasionally reflouring hands. (Stretching may take as long as 20 minutes; try not to make any holes in dough, but if you do, cut off pieces from overhang to patch them.) Let dough stand 5 minutes to dry.

ASSEMBLE STRUDELS:

▶ Very gently brush dough with ⅓ cup melted butter and sprinkle evenly with reserved almond mixture. Mound filling in 2 (11- by 3-inch) strips, end to end, along edge of dough nearest you, leaving 3 inches between strips and a 4-inch border along sides and edge of dough nearest you. Cut off dough overhang to table edge with kitchen shears. Fold edge of dough nearest you over filling, and, holding sheet tautly, use sheet to make dough roll over filling, away from you.

▶ Brush strudel all over with remaining melted butter and cut into 2 pieces through space between mounds. Using 2 metal spatulas, carefully transfer strudels to baking sheet, arranging them 4 inches apart, and sprinkle with 2 tablespoons confectioners sugar. Cut 3 or 4 steam vents about 2 inches apart in top of each strudel and bake until golden, 40 to 45 minutes. Cool for 10 minutes on sheet on a rack, then carefully transfer to rack and cool to warm or room temperature, about 30 minutes. Dust evenly with remaining 2 tablespoons confectioners sugar. If desired, carefully move blowtorch flame evenly back and forth over sugar until sugar is melted and caramelized.

▶ Cut strudels into 2-inch-wide pieces and serve with ice cream and star-fruit chips. Drizzle with reserved quince syrup.

COOKS' NOTES: To make syrup (if not making star-fruit chips), bring 2 cups water and 2 cups sugar to a boil in a 3-quart heavy saucepan, stirring until sugar is dissolved, then add quince and proceed with recipe.

• Quince syrup and filling (including apples and cherries) can be made 3 days ahead and cooled completely, uncovered, then chilled, covered. Bring to room temperature before using.

• Nut mixture can be made 2 days ahead and kept in an airtight container at room temperature.

• Strudels are best eaten the same day they're made but can be made 1 day ahead and kept at room temperature, covered. Reheat in a preheated 350°F oven 15 minutes.

• Strudels can be assembled (but not baked) and frozen on baking sheet, covered tightly with foil, until frozen hard, then kept frozen, wrapped in parchment and then foil, 2 weeks ahead. Thaw, uncovered, on baking sheet at least 1 hour before baking.

STAR-FRUIT CHIPS
MAKES ABOUT 32 CHIPS
ACTIVE TIME: 10 MIN START TO FINISH: 2¼ HR

2 firm-ripe yellow star fruit (½ lb total)
2 cups sugar
2 cups water

SPECIAL EQUIPMENT: an adjustable-blade slicer; a 17- by 11-inch nonstick bakeware liner such as Silpat

▶ Slice star fruit crosswise with slicer into 1⁄16-inch-thick slices.

▶ Bring sugar and water to a boil in a 2-quart heavy saucepan, stirring until sugar is dissolved. Add star fruit, then remove from heat and let stand, uncovered, 15 minutes. Pour star fruit into a sieve set over a bowl and drain 15 minutes. Reserve syrup for strudel (recipe precedes).

▶ Put oven rack in middle position and preheat oven to 200°F. Put liner on a large (17- by 11-inch) baking sheet, then arrange star-fruit slices in 1 layer on liner (discard extra along with any broken slices). Bake until dry, 1 to 1¼ hours. Immediately transfer chips to a rack to cool.

COOKS' NOTE: Chips can be made 1 week ahead and cooled completely, uncovered, then layered between sheets of wax paper in an airtight container at room temperature. Chill syrup, covered.

GAME PLAN

2 WEEKS AHEAD
-Assemble and freeze strudels

1 WEEK AHEAD
-Make consommé
-Assemble and freeze *pirozhki*
-Make star-fruit chips

3 DAYS AHEAD
-Make toasts

2 DAYS AHEAD
-Make lobster gelées
-Make tarragon oil
-Make wine sauce for roast
-Blanch and peel onions

1 DAY AHEAD
-Prepare gratin (do not bake)
-Wash and dry lettuces and greens for salad
-Cook onions

CHRISTMAS DAY

6 HOURS AHEAD
-Thaw and bake strudels

4 HOURS AHEAD
-Bring beef to room temperature, then roast

2 HOURS AHEAD
-Bring gratin to room temperature, then bake while beef stands

1 HOUR AHEAD
-Thaw and bake *pirozhki*

JUST BEFORE SERVING
-Unmold gelées and drizzle plates with tarragon oil
-Reheat consommé
-Reheat wine sauce
-Reheat glazed onions
-Make salad

THE RECIPE COMPENDIUM

Since this volume is all about sharing our favorite dishes, we'd like to draw your attention to the last chapter of this section where you'll find our recipe for pastry dough. Perfected after years of experimenting, it rolls out like a dream, and bakes into a tender, flaky, buttery crust. It's the ideal embrace for any fruit, or, if sweets aren't your thing, you can use this dough for a savory pot pie. And it comes together equally well whether you mix it by hand or whiz it in a food processor. This dough will never let you down.

In fact, this entire section is brimming with recipes that you'll find so easy and delicious that you'll make them again and again. Imagine quick-cooking pork chops bathed in a deeply flavored balsamic glaze, or bacon-wrapped salmon, which gets an extra jolt of flavor and moistness from a dab of coarse-grain mustard. Or chicken with black-pepper maple sauce: Friends and family will rave about its crisp skin and juicy, sweet-spicy meat, and you'll love how quickly and evenly it cooks because the whole chicken is spatchcocked, or flattened, allowing more of the bird to come in direct contact with a hot skillet.

Like our readers, we realize that serious cooking doesn't happen only in the kitchen. You'll find many grilling recipes that merit a trip outside, no matter the season. Garlicky lamb kebabs, burgers stuffed with salty tapenade, and arctic char in a smoky chipotle-lime sauce are just a few dishes you'll find here.

And because every cook seeks exceptional one-dish meals that can be put on the table in minutes, not hours, we've also included many recipes from our Ten-Minute Mains column. In just ten minutes of active time, you can pull together dinners like spicy wok shrimp, scallop chowder with bacon, or *straccetti di manzo*, a classic Roman dish of sliced steak and warm dressing laid over pungent arugula. These quick recipes (and any other recipe that takes thirty minutes or less) are indicated in the index by a clock symbol.

Vegetarian dishes are also denoted in the index, by a V. With recipes for steaming calzones stuffed with arugula and ricotta, cheesy quiche studded with roasted poblano chiles, and fettuccine tossed with a woodsy mix of wild mushrooms, you'll be able to mix up your meal plans and take a break from meat dishes. Plus, you'll always be ready for vegetarian guests.

And, of course, that fabulous pastry dough isn't the only gem you'll find in the desserts chapter. The pomegranate gelato is heavenly, as are the passion-fruit gelée with basil cream and moist lemon olive-oil cake, which boasts such an intriguing fruitiness you won't believe it's made with only five ingredients.

As you can see, this delicious collection is filled with classics-in-the-making. Have fun discovering your own personal favorites.

APPETIZERS

HORS D'OEUVRES

PROSCIUTTO-WRAPPED ASPARAGUS WITH TRUFFLE BUTTER
MAKES 18 TO 20 HORS D'OEUVRES
ACTIVE TIME: 30 MIN   START TO FINISH: 40 MIN

 1 lb medium asparagus (18 to 20)
½ teaspoon white-truffle oil
 2 tablespoons unsalted butter, softened
 9 or 10 large thin slices prosciutto (⅓ lb)

▶ Prepare a large bowl of ice and cold water. Trim asparagus to 5 inches long, then steam in a steamer over boiling water until crisp-tender, about 4 minutes. Transfer to cold water to stop cooking. Drain and pat dry. Season with salt.
▶ Stir oil into butter until incorporated.
▶ Cut prosciutto slices into roughly 3- by 3-inch pieces, then thinly coat 1 slice with truffle butter and place an asparagus stalk at one edge. Roll up, leaving tip and end of asparagus visible. Repeat with remaining asparagus and prosciutto.

ALSATIAN CHEESE TART
MAKES 36 HORS D'OEUVRES
ACTIVE TIME: 20 MIN   START TO FINISH: 50 MIN

 1 sheet frozen puff pastry (from a 17¼-oz package), thawed
½ cup whole-milk cottage cheese
¼ cup sour cream
¼ teaspoon salt
¼ teaspoon black pepper
 6 bacon slices (6 oz), cut crosswise into ½-inch pieces
⅓ cup packed thinly sliced onion
 1 tablespoon finely grated Parmigiano-Reggiano (see Tips, page 8)

▶ Put oven rack in middle position and preheat oven to 400°F.
▶ Roll out pastry on a lightly floured work surface with a lightly floured rolling pin into a 12-inch square, then transfer to a large baking sheet.
▶ Blend cottage cheese, sour cream, salt, and pepper in a blender until smooth.

▶ Cook bacon in a 10-inch heavy skillet over moderate heat, stirring occasionally, until it just begins to brown, about 5 minutes. (Bacon should be tender, not crisp.) Remove from heat.
▶ Spread cheese mixture evenly over pastry, leaving a 1-inch border all around. Scatter bacon and onion on top, then sprinkle with Parmigiano-Reggiano. Bake until pastry is golden brown, 20 to 25 minutes. Cut into 36 pieces and serve warm.

CRISP EGGPLANT CHIPS
SERVES 6
ACTIVE TIME: 30 MIN   START TO FINISH: 45 MIN

Here, something savory becomes addictively sweet and salty. The confectioners sugar helps brown the eggplant, and panko *adds crunch.*

 6 tablespoons confectioners sugar
 6 tablespoons cornstarch
 1 cup *panko* (Japanese bread crumbs; see Sources)
¼ teaspoon salt
½ lb thin Asian eggplant (2 inches in diameter; about 2 medium), trimmed
   About 3 cups vegetable oil

SPECIAL EQUIPMENT: an adjustable-blade slicer; a deep-fat thermometer

▶ Stir together confectioners sugar, cornstarch, *panko*, and salt in a wide shallow bowl. Cut eggplant crosswise into paper-thin rounds with slicer.
▶ Fill a deep 10- to 12-inch heavy skillet (preferably cast-iron) halfway with oil and heat over moderate heat until it registers 360°F on thermometer (see cooks' note, below).
▶ Dredge one fourth of slices in cornstarch mixture, tossing until thoroughly coated and lightly pressing to help coating adhere, then gently shake in a large sieve to remove excess.
▶ Fry coated slices in oil, turning and separating with a slotted spoon, until golden brown, 1 to 2 minutes. Transfer eggplant chips with a wire-mesh or slotted spoon to paper towels to drain, then season lightly with salt. Coat and fry remaining slices in 3 batches in same manner, transferring to paper towels. Return oil to 360°F between batches. Chips will crisp as they cool. Serve at room temperature.

COOKS' NOTES: To take the temperature of a shallow amount of oil with a metal flat-framed deep-fat thermometer, put bulb of thermometer in skillet and turn thermometer facedown, resting other end (not plastic handle) against rim of skillet. Check temperature frequently.

• Chips can be made up to 2 hours ahead and kept at room temperature.

PARMESAN ONION PUFFS

MAKES 40 HORS D'OEUVRES
ACTIVE TIME: 25 MIN   START TO FINISH: 30 MIN

  2   oz finely grated Parmigiano-Reggiano (1 cup; see Tips, page 8)
  ½   cup mayonnaise
  1   tablespoon minced onion
  ⅛   teaspoon cayenne
  10   slices firm white sandwich bread

SPECIAL EQUIPMENT: a 1¾-inch round cookie cutter

▶ Put oven rack in upper third of oven and preheat oven to 400°F.
▶ Stir together cheese, mayonnaise, onion, and cayenne.
▶ Cut out 4 rounds from each bread slice using cutter and arrange on a baking sheet. Bake toasts until tops are crisp and just golden, 3 to 4 minutes. Cool toasts slightly on baking sheet on a rack. (Leave oven on.)
▶ Top each toast with a rounded ½ teaspoon cheese mixture, spreading to edge with a small offset spatula or knife. Bake toasts until topping is puffed and golden, about 6 minutes.

SEA SCALLOPS WITH SPICED BACON

MAKES 28 HORS D'OEUVRES
ACTIVE TIME: 35 MIN   START TO FINISH: 35 MIN

  6   tablespoons packed dark brown sugar
  1   tablespoon curry powder (preferably Madras)
  ½   teaspoon cayenne
  14   bacon slices (¾ lb)
  14   large sea scallops (1 lb), tough ligament removed from side of each if attached and scallops halved

SPECIAL EQUIPMENT: 28 wooden toothpicks

▶ Stir together brown sugar, curry powder, and cayenne in a bowl until combined well.

▶ Cook bacon in 2 batches in a 12-inch heavy skillet over moderate heat until some fat has rendered and edges begin to brown but bacon is still flexible, about 2 minutes per batch. Transfer bacon to paper towels as cooked to drain and cool.
▶ Preheat broiler and lightly oil rack of a broiler pan (do not line with foil).
▶ Cut bacon slices in half crosswise. Divide sugar mixture among slices, spreading evenly and lightly pressing to help it adhere. Place 1 scallop half, cut side down, on each slice of sugar-coated bacon, then wrap bacon around scallop and secure with a toothpick. Transfer to rack of broiler pan.
▶ Broil scallops, bacon side down, 4 to 5 inches from heat, turning over once, until bacon is browned and scallops are opaque, about 6 minutes total. Serve immediately.

KITCHEN NOTE

WHEN BUYING **PARMIGIANO-REGGIANO**, MAKE SURE YOU ARE GETTING THE GENUINE ARTICLE. IT'S A PART-SKIM COW'S-MILK CHEESE ARTISANALLY MADE ONLY IN EMILIA-ROMAGNA AND A SMALL AREA OF LOMBARDY. PRODUCTION IS CLOSELY REGULATED, SO LOOK FOR THE WORDS "PARMIGIANO-REGGIANO" STAMPED ON THE RIND. WRAP IT IN PARCHMENT OR WAX PAPER, NOT PLASTIC, AND STORE IT IN THE CRISPER DRAWER OF YOUR FRIDGE TO KEEP IT MOIST.

LACY PARMESAN CRISPS

MAKES 12 HORS D'OEUVRES
ACTIVE TIME: 10 MIN   START TO FINISH: 35 MIN

  1   (3-oz) piece Parmigiano-Reggiano

SPECIAL EQUIPMENT: a nonstick bakeware liner such as Silpat

▶ Put oven rack in middle position and preheat oven to 375°F. Line a baking sheet with nonstick liner.
▶ Grate 1 cup cheese using large holes of a box grater.
▶ Arrange 6 mounds (1 rounded tablespoon each) of cheese 3 inches apart on liner, then flatten each mound lightly with a metal spatula to form a 3-inch round.
▶ Bake until golden, 7 to 10 minutes, then transfer crisps with spatula to a rack to cool completely, about 5 minutes.
▶ Repeat procedure with remaining cheese to make more crisps.

SEVEN-LAYER SALMON BITES

MAKES 48 HORS D'OEUVRES

ACTIVE TIME: 45 MIN   START TO FINISH: 1 ¾ HR

10 oz whipped cream cheese
 1 teaspoon finely grated fresh lemon zest (see Tips, page 8)
 2 teaspoons fresh lemon juice
 2 tablespoons finely chopped fresh chives
 ¼ teaspoon salt
 ¼ teaspoon black pepper
 6 (6- by 5-inch) oval slices dark pumpernickel
     sandwich bread (about ⅓ inch thick)
 ½ lb thinly sliced Scottish smoked salmon
 ¼ cup salmon roe (2 oz)

▶ Stir together cream cheese, zest, lemon juice, chives, salt, and pepper in a small bowl. Stack bread slices, then trim to form 4¼- by 3¼-inch rectangles. Arrange rectangles in 1 layer. Spread each with 1 heaping tablespoon cheese mixture and top with a thin layer of smoked salmon (cut to fit with kitchen shears). Make 1 more layer each of cheese and salmon, then top with remaining cheese. Trim edges to make uniform and chill rectangles on a platter until tops are firm, about 1 hour. Cut rectangles into 8 (1½- by 1-inch) pieces, then top each piece with a rounded ¼ teaspoon roe.

DIPS AND SPREADS

GARLICKY CHEESE DIP

MAKES ABOUT 1¼ CUPS

ACTIVE TIME: 20 MIN   START TO FINISH: 20 MIN

 1 cup whole-milk cottage cheese
 2 tablespoons sour cream
 1 hard-boiled large egg, forced through a
     medium-mesh sieve
 1 tablespoon chopped fresh chives
 1 teaspoon finely chopped fresh dill
 ½ teaspoon finely chopped garlic
 ¼ teaspoon salt
 ⅛ teaspooon black pepper
 ⅛ teaspoon ground cumin

▶ Blend together all ingredients in a food processor until smooth, then chill, covered, until ready to serve.

SPICY RED-PEPPER AND EGGPLANT CONFIT

MAKES ABOUT 3 CUPS

ACTIVE TIME: 30 MIN   START TO FINISH: 2½ HR (INCLUDES ROASTING PEPPERS)

This Mediterranean dish can be served with bread or crackers as a meze (appetizer), and it's also great as a sandwich filling.

 2 lb red bell peppers, tender-roasted (see Tips, page 8)
 1 (1½-lb) eggplant, peeled and cut into 1-inch pieces
 4 large garlic cloves, smashed
 1 (28-oz) can whole tomatoes in juice, drained and
     coarsely chopped
 1 cup extra-virgin olive oil
 ¾ teaspoon salt
 ½ teaspoon dried hot red-pepper flakes

▶ Put oven rack in middle position and preheat oven to 400°F.
▶ Cut bell peppers into 1-inch pieces. Toss together all ingredients in a large roasting pan, then spread evenly. Roast, stirring occasionally, until vegetables are very tender, about 1 hour. Cool to room temperature before serving.

COOKS' NOTE: Confit can be made 1 week ahead and cooled completely, uncovered, then chilled, covered. Bring to room temperature and stir before serving.

ROASTED-GARLIC HERB DIP

MAKES ABOUT ½ CUP

ACTIVE TIME: 10 MIN   START TO FINISH: 1½ HR

 2 heads garlic (3 inches wide)
 ½ cup extra-virgin olive oil
 6 (4-inch) sprigs fresh thyme
 3 (4-inch) sprigs fresh rosemary
 ½ teaspoon salt
 ¼ teaspoon black pepper

▶ Put oven rack in middle position and preheat oven to 425°F.
▶ Cut off and discard ½ inch from tops of garlic heads, exposing cloves. Put garlic in a pie plate with oil, herbs, salt, and pepper and cover plate tightly with a double layer of foil. Roast until garlic is golden and tender, 1 to 1¼ hours.
▶ When garlic is cool enough to handle, squeeze cloves into a bowl and pour oil through a fine-mesh sieve onto garlic, discarding herbs. Mash well with a fork and season with salt.

FIRST COURSES

GORGONZOLA AND GRAPE PIZZA

SERVES 6
ACTIVE TIME: 30 MIN   START TO FINISH: 1¾ HR (INCLUDES RISING)

Grape focaccia is a Tuscan classic. Here, we've reworked it with two kinds of cheese and a dash of sweet wine.

FOR DOUGH
- 1 (¼-oz) package active dry yeast (2¼ teaspoons)
- 1¾ cups unbleached all-purpose flour
- ¾ cup warm water (105–115°F)
- 1 teaspoon salt
- ½ tablespoon olive oil

FOR TOPPING
- ⅓ cup Vin Santo
- 1 tablespoon sugar
- 1½ cups red seedless grapes (9 oz), halved lengthwise
- 5 oz Italian Fontina, rind discarded and cheese cut into ¼-inch dice (1 cup)
- 2 oz Gorgonzola *dolce*, crumbled
- ½ teaspoon coarsely ground black pepper

SPECIAL EQUIPMENT: **a pizza stone; parchment paper**

MAKE DOUGH:

▶ Stir together yeast, 1 tablespoon flour, and ¼ cup warm water in a cup and let stand until mixture appears creamy on surface, about 5 minutes. (If mixture doesn't appear creamy, discard and start over with new yeast.)

▶ Whisk salt into 1¼ cups flour in a large bowl, then add yeast mixture, oil, and remaining ½ cup warm water and stir until smooth. Stir in enough flour (¼ to ½ cup) for dough to begin to pull away from side of bowl. (This pizza dough will be slightly wetter than others you may have made.)

▶ Knead dough on a floured work surface with floured hands, reflouring when dough becomes too sticky, but using as little flour as possible, until dough is smooth, soft, and elastic, about 8 minutes. Form dough into a ball and dust generously with flour. Put dough in a medium bowl and cover bowl with plastic wrap, then let dough rise in a draft-free place at warm room temperature until doubled in bulk, about 1¼ hours.

SHAPE DOUGH AND MAKE TOPPING:

▶ At least 45 minutes before baking pizza, put pizza stone on oven rack in lower third of oven and preheat oven to 500°F.

▶ Do not punch down dough. Gently dredge dough in a bowl of flour to coat, then transfer to a parchment-lined pizza peel or baking sheet (without sides). Lightly flour parchment (around dough). Pat out dough evenly with your fingers and stretch into a 13-inch round. (Do not handle dough more than necessary. If dough is sticky, dust it lightly with flour.)

▶ Bring Vin Santo with sugar to a boil in a small heavy saucepan over moderate heat, stirring until sugar is dissolved. Boil, uncovered, until reduced to about 1 tablespoon, about 5 minutes. Add grapes and stir gently to coat with syrup, then transfer to a bowl. Stir in cheeses and pepper until combined.

ASSEMBLE PIZZA:

▶ Arrange topping on dough, leaving a 1-inch border.

▶ Slide pizza on parchment onto pizza stone. Bake pizza until dough is crisp and browned and cheese is golden and bubbling in spots, 14 to 16 minutes. Using peel or baking sheet, transfer pizza on parchment to a cutting board. Cool 5 minutes and remove parchment before slicing.

COOKS' NOTE: Dough can rise slowly, covered and chilled, 1 day ahead. Bring to room temperature before shaping.

KITCHEN NOTE

GORGONZOLA, A BLUE-VEINED COW'S-MILK CHEESE, IS CREAMIER THAN ROQUEFORT AND STILTON. WE LIKE TO BUY IT AND ENJOY IT BEFORE THE VEINING BLOOMS THROUGH THE RIND. THE MOST COMMON TYPE, GORGONZOLA *DOLCE*, IS MILDER AND SWEETER THAN THE MORE ASSERTIVE *NATURALE* TYPE. TO KEEP IT MOIST, STORE IT IN THE VEGETABLE CRISPER, WRAPPED IN PLASTIC OR IN WAX PAPER IN A PARTIALLY CLOSED SEALABLE PLASTIC BAG.

STEWED-TOMATO BRUSCHETTA

SERVES 6

ACTIVE TIME: 40 MIN   START TO FINISH: 1 HR

Breaking down the season's freshest tomatoes and piling them on sourdough toast creates a simple and flavorful first course.

- ½ cup extra-virgin olive oil
- 3 large garlic cloves, thinly sliced lengthwise
- 2 Turkish bay leaves or 1 California bay leaf
- 2 whole cloves
- 1 celery rib, finely chopped
- 1 medium onion, finely chopped (1 cup)
- ½ Italian frying pepper, finely chopped (½ cup)
- 1 teaspoon curry powder (preferably Madras)
- ¾ teaspoon salt
- ¼ teaspoon black pepper
- 2 lb tomatoes, cored and cut into 1-inch-wide wedges
- 2 to 3 teaspoons packed dark brown sugar
- 3 large slices sourdough (cut from center of a 9- to 10-inch round loaf)

SPECIAL EQUIPMENT: **a well-seasoned ridged grill pan**

▶ Heat oil in a 12-inch heavy skillet over moderate heat until hot but not smoking, then cook garlic, bay leaves, and cloves, stirring, until garlic is golden, 35 to 40 seconds. Remove from heat, then transfer garlic, bay leaves, and cloves with a slotted spoon to paper towels to drain. Reserve all but 2 tablespoons oil in a heatproof bowl, then add celery, onion, frying pepper, curry powder, salt, pepper, and reserved bay leaves and cloves to oil remaining in skillet and cook, stirring occasionally, until vegetables are softened, about 5 minutes.
▶ Add tomatoes and 1 teaspoon brown sugar and cook, stirring occasionally, until tomatoes are just beginning to break down, about 20 minutes. Remove skillet from heat and stir in half of reserved garlic slices. Add remaining 1 to 2 teaspoons brown sugar, if desired.
▶ Heat grill pan over moderately high heat until hot but not smoking.
▶ Meanwhile, brush both sides of bread slices with reserved olive oil, then grill in hot grill pan, turning over once, until pale golden and grill marks appear, about 4 minutes total.
▶ Spoon tomato mixture onto toast on plates and sprinkle with remaining garlic slices.

SMOKED SALMON COEURS À LA CRÈME

SERVES 6

ACTIVE TIME: 15 MIN   START TO FINISH: 4¼ HR

- ½ cup whole-milk cottage cheese
- 2 oz cream cheese
- 2 tablespoons heavy cream
- 1 teaspoon fresh lime juice
- ⅛ teaspoon salt
  Pinch of cayenne
- ¼ lb smoked wild salmon, finely chopped
- 1 tablespoon finely chopped fresh chives

SPECIAL EQUIPMENT: **3 (⅓-cup)** *coeur à la crème* **molds; cheesecloth**
ACCOMPANIMENT: **toast points or crackers**

▶ Blend together cheeses, heavy cream, lime juice, salt, and cayenne in a blender until smooth. Transfer cheese mixture to a bowl, then stir in salmon and chives until just combined.
▶ Line each mold with a single layer of rinsed and squeezed cheesecloth, leaving a 1-inch overhang. Pack salmon mixture into molds. (It will mound slightly.) Fold overhanging cheesecloth over tops. Transfer molds to a plate and chill, covered, at least 3 but no more than 24 hours.

KITCHEN NOTE

CREMINI, (SOMETIMES LABELED "BABY BELLAS"), PORTABELLA, AND WHITE BUTTON MUSHROOMS ARE ESSENTIALLY THE SAME VARIETY. THE COCOA-COLORED CREMINI, AN IMMATURE PORTABELLA, IS ACTUALLY THE REINTRODUCTION OF A BROWN MUSHROOM THAT WAS POPULAR IN THE UNITED STATES BEFORE THE WHITE STRAIN WAS DEVELOPED IN THE 1920S. IT HAS A DENSER TEXTURE AND RICHER FLAVOR THAN THE WHITE BUTTONS.

PECAN-STUFFED MUSHROOMS

SERVES 8

ACTIVE TIME: 25 MIN   START TO FINISH: 1 HR

- 24 (1½- to 2-inch-wide) cremini or baby bella mushrooms with stems
- 2 tablespoons unsalted butter plus additional for buttering dish
- 1 large garlic clove, minced
- 1½ teaspoons finely chopped fresh oregano
- 4 oz pecans (1 cup), finely chopped
- ½ teaspoon salt
- ¼ teaspoon black pepper
- 1 cup heavy cream

▶ Put oven rack in middle position and preheat oven to 400°F.

▶ Trim ends of mushroom stems and carefully separate caps and stems, reserving both. Arrange caps, stemmed sides up, in a buttered 13- by 9-inch shallow baking dish.

▶ Finely chop stems, then cook with garlic and oregano in butter in a 10-inch heavy skillet over moderate heat, stirring frequently, until lightly browned, about 5 minutes. Stir in pecans, ¼ teaspoon salt, and ⅛ teaspoon pepper and cook, stirring frequently, 1 minute. Stir in ⅓ cup cream and bring to a simmer, then remove from heat.

▶ Sprinkle insides of caps with remaining ¼ teaspoon salt and ⅛ teaspoon pepper, then divide filling among caps. Drizzle mushrooms with remaining ⅔ cup cream and bake until filling is browned and caps are tender, about 30 minutes. Serve mushrooms drizzled with juices in baking dish.

COOKS' NOTE: Stuffed mushrooms can be assembled (but not baked) 1 day ahead and chilled, covered. Bring to room temperature before baking.

SCALLOPS WITH CILANTRO SAUCE AND ASIAN SLAW

SERVES 6

ACTIVE TIME: 20 MIN   START TO FINISH: 35 MIN

- 1 large carrot
- ⅓ lb daikon radish, peeled
- 1 unpeeled Granny Smith apple
- 1 scallion, cut into julienne (with a knife)
- 3 tablespoons rice vinegar (not seasoned)
- 1½ tablespoons sugar
- 1 teaspoon salt
- ½ cup finely chopped fresh cilantro
- 3 tablespoons fresh lime juice
- 1 to 2 teaspoons minced fresh serrano chile
- 1 teaspoon Asian fish sauce
- ¼ cup vegetable oil
- 1½ lb sea scallops, tough ligament discarded from each

SPECIAL EQUIPMENT: an adjustable-blade slicer with ¼-inch julienne blade

▶ Cut carrot, radish, and apple into julienne, with slicer, then toss together with scallion, vinegar, 1 tablespoon sugar, and ½ teaspoon salt in a bowl. Let stand, tossing occasionally, 15 minutes to soften.

▶ Stir together cilantro, lime juice, serrano chile, fish sauce, 3 tablespoons oil, and remaining ½ tablespoon sugar, or to taste.

▶ Pat scallops dry. Sprinkle with remaining ½ teaspoon salt. Heat remaining tablespoon oil in a 12-inch heavy skillet over moderately high heat until hot but not smoking, then sauté scallops, turning over once, until golden and just cooked through, about 4 minutes total.

▶ Drain slaw, discarding liquid. Divide among 6 plates and top with scallops. Drizzle with cilantro sauce.

BREADS

PORTUGUESE HONEY BREAD

MAKES 6 SMALL LOAVES
ACTIVE TIME: 40 MIN   START TO FINISH: 2½ HR

We like to bake this lightly spiced bread, filled with bits of flavorful candied fruit, in small loaves—perfect for gift giving. Mild honey lends sweetness, while molasses adds notes of caramel.

2½ sticks (1¼ cups) unsalted butter, softened, plus additional for buttering pans
¾ cup dried cranberries or dried sour cherries
¾ cup chopped mixed fine-quality candied fruit such as pear, citron, and candied orange peel (not a supermarket brand; see Sources; ¼ lb)
¼ cup Port
1¼ cups walnuts (4¼ oz)
4½ cups all-purpose flour
1 teaspoon salt
1 teaspoon baking soda
½ teaspoon ground ginger
½ teaspoon ground cinnamon
¼ teaspoon ground cloves
1 cup sugar
3 large eggs
3 teaspoons active dry yeast (from two ¼-oz packages)
¼ cup warm water (105–115°F)
¾ cup molasses (not blackstrap)
½ cup mild honey

SPECIAL EQUIPMENT: 6 (6- by 3¼- by 2-inch) metal loaf pans (2- to 2¼-cup capacity)

▶ Put oven rack in middle position and preheat oven to 325°F. Butter loaf pans.
▶ Bring cranberries, candied fruit, and Port to a simmer in a small saucepan. Remove from heat and set aside, covered.
▶ Pulse walnuts in a food processor until just coarsely chopped. Add flour, salt, baking soda, and spices and pulse to combine.
▶ Beat together butter (2½ sticks) and sugar in a large bowl with an electric mixer at medium-high speed until pale and fluffy, about 4 minutes in a stand mixer or 6 with a handheld. Add eggs 1 at a time, beating well after each addition.
▶ Stir together yeast and warm water in a small bowl and let stand until foamy, about 5 minutes. (If mixture doesn't foam, discard and start over with new yeast.)

▶ Add one third of flour mixture to butter mixture and mix at low speed until combined, then add molasses and mix until incorporated. Add half of remaining flour mixture and mix until combined, then add honey and mix until incorporated. Add yeast mixture and remaining flour mixture and mix until combined, then stir in candied-fruit mixture.
▶ Divide batter among pans, smoothing tops. (Do not let batter rise.) Bake until a wooden pick or skewer inserted in centers of loaves comes out clean, 50 to 60 minutes. Cool in pans on a rack 10 minutes, then remove loaves from pans and cool completely on rack.

COOKS' NOTE: Breads keep, wrapped tightly in plastic wrap and then foil, at room temperature 1 week.

GARLIC KNOTS

MAKES ABOUT 5 DOZEN KNOTS
ACTIVE TIME: 40 MIN   START TO FINISH: 1 HR

2 tablespoons olive oil plus additional for greasing pan
2 lb frozen pizza dough, thawed
1 garlic clove
¼ teaspoon salt
1 tablespoon finely chopped fresh flat-leaf parsley
1 oz Parmigiano-Reggiano, finely grated (½ cup; see Tips, page 8)

▶ Put oven racks in upper and lower thirds of oven and preheat oven to 400°F. Lightly oil 2 large (17- by 13-inch) baking sheets.
▶ Divide dough in half. Keep half of dough covered with a clean kitchen towel (not terry cloth). Gently roll out other half into a 10-inch square on a lightly floured surface with a lightly floured rolling pin. (Use your hands to pull corners. If dough is very elastic, cover with a clean kitchen towel and let rest about 3 minutes.)
▶ Cut square in half with a pizza wheel or a sharp heavy knife, then cut each half crosswise into 15 strips (about ⅔ inch wide). Cover strips with a clean kitchen towel.
▶ Keeping remaining strips covered, gently tie each strip into a knot, pulling ends slightly to secure (if dough is sticky, dust lightly with flour) and arranging knots 1 inch apart in staggered rows on 1 baking sheet. Keep knots covered with clean kitchen towels (not terry cloth).

▶ Roll out and cut remaining dough, then form into knots in same manner, arranging 1 inch apart in staggered rows on second baking sheet. Bake, switching position of sheets halfway through baking, until golden, 20 to 25 minutes total.

▶ While knots bake, mince garlic and mash to a paste with salt, then stir together with oil (2 tablespoons) in a very large bowl. Immediately after baking, toss knots in garlic oil, then sprinkle with parsley and cheese and toss to coat. Serve warm or at room temperature.

MAPLE SUGAR RAGAMUFFINS

MAKES 12 MUFFINS

ACTIVE TIME: 25 MIN   START TO FINISH: 1 HR (INCLUDES COOLING)

These buttery roll-ups feature maple in the dough and the filling.

FOR DOUGH

- 2 cups all-purpose flour
- 1 tablespoon granulated maple sugar (see cooks' note, below, and Sources)
- 1 tablespoon baking powder
- ½ teaspoon salt
- 5 tablespoons cold unsalted butter, cut into small pieces
- ¾ cup whole milk

FOR FILLING

- ¾ stick (6 tablespoons) unsalted butter, well softened
- 1 cup granulated maple sugar (6 oz)

SPECIAL EQUIPMENT: **parchment paper**

MAKE DOUGH:

▶ Put oven rack in middle position and preheat oven to 400°F. Line a large (17- by 13-inch) baking sheet with parchment.

▶ Whisk together flour, maple sugar, baking powder, and salt in a large bowl. Blend in butter with a pastry blender or your fingertips until most of mixture resembles coarse meal with some small (roughly pea-size) butter lumps. Add milk and stir with a fork until a shaggy dough forms. Gently knead dough 8 to 10 times with floured hands on a lightly floured surface.

ROLL OUT AND FILL DOUGH:

▶ Roll out dough on a lightly floured surface with a floured rolling pin into a 13- by 11-inch rectangle. Spread softened butter evenly over dough and sprinkle all over with maple sugar, pressing firmly to help adhere. Beginning with one long side, roll up dough snugly, jelly-roll style. Cut roll crosswise into 12 slices with a sharp knife. Arrange slices, cut sides down, 2 inches apart on baking sheet. Gather any maple sugar from work surface and sprinkle on top of rolls.

BAKE DOUGH:

▶ Bake rolls until puffed and golden, 18 to 20 minutes. Transfer to a rack to cool until warm, about 15 minutes.

COOKS' NOTE: Maple sugar is usually sold granulated, but if you find a brand sold as very large granules, pulse the sugar in a blender until it becomes more finely granulated.

FIGGY SCONES

MAKES 20 SCONES

ACTIVE TIME: 25 MIN   START TO FINISH: 1 HOUR

- ¾ cup well-shaken buttermilk
- ¼ cup pure maple syrup
- ½ cup plus 2 tablespoons heavy cream
- 3½ cups all-purpose flour
- ¾ cup sugar
- 1 teaspoon salt
- 1 teaspoon baking powder
- ½ teaspoon baking soda
- 2 sticks (1 cup) unsalted butter, cut into ½-inch cubes
- ½ lb dried Calmyrna figs, stems discarded and figs cut into ½-inch pieces (about 1½ cups)
- 2 large egg yolks

SPECIAL EQUIPMENT: **parchment paper**

▶ Put oven racks in upper and lower thirds of oven and preheat oven to 400°F.

▶ Whisk together buttermilk, syrup, and ½ cup cream in a small bowl. Mix together flour, sugar, salt, baking powder, and baking soda in bowl of a stand mixer with paddle attachment at low speed (or whisk in a large bowl) until combined. Add butter and mix (or blend with your fingertips or a pastry blender) until mixture resembles coarse meal with some small (roughly pea-size) butter lumps. Mix in figs, then add buttermilk mixture and mix until just combined. (Do not overmix.)

▶ Line 2 large baking sheets with parchment paper and drop 10 (¼-cup) mounds of batter onto each sheet, leaving 1 inch between mounds.

▶ Whisk together yolks and remaining 2 tablespoons cream, then brush over tops of scones (use all of egg wash).

▶ Bake, switching position of baking sheets halfway through baking, until scones are puffed and golden, 20 to 25 minutes total. Transfer to a rack and cool to warm.

COOKS' NOTE: Scones are best eaten the day they're made.

CINNAMON BLUEBERRY MUFFINS

MAKES 12 MUFFINS

ACTIVE TIME: 25 MIN   START TO FINISH: 1¼ HR (INCLUDES COOLING)

¾ stick (6 tablespoons) unsalted butter, melted and cooled
1 cup packed light brown sugar
½ cup whole milk
1 large egg
1½ cups all-purpose flour
1½ teaspoons baking powder
1 teaspoon cinnamon
½ teaspoon salt
1½ cups blueberries (7½ oz)

SPECIAL EQUIPMENT: a muffin pan with 12 (½-cup) muffin cups;
12 foil or paper muffin liners

▶ Put oven rack in middle position and preheat oven to 400°F.
Put liners in muffin cups.
▶ Whisk together butter, brown sugar, milk, and egg in a bowl
until combined well. Whisk together flour, baking powder,
cinnamon, and salt in a large bowl. Add milk mixture and stir
until just combined. Fold in blueberries gently.
▶ Divide batter among muffin cups and bake until golden brown
and a wooden pick or skewer inserted into center of a muffin
comes out clean, 25 to 30 minutes. Transfer to a rack and cool
until warm, about 15 minutes.

COFFEE-GLAZED DOUGHNUTS

MAKES ABOUT 1 DOZEN

ACTIVE TIME: 45 MIN   START TO FINISH: 3¾ HR (INCLUDES RISING)

FOR DOUGHNUTS
1 (¼-oz) package active dry yeast (2½ teaspoons)
2 tablespoons warm water (105–115°F)
3¼ cups all-purpose flour plus additional for sprinkling
    and rolling out dough
1 cup whole milk at room temperature
½ stick (¼ cup) unsalted butter, softened
3 large egg yolks
2 tablespoons sugar
1½ teaspoons salt
½ teaspoon cinnamon
    About 10 cups vegetable oil for deep frying

FOR GLAZE
¼ cup boiling-hot water
5 teaspoons instant-espresso powder or
    instant-coffee granules

1½ cups confectioners sugar
1 tablespoon light corn syrup
¼ teaspoon pure vanilla extract
¼ teaspoon salt
    About ¼ cup sanding sugar (optional; see Sources)

SPECIAL EQUIPMENT: a stand mixer fitted with paddle
attachment; a 3-inch and a 1-inch round cookie cutter; a deep-
fat thermometer

MAKE DOUGH:

▶ Stir together yeast and warm water in a small bowl until yeast
is dissolved. Let stand until foamy, about 5 minutes. (If yeast
doesn't foam, discard and start over with new yeast.)
▶ Mix together flour, milk, butter, yolks, sugar, salt, cinnamon,
and yeast mixture in mixer at low speed until a soft dough forms.
Increase speed to medium-high and beat 3 minutes more.
▶ Scrape dough down side of bowl (all around) into center, then
sprinkle lightly with flour (to keep a crust from forming). Cover
bowl with a clean kitchen towel (not terry cloth) and let dough
rise in a draft-free place at warm room temperature until doubled
in bulk, 1½ to 2 hours. (Alternatively, let dough rise in bowl in
refrigerator 8 to 12 hours.)
▶ Turn dough out onto a lightly floured surface and roll out
with a lightly floured rolling pin into a 12-inch round (½ inch
thick). Cut out as many rounds as possible with 3-inch cutter,
then cut a hole in center of each round with 1-inch cutter and
transfer doughnuts to a lightly floured large baking sheet. Cover
doughnuts with a clean kitchen towel and let rise in a draft-free
place at warm room temperature until slightly puffed, about
30 minutes (45 minutes if dough was cold when cutting out
doughnuts). Do not reroll scraps.
▶ Heat 2½ inches oil in a deep 4-quart heavy pot until it registers
350°F on thermometer. Fry doughnuts, 2 at a time, turning
occasionally with a wire or mesh skimmer or a slotted spoon,
until puffed and golden brown, about 2 minutes per batch.
Transfer to paper towels to drain. (Return oil to 350°F
between batches.)

MAKE GLAZE:

▶ Stir together boiling-hot water and espresso powder
in a medium bowl until powder is dissolved, then stir in
confectioners sugar, corn syrup, vanilla, and salt until smooth.
▶ Dip doughnuts into glaze, turning to coat well, then put on a
rack set in a shallow baking pan (to catch any drips). While
glaze is wet, sprinkle doughnuts with sanding sugar (if using).
Let stand until glaze is set, about 20 minutes.

COOKS' NOTE: Doughnuts are best eaten the day they're fried.

SOUPS

BEEF, MUSHROOM, AND BARLEY SOUP

SERVES 8 TO 10 (MAIN COURSE)

ACTIVE TIME: 45 MIN START TO FINISH: 2¼ HR

Tender pieces of short rib and barley add body to a delicate herbal broth you can make ahead and enjoy for days.

1½ oz dried mushrooms

3 cups boiling-hot water plus 8 cups cold water

1 lb cross-cut beef short ribs or flanken

2½ teaspoons salt

½ teaspoon black pepper

1 large onion, chopped (2 cups)

2 carrots, cut into ¼-inch dice

2 celery ribs, cut into ¼-inch dice

½ lb fresh cremini mushrooms, trimmed and quartered

2 tablespoons vegetable oil

½ cup pearl barley

¼ cup chopped fresh dill

▶ Soak dried mushrooms in boiling-hot water in a bowl until softened, about 20 minutes. Drain in a paper-towel-lined sieve set over a bowl and reserve soaking liquid. Rinse mushrooms, then pat dry and finely chop.

▶ Bring soaked mushrooms, soaking liquid, ribs, salt, pepper, and remaining 8 cups water to a boil in a 6- to 8-quart pot, then reduce heat and simmer, partially covered, skimming foam, until meat is just tender, about 1 hour. Transfer ribs with a slotted spoon to a cutting board to cool, reserving broth.

▶ While meat simmers, cook onion, carrots, celery, and creminis in oil in a 12-inch heavy skillet over moderate heat, stirring occasionally, until well browned, 15 to 20 minutes, Stir in barley and cook, stirring, 1 minute.

▶ Discard bones, fat, and gristle from meat, then cut meat into ½-inch pieces and add to broth along with barley mixture. Simmer, uncovered, until barley is tender, about 40 minutes. Skim fat from surface, then stir in dill and salt to taste.

COOKS' NOTE: Soup, without dill, can be made 3 days ahead and cooled, uncovered, then chilled, covered. Remove any solidified fat before reheating.

KITCHEN NOTE

DRIED MUSHROOMS ARE MORE INTENSELY FLAVORED THAN FRESH. AFTER SOAKING, RINSE THEM TO REMOVE ANY GRIT. (STRAIN THE FLAVORFUL SOAKING LIQUID AND INCORPORATE IT IN THE DISH IF POSSIBLE.) AND ALTHOUGH SOME OF THE CULTIVATED EXOTICS MAY LOSE THEIR COLOR AND SHAPE WHEN COOKED, DON'T BE TEMPTED TO SERVE THEM RAW. THEY CONTAIN NATURAL TOXINS (DESTROYED BY COOKING) THAT WILL CAUSE INDIGESTION.

SOUTHWESTERN CORN AND POTATO SOUP

SERVES 6 (MAIN COURSE)

ACTIVE TIME: 20 MIN START TO FINISH: 35 MIN

3 tablespoons olive oil

1 large onion, chopped

1 fresh jalapeño, seeded and finely chopped

½ teaspoon salt

¼ teaspoon black pepper

1½ lb large yellow-fleshed potatoes such as Yukon Gold (about 2)

3¼ cups reduced-sodium chicken broth (26 fl oz)

1 cup water

1 (10-oz) package frozen corn (not thawed)

3 tablespoons fresh lime juice

¼ cup finely chopped fresh cilantro

ACCOMPANIMENTS: ½-inch cubes of California avocado; chopped fresh cilantro; tortilla chips; lime wedges

▶ Heat oil in a 5- to 6-quart heavy pot over moderate heat until hot but not smoking, then cook onion, jalapeño, salt, and pepper, stirring occasionally, until onion is pale golden, about 8 minutes.

▶ Meanwhile, peel potatoes and cut into 1-inch pieces.

▶ Add broth, water, and potatoes to onion mixture and cover pot, then bring to a boil over high heat.

▶ Reduce heat and simmer, uncovered, stirring occasionally, until potatoes are very tender, 12 to 14 minutes.

▶ Coarsely mash potatoes in pot with a potato masher. Stir in corn and simmer, uncovered, 3 minutes.

▶ Stir in lime juice, cilantro, and salt to taste.

CURRIED PEANUT AND TOMATO SOUP

SERVES 4 (FIRST COURSE)
ACTIVE TIME: 15 MIN   START TO FINISH: 30 MIN

*Fresh cilantro and curry powder, along with the unexpected
addition of peanut butter, turn a simple tomato-based soup
into something special.*

  1 medium onion, chopped (1 cup)
 ¼ teaspoon salt
 ⅛ teaspoon black pepper
  2 tablespoons vegetable oil
  2 teaspoons curry powder (preferably Madras)
  1 (14-oz) can diced tomatoes in juice, chopped if large,
     reserving juice
1¾ cups reduced-sodium chicken broth (14 fl oz)
  1 cup hot water
 ¼ cup smooth peanut butter
  2 tablespoons chopped fresh cilantro

▶Cook onion, salt, and pepper in oil in a 2- to 3-quart heavy
saucepan over moderate heat, stirring occasionally, until
softened, 4 to 5 minutes. Add curry powder and cook, stirring
frequently, 2 minutes. Add tomatoes (with their juice) and broth
and simmer, uncovered, 5 minutes. Stir hot water into peanut
butter until smooth and add to soup. Simmer, uncovered, stirring
occasionally, 5 minutes. Stir in cilantro before serving.

SMOKY RED-LENTIL SOUP WITH CHEDDAR TOASTS

SERVES 6 (MAIN COURSE)
ACTIVE TIME: 15 MIN   START TO FINISH: 45 MIN

  2 bacon slices, finely chopped
  1 cup finely chopped onion (1 large)
  2 large carrots, quartered and cut into ¼-inch dice
  1 cup red lentils (7 oz)
  1 qt water
 ¾ teaspoon salt
1½ teaspoons black pepper
  6 (1-inch-thick) baguette slices, cut on a long diagonal
  1 tablespoon unsalted butter
  1 to 2 teaspoons Dijon mustard
 ¼ lb extra-sharp Cheddar, cut into 12 (¼-inch-thick) slices

▶Cook bacon in a 4-quart heavy pot over moderate heat, stirring
occasionally, until fat is rendered and bacon is golden brown,
about 6 minutes. Pour off all but 2 tablespoons fat from pot (if

your bacon renders less fat, add enough olive oil to bring total to
2 tablespoons), then add onion and carrots to bacon and cook
over moderate heat, stirring frequently, until onion is softened
and golden, about 5 minutes. Add lentils and cook, stirring,
1 minute. Add water, stirring and scraping up any brown bits
from bottom of pot, then reduce heat to moderately low and
simmer, covered, until lentils are very tender, 15 to 25 minutes.
Stir in salt and pepper.
▶Preheat broiler. Arrange baguette slices on a baking sheet or
broiler pan and spread top of each slice with butter. Broil slices
6 inches from heat until pale golden, about 1 minute. Spread
buttered sides with a thin layer of mustard, then top each toast
with 2 slices of cheese and broil until cheese is melted and
bubbling, about 1 minute.
▶Serve soup with Cheddar toasts.

QUICK MINESTRONE SOUP

SERVES 4 (MAIN COURSE)
ACTIVE TIME: 10 MIN   START TO FINISH: 30 MIN

 ¼ cup olive oil
  1 small onion, coarsely chopped
  4 garlic cloves, crushed in a garlic press
  4 oz prewashed and cut kale (6 cups)
  1 (1-lb) bag frozen mixed Italian vegetables such as
     zucchini, green beans, cauliflower, and broccoli
  1 (14½-oz) can "petite" diced tomatoes in juice
  1 cup *ditalini* pasta or small elbow macaroni
5¼ cups reduced-sodium chicken broth (42 fl oz)
  2 cups water
 ¾ teaspoon salt
 ½ teaspoon black pepper
  1 (19-oz) can cannellini beans, rinsed and drained

ACCOMPANIMENT: grated Parmigiano-Reggiano

▶Heat oil in a 5- to 6-quart heavy pot over moderately high heat
until hot but not smoking, then sauté onion and garlic, stirring
occasionally, until golden, about 3 minutes. Add kale and sauté,
stirring, 1 minute. Add frozen vegetables, tomatoes with juice,
pasta, broth, water, salt, and pepper and simmer, uncovered,
stirring occasionally, until vegetables are tender and pasta is
al dente, about 10 minutes.
▶Meanwhile, transfer half of beans to a wide shallow bowl and
coarsely mash with a fork or a potato masher, then stir mashed
and whole beans into soup and simmer, stirring occasionally,
until soup is slightly thickened, about 5 minutes. Season with
salt and pepper.

MUSHROOM AND OYSTER SOUP

SERVES 6 TO 8 (MAIN COURSE)

ACTIVE TIME: 20 MIN   START TO FINISH: 40 MIN

    3   medium leeks (white and pale green parts only),
          chopped (2 cups)
    3   tablespoons unsalted butter
  ½   lb cremini mushrooms, trimmed
    1   garlic clove, smashed
  ¾   teaspoon salt
  ½   teaspoon freshly grated nutmeg
  ¼   teaspoon black pepper
2½   cups half-and-half
    2   cups shucked oysters with ½ cup of their liquor
          (see cooks' note, below)
    2   tablespoons chopped fresh chives

▶ Wash leeks in a bowl of cold water, agitating them, then lift out and pat dry.

▶ Heat butter in a 2½- to 3-quart heavy saucepan over moderate heat until foam subsides, then cook leeks, mushrooms, garlic, salt, nutmeg, and pepper, stirring occasionally, until leeks are softened and any liquid mushrooms give off is evaporated, about 10 minutes.

▶ Transfer half of mushroom mixture to blender and purée with half-and-half until very smooth, about 1 minute. Return purée to saucepan.

▶ Bring soup just to a simmer, stirring occasionally, then add oysters and their liquor and cook, stirring, until oysters become plump and edges begin to curl, about 3 minutes. Sprinkle soup with chives.

COOKS' NOTE: If you don't have enough oyster liquor, add enough bottled clam juice to bring total to ½ cup.

SCALLOP CHOWDER WITH BACON

SERVES 4 (MAIN COURSE)

ACTIVE TIME: 10 MIN   START TO FINISH: 15 MIN

This light chowder with a subtle note of smokiness really lets the scallops shine.

    4   bacon slices, chopped
    1   cup frozen chopped onions (about 6 oz)
    1   large boiling potato, peeled and cut into
          ¼-inch pieces
    1   tablespoon all-purpose flour
    2   cups whole milk
    1   (10-oz) package frozen mixed vegetables
    1   sprig fresh thyme or ¼ teaspoon dried thyme,
          crumbled
  ½   teaspoon salt
  ¼   teaspoon black pepper
    1   lb sea scallops, tough ligament removed from side
          of each if attached

▶ Cook chopped bacon in a 2-quart heavy saucepan over moderately high heat, stirring occasionally, until crisp, about 2 minutes. Transfer with a slotted spoon to paper towels to drain.

▶ Add onions and potato to fat in pan and cook over moderately high heat, stirring frequently, until onions are thawed, about 1 minute, then sprinkle in flour and cook, stirring, 1 minute. Slowly whisk in milk and bring to a boil, whisking constantly. Add vegetables, thyme, salt, and pepper and simmer, uncovered, stirring occasionally, 3 minutes.

▶ Cut scallops in half (or quarters if large) and add to soup, then simmer just until scallops are cooked through, about 3 minutes. Discard thyme sprig (if using), then season soup with salt and sprinkle with bacon.

CELERY APPLE GAZPACHO

SERVES 4 (FIRST COURSE)

ACTIVE TIME: 15 MIN   START TO FINISH: 1¼ HR (INCLUDES CHILLING)

    8   to 9 celery ribs, chopped (3 cups)
    1   Granny Smith apple, peeled and cored
1½   cups cold water
    1   tablespoon fresh lemon juice
    1   teaspoon salt
    1   (3-inch) piece baguette, crust discarded
  ¼   cup blanched almonds, chopped
    2   tablespoons extra-virgin olive oil

GARNISH: thin celery matchstick curls

▶ Purée celery, apple, water, lemon juice, and salt in a blender until smooth. Chill mixture in blender, covered, 1 hour. Reblend, then pour through a fine-mesh sieve into a bowl. Soak bread in strained soup 3 minutes. Rinse blender and pulse almonds until finely ground. Add soup with bread and blend until smooth. Then, with motor running, add oil in a slow stream, blending until emulsified.

GINGERED CARROT SOUP

SERVES 4 (FIRST COURSE)

ACTIVE TIME: 10 MIN   START TO FINISH: 10 MIN

    2 (7- to 8-oz) firm-ripe California avocados
    3 cups fresh carrot juice
    ¾ teaspoon salt
    5 teaspoons fresh lime juice
  2¼ teaspoons finely grated peeled fresh ginger
       Pinch of curry powder

▶ Quarter avocados, then pit and peel.

▶ Purée 1 avocado with carrot juice, salt, 4 teaspoons lime juice, and 2 teaspoons ginger in a blender until very smooth.

▶ Cut remaining avocado into ¼-inch dice. Gently toss with remaining teaspoon lime juice, ¼ teaspoon ginger, curry powder, and a pinch of salt.

▶ Serve soup garnished with seasoned avocado dice.

KITCHEN NOTE

WE PREFER **CALIFORNIA AVOCADOS.** THEIR TEXTURE IS CREAMY, AND WE FIND THEIR NUTTY FLAVOR SUPERIOR TO THAT OF AVOCADOS GROWN IN FLORIDA. THE MOST WIDELY AVAILABLE CALIFORNIA VARIETY, THE OVAL-SHAPED HAAS, IS IN SEASON YEAR-ROUND, ALTHOUGH IT ACTUALLY COMES FROM CALIFORNIA ONLY FROM JANUARY TO SEPTEMBER OR OCTOBER. IT'S IMPORTED FROM CHILE AND MEXICO FOR THOSE FEW REMAINING MONTHS. THE BEST WAY TO TEST AN AVOCADO'S RIPENESS IS TO PRESS IT VERY GENTLY; IF IT YIELDS TO PRESSURE, IT'S RIPE.

CHILLED RADISH BUTTERMILK SOUP

SERVES 4 (FIRST COURSE)

ACTIVE TIME: 10 MIN   START TO FINISH: 10 MIN

    ½ lb trimmed radishes, quartered (1¼ cups)
    ¾ lb seedless cucumber (usually plastic-wrapped),
       peeled and chopped (2 cups)
    2 cups well-shaken chilled buttermilk
    1 teaspoon salt
    1 teaspoon seasoned rice vinegar
    ½ teaspoon sugar

GARNISH: thin slices of cucumber and radish

▶ Purée all ingredients in a blender until very smooth. Serve immediately.

ZUCCHINI CUCUMBER SOUP

SERVES 4 (FIRST COURSE)

ACTIVE TIME: 15 MIN   START TO FINISH: 15 MIN

    1 lb zucchini, chopped
    ¾ lb seedless cucumber (usually plastic-wrapped), peeled
       and chopped (2 cups)
    ⅓ cup chopped sweet onion such as Vidalia
    ¼ cup white-wine vinegar
    ¼ cup cold water
    1 teaspoon chopped fresh hot green chile
  1⅛ teaspoons salt
    1 teaspoon ground coriander
    ½ cup crème fraîche (4 oz)

▶ Purée zucchini, cucumber, onion, vinegar, water, chile, 1 teaspoon salt, and ½ teaspoon coriander in a blender until very smooth.

▶ Whisk remaining ⅛ teaspoon salt and ½ teaspoon coriander into crème fraîche. Serve soup topped with dollops of seasoned crème fraîche.

FISH AND SHELLFISH

FISH

MAPLE-SOY-GLAZED MACKEREL FILLETS WITH AVOCADO

SERVES 4

ACTIVE TIME: 25 MIN   START TO FINISH: 35 MIN

- ⅔ cup rice vinegar (not seasoned)
- ½ cup soy sauce
- ½ cup dry Sherry
- ½ cup dark amber or Grade B maple syrup
- 1 firm-ripe large California avocado
- 2 teaspoons fresh lemon juice
- 2 teaspoons extra-virgin olive oil
- ¼ teaspoon salt
- ⅛ teaspoon black pepper
- 4 (7- to 8-oz) Spanish mackerel fillets with skin (about ½ inch thick)

ACCOMPANIMENTS: rice; lemon wedges

MAKE GLAZE:

▶ Briskly simmer vinegar, soy sauce, Sherry, and maple syrup in a 9- to 10-inch heavy skillet over moderately low heat until reduced to about ⅓ cup, 20 to 25 minutes. Keep warm.

PREPARE AVOCADO WHILE GLAZE REDUCES:

▶ Quarter avocado lengthwise, then pit and peel. Cut lengthwise into ½-inch-thick slices, then gently toss together with lemon juice, oil, salt, and pepper in a small bowl.

GLAZE AND BAKE FISH:

▶ Preheat broiler. Line a large (15- by 10-inch) shallow baking pan with foil.

▶ Reserve about one fourth of glaze in a small bowl.

▶ Arrange fillets, skin sides down, in 1 layer in baking pan. Spoon about one third of remaining glaze over fillets, then spread with back of spoon to coat evenly.

▶ Broil fish 5 to 6 inches from heat, without turning, 2 minutes. Remove pan from broiler and coat with another layer of glaze, then broil 2 minutes more. Remove fillets from broiler and apply a third coat of glaze, then broil 1 minute more (for a total of 5 minutes). Remove from broiler and, with a clean spoon, apply reserved glaze.

▶ Serve fish with avocado salad.

PAN-COOKED BASS WITH DILL AND CUCUMBER

SERVES 4

ACTIVE TIME: 10 MIN   START TO FINISH: 15 MIN

Cucumbers provide visual appeal and help keep the fish fillets delightfully moist.

- 3 tablespoons unsalted butter
- 4 (5- to 7-oz) black sea bass or striped bass fillets (½ to ¾ inch thick) with skin
- ½ teaspoon salt
- ¼ teaspoon black pepper
- 1½ tablespoons finely chopped fresh dill
- ½ seedless cucumber (usually plastic-wrapped), very thinly sliced

SPECIAL EQUIPMENT: parchment paper

▶ Melt butter in a 12-inch heavy nonstick skillet, then remove from heat and cool. Put fillets, flesh sides down, in butter, then turn over so skin sides are down. Sprinkle fish with salt (½ teaspoon), pepper (¼ teaspoon), and 1 tablespoon dill. Arrange cucumber slices overlapping on fish (like scales) and season with salt and pepper. Cover fish directly with a piece of buttered parchment paper (buttered side down) large enough to cover it, then tightly cover skillet with lid or foil.

▶ Cook fish over moderately high heat until just cooked through, 3 to 5 minutes, depending on thickness of fish. Remove parchment, then sprinkle fish with remaining ½ tablespoon dill and drizzle with some pan juices.

KITCHEN NOTE

FULL-FLAVORED **SPANISH MACKEREL** IS CAUGHT IN ATLANTIC WATERS FROM THE CHESAPEAKE BAY DOWN TO FLORIDA AND THE GULF OF MEXICO. BECAUSE IT IS MEATY AND OILY, IT'S A VERY FORGIVING FISH TO COOK, AND IT TAKES WELL TO STRONG ASIAN AND MEDITERRANEAN FLAVORS. SPANISH MACKEREL IS AT ITS BEST WHEN ULTRAFRESH, SO BUY IT FROM A SEAFOOD STORE WITH HIGH TURNOVER.

GRILLED CHILE-LIME ARCTIC CHAR

SERVES 4 GENEROUSLY

ACTIVE TIME: 40 MIN   START TO FINISH: 40 MIN

Its firm flesh and assertive taste make arctic char a great choice for the grill. The ground chipotle offers a hint of smoky heat.

  7   medium garlic cloves
  2   tablespoons salt
  ¼   cup fresh lime juice
  2   tablespoons olive oil
1¾   teaspoons sugar
1¼   teaspoons ground chipotle chile
  2   (1-lb) arctic char fillets with skin (about 1¼ inches thick)

SPECIAL EQUIPMENT: **tweezers or needlenose pliers**
ACCOMPANIMENT: **lime wedges**

▶ Mince garlic and mash to a paste with salt using a large heavy knife.

▶ Stir together garlic paste, lime juice, oil, sugar, and chipotle chile in a small bowl until sugar is dissolved.

▶ Remove any bones from fish with tweezers, then pat fish dry and place, skin side down, on a plastic-wrap-lined large tray.

▶ Rub chile mixture all over flesh side of fish, then wrap plastic around fish and marinate at cool room temperature 15 minutes.

▶ While fish is marinating, prepare grill for cooking over indirect heat with medium-hot charcoal (moderately high heat for gas); see Tips, page 8.

TO COOK FISH USING A CHARCOAL GRILL:

▶ Lightly oil grill rack, then put fish, skin side down, on grill rack with no coals underneath and grill, covered with lid, 4 minutes. Using 2 metal spatulas, loosen fish from grill rack and turn fish over, rotating 180 degrees. Grill fish, covered with lid, until just cooked through, 3 to 5 minutes more, then loosen from grill rack with spatulas and transfer to a clean platter. If desired, lift skin from fish with tongs and cook skin on rack directly over coals, turning over occasionally, until lightly browned and crisp, 1 to 2 minutes, then serve over fish.

TO COOK FISH USING A GAS GRILL:

▶ Lightly oil grill rack, then put fish, skin side down, on rack above shut-off burner and grill, covered with lid, 4 minutes. Using 2 metal spatulas, loosen skin from grill rack and turn fish over. Grill fish, covered with lid, until just cooked through, 3 to 5 minutes more, then loosen from grill rack with spatulas and transfer to a clean platter. If desired, lift skin from fish with tongs and cook skin directly over a burner, uncovered, turning over occasionally, until lightly browned and crisp, 1 to 2 minutes, then serve over fish.

COOKS' NOTES: If you aren't able to grill outdoors, fish can be broiled, skin side down, without turning, on oiled rack of a broiler pan 5 to 6 inches from preheated broiler, about 6 minutes total. (Skin cannot be crisped in broiler.)
• You can substitute 2 (1-lb) pieces of salmon fillet (about 1½ inches thick) for the arctic char. Grill, turning over once, about 12 minutes total.

FISH FILLETS WITH OLIVES AND OREGANO

SERVES 4

ACTIVE TIME: 15 MIN   START TO FINISH: 30 MIN

Elegant but easy, this fast fish dinner is simple enough to prepare on a weeknight and special enough to serve to company.

  4   (1¼-inch-thick) pieces skinless white-fleshed fish fillets such as halibut (6 oz each)
  1   teaspoon salt
  ¼   teaspoon black pepper
  3   tablespoons extra-virgin olive oil
  4   very thin lemon slices
  ½   cup dry white wine
  ⅓   cup pitted brine-cured green olives such as *picholine*, halved lengthwise (2 oz)
  1   to 1½ teaspoons fresh lemon juice
  2   tablespoons finely chopped fresh oregano or ¾ teaspoon dried oregano, crumbled

SPECIAL EQUIPMENT: **a 2½-qt shallow ceramic or glass baking dish**

▶ Put oven rack in upper third of oven and preheat oven to 450°F.

▶ Pat fish dry and sprinkle with salt and pepper. Heat 1 tablespoon oil in a 12-inch heavy skillet over moderately high heat until hot but not smoking, then sear fillets, skinned sides down, until browned well, 3 to 4 minutes. Transfer, seared sides up, to baking dish (reserve skillet), then top each fillet with a slice of lemon.

▶ Add wine to skillet and bring to a boil, scraping up any brown bits. Boil 30 seconds, then pour around fish. Scatter olives around fish and bake, uncovered, until fish is just cooked through, 8 to 12 minutes.

▶ Transfer fish to a platter, then whisk lemon juice, oregano, and remaining 2 tablespoons oil into cooking liquid in baking dish. Season sauce with salt and pepper and spoon over fish.

BROILED BLUEFISH WITH TOMATO AND HERBS

SERVES 4 TO 6

ACTIVE TIME: 20 MIN   START TO FINISH: 35 MIN

  2 lb bluefish or Spanish mackerel fillets with skin, cut into
      portions if desired
 ¼ teaspoon black pepper
 ½ teaspoon salt
 ⅓ cup mayonnaise
  1 teaspoon fresh lemon juice
  2 tablespoons chopped fresh dill
  2 tablespoons chopped fresh chives
  3 medium tomatoes (¾ lb total), cut into ⅛-inch-thick slices

▶ Preheat broiler. Line rack of a broiler pan with foil.
▶ Put fish, skin sides down, on foil and sprinkle with pepper and
¼ teaspoon salt.
▶ Whisk together mayonnaise, lemon juice, dill, and chives in
a small bowl. Spread evenly over fish, then cover with tomato
slices, overlapping slightly, and sprinkle with remaining
¼ teaspoon salt.
▶ Broil fish 3 to 4 inches from heat until just cooked through,
12 to 15 minutes.

KITCHEN NOTE

MEATY, SATISFYING, AND PACKED WITH FLAVOR,
BLUEFISH LEND THEMSELVES BRILLIANTLY TO STRONG
MEDITERRANEAN-INSPIRED FLAVORINGS—BAY AND
CORIANDER OR TOMATOES AND HERBS. ALTHOUGH
CATEGORIZED AS AN OILY FISH, BLUEFISH IS NOT
REALLY THAT OILY; AT ITS PEAK OF FRESHNESS, IT
HAS A YIELDING, LUXURIOUS BASSLIKE TEXTURE.

GRILLED TUNA AND PEPPERS WITH CAPER VINAIGRETTE

SERVES 4

ACTIVE TIME: 10 MIN   START TO FINISH: 25 MIN

 ¾ lb Italian frying peppers (light green)
  2 (¾-lb) sushi-grade tuna steaks (1 inch thick)
1¼ teaspoons salt
  1 teaspoon black pepper
1½ tablespoons fresh lemon juice
 ½ teaspoon Dijon mustard
 ¼ cup olive oil
1½ tablespoons small capers in brine, drained and chopped
  2 tablespoons chopped fresh flat-leaf parsley

▶ Prepare gas grill for cooking over direct high heat (see Tips,
page 8).
▶ While grill heats, cut peppers lengthwise into quarters,
discarding stems and seeds. Trim ends so that quarters lie flat.
▶ Sprinkle tuna all over with 1 teaspoon salt and ½ teaspoon
pepper. Cook tuna and peppers on lightly oiled grill rack, turning
over once, until tuna is pink only in center and peppers are just
tender, 4 to 6 minutes total (peppers may take longer than tuna).
Transfer tuna and peppers as cooked to a serving plate.
▶ While tuna cooks, whisk together lemon juice, mustard, and
remaining ¼ teaspoon salt and ½ teaspoon pepper in a small
bowl, then add oil in a slow stream, whisking until emulsified.
Whisk in capers and parsley.
▶ Serve tuna topped with peppers and caper vinaigrette.

COOKS' NOTE: If you don't have a gas grill or aren't able to
grill outdoors, cook tuna and peppers in a lightly oiled
well-seasoned large (2-burner) ridged grill pan (preferably
cast iron) over moderately high heat, turning over once, 4 to
6 minutes total.

BEER-BATTERED FISH WITH SMOKED-PAPRIKA MAYONNAISE

SERVES 4

ACTIVE TIME: 10 MIN   START TO FINISH: 20 MIN

  6 to 8 cups vegetable oil for frying
 ¾ cup all-purpose flour
 ¾ teaspoon salt
 ¾ cup beer (not dark)
  8 (2½-oz) pieces of pollack, Pacific cod, or catfish fillet
      (¾ to 1 inch thick)
 ¼ cup drained bottled capers, coarsely chopped
 ¾ teaspoon hot Spanish smoked paprika
 ½ cup mayonnaise

SPECIAL EQUIPMENT: a deep-fat thermometer
GARNISH: lemon wedges

▶ Heat 2 inches oil in a wide 5- to 6-quart heavy pot over high
heat until it registers 380°F on thermometer.
▶ While oil is heating, whisk together flour and salt in a shallow
bowl, then whisk in beer (batter will be thick). Coat each piece
of fish with batter and transfer to hot oil with tongs (remove
thermometer). Cook over high heat, turning over once, until
golden and just cooked through, 5 to 6 minutes total, then
transfer fish to paper towels to drain.
▶ While fish fries, whisk capers and paprika into mayonnaise
in a bowl. Serve with fish.

CATFISH AND OKRA WITH PECAN BUTTER SAUCE

SERVES 4

ACTIVE TIME: 10 MIN   START TO FINISH: 30 MIN

   1   (10-oz) package frozen whole baby okra, thawed and rinsed
 12   oz grape tomatoes (2 cups)
   2   tablespoons vegetable oil
  ½   teaspoon salt
  ¼   teaspoon black pepper
   4   (½-lb) catfish fillets
   2   teaspoons Old Bay seasoning
   1   (10-oz) package frozen corn, thawed
  ¾   stick (6 tablespoons) unsalted butter
  ½   cup pecans (2 oz), coarsely chopped
   1   teaspoon fresh lemon juice

GARNISH: **lemon wedges**

▶ Put oven racks in upper and lower thirds of oven and preheat oven to 500°F.

▶ Toss okra and tomatoes with oil, salt, and pepper in a bowl. Spread in a large shallow baking pan and roast in lower third of oven until tomato skins begin to burst, about 10 minutes.

▶ Meanwhile, pat fillets dry and arrange in another large shallow baking pan. Sprinkle both sides with 1½ teaspoons (total) Old Bay seasoning.

▶ When tomato skins begin to burst, add corn to vegetables in lower third of oven and put fish in upper third of oven. Roast fish and vegetables until fish is just cooked through, about 10 minutes.

▶ While fish roasts, melt butter in a 10-inch heavy skillet over moderate heat, then add nuts and remaining ½ teaspoon Old Bay seasoning. Cook, stirring occasionally, until nuts are golden and butter is deep golden, about 3 minutes. Remove from heat and stir in juice. Serve fish over vegetables and top with sauce.

KITCHEN NOTE

THE BLEND OF CELERY SALT, MUSTARD, PEPPER, BAY LEAVES, CLOVES, ALLSPICE, GINGER, MACE, CARDAMOM, CINNAMON, AND PAPRIKA CALLED **OLD BAY SEASONING** ADDS PEP TO MANY FISH DISHES. IT WAS CREATED BY SAUSAGEMAKER GUSTAV BRUNN, WHO ARRIVED IN BALTIMORE IN 1938 AND STARTED MAKING SEASONINGS FOR LOCAL FISHMONGERS.

MAHIMAHI WITH ONION, CAPERS, AND LEMON

SERVES 4

ACTIVE TIME: 35 MIN   START TO FINISH: 35 MIN

    3   tablespoons olive oil
    1   large onion, halved lengthwise, then thinly sliced crosswise
    3   tablespoons water
   ½   teaspoon black pepper
    3   tablespoons unsalted butter
    3   tablespoons capers (in brine), rinsed, drained, and coarsely chopped
 2½   tablespoons fresh lemon juice
    4   (6-oz) pieces mahimahi fillet (1½ to 2 inches thick) with skin
   ¾   teaspoon salt
    2   tablespoons chopped fresh flat-leaf parsley

▶ Heat 2 tablespoons oil in a 12-inch heavy skillet over moderately high heat until hot but not smoking, then sauté onion, stirring frequently, until golden, about 6 minutes. Stir in water and ¼ teaspoon pepper and cook, stirring, until onion is softened, about 1 minute. Stir in butter until melted, then stir in capers and lemon juice. Remove from heat and keep warm, covered.

▶ Preheat broiler.

▶ Pat fish dry, then brush all over with remaining tablespoon oil and sprinkle with salt and remaining ¼ teaspoon pepper. Put fillets, skin sides down, on rack of a broiler pan and broil about 5 inches from heat until just cooked through, 6 to 8 minutes.

▶ Serve fish topped with onion mixture and sprinkled with chopped parsley.

HAKE WITH CHUNKY "ROMESCO"

SERVES 6

ACTIVE TIME: 25 MIN   START TO FINISH: 1 HR

   ½   cup extra-virgin olive oil
 2½   lb (1½- to 1¾-inch-thick) skinless hake fillets
    1   teaspoon salt
   ½   teaspoon black pepper
    2   garlic cloves, minced
   ½   cup whole almonds with skin, coarsely chopped
 2¼   cups (½-inch) torn pieces of baguette
    3   tablespoons chopped fresh flat-leaf parsley
    1   (12-oz) jar roasted red peppers, rinsed and patted dry
 1½   tablespoons Sherry vinegar
   ¼   teaspoon cayenne

▸ Put oven rack in upper third of oven and preheat oven to 450°F.

▸ Coat bottom of a 13- by 9-inch baking dish with 1 tablespoon oil and add fish, skinned side down. Sprinkle fish with salt and black pepper.

▸ Cook garlic, almonds, and bread in 2 tablespoons oil in a 12-inch heavy skillet over moderate heat, stirring, until pale golden, 6 to 8 minutes. Stir in parsley and spoon over fish. Bake fish, uncovered, 5 minutes. Loosely cover with foil and bake until fish is just cooked through, 20 to 28 minutes more (depending on thickness of fish). Drizzle with 1 tablespoon oil.

▸ Coarsely chop red peppers in a food processor. Add Sherry vinegar, cayenne, and remaining ¼ cup oil and pulse until just combined.

▸ Serve fish topped with sauce.

CRUNCHY WASABI-CRUSTED FISH WITH RED-CABBAGE SLAW

SERVES 4

ACTIVE TIME: 10 MIN START TO FINISH: 20 MIN

FOR FISH

4 (¾- to 1-inch-thick) skinless white-fleshed fish fillets such as Pacific cod or halibut (6 oz each)
½ teaspoon salt
1½ teaspoons wasabi paste (from a tube)
½ cup mayonnaise
1 to 1¼ cups *panko* (Japanese bread crumbs; see Sources)

FOR SLAW

¼ cup distilled white vinegar
1 teaspoon sugar
½ teaspoon dry mustard
¾ teaspoon salt
1 seedless cucumber (usually plastic-wrapped)
8 oz shredded red cabbage (4 cups; from a 10-oz package)

ACCOMPANIMENT: pickled ginger (sushi ginger)

PREPARE FISH:

▸ Put oven rack in upper third of oven and preheat oven to 400°F. Line a shallow baking pan with foil.

▸ Pat fillets dry, then arrange in baking pan. Sprinkle salt all over fillets. Stir together wasabi paste and mayonnaise in a small bowl, then spread tops of fillets with half of mayonnaise mixture and sprinkle with half of *panko*. Turn fillets over and spread with remaining mayonnaise mixture, then sprinkle with remaining *panko*.

▸ Bake until fish is just cooked through, 12 to 16 minutes, then broil 4 to 6 inches from heat until crumbs on top are golden brown, 1 to 2 minutes.

MAKE SLAW WHILE FISH BAKES:

▸ Stir together vinegar, sugar, mustard, and salt in a bowl until sugar is dissolved. Halve cucumber lengthwise, then thinly slice. Add to dressing along with cabbage and stir to coat. Serve slaw alongside fish.

BACON-WRAPPED SALMON WITH WILTED SPINACH

SERVES 4

ACTIVE TIME: 15 MIN START TO FINISH: 25 MIN

Wrapped with bacon, these delicious fillets self-baste during broiling, eliminating the need for a sauce.

4 (5- to 6-oz) center-cut pieces skinless salmon fillet (about 1½ inches thick)
½ teaspoon salt
¼ teaspoon black pepper
4 teaspoons whole-grain or coarse-grain mustard
4 bacon slices
⅔ cup sliced shallots (2 large)
2 tablespoons olive oil
10 oz baby spinach (16 cups packed), rinsed but not dried

SPECIAL EQUIPMENT: 4 (10- to 12-inch) metal skewers

▸ Preheat broiler and put broiler pan under broiler so that its rack is about 4 inches from heat.

▸ Pat fish dry and sprinkle with salt and pepper, then spread curved sides with mustard. Lay 1 bacon slice lengthwise along top of each fillet, tucking ends of bacon under fillet (ends will not meet). Thread 1 skewer through length of each fillet, entering and exiting fish through bacon to secure it.

▸ Arrange fish, bacon sides down, on preheated rack of broiler pan and broil 3 minutes, then turn over and broil until fish is just cooked through and bacon is crisp, 3 to 4 minutes more.

▸ While salmon broils, cook shallots in oil in a 12-inch heavy skillet over moderate heat, stirring occasionally, until beginning to brown, 3 to 5 minutes. Add spinach and cook, covered, stirring occasionally, until spinach is just wilted, 1 to 2 minutes. Season with salt and pepper.

▸ Serve salmon with spinach.

SHELLFISH

LOBSTER CANTONESE

SERVES 4

ACTIVE TIME: 40 MIN   START TO FINISH: 45 MIN

- 1 tablespoon cornstarch
- ¾ cup reduced-sodium chicken broth
- ¼ cup Chinese rice wine or medium-dry Sherry
- 3 tablespoons soy sauce
- 1 teaspoon sugar
- ¼ teaspoon black pepper
- 2 (1½-lb) live lobsters
- 2 tablespoons vegetable oil
- 2 tablespoons Chinese fermented black beans (see Sources), rinsed and finely chopped
- 2 teaspoons finely chopped garlic
- 2 teaspoons finely chopped peeled fresh ginger
- 4 scallions, trimmed and cut into 1½-inch pieces
- ¼ lb ground fatty pork
- 2 large eggs, lightly beaten
- 2 teaspoons Asian sesame oil

SPECIAL EQUIPMENT: kitchen shears; a well-seasoned 14-inch flat-bottomed wok with a lid

▸ Bring 6 quarts water with 3 tablespoons salt to a boil in an 8- to 10-quart pot over high heat.
▸ Meanwhile, stir together cornstarch, broth, rice wine, soy sauce, sugar, and pepper in a small bowl until sugar is dissolved.
▸ Plunge lobsters headfirst into boiling water, then cover tightly and cook for 2 minutes from time lobsters enter water. Transfer lobsters with tongs to a large bowl of ice and cold water to stop cooking (lobsters will not be fully cooked), then drain lobsters in a colander. When cool enough to handle, twist off tail and claws (including joints) of 1 lobster. Cut body in half lengthwise through shell with shears, then remove and discard sand sacs from inside head. Cut body in half again crosswise. Halve tail lengthwise through shell with a cleaver or large heavy knife, then cut each half crosswise into 4 pieces. Working with same lobster, 1 claw at a time, wrap claws with joints in a kitchen towel and twist off claws from joints. Unwrap claws, then crack joints with a mallet or back of a large heavy knife. Chop claws in half lengthwise between pincers with a cleaver or large heavy knife. Transfer lobster pieces to a bowl, keeping meat in shells. Repeat with second lobster, putting pieces of second lobster in another bowl.

▸ Heat wok over high heat until a drop of water evaporates instantly. Pour 1 tablespoon vegetable oil down side of wok, then tilt wok to swirl oil, coating side. When oil begins to smoke, add pieces of 1 lobster and stir-fry just until meat starts to turn opaque, about 1½ minutes. Transfer cooked lobster with a slotted spoon to a large bowl. Repeat with second lobster, transferring cooked pieces to same bowl.
▸ Add remaining tablespoon vegetable oil to wok, swirling to coat, then add beans, garlic, ginger, scallions, and pork and stir-fry until pork is no longer pink, about 1 minute.
▸ Stir cornstarch mixture, then add to pork in wok and bring to a boil. Add lobster and stir to coat, then reduce heat and simmer, covered, 2 minutes. Remove lid and pour eggs over lobster mixture in a thin circular stream. Cover wok and simmer just until eggs begin to set, 1 to 2 minutes. Drizzle with sesame oil, then gently toss. Serve immediately.

LEMON CAPER CALAMARI STEAKS WITH BROCCOLINI

SERVES 4

ACTIVE TIME: 10 MIN   START TO FINISH: 20 MIN

Meaty, sweet squid steaks offer a variation of chicken francese.

- ¼ cup olive oil
- 3 garlic cloves, crushed in a garlic press
- ¼ teaspoon dried hot red-pepper flakes
- 1 lb Broccolini, trimmed
- ¼ teaspoon salt
- ⅓ cup plus 1 tablespoon water
- 3 tablespoons all-purpose flour
- ¼ cup finely grated Parmigiano-Reggiano
- ¼ teaspoon black pepper
- 1 large egg
- 4 frozen calamari steaks (1 lb total), thawed
- 2 tablespoons unsalted butter
- 1 to 1½ tablespoons fresh lemon juice
- 1 tablespoon bottled capers in brine, rinsed and drained

ACCOMPANIMENT: lemon wedges

▸ Heat 2 tablespoons oil in a 12-inch heavy skillet over moderate heat until hot but not smoking, then cook garlic and red-pepper flakes, stirring, until golden, about 30 seconds. Add Broccolini and cook, turning with tongs, until coated with oil, then add salt and ⅓ cup water and cook, covered, stirring occasionally, until Broccolini is crisp-tender, 8 to 10 minutes. Transfer to a platter with tongs and keep warm, loosely covered with foil.

▸ Heat remaining 2 tablespoons oil in a 10-inch heavy skillet over moderately high heat until hot but not smoking. While oil heats, stir together flour, cheese, and pepper in a wide shallow bowl, then lightly beat egg with remaining tablespoon water in another wide shallow bowl. Dredge 1 calamari steak in flour mixture, shaking off excess, then dip in egg mixture, letting excess drip off, and transfer to a plate. Dredge another steak in flour and dip in egg in same manner, then sauté coated steaks in hot oil over moderately high heat, turning over once, until golden, about 1½ minutes total. Transfer to platter with Broccolini and keep warm, loosely covered. Dredge, dip, and sauté remaining 2 steaks in same manner, transferring to platter.

▸ Pour off fat from skillet, then add butter, lemon juice (to taste), and capers to skillet and cook over moderate heat just until butter melts, about 45 seconds. Pour lemon caper sauce over calamari steaks and serve immediately.

KITCHEN NOTE

AVAILABLE AT FISH STORES AND SOME SUPERMARKETS, MEATY **CALAMARI STEAKS** (A.K.A. "SQUID STEAKS" AND, IN CALIFORNIA, "POOR MAN'S ABALONE") CAN BE SAUTÉED IN NO TIME. THE STEAKS ARE MADE FROM SUSTAINABLE WILD-CAUGHT LARGE SPECIES OF SQUID THAT HAVE BEEN TENDERIZED, USUALLY WITH A CUBE-STEAKING MACHINE OR AN ENZYME LIKE PAPAYIN. LOOK FOR STEAKS FROM TAIWAN AND ARGENTINA, SINCE THEY ARE SAID TO BE THE BEST.

MUSSELS WITH SAFFRON CREAM

SERVES 4
ACTIVE TIME: 10 MIN START TO FINISH: 25 MIN

Just a small amount of precious saffron turns this weeknight supper into something out of the ordinary.

- 1 large onion, halved lengthwise
     Rounded ¼ teaspoon crumbled saffron threads
- ¾ teaspoon salt
- 3 tablespoons olive oil
- 1 cup dry white wine
- 1 cup heavy cream
- ¼ teaspoon black pepper
- 4 lb cultivated mussels, rinsed well
- 2 tablespoons chopped fresh flat-leaf parsley

SPECIAL EQUIPMENT: **an adjustable-blade slicer**
ACCOMPANIMENT: **prepared garlic bread**

▸ Cut onion halves crosswise into less than ¹⁄₁₆-inch-thick slices with slicer.
▸ Cook onion with saffron and ½ teaspoon salt in oil in a wide 6- to 8-quart heavy pot over moderately high heat, covered, stirring occasionally, until onion is softened, about 5 minutes.
▸ Add wine and bring to a boil, then stir in cream, pepper, remaining ¼ teaspoon salt, and mussels. Cook, covered, checking after 6 minutes and transferring opened mussels to soup bowls with a slotted spoon. (Discard any that remain unopened after 8 minutes.)
▸ Stir parsley into broth and pour over mussels.

MOROCCAN-STYLE MUSSELS

SERVES 4
ACTIVE TIME: 30 MIN START TO FINISH: 40 MIN

Chickpeas transform saucy mussels into a meal that's as hearty as it is seductive.

- 1 medium onion, coarsely chopped (1 cup)
- 2 garlic cloves, thinly sliced
- 1¼ teaspoons ground cumin
- 1 teaspoon paprika (preferably hot)
- 1 teaspoon ground ginger
- ⅜ teaspoon ground cinnamon
- ⅛ teaspoon cayenne
- 3 tablespoons olive oil
- 1 tablespoon cider vinegar
- 1 (15- to 19-oz) can chickpeas, rinsed and drained
- 2 teaspoons sugar
- 1 (28-oz) can whole tomatoes in juice, juice reserved and tomatoes coarsely chopped
- 3 lb cultivated mussels, scrubbed and beards removed
- 2 tablespoons chopped fresh flat-leaf parsley

▸ Cook onion, garlic, and spices in oil in a 5- to 6-quart heavy pot over moderately low heat, stirring, until onion is softened, about 6 minutes. Stir in vinegar and simmer 1 minute. Add chickpeas, sugar, and tomatoes with their juice, then increase heat to moderate and gently simmer, uncovered, stirring occasionally, until slightly thickened, about 15 minutes. Add mussels and return to a simmer. Cover tightly with lid and cook until mussels just open wide, 3 to 6 minutes. (Discard any mussels that remain unopened after 6 minutes.) Stir in parsley and serve in shallow bowls.

SHRIMP WITH SHERRY-TOMATO SAUCE

SERVES 4

ACTIVE TIME: 10 MIN   START TO FINISH: 25 MIN

- 1 large onion, quartered
- 1 (28-oz) can whole tomatoes in juice
- 3 tablespoons extra-virgin olive oil
- 1½ lb peeled and deveined large shrimp (not cooked)
- ¾ teaspoon salt
- ½ teaspoon black pepper
- 4 garlic cloves
- ⅓ cup Sherry
- ¾ cup pitted green olives (from an 8-oz jar), chopped if large

ACCOMPANIMENT: **white rice**

▶ Pulse onion in a food processor until finely chopped, then transfer to a bowl. Add tomatoes with juice to processor and pulse until chopped.

▶ Heat oil in a 12-inch heavy skillet over high heat until hot but not smoking. Toss shrimp with ½ teaspoon salt and ¼ teaspoon pepper, then add to skillet and sauté, turning over once, until just cooked through, about 3 minutes total. Transfer shrimp to a plate with tongs (do not clean skillet).

▶ Force garlic through a garlic press into skillet and cook, stirring, until golden, about 15 seconds. Stir in Sherry, scraping up any brown bits from bottom of skillet, then add onion and remaining ¼ teaspoon salt and ¼ teaspoon pepper and cook, stirring occasionally, until all of liquid is evaporated and onion is just tender, 5 to 6 minutes.

▶ Add tomatoes and olives and simmer, stirring occasionally, until sauce is slightly thickened, 5 to 7 minutes.

▶ Stir in shrimp with any juices accumulated on plate and heat through. Season with salt.

CAJUN SHRIMP STEW

SERVES 4

ACTIVE TIME: 25 MIN   START TO FINISH: 35 MIN

- 2 tablespoons vegetable oil
- ¼ cup all-purpose flour
- 1 medium onion, chopped
- 1 small celery rib, finely chopped
- ½ cup finely chopped green bell pepper
- 1 cup bottled clam juice (8 fl oz)
- ¾ cup water
- ¼ teaspoon salt
- ¼ teaspoon cayenne
- 1¼ lb peeled and deveined large shrimp (21 to 25 per lb)
- ⅓ cup thinly sliced scallion greens

ACCOMPANIMENT: **white rice**

▶ Stir together oil and flour in a 10-inch heavy skillet (preferably cast iron) with a metal or wooden spatula, then cook over moderate heat, scraping back and forth constantly, until roux is the color of light milk chocolate, 10 to 12 minutes.

▶ Add onion, celery, and bell pepper and cook, scraping back and forth occasionally, until bell pepper is softened, about 8 minutes. Stir in clam juice, water, salt, and cayenne and simmer, stirring occasionally, until liquid is thickened, 8 to 10 minutes. Stir in shrimp and simmer, stirring occasionally, until shrimp is just cooked through, 3 to 4 minutes. Stir in scallion greens and salt to taste.

BEEF

GRILLED PORTERHOUSE STEAK WITH HORSERADISH CREAM

SERVES 6
ACTIVE TIME: 25 MIN START TO FINISH: 35 MIN

A simple seasoning of salt and pepper leaves this steak ready for an assertive horseradish sauce.

2	(1¼-inch-thick) porterhouse steaks (4 lb total)
1	cup sour cream
¼	cup undrained horseradish (from a new jar)
4	scallions, chopped
1½	teaspoons salt
1½	teaspoons black pepper

SPECIAL EQUIPMENT: **an instant-read thermometer**

▸ Prepare grill for cooking over direct heat with medium-hot charcoal (moderate heat for gas); see Tips, page 8.
▸ While coals are lighting, let steaks stand at room temperature about 15 minutes. Stir together sour cream, horseradish, scallions, ½ teaspoon salt, and ½ teaspoon pepper in a bowl.
▸ Pat steaks dry and sprinkle all over with remaining teaspoon each of salt and pepper. Grill steaks on lightly oiled grill rack, covered only if using a gas grill, turning steaks over once and moving them around grill to avoid flare-ups if necessary, until thermometer inserted horizontally 2 inches into meat (do not touch bone) registers about 120°F for rare, 9 to 12 minutes total. Transfer steaks to a cutting board and let stand 10 minutes before slicing. (Internal temperature will rise to 125 to 128°F while steaks stand.) Thinly slice meat and serve with sauce.

COOKS' NOTE: If you aren't able to grill outdoors, steaks can be seared in a hot lightly oiled well-seasoned large (2-burner) ridged grill pan (preferably cast iron) over moderately high heat, turning over once, until grill marks form, 4 to 6 minutes total. Reduce heat to moderately low, then cover with 2 large overturned metal bowls and cook, turning over once, about 12 minutes total.

FILETS MIGNONS WITH STROGANOV SAUCE

SERVES 4
ACTIVE TIME: 10 MIN START TO FINISH: 30 MIN

We couldn't improve much on traditional beef Stroganov, but we did decide to trade up: The usual small tenderloin pieces are replaced by whole steaks, which make for a more striking presentation on the plate.

6	oz dried egg noodles
1	medium onion, halved lengthwise
2	tablespoons vegetable oil
4	(1¼-inch-thick) beef tenderloin steaks (filets mignons)
1¼	teaspoons salt
¾	teaspoon black pepper
2	garlic cloves, thinly sliced
½	lb sliced white mushrooms
¼	cup brandy
¾	cup reduced-sodium beef broth
2	tablespoons Worcestershire sauce
¾	cup sour cream

SPECIAL EQUIPMENT: **an adjustable-blade slicer**

▸ Cook noodles in a 6- to 8-quart pot of boiling salted water (see Tips, page 8) until just tender. Drain in a colander.
▸ Meanwhile, thinly slice onion using slicer. Heat oil in a 12-inch heavy skillet over high heat until hot but not smoking. While oil heats, pat steaks dry. Sprinkle ¾ teaspoon salt and ¼ teaspoon pepper on steaks, then add to skillet and sauté, turning over once with tongs, about 6 minutes total for medium-rare. Transfer to a plate with tongs.
▸ Add onion, garlic, and remaining ½ teaspoon salt and ½ teaspoon pepper to oil in skillet and sauté, scraping up any brown bits with a wooden spoon, until onion begins to brown, about 3 minutes. Add mushrooms and sauté, stirring occasionally, until liquid given off by mushrooms is evaporated, about 4 minutes.
▸ Add brandy and boil until evaporated, about 1 minute. Add broth and Worcestershire sauce, then cover and cook until onion is softened, about 4 minutes.
▸ Remove from heat and stir in sour cream.
▸ Toss noodles with some of sauce and serve remaining sauce over steaks.

RIB-EYE STEAKS WITH HARISSA-STYLE RELISH

SERVES 4

ACTIVE TIME: 25 MIN   START TO FINISH: 35 MIN

　1　garlic clove
　1　teaspoon cumin seeds
　½　teaspoon coriander seeds
　½　teaspoon caraway seeds
　1　cup drained bottled roasted red peppers (from a 7-oz jar),
　　　rinsed well, patted dry, and finely chopped
　2　tablespoons olive oil
　¾　to 1 teaspoon dried hot red-pepper flakes
　½　teaspoon sugar
　¾　teaspoon salt
　2　lb (¾- to 1-inch-thick) boneless rib-eye steaks
　½　teaspoon black pepper

SPECIAL EQUIPMENT: an electric coffee/spice grinder

▸ Mince garlic and mash to a paste with a pinch of salt using a large heavy knife, then transfer to a bowl.

▸ Heat a dry small heavy skillet over moderately low heat until hot, then toast cumin, coriander, and caraway seeds, shaking skillet frequently, until fragrant, about 1 minute. Transfer seeds to grinder and pulse until coarsely ground.

▸ Add spices to garlic paste along with roasted peppers, oil, red-pepper flakes (to taste), sugar, and ¼ teaspoon salt.

▸ Pat steaks dry and sprinkle all over with pepper and remaining ½ teaspoon salt.

▸ Prepare grill for cooking with medium-hot charcoal (moderately high heat for gas); see Tips, page 8.

▸ Grill steaks on lightly oiled grill rack, turning over once and moving around rack to avoid flare-ups, 5 to 6 minutes total for medium-rare. If using a gas grill, cook covered, turning over once and moving around rack to avoid flare-ups, 4 to 5 minutes total for medium-rare.

▸ Transfer steaks to a cutting board and let stand, uncovered, 5 minutes.

COOKS' NOTE: If you aren't able to grill outdoors, steaks can be cooked in a hot, lightly oiled well-seasoned large (2 burner) ridged grill pan (preferably cast iron) over moderately high heat, turning over once, 10 to 12 minutes total.

TRI-TIP ROAST WITH PARSLEY CHERRY-TOMATO SAUCE

SERVES 4 TO 6

ACTIVE TIME: 15 MIN   START TO FINISH: 55 MIN

This cut of meat yields a juicy roast with no fuss. And the spicy parsley sauce is tasty enough to keep some on hand for chicken, fish, or pasta.

FOR ROAST
　1　(2- to 2¼-lb) tri-tip beef roast (also called triangular roast;
　　　about 2 inches thick)
　1½　teaspoons salt
　¼　teaspoon black pepper
　1　tablespoon olive oil

FOR PARSLEY CHERRY-TOMATO SAUCE
　1½　lb cherry tomatoes (5 cups)
　½　teaspoon salt
　¼　teaspoon dried hot red-pepper flakes
　¼　cup plus 2 tablespoons extra-virgin olive oil
　1　cup firmly packed fresh flat-leaf parsley leaves
　1　garlic clove, sliced
　1　tablespoon red-wine vinegar

SPECIAL EQUIPMENT: a well-seasoned 10-inch cast-iron skillet; an instant-read thermometer

MAKE ROAST:
▸ Put oven racks in upper and lower thirds of oven and preheat oven to 425°F.

▸ Pat roast dry and sprinkle with salt and pepper. Heat oil in skillet over moderately high heat until hot but not smoking, then sear roast until underside is browned, about 4 minutes. Turn meat over, then transfer skillet to upper rack of oven and roast until thermometer inserted 2 inches into center of meat registers 120°F, 20 to 25 minutes. Transfer to a cutting board and let stand 15 minutes. (Internal temperature of meat will rise to 130 to 135°F for medium-rare.)

MAKE SAUCE WHILE MEAT COOKS:
▸ Toss together tomatoes, salt, red-pepper flakes, and ¼ cup oil in a 13- by 9-inch glass baking dish. Roast on lower rack until tomatoes burst and release their juices, about 30 minutes.

▸ Meanwhile, pulse parsley and garlic with vinegar and remaining 2 tablespoons oil in a food processor until chopped, then transfer to a bowl.

▸ Stir tomatoes with their juices into parsley mixture. Slice roast across the grain and serve with sauce.

COOKS' NOTE: Leftover sauce keeps, covered and chilled, 5 days.

COFFEE-BRAISED BEEF WITH CINNAMON AND ORANGE

SERVES 4

ACTIVE TIME: 15 MIN   START TO FINISH: 4¼ HR

 1   large onion, chopped (1½ cups)
1½ tablespoons olive oil
 2   garlic cloves, thinly sliced
1¼ cups strong brewed coffee
 3   (3- by 1-inch) strips fresh orange zest (see Tips, page 8)
 1   (3-inch) cinnamon stick
 2   teaspoons packed brown sugar
 1   (3½-lb) boneless beef chuck roast
1½ teaspoons salt
½   teaspoon black pepper

▶ Put oven rack in middle position and preheat oven to 325°F.
▶ Cook onion in oil in a 4- to 5-quart heavy pot over moderately high heat, stirring, until golden, about 6 minutes. Add garlic and cook, stirring, 1 minute. Stir in coffee, zest, cinnamon stick, and brown sugar, then bring to a simmer. Sprinkle beef all over with salt and pepper, then add to pot. Transfer pot to oven and braise, tightly covered, until meat is very tender, 3½ to 4 hours.
▶ Skim fat from sauce and discard cinnamon stick.

SKIRT STEAK WITH HARICOTS VERTS, CORN, AND PESTO

SERVES 4

ACTIVE TIME: 10 MIN   START TO FINISH: 30 MIN

1½ lb skirt steak
¾   teaspoon salt
¼   teaspoon black pepper
1½ tablespoons olive oil
 1   ear corn, kernels cut off
¾   lb haricots verts, trimmed
½   cup prepared basil pesto

▶ Pat steak dry and cut into 4 pieces, then sprinkle all over with salt and pepper.

▶ Heat ½ tablespoon olive oil in a 12-inch heavy skillet over moderately high heat until hot but not smoking, then sauté corn, stirring, until just starting to brown, 1 to 2 minutes. Transfer to a large bowl.
▶ Add remaining tablespoon oil to skillet and sauté steaks, in batches if necessary, turning over once, 3 to 5 minutes per batch for thin pieces and 5 to 7 minutes per batch for thicker pieces (for medium-rare). Transfer steaks to a cutting board and let stand 5 minutes before slicing.
▶ While steaks stand, cook haricots verts in a large pot of well-salted boiling water (see Tips, page 8), uncovered, until just tender, about 4 minutes, then drain well in a colander. Add beans to corn, then add pesto, stirring to coat. Serve vegetables topped with sliced steak.

STRACCETTI DI MANZO

Sliced Steak with Arugula

SERVES 4

ACTIVE TIME: 10 MIN   START TO FINISH: 10 MIN

Generations of Roman cooks have relied on this trattoria favorite for dinner in a hurry.

 5   oz baby arugula
⅓   cup extra-virgin olive oil
 2   large garlic cloves, smashed
 1   large sprig fresh rosemary
 1   lb boneless top loin steak (New York strip) or sirloin (1 inch thick)
 1   teaspoon salt
¾   teaspoon black pepper
 1   large shallot, thinly sliced crosswise
1½ tablespoons balsamic vinegar
1½ tablespoons red-wine vinegar

GARNISH: freshly ground black pepper

▶ Mound arugula on a large platter.
▶ Heat oil with garlic and rosemary in a 12-inch heavy skillet over high heat, turning garlic once or twice, until garlic is golden, about 4 minutes. Discard garlic and rosemary.
▶ Meanwhile, cut steak crosswise into ⅛-inch-thick slices and toss with ¾ teaspoon salt and ½ teaspoon pepper. Add meat to skillet all at once and sauté over high heat, tossing with tongs to color evenly, about 1 minute for medium-rare. Arrange steak over arugula using tongs, then add shallot to oil in skillet along with vinegars and remaining ¼ teaspoon each of salt and pepper and boil 2 minutes. Pour dressing over steak and serve immediately.

GREEN-CHILE BEEF STEW

SERVES 6

ACTIVE TIME: 1 HR (INCLUDES ROASTING CHILES)   START TO FINISH: 4 HR

This stew has "family favorite" written all over it. The simplicity of the ingredients, along with its versatility, add up to a dish that is fabulous for a casual dinner at home or to serve to guests.

- 3   lb boneless beef chuck, trimmed and cut into 1½-inch pieces
- ½   teaspoon black pepper
- 2   teaspoons salt
- 2   tablespoons vegetable oil
- 2   large white onions, chopped (4 to 5 cups)
- 3   garlic cloves, finely chopped (about 1 tablespoon)
- 1   tablespoon ground cumin
- 1   (28-oz) can whole tomatoes in juice
- 2   to 2½ cups water
- 1   lb fresh New Mexico green chiles or Anaheim chiles (8 to 10), roasted and peeled (see Tips, page 8)

ACCOMPANIMENTS: **cooked pinto beans and rice**

▶ Pat beef dry and season with pepper and 1 teaspoon salt.

▶ Heat oil in a 10- to 11-inch-wide (5- to 7-quart) heavy pot over moderately high heat until hot but not smoking, then cook beef in 2 or 3 batches, turning occasionally, until browned, 6 to 8 minutes per batch. Transfer as browned to a bowl using a slotted spoon.

▶ Add onions and garlic to fat in pot and cook over moderately high heat, stirring and scraping up brown bits, until softened, about 8 minutes. Add cumin and remaining teaspoon salt and cook, stirring, 2 minutes. Return beef (with any juices accumulated in bowl) to pot and stir in tomatoes with juice and enough water to cover meat, then bring to a simmer.

▶ Discard seeds, ribs, and stems from chiles, then cut lengthwise into ⅓-inch-wide strips. Add chiles to stew and gently simmer, uncovered, stirring occasionally to break up tomatoes, until meat is very tender, about 3 hours.

COOKS' NOTE: Stew is best made 1 day ahead to allow flavors to develop. Cool completely, uncovered, then chill, covered. Reheat before serving.

TAPENADE-FILLED BURGERS

SERVES 6

ACTIVE TIME: 50 MIN   START TO FINISH: 50 MIN

Tucked inside these juicy chuck burgers is a pocket of rich, salty tapenade. To experience the full range of flavors, build your burger with all the accompaniments—the bite of red onion and the sweet crunch of gherkin pickles are key.

- 2¼   lb lean ground beef chuck
- 9   tablespoons black or green olive tapenade (sometimes labeled "olive paste")
- ¾   teaspoon salt
- 1   teaspoon black pepper
- 6   grilled or toasted hamburger buns or kaiser rolls

ACCOMPANIMENTS: **mayonnaise; coarse-grain mustard; thinly sliced red onion; thinly sliced sweet gherkin pickles; about 2 cups baby romaine lettuce**

▶ Divide beef into 6 portions. Divide 1 portion in half, then flatten 1 half into a 4-inch patty and form a ¼-inch rim around patty. Spread 1½ tablespoons of tapenade onto patty within rim. Flatten remaining half into a 4-inch patty, then lay on top of tapenade-covered half and pinch edges together to seal. Pat side to form a straight-sided edge all around and transfer to a large tray. Make 5 more tapenade patties in same manner and transfer to tray, then chill patties, covered, until ready to grill.

▶ Prepare grill for cooking over direct heat with medium-hot charcoal (moderately high heat for gas); see Tips, page 8.

▶ Sprinkle patties on both sides with salt and pepper. Lightly oil grill rack, then grill patties, covered only if using a gas grill, turning over once, 3 minutes total for medium-rare. (Burgers will continue to cook slightly after being removed from grill.)

▶ Spread mayonnaise and mustard on buns, then assemble burgers with onion, pickles, and romaine.

COOKS' NOTES: Patties can be chilled up to 8 hours.
• If you aren't able to grill outdoors, patties can be cooked in a lightly oiled well-seasoned large (2-burner) ridged grill pan (preferably cast iron) over moderately high heat, turning over once, 4 minutes total for medium-rare.

SPICED BEEF CORN BREAD COBBLER

SERVES 4

ACTIVE TIME: 35 MIN   START TO FINISH: 50 MIN

Think of this dish as a sloppy joe with a corn bread and Cheddar crust—a welcome twist to an American classic.

- 1   medium onion, chopped
- 4   tablespoons vegetable oil
- 2   garlic cloves, finely chopped
- 1   lb ground beef chuck
- 1   teaspoon sugar
- ½   teaspoon ground cinnamon
- ½   teaspoon cayenne
- ¼   teaspoon ground allspice
- ¼   teaspoon black pepper
- ⅛   teaspoon ground ginger
- 1¼ teaspoons salt
- 1   (14- to 15-oz) can diced tomatoes in juice
- ⅔   cup yellow cornmeal
- ⅓   cup all-purpose flour
- 1   teaspoon baking powder
- ⅓   cup whole milk
- 1   large egg
- 2   oz coarsely grated sharp Cheddar (½ cup plus 2 tablespoons)

▶ Put oven rack in middle position and preheat oven to 400°F. Lightly oil a 9½-inch (6-cup capacity) pie plate.

▶ Cook onion in 2 tablespoons oil in a deep 10-inch heavy skillet over moderate heat, stirring occasionally, until edges are golden, 3 to 4 minutes. Add garlic and cook, stirring, 1 minute. Add beef and cook, breaking up large lumps, until no longer pink, 4 to 5 minutes. Add sugar, spices, and 1 teaspoon salt and cook, stirring, 1 minute. Add tomatoes with juice and briskly simmer, stirring occasionally, until liquid is reduced to about ¼ cup, 8 to 10 minutes.

▶ While beef simmers, whisk together cornmeal, flour, baking powder, and remaining ¼ teaspoon salt in a medium bowl. Whisk together milk, egg, and remaining 2 tablespoons oil in a small bowl, then stir into cornmeal mixture until just combined. Fold in ½ cup cheese.

▶ Spoon cooked spiced beef into pie plate with a slotted spoon, reserving juices in skillet. Skim off and discard fat from juices if desired, then pour juices over beef in pie plate.

▶ Spoon 4 mounds of corn bread batter over beef, then sprinkle remaining 2 tablespoons cheese over batter. Bake until a wooden pick or skewer inserted into center of corn bread comes out clean, 15 to 25 minutes.

▶ Serve cobbler warm.

VEAL

SAUTÉED VEAL CHOPS WITH MUSHROOMS

SERVES 4

ACTIVE TIME: 40 MIN   START TO FINISH: 45 MIN

There is a reason for the enduring popularity of veal with mushrooms—they just work so well together.

- 1   teaspoon cornstarch
- 2   teaspoons Worcestershire sauce
- 1   cup reduced-sodium chicken broth
- 4   (½-inch-thick) veal loin chops (1¾ lb total)
- ¾   teaspoon salt
- ¾   teaspoon black pepper
- 2   tablespoons olive oil
- 2   tablespoons unsalted butter
- 1   medium onion, finely chopped
- 10 oz cremini mushrooms, thinly sliced (3 cups)
- 2   garlic cloves, finely chopped
- ¼   cup heavy cream
- ¼   cup finely chopped fresh flat-leaf parsley

▶ Put oven rack in middle position and preheat oven to 200°F.

▶ Stir together cornstarch, Worcestershire sauce, and broth in a small bowl until combined well.

▶ Pat 2 chops dry, then sprinkle both sides with ¼ teaspoon salt and ¼ teaspoon pepper (total). Heat 1 tablespoon oil in a 12-inch heavy skillet over moderately high heat until hot but not smoking, then sauté seasoned chops, turning over once, until golden and almost cooked through, 4 to 5 minutes total. Transfer to a shallow baking pan and keep warm in oven. Season remaining 2 chops and sauté in remaining tablespoon oil in same manner, transferring to shallow baking pan.

▶ Pour off oil from skillet, then add butter and onion to skillet and cook over moderate heat, stirring occasionally, until onion is softened, about 3 minutes. Add mushrooms and remaining ¼ teaspoon salt and ¼ teaspoon pepper and increase heat to moderately high. Cook, stirring occasionally, until any liquid mushrooms give off is evaporated and mushrooms are just tender, 4 to 5 minutes. Add garlic and cook, stirring, 1 minute. Stir broth mixture, then add to mushrooms and bring to a boil, stirring occasionally. Reduce head and simmer, stirring occasionally, until sauce is very thick, 2 to 3 minutes. Add cream and any meat juices accumulated in baking pan, then bring to a boil, stirring occasionally.

▶ Stir in parsley and salt and pepper to taste. Serve chops with mushroom sauce.

VEAL PATTIES WITH MUSHROOMS AND CHIVES

SERVES 4

ACTIVE TIME: 30 MIN   START TO FINISH: 30 MIN

An adaptation of Viennese butterschnitzel, *these individual meatloaves are incredibly moist and juicy.*

    2 slices firm white sandwich bread, coarsely crumbled
    ¼ cup heavy cream
    1 large egg, lightly beaten
    ¾ teaspoon salt
    ¼ teaspoon black pepper
   2½ tablespoons finely chopped fresh chives
   1¼ lb ground veal
    ½ cup fine dry bread crumbs (not seasoned)
    2 tablespoons vegetable oil
    ½ stick (¼ cup) unsalted butter
    ½ lb cremini mushrooms, trimmed and cut into sixths

SPECIAL EQUIPMENT: **an instant-read thermometer**

ACCOMPANIMENT: **lemon wedges**

▶ Put oven rack in middle position and preheat oven to 200°F.

▶ Soak bread in cream in a large bowl 5 minutes. Stir in egg, salt, pepper, and 1 tablespoon chives until blended well. Add veal and mix with your hands until combined well. Form veal mixture into 4 (4-inch) patties. Spread dry bread crumbs on a sheet of wax paper and coat patties all over.

▶ Heat oil with 2 tablespoons butter in a 12-inch nonstick skillet over moderately high heat until foam subsides, then cook patties, carefully turning over once, until golden brown, firm to the touch, and thermometer inserted into center of each registers 148°F, 8 to 10 minutes total. Transfer patties to an ovenproof platter and keep warm, covered with foil, in oven. Do not clean skillet.

▶ Heat remaining 2 tablespoons butter in skillet over moderately high heat until foam subsides, then sauté mushrooms, stirring occasionally, until browned and tender, 3 to 5 minutes. Stir in remaining 1½ tablespoons chives and salt and pepper to taste.

▶ Serve veal patties topped with mushrooms.

PORK

PORK TENDERLOIN WITH POMEGRANATE SAUCE

SERVES 4

ACTIVE TIME: 10 MIN   START TO FINISH: 35 MIN

    ¾ teaspoon ground cumin
    ¾ teaspoon ground coriander
    ¾ teaspoon black pepper
    ½ teaspoon ground cinnamon
    ½ teaspoon salt
    2 pork tenderloins (each about ¾ lb)
    2 tablespoons olive oil
    1 cup plain pomegranate juice (such as POM Wonderful)
    ¾ teaspoon cornstarch
    1 tablespoon water
    1 to 2 teaspoons Sherry vinegar
    1 tablespoon unsalted butter

SPECIAL EQUIPMENT: **an instant-read thermometer**

▶ Stir together cumin, coriander, pepper, cinnamon, and salt in a shallow bowl. Pat tenderloins dry and dredge in spice mixture until evenly coated.

▶ Heat oil in a 12-inch heavy skillet over moderately high heat until hot but not smoking. Reduce heat to moderate and cook pork, turning occasionally, until meat is browned on all sides and thermometer inserted diagonally into center of each tenderloin registers 145°F, 20 to 25 minutes. Transfer pork with tongs to a cutting board (reserve skillet) and let stand 10 minutes.

▶ While pork stands, pour off and discard any fat from skillet, then add pomegranate juice to skillet and boil over moderately high heat until reduced to about ⅔ cup, about 3 minutes (if side of skillet begins to scorch, reduce heat to moderate). Stir together cornstarch and water and whisk into juice, then boil sauce until thickened slightly, 1 to 2 minutes.

▶ Remove from heat and add Sherry vinegar to taste, then swirl in butter until incorporated. Pour sauce through a fine-mesh sieve into a bowl and skim off any fat. Season with salt.

▶ Slice pork and serve with sauce.

JERK PORK CHOPS WITH HEARTS OF PALM SALAD AND SWEET PLANTAINS

SERVES 4
ACTIVE TIME: 10 MIN START TO FINISH: 20 MIN

FOR SALAD
1 (14-oz) can hearts of palm (not salad-cut), drained
¼ medium red onion, thinly sliced
¼ cup coarsely chopped fresh cilantro
1 tablespoon fresh lime juice
1 tablespoon olive oil
¼ teaspoon salt
⅛ teaspoon black pepper

FOR PLANTAINS
1 (11-oz) box frozen ripe plantains

FOR PORK
3 to 4 teaspoons Walkerswood Traditional Jamaican Jerk Seasoning (see Sources)
1 tablespoon olive oil
8 thin boneless center-cut pork chops (about ¼ inch thick)

SPECIAL EQUIPMENT: a well-seasoned large (2-burner) ridged grill pan (preferably cast iron)

▶ Put oven rack in middle position and preheat oven to 375°F. Line a baking sheet with aluminum foil.
▶ Thinly slice hearts of palm on the diagonal and put in a colander along with sliced onion. Rinse well under cold water and pat dry. Transfer to a large bowl and toss together with remaining salad ingredients.
▶ Spread plantains on foil-lined baking sheet and bake until hot, 5 to 10 minutes.
▶ While plantains bake, lightly oil grill pan and heat over moderately high heat until hot but not smoking.
▶ Meanwhile, stir together jerk seasoning and oil in a small bowl and rub all over pork to coat. Grill pork, turning over once, until just cooked through, about 3 minutes total. Serve pork with salad and plantains.

GRILLED PORK CHOPS WITH PINEAPPLE SALSA

SERVES 4
ACTIVE TIME: 35 MIN START TO FINISH: 40 MIN

Cumin and time over the coals give these hearty thick-cut pork chops deep flavor. A spicy-sweet tropical salsa made with fresh pineapple balances the dish.

1 tablespoon vegetable oil
2½ teaspoons ground cumin
½ teaspoon black pepper
1½ teaspoons salt
4 (1-inch-thick) bone-in rib pork chops (about 2¼ lb total)
½ pineapple, peeled, cored, and cut into ¼-inch dice (1¼ cups)
½ cup finely chopped red onion
1 fresh serrano chile, minced, including seeds
1 tablespoon fresh lime juice

▶ Prepare grill for cooking over direct heat with medium-hot charcoal (moderate heat for gas); see Tips, page 8.
▶ Stir together oil, cumin, pepper, and 1 teaspoon salt in a small bowl, then rub all over pork chops, transferring chops as coated to a tray. Stir together pineapple, onion, chile, lime juice, and remaining ½ teaspoon salt in another bowl.
▶ Lightly oil grill rack and grill pork chops, covered only if using a gas grill, turning over once, until just cooked through, 6 to 9 minutes total. Transfer to a clean platter and let stand 5 minutes. Serve with pineapple salsa.

COOKS' NOTE: If you aren't able to grill outdoors, pork chops can be cooked in a lightly oiled well-seasoned large (2-burner) ridged grill pan (preferably cast iron) over moderately high heat, turning over once, about 12 minutes total.

SMOKED PORK CHOPS WITH ONION-AND-CIDER GLAZE

SERVES 4

ACTIVE TIME: 15 MIN START TO FINISH: 35 MIN

  4 (1-inch-thick) bone-in smoked pork chops
  1 tablespoon vegetable oil
  1 tablespoon unsalted butter
  1 large onion, halved lengthwise, then thinly
      sliced crosswise
  1 teaspoon sugar
  ¼ teaspoon salt
  2 cups unfiltered apple cider
  2 tablespoons cider vinegar

▶ Put oven rack in middle position and preheat oven to 350°F.

▶ Pat chops dry. Heat oil in a 12-inch heavy skillet over moderately high heat until hot but not smoking, then brown chops in 2 batches on one side only, 3 to 4 minutes per batch. Transfer chops, browned sides up, to a large shallow baking pan, reserving skillet (do not clean). Bake chops until heated through, about 20 minutes.

▶ While chops bake, melt butter in skillet over moderate heat until foam subsides, then cook onion with sugar and salt, scraping up brown bits and stirring occasionally with a wooden spoon, until onion is softened, 8 to 10 minutes.

▶ Add cider and vinegar and boil mixture, stirring occasionally, until onions are tender and liquid is reduced to a glaze, about 10 minutes more. Serve chops with glaze.

BALSAMIC-GLAZED PORK CHOPS

SERVES 4

ACTIVE TIME: 25 MIN START TO FINISH: 25 MIN

Caramelized shallots and a dark vinegar glaze turn chops into an extremely flavorful sweet-and-sour dish.

  4 (¾-inch-thick) center-cut pork chops (about 2 lb total)
  1 teaspoon salt
  ½ teaspoon black pepper
  2 tablespoons olive oil
  6 oz small shallots (about 8), quartered and peeled,
      leaving root ends intact
  ⅔ cup balsamic vinegar
  1½ teaspoons sugar

▶ Pat pork chops dry and sprinkle with ½ teaspoon salt and ¼ teaspoon pepper.

▶ Heat oil in a 12-inch heavy skillet over moderately high heat until hot but not smoking, then cook pork (in 2 batches if necessary) along with shallots, turning pork over once and stirring shallots occasionally, until pork is browned and shallots are golden brown and tender, about 5 minutes total. Transfer pork with tongs to a plate and add vinegar, sugar, and remaining ½ teaspoon salt and ¼ teaspoon pepper to shallots in skillet. Cook, stirring until sugar is dissolved and liquid is thickened slightly, about 1 minute.

▶ Reduce heat to moderate, then return pork along with any juices accumulated on plate to skillet and turn 2 or 3 times to coat with sauce. Cook, turning over once, until pork is just cooked through, about 3 minutes total. Transfer pork to a platter and boil sauce until thickened and syrupy, 1 to 2 minutes. Pour sauce over pork.

KIELBASA WITH GOLDEN ONIONS AND APPLE

SERVES 6

ACTIVE TIME: 25 MIN START TO FINISH: 50 MIN

  2 lb smoked kielbasa (preferably beef and pork), cut
      crosswise into 3-inch lengths
  2 tablespoons olive oil
  3 large onions, chopped (6 cups)
  ½ teaspoon salt
  1 teaspoon black pepper
  ½ stick (¼ cup) unsalted butter
  1 large Granny Smith apple
  1¾ cups reduced-sodium chicken broth (14 fl oz)

ACCOMPANIMENT: **mashed potatoes**

▶ Lightly score each piece of sausage in several places with a sharp paring knife. Heat 1 tablespoon oil in a 12-inch heavy skillet over moderate heat until hot but not smoking, then brown half of sausage, turning occasionally, until golden, about 4 minutes. Transfer to a bowl and cover to keep warm. Pour off fat from skillet and wipe skillet clean. Add remaining tablespoon oil to skillet and brown remaining sausage in same manner, transferring to bowl as cooked.

▶ Wipe skillet clean again, then cook onions with salt and pepper in butter over moderate heat, stirring occasionally, until golden brown, 15 to 20 minutes. Meanwhile, peel, core, and finely chop apple. Stir apple and broth into onion mixture and simmer briskly, uncovered, stirring occasionally, until apple is tender, 6 to 7 minutes. Add sausage and simmer, stirring, until heated through, about 1 minute.

LAMB

GRILLED LAMB CHOPS WITH CURRIED COUSCOUS AND ZUCCHINI RAITA

SERVES 4
ACTIVE TIME: 10 MIN   START TO FINISH: 25 MIN

- ¾   teaspoon curry powder
- ¼   teaspoon turmeric (optional)
- ⅛   teaspoon cinnamon
- ½   teaspoon black pepper
- 1½   cups water
- 1¼   teaspoons salt
- 2   tablespoons unsalted butter
- 1¼   cups couscous (8 oz)
- 1¼   lb (½-inch-thick) lamb shoulder blade chops
- 1   cup plain Greek yogurt
- 1   medium zucchini (½ lb), coarsely grated (about 1 cup)
- ¼   teaspoon dried mint, crumbled

SPECIAL EQUIPMENT: a well-seasoned large (2-burner) ridged grill pan (preferably cast iron)

▶ Heat lightly oiled grill pan over moderately high heat until hot but not smoking.
▶ Meanwhile, toast curry, turmeric (if using), cinnamon, and ¼ teaspoon pepper in a small heavy saucepan over moderate heat, stirring constantly, until fragrant, about 1 minute. Add water, ½ teaspoon salt, and butter and bring to a boil. Place couscous in a heatproof bowl and pour in boiling water mixture, then quickly cover with a plate or plastic wrap and let stand 5 minutes.
▶ While couscous stands, pat chops dry and sprinkle on both sides with ¼ teaspoon salt and remaining ¼ teaspoon pepper (total). Grill chops, turning over once, about 6 minutes total for medium-rare. Transfer to a serving plate.
▶ For raita, stir together yogurt, zucchini, mint, and remaining ½ teaspoon salt.
▶ Fluff couscous with a fork and serve with lamb and raita.

KITCHEN NOTE

WHEN GRILLING WITH CHARCOAL, USE A **CHIMNEY STARTER** (AN INEXPENSIVE TOOL AVAILABLE AT MOST HARDWARE STORES) TO LIGHT YOUR FIRE. CRUMPLED NEWSPAPER GOES IN THE BOTTOM OF THE STARTER; CHARCOAL GOES ON TOP. LIGHT THE PAPER AND THE FLAMES WILL IGNITE THE CHARCOAL, WHICH WILL BE RED-HOT IN FIVE MINUTES OR SO. DUMP IT OUT INTO THE GRILL AND YOU'RE GOOD TO GO.

GRILLED LAMB SKEWERS WITH WHITE-BEAN SALAD

SERVES 4 TO 6
ACTIVE TIME: 30 MIN   START TO FINISH: 40 MIN

- 4   large garlic cloves
- 2   teaspoons salt
- 1   teaspoon black pepper
- ¼   cup plus 2 tablespoons extra-virgin olive oil
- 2   lb boneless lamb shoulder, cut into 1-inch cubes
- 2   tablespoons Sherry vinegar or red-wine vinegar
- 2   (15- to 19-oz) cans cannellini beans, rinsed and drained (about 3 cups)
- 1   celery rib, thinly sliced
- ¼   cup brine-cured black olives such as Kalamata, pitted and quartered
- ½   cup pine nuts (2¼ oz), toasted (see Tips, page 8)
- ½   cup chopped fresh mint

SPECIAL EQUIPMENT: 6 to 8 metal skewers

▶ Prepare grill for cooking over medium-hot charcoal (moderate heat for gas); see Tips, page 8.
▶ While grill is heating, mince garlic, then mash to a paste with salt and pepper using a large heavy knife. Reserve half of garlic paste in a large salad bowl.
▶ Whisk together 2 tablespoons oil and remaining garlic paste in another large bowl, then add lamb and toss to coat.
▶ Divide lamb among skewers, leaving a little space between pieces (for even cooking).
▶ Whisk vinegar into reserved garlic paste, then add remaining ¼ cup oil in a slow stream, whisking until emulsified. Add beans, celery, olives, pine nuts, and mint, then toss to coat.
▶ Grill lamb, turning as grill marks appear on each side, about 6 minutes total for medium-rare. Serve with bean salad.

GRILLED LEMONGRASS LAMB CHOPS WITH HERBS

SERVES 6

ACTIVE TIME: 45 MIN   START TO FINISH: 13 HR (INCLUDES MARINATING)

Aromatic without being spicy, this dish has a touch of the exotic but will please traditionalists, too. The spice paste hits on sweet, hot, salty, and sour, and the lamb is wonderfully tender.

1½ teaspoons cumin seeds, toasted (see Tips, page 8) and cooled

3 fresh lemongrass stalks, root ends trimmed and 1 or 2 tough outer leaves discarded from each

2 large shallots, chopped (½ cup)

4 garlic cloves, chopped

1½ tablespoons chopped peeled fresh ginger

1½ tablespoons sugar

1 teaspoon salt

½ teaspoon turmeric

¼ teaspoon cayenne

3 tablespoons water

¼ cup plus 3 tablespoons vegetable oil

6 (1¼-inch-thick) loin lamb chops (2 to 2½ lb total), end flaps secured with wooden picks

¼ teaspoon finely grated fresh lime zest (see Tips, page 8)

1 tablespoon fresh lime juice

½ cup small fresh basil leaves

¼ cup small fresh mint leaves

¼ cup fresh cilantro leaves

▶ Finely grind cumin seeds in an electric coffee/spice grinder or with a mortar and pestle.

▶ Thinly slice bottom 6 inches of lemongrass, discarding remainder. Purée lemongrass, shallots, garlic, ginger, cumin, sugar, salt, turmeric, cayenne, and water in a food processor, scraping down side occasionally, until as smooth as possible, about 2 minutes. (Paste will not be completely smooth.)

▶ Heat 3 tablespoons oil in a 10-inch heavy skillet over moderate heat until hot but not smoking. Add lemongrass paste, then reduce heat to moderately low and cook, stirring constantly, until paste begins to stick to bottom of skillet and is very thick, 8 to 12 minutes. Transfer paste to a bowl and cool to room temperature, about 10 minutes.

▶ Pat lamb chops dry and rub lemongrass paste all over them, then arrange in 1 layer in a 13- by 9-inch dish. Marinate, covered and chilled, at least 12 and up to 24 hours.

▶ Prepare grill for cooking over direct heat with medium-hot charcoal (moderate heat for gas); see Tips, page 8.

▶ Grill lamb on a lightly oiled grill rack, covered only if using a gas grill, loosening lamb from grill with a metal spatula, turning over occasionally, and moving around on grill when flare-ups occur, 9 to 11 minutes total for medium-rare. (Some of lemongrass paste will fall off.) Transfer chops to a platter and let stand, loosely covered with foil, 10 minutes. Discard wooden picks.

▶ Whisk together lime zest and juice, remaining ¼ cup oil, and salt and pepper to taste. Spoon over chops and sprinkle with herbs.

COOKS' NOTE: If you aren't able to grill outdoors, preheat an oiled shallow heavy baking pan 5 minutes in lower third of a 450°F oven. Add chops and roast until undersides are golden, about 15 minutes, then turn over and roast 5 to 6 minutes more for medium-rare.

POULTRY

CHICKEN

RED-COOKED CHICKEN WITH SHIITAKES

SERVES 4
ACTIVE TIME: 30 MIN   START TO FINISH: 1¾ HR

Falling-off-the-bone chicken is cooked in a Chinese-inspired citrus sauce—the source of its reddish-brown color.

 5 cups water
 1 cup soy sauce
 1 cup Chinese rice wine (preferably Shaoxing) or
    medium-dry Sherry
¼ cup packed light brown sugar
 1 (1-inch) cube peeled fresh ginger, smashed
 3 garlic cloves, peeled and smashed
 2 (2-inch-long) pieces Asian dried tangerine peel
    (see Sources)
 4 whole star anise (1 tablespoon)
 2 bunches scallions, cut into 1-inch pieces (4 cups)
 1 (3- to 3½-lb) chicken
 1 teaspoon Asian sesame oil
1½ tablespoons vegetable oil
½ lb fresh shiitakes, stems discarded and caps cut into
    ¼-inch slices
¼ teaspoon salt

▶ Bring water, soy sauce, rice wine, brown sugar, ginger, garlic, tangerine peel, star anise, and 2 cups scallions to a boil in an 8-quart pot, then reduce heat and simmer 10 minutes. Add whole chicken and simmer, covered, turning once, until just cooked through, 50 to 60 minutes. Transfer chicken with a large slotted spoon to a platter and brush with sesame oil. Keep warm, covered with foil.

▶ Pour cooking liquid through a sieve into a large bowl, discarding solids. Skim fat from surface and reserve 1 cup cooking liquid. (Cool remainder, uncovered, then freeze for another use.) Heat vegetable oil in a 12-inch heavy skillet over moderately high heat until hot but not smoking, then stir-fry shiitakes and remaining 2 cups scallions with salt, stirring frequently, until mushrooms are tender, 3 to 5 minutes. Add reserved cooking liquid and boil until reduced by half, about 3 minutes. Cut chicken into serving pieces and serve with sauce.

CRISP CHICKEN WITH SHERRY-VINEGAR SAUCE

SERVES 4
ACTIVE TIME: 20 MIN   START TO FINISH: 45 MIN

The tangy honey-vinegar sauce that tops this crisp-skinned chicken is also great on pork, duck, or even a meaty fish.

 4 chicken breast halves (2 to 2½ lb total), with skin
    and bone
 1 teaspoon salt
½ teaspoon black pepper
 2 tablespoons olive oil
 4 garlic cloves, finely chopped
¾ teaspoon paprika
⅓ cup Sherry vinegar
⅓ cup reduced-sodium chicken broth
 2 teaspoons mild honey
 2 tablespoons unsalted butter

▶ Put oven rack in upper third of oven and preheat oven to 450°F.

▶ Pat chicken dry and sprinkle evenly with salt and pepper.

▶ Heat oil in a 12-inch heavy skillet over moderately high heat until hot but not smoking, then sear skin side of chicken until golden brown, 4 to 6 minutes. Transfer chicken, skin side up, with tongs to a large shallow baking pan (reserve skillet; do not clean) and roast until chicken is just cooked through, 20 to 25 minutes. Let chicken stand 5 minutes.

▶ Meanwhile, cook garlic in reserved skillet over moderately high heat, stirring, until pale golden, 15 to 30 seconds. Add paprika, then immediately add vinegar, stirring and scraping up any brown bits, and boil 1 minute. Add broth and honey and simmer, stirring occasionally, until liquid is reduced to about ½ cup, about 2 minutes. Remove from heat and whisk in butter, 1 tablespoon at a time, until incorporated. Season sauce with salt and serve with chicken.

MOROCCAN-SPICED CHICKEN PAILLARDS

SERVES 4

ACTIVE TIME: 35 MIN START TO FINISH: 35 MIN

FOR SAUCE

¼ cup orange juice
1 tablespoon mild honey
1 teaspoon fresh lemon juice
1 (3-inch) cinnamon stick
¼ teaspoon dried hot red-pepper flakes
2 tablespoons unsalted butter

FOR PAILLARDS

½ teaspoon ground cumin
½ teaspoon paprika (not hot)
¼ teaspoon black pepper
2 tablespoons olive oil
1¾ lb boneless chicken breast slices (¼ inch thick; see cooks' note, below)
1¼ teaspoons salt

SPECIAL EQUIPMENT: a well-seasoned large (2-burner) ridged grill pan (preferably cast iron)

PREPARE GRILL PAN AND START SAUCE:

▶Heat grill pan over moderate heat until hot.

▶Meanwhile, simmer all sauce ingredients except butter in a 1-quart saucepan, uncovered, stirring occasionally, 2 minutes. Set aside while cooking chicken.

MAKE PAILLARDS:

▶Cook cumin, paprika, and pepper in oil in a small skillet over moderately low heat, stirring, until fragrant, about 2 minutes. Transfer to a small bowl, reserving skillet for sauce (do not clean). Brush some spiced oil on 1 side of each paillard, then sprinkle with some salt. Arrange 2 paillards in grill pan, oiled sides down, and brush tops with some of spiced oil, then sprinkle with some salt. Grill 2 minutes, then turn over and grill until just cooked through, about 3 minutes more. Transfer to a platter and cover with foil. Grill remaining paillards in same manner, transferring to platter.

FINISH SAUCE:

▶Pour sauce through a medium-mesh sieve into reserved small skillet, discarding solids. Add any juices from chicken accumulated on platter to sauce and bring to a boil. Remove from heat, then add butter and swirl skillet until butter is just incorporated. Season sauce with salt and spoon over chicken.

COOKS' NOTE: If chicken slices are not of an even thickness, put each paillard between 2 sheets of plastic wrap and pound with flat side of a meat pounder until about ¼ inch thick.

CHICKEN WITH BLACK-PEPPER MAPLE SAUCE

SERVES 4

ACTIVE TIME: 20 MIN START TO FINISH: 40 MIN

This dish, inspired by a recipe from Gray Kunz's Elements of Taste, *is a great alternative to roasting a whole chicken. To ensure that the bird lies flat and cooks evenly in the pan, we've used the spatchcock technique, which entails removing the backbone of the chicken and tucking the legs up and out of the way.*

1 (3- to 3½-lb) whole chicken
1 teaspoon salt
¼ teaspoon black pepper
5 tablespoons unsalted butter
2 (3-inch-long) sprigs fresh rosemary plus 1 (1-inch-long) sprig
1 tablespoon whole black peppercorns
¼ cup dark amber or Grade B maple syrup
¾ cup reduced-sodium chicken broth
¼ cup cider vinegar

SPECIAL EQUIPMENT: kitchen shears; 2 (10-inch) heavy skillets (one well-seasoned cast-iron or heavy nonstick); a 10-inch round of parchment paper; 5 to 6 lb of weights such as 3 (28-oz) cans of tomatoes

▶Cut out backbone from chicken with kitchen shears and discard. Pat chicken dry, then spread flat, skin side up, on a cutting board. Cut a ½-inch slit on each side of chicken in center of triangle of skin between thighs and breast (near drumstick), then tuck bottom knob of each drumstick through slit. Tuck wing tips under breast. Sprinkle chicken all over with salt and pepper.

▶Heat 3 tablespoons butter in 10-inch cast-iron or heavy nonstick skillet over moderate heat until foam subsides. Add chicken, skin side down, and arrange larger rosemary sprigs over chicken. Cover with parchment round and second skillet, then top with weights. Cook chicken until skin is browned, about 15 minutes. Remove and reserve weights, top skillet, parchment, and rosemary, then carefully loosen chicken from skillet with a spatula. Turn chicken over and re-place rosemary sprigs, then re-cover with parchment, skillet, and weights. Cook until chicken is just cooked through, 15 to 20 minutes more.

MAKE SAUCE WHILE CHICKEN COOKS:

▶Toast peppercorns in a dry 1-quart heavy saucepan over moderate heat, shaking pan occasionally, until fragrant, about 3 minutes. Transfer to a clean cutting board and coarsely crush with a rolling pin. Return peppercorns to saucepan and bring to a simmer with syrup, ½ cup broth, and small rosemary sprig, then reduce heat and simmer 20 minutes.

▶ Transfer chicken to a platter and loosely cover with foil. Add vinegar to skillet and deglaze, boiling and scraping up brown bits with a wooden spoon until liquid is reduced by half. Stir in maple mixture and remaining ¼ cup broth and boil until slightly syrupy, about 3 minutes. Reduce heat to low and swirl in remaining 2 tablespoons butter. Season sauce with salt and pour through a fine-mesh sieve into a bowl, discarding solids. Serve chicken with sauce.

KITCHEN NOTE

THE TECHNIQUE OF SPLITTING AND FLATTENING A BIRD SO THAT IT IS UNIFORMLY THICK AND THUS COOKS MORE QUICKLY AND EVENLY IS CALLED **SPATCHCOCKING.** IT ALLOWS AS MUCH SKIN AS POSSIBLE TO COME IN DIRECT CONTACT WITH A HOT SKILLET, ESPECIALLY WHEN YOU WEIGHT THE BIRD. SPATCHCOCKED CHICKENS ARE ALSO GREAT ON THE GRILL.

GRILLED LEMON-CORIANDER CHICKEN

SERVES 4

ACTIVE TIME: 25 MIN   START TO FINISH: 1½ HR

- ¾ cup loosely packed fresh cilantro sprigs
- ¼ cup olive oil
- 2 shallots, chopped (½ cup)
- 1 large garlic clove, chopped
- 1 teaspoon finely grated fresh lemon zest (see Tips, page 8)
- 2 teaspoons fresh lemon juice
- 1 fresh serrano chile, minced, including seeds
- 1 teaspoon ground coriander
- 1 teaspoon sugar
- ¾ teaspoon salt
- 1 (3- to 3½-lb) chicken, rinsed and patted dry
- ¼ teaspoon black pepper
- 1 tablespoon unsalted butter, melted and cooled

SPECIAL EQUIPMENT: **kitchen string; a large chimney starter (if using charcoal); an instant-read thermometer**

▶ Purée cilantro, oil, shallots, garlic, lemon zest and juice, chile, coriander, sugar, and ½ teaspoon salt in a food processor until it forms a paste. Leave any fat in opening of chicken cavity and sprinkle cavity with pepper and remaining ¼ teaspoon salt. Starting at cavity end, gently slide an index finger between skin and flesh of breast and legs to loosen skin (be careful not to tear skin). Using a small spoon, slide cilantro purée under skin over breast and drumsticks, using your finger on outside of skin to push purée out of spoon and distribute evenly. Tie legs together with kitchen string and tuck wing tips under. Brush outside of chicken all over with butter.

▶ Prepare grill for cooking over indirect heat with medium-hot charcoal (moderate heat for gas); see Tips, page 8.

TO COOK CHICKEN USING A CHARCOAL GRILL:

▶ Lightly oil grill rack, then put chicken on rack with no coals directly underneath and cook, covered with lid, until thermometer inserted into fleshy part of thigh (do not touch bone) registers 170°F, 40 to 50 minutes. (Add more briquettes during grilling if necessary to maintain heat.) Transfer chicken to a platter and let stand 15 minutes.

TO COOK CHICKEN USING A GAS GRILL:

▶ Lightly oil grill rack, then put chicken above shut-off burner. Grill, covered with lid, turning chicken 180 degrees halfway through cooking if using a 2-burner grill, until thermometer inserted into fleshy part of thigh (do not touch bone) registers 170°F, 35 to 45 minutes.

COOKS' NOTE: Chicken can be prepared (but not grilled) 1 day ahead and chilled, covered with plastic wrap. Let stand at cool room temperature 30 minutes before grilling.

INSTANT CHICKEN MOLE POBLANO

SERVES 4

ACTIVE TIME: 10 MIN   START TO FINISH: 30 MIN

- 1½ cups long-grain white rice
- 2½ cups water
- ¾ teaspoon salt
- 1 (8¼-oz) jar *mole poblano* such as Doña María brand (see Sources)
- 2 (14-oz) cans reduced-sodium chicken broth (3½ cups)
- 4 small skinless boneless chicken breast halves (1¼ to 1½ lb total)

GARNISH: 1 tablespoon sesame seeds, toasted (see Tips, page 8)

▶ Combine rice, water, and salt in a 2-quart heavy saucepan and bring to a boil. Reduce heat to low and cook, covered, until rice is tender and liquid is absorbed, about 18 minutes. Remove from heat and let stand, covered and undisturbed, 5 minutes. Fluff with a fork.

▶ While rice cooks, blend *mole* and broth in a blender until smooth, then bring to a boil in a 12-inch skillet, stirring occasionally. Add chicken, then reduce heat and cook at a bare simmer, uncovered, turning chicken over once, until just cooked through, about 15 minutes total (sauce will thicken slightly).

CHIPOTLE-LIME GRILLED CHICKEN

SERVES 6

ACTIVE TIME: 15 MIN   START TO FINISH: 35 MIN

¼   cup fresh lime juice
¼   cup olive oil
2½ tablespoons chipotle Tabasco
¾   teaspoon salt
6   large skinless boneless chicken thighs (2½ lb total)
2   teaspoons mild honey

▶ Prepare grill for cooking over direct heat with medium-hot charcoal (moderate heat for gas); see Tips, page 8.

▶ While coals are lighting, stir together lime juice, oil, Tabasco, and salt in a liquid-measuring cup. Put chicken in a large sealable bag and add ⅓ cup marinade (reserve remainder in cup). Seal bag, forcing out excess air, and marinate chicken at room temperature, about 15 minutes. Stir honey into remaining marinade until dissolved to make sauce.

▶ Grill chicken (discarding marinade in bag) on lightly oiled grill rack, covered only if using a gas grill, turning chicken over occasionally and moving it to avoid flare-ups if necessary, until just cooked through, 8 to 10 minutes total.

▶ Brush both sides of chicken with some of reserved sauce, then continue to grill, turning over once, until lightly browned, about 1 minute more. Serve chicken drizzled with remaining sauce.

COOKS' NOTE: If you aren't able to grill outdoors, chicken can be cooked in batches in a hot, lightly oiled, well-seasoned large (2-burner) ridged grill pan (preferably cast iron) over moderate heat, about 15 minutes (before brushing with sauce).

STICKY SESAME CHICKEN WINGS

SERVES 4

ACTIVE TIME: 15 MIN   START TO FINISH: 50 MIN

1   large garlic clove
¾   teaspoon salt
2   tablespoons soy sauce
2   tablespoons hoisin sauce
2   tablespoons mild honey
1   teaspoon Asian sesame oil
    Pinch of cayenne
3   lb chicken wingettes or chicken wings (see cooks' note, below)
1½ tablespoons sesame seeds, lightly toasted (see Tips, page 8)
1   scallion (green part only), finely chopped

▶ Put oven rack in upper third of oven and preheat oven to 425°F. Line a large shallow baking pan (17 by 12 inches) with foil and lightly oil foil.

▶ Mince garlic and mash to a paste with salt using a large heavy knife. Transfer garlic paste to a large bowl and stir in soy sauce, hoisin, honey, oil, and cayenne. Add wingettes to sauce, stirring to coat.

▶ Arrange wingettes in 1 layer in baking pan and roast, turning over once, until cooked through, about 35 minutes total. Transfer wingettes to a large serving bowl and toss with sesame seeds and scallion.

COOKS' NOTE: If using chicken wings instead of wingettes, cut off and discard tips from chicken wings with kitchen shears or a large heavy knife, then halve wings at joint.

HOISIN CHICKEN IN LETTUCE LEAVES

SERVES 4

ACTIVE TIME: 10 MIN   START TO FINISH: 10 MIN

2   tablespoons vegetable oil
1   tablespoon finely chopped peeled fresh ginger
½   teaspoon salt
2   scallions, chopped (¼ cup)
2   skinless boneless chicken breast halves (about 1 lb total), cut into ½-inch pieces
1   (8-oz) can sliced water chestnuts, rinsed and coarsely chopped
¼   cup bottled hoisin sauce (preferably Lee Kum Kee, House of Tsang, or Koon Chun brand)
1½ teaspoons Worcestershire sauce
1   teaspoon rice vinegar (not seasoned)
½   cup pine nuts (2½ oz)
12 large red- or green-leaf lettuce leaves

▶ Heat a wok (preferably flat-bottomed) or a 12-inch heavy skillet (not nonstick) over moderately high heat until just smoking, then add oil. Add ginger, salt, and 2 tablespoons scallions and stir-fry until ginger is fragrant, about 45 seconds. Add chicken and stir-fry until just cooked through, about 2 minutes. Add water chestnuts, hoisin sauce, Worcestershire sauce, vinegar, and pine nuts and stir-fry until heated through, about 1 minute. Transfer to a bowl and sprinkle with remaining 2 tablespoons scallions.

▶ Have guests serve themselves by spooning chicken mixture into lettuce leaves and wrapping leaves around filling to enclose.

BAKED CHICKEN AND BACON-WRAPPED LADY APPLES

SERVES 4 TO 6

ACTIVE TIME: 25 MIN START TO FINISH: 45 MIN

  8 thin bacon slices (from a ½-lb package)
 12 lady apples (about 1½ to 2 inches in diameter; see Sources)
  6 chicken thighs (2 lb; with skin and bones)
 ½ teaspoon salt
 ½ teaspoon black pepper
  1 cup unfiltered apple cider
 ½ cup cider vinegar
  2 sprigs fresh marjoram plus 2 teaspoons chopped fresh marjoram, or to taste
  1 tablespoon cold unsalted butter

▸ Put oven rack in middle position and preheat oven to 400°F.
▸ Cook bacon in a 12-inch heavy skillet over moderate heat, turning over once, until edges are lightly browned but bacon is still flexible (it will continue to cook in oven), 6 to 8 minutes total. Transfer to paper towels to drain, reserving fat in skillet.
▸ While bacon cooks, core apples, if desired, from bottom, with pointed end of a vegetable peeler or a paring knife, leaving stems intact. Wrap a slice of bacon around each of 8 apples, securing ends of bacon by piercing with stem or using half a wooden pick.
▸ Brush a 3-quart (13- by 9-inch) shallow baking dish with some bacon fat, then add apples to dish and bake, uncovered, 10 minutes.
▸ Meanwhile, pat chicken dry and sprinkle with salt and pepper. Heat bacon fat in skillet over moderately high heat until hot but not smoking, then cook chicken, turning over once, until browned, about 8 minutes total. Transfer chicken with tongs to baking dish, rearranging some of apples so that chicken fits in bottom of dish, and bake, uncovered, 5 minutes.
▸ While chicken bakes, pour off fat from skillet and add cider, vinegar, and marjoram sprigs to skillet. Boil, stirring and scraping up brown bits, until reduced by half (about ¾ cup), about 5 minutes. Pour sauce through a fine-mesh sieve into a glass measuring cup, pressing on and then discarding solids.

Add butter and chopped marjoram to sauce, stirring until butter is melted. Pour sauce over chicken and apples and continue to bake, uncovered, until chicken is cooked through and apples are tender, about 20 minutes more.

ASSORTED FOWL

TURKEY CUTLETS WITH CILANTRO-ALMOND SAUCE

SERVES 4

ACTIVE TIME: 20 MIN START TO FINISH: 35 MIN

  3 tablespoons red-wine vinegar
  1 large garlic clove, finely chopped
 ¼ teaspoon dried hot red-pepper flakes
 ¾ teaspoon salt
 ¼ cup extra-virgin olive oil
 ½ cup sliced almonds, toasted (see Tips, page 8)
 ⅓ cup chopped fresh cilantro
 ½ teaspoon ground coriander
 ¼ teaspoon cinnamon
  4 (¼-inch-thick) turkey breast cutlets (about 1¼ lb)

▸ Whisk together vinegar, garlic, red-pepper flakes, and ¼ teaspoon salt until salt is dissolved. Add 3 tablespoons oil in a slow stream, whisking until combined well, then whisk in almonds and cilantro.
▸ Prepare grill for cooking with hot charcoal (high heat for gas); see Tips, page 8.
▸ While coals are lighting, whisk together coriander, cinnamon, remaining tablespoon oil, and remaining ½ teaspoon salt in a shallow bowl. Turn cutlets to coat in spice mixture.
▸ Grill turkey, covered only if using a gas grill, turning over once, until just cooked through, about 3 minutes total. Transfer to a platter.
▸ Spoon almond sauce over turkey.

COOKS' NOTE: If you aren't able to grill outdoors, turkey can be cooked in a hot lightly oiled well-seasoned large (2-burner) ridged grill pan (preferably cast iron) over moderately high heat, turning over once, until just cooked through, about 6 minutes total.

DUCK AND SHRIMP GUMBO

SERVES 6 TO 8

ACTIVE TIME: 1¼ HR   START TO FINISH: 2¾ HR

1   (5½- to 6-lb) Long Island duck (also called Pekin), excess
      fat discarded and duck cut into 6 pieces
1   tablespoon vegetable oil
½   cup all-purpose flour
2   medium onions, finely chopped (2 cups)
2   celery ribs, finely chopped (1 cup)
1   large red bell pepper, finely chopped (1 cup)
1   large green bell pepper, finely chopped (1 cup)
4   Turkish or 2 California bay leaves
2   teaspoons salt
6   cups reduced-sodium chicken broth (48 fl oz)
4   cups water
1   lb medium shrimp in shell (31 to 35 per lb), peeled
      and deveined
1   cup thinly sliced scallion greens (from 2 bunches)
¼   teaspoon cayenne

ACCOMPANIMENT: white rice

▶ Pat duck dry, then prick skin all over with tip of a knife.
▶ Heat oil in a wide 6-quart heavy pot over moderately high heat,
then brown duck in 3 batches, skin side down, turning over
once, 8 to 10 minutes per batch. Transfer duck to a bowl as
browned. Pour off all but ¼ cup fat from pot and reduce heat to
moderately low, then add flour to fat in pot. Cook roux, stirring
constantly with a wooden spatula or spoon, until well browned
(a shade darker than peanut butter), about 20 minutes. Add
onions, celery, bell peppers, bay leaves, and salt and cook
over moderately low heat, stirring occasionally, until vegetables
are crisp-tender, 6 to 10 minutes. Add broth, water, and duck
with any juices accumulated in bowl and bring to a boil, then
reduce heat and simmer, uncovered, until duck is tender,
1¼ to 1½ hours.
▶ Remove gumbo from heat, then transfer duck to a cutting
board with a slotted spoon and, when cool enough to handle,
shred meat into large pieces, discarding bones and skin. Skim
fat from surface of gumbo, then return duck to gumbo. Bring
to a boil, then reduce to a simmer and stir in shrimp, scallions,
and cayenne. Simmer gumbo until shrimp is just cooked
through, about 2 minutes. Discard bay leaves. Serve gumbo
over white rice.

COOKS' NOTE: Gumbo, without shrimp, scallions, and cayenne,
can be made 3 days ahead and cooled completely, uncovered,
then chilled, covered. Bring to a boil, then reduce to a simmer
and add shrimp, scallions, and cayenne and simmer until shrimp
is just cooked through, about 2 minutes.

CORNISH HENS WITH ROASTED-GARLIC AIOLI

SERVES 4

ACTIVE TIME: 20 MIN   START TO FINISH: 1¼ HR

*Roasting the garlic mellows the flavor, which results in an aioli
that is less pungent than traditional ones. It also makes a great
accompaniment to vegetables, lamb, and fish.*

2   whole heads of garlic
2   teaspoons extra-virgin olive oil
2   Cornish hens (1¼ to 1½ lb each), rinsed and patted dry
1½   teaspoons salt
½   teaspoon black pepper
1   cup bottled mayonnaise
1   teaspoon finely grated fresh lemon zest (see Tips, page 8)
2   tablespoons fresh lemon juice
2   tablespoons finely chopped fresh chives

SPECIAL EQUIPMENT: kitchen string; a small (13- by 9-inch)
roasting pan; an instant-read thermometer

▶ Put oven rack in middle position and preheat oven to 500°F.
▶ Trim off and discard about ¼ inch from top of garlic heads to
expose cloves, then put heads on a sheet of foil. Spoon oil over
garlic, then wrap up foil tightly to enclose. Roast garlic on oven
rack until very soft, about 40 minutes.
▶ Meanwhile, season hens inside and out with 1 teaspoon salt
and ¼ teaspoon pepper (total). Tie legs together with string
and tuck wing tips under. Transfer to roasting pan and roast
alongside garlic until hens are golden brown and thermometer
registers 170°F when inserted into leg joint, 30 to 40 minutes.
Let stand, loosely covered with foil, 15 minutes.
▶ Unwrap garlic carefully and cool slightly, then squeeze pulp
into a bowl. Add mayonnaise, lemon zest and juice, chives,
remaining ½ teaspoon salt, and remaining ¼ teaspoon pepper
(plus 2 tablespoons pan juices from hens if desired) and stir
until combined well.
▶ Halve hens lengthwise. Serve with aioli.

BREAKFAST, BRUNCH, AND SANDWICHES

BREAKFAST AND BRUNCH DISHES

CHEESE AND CHILE QUICHE

SERVES 6 TO 8

ACTIVE TIME: 1 HR   START TO FINISH: 4 HR   (INCLUDES MAKING DOUGH)

Pastry dough for a single-crust pie (page 275)
1 large garlic clove
¾ teaspoon salt
1 lb poblano chiles (about 4 large), roasted and peeled (see Tips, page 8)
6 large eggs
1 cup whole milk
½ cup Mexican *crema* or heavy cream
2 tablespoons finely grated white onion (using small teardrop holes of a box grater)
½ teaspoon black pepper
½ lb Monterey Jack cheese, coarsely grated (2½ to 3 cups)

SPECIAL EQUIPMENT: a 9-inch (2-inch-deep) round fluted tart pan with a removable bottom; pie weights or raw rice

▸ Put oven rack in middle position and preheat oven to 375°F.
▸ Roll out dough into a 13-inch round on a lightly floured surface with a floured rolling pin. Fit dough into tart pan, without stretching, letting excess dough hang over edge. Fold overhang inward and press against side of pan to reinforce edge. Prick bottom all over with a fork. Chill until firm, about 30 minutes.
▸ Line shell with foil or parchment paper and fill with pie weights. Bake until pastry is set and pale golden along rim, 20 to 25 minutes.
▸ Carefully remove weights and foil and bake shell until deep golden all over, 15 to 20 minutes more. Put tart pan in a shallow baking pan. Leave oven on.
▸ Mince garlic and mash to a paste with ¾ teaspoon salt using a large heavy knife.
▸ Discard seeds, ribs, and stems from chiles, then pat dry if necessary and cut into ⅓-inch-wide strips.
▸ Whisk together eggs, milk, *crema*, onion, garlic paste, and pepper in a large bowl until just combined, then pour into baked tart shell.

▸ Sprinkle cheese and chiles over custard (chiles will sink slightly) and bake until custard is just set, 50 to 60 minutes. (Center will jiggle slightly; filling will continue to set as it cools.)
▸ Transfer quiche in tart pan to a rack to cool at least 20 minutes before serving.
▸ To remove side of tart pan, center a large can under tart pan and let side of pan drop. Serve warm or at room temperature.

COOKS' NOTE: Quiche can be baked 1 day ahead and cooled completely, uncovered, then chilled, covered. Reheat, uncovered, in a preheated 325°F oven until just heated through, about 25 minutes.

COTTAGE CHEESE PANCAKES

SERVES 4

ACTIVE TIME: 40 MIN   START TO FINISH: 40 MIN

Versatile cottage cheese lends creaminess to this savory dish. Think of these pancakes as an easy omelet substitute.

⅓ cup chopped onion
¼ teaspoon salt
¼ teaspoon black pepper
7 tablespoons unsalted butter, melted
1½ cups whole-milk cottage cheese
3 large eggs
6 tablespoons all-purpose flour

▸ Preheat oven to 200°F.
▸ Cook onion, ⅛ teaspoon salt, and ⅛ teaspoon pepper in 2 tablespoons butter in a small heavy skillet over moderately low heat, stirring occasionally, until golden brown, about 12 minutes. Transfer to a bowl, then add cottage cheese, eggs, flour, ¼ cup butter, remaining ⅛ teaspoon salt, and remaining ⅛ teaspoon pepper and whisk until combined.
▸ Brush a 12-inch nonstick skillet with some of remaining butter and heat over moderate heat until hot but not smoking. Working in batches of 5, scoop ⅛-cup measures of batter into skillet and cook until undersides are golden brown, 1 to 2 minutes. Flip and cook until undersides are golden brown and pancakes are cooked through, 1 to 2 minutes more. Transfer to a baking sheet as cooked and keep warm in oven. Brush skillet with butter between batches if necessary.

BUCKWHEAT BACON PANCAKES

SERVES 4
ACTIVE TIME: 25 MIN START TO FINISH: 25 MIN

- ½ cup buckwheat flour
- ½ cup all-purpose flour
- 1 teaspoon sugar
- 1 teaspoon baking powder
- ½ teaspoon baking soda
- ¼ teaspoon salt
- 1 large egg, lightly beaten
- 1¼ cups well-shaken buttermilk
- 2½ tablespoons vegetable oil
- ¼ lb sliced Canadian bacon, cut into ⅛-inch pieces

▸ Preheat oven to 200°F.

▸ Stir together flours, sugar, baking powder, baking soda, and salt. Add egg, buttermilk, and 2 tablespoons oil and stir just until blended. Stir in bacon.

▸ Heat a griddle or large heavy skillet over moderate heat until hot, then lightly brush with remaining ½ tablespoon oil. Working in batches and using a scant ¼ cup per pancake, pour batter onto griddle and cook, turning over once, until golden, about 4 minutes total per batch. Transfer to a baking sheet as cooked and keep warm, covered, in oven. Brush griddle with oil between batches if necessary.

ALMOND FRENCH TOAST

SERVES 4
ACTIVE TIME: 25 MIN START TO FINISH: 25 MIN

- 4 large eggs
- 1⅓ cups half-and-half
- 4 teaspoons sugar
- ½ teaspoon pure vanilla extract
- ⅛ teaspoon salt
- 1¼ cups sliced almonds (5 oz)
- 8 (¾-inch-thick) slices brioche or challah from a 4- to 5-inch-wide loaf
- 3 tablespoons unsalted butter

ACCOMPANIMENTS: **maple syrup; confectioners sugar (optional)**

▸ Put oven rack in middle position and preheat oven to 275°F.

▸ Whisk together eggs, half-and-half, sugar, vanilla, and salt in a large shallow dish until combined well. Spread almonds on a large plate. Soak 4 slices of bread in egg mixture, turning over once, until saturated. Working with 1 slice at a time, remove bread, letting excess egg mixture drip off, then dredge

in almonds to coat both sides, gently pressing to help adhere. Transfer to a plate or wax paper. Repeat procedure with remaining 4 slices.

▸ Heat 1½ tablespoons butter in a 12-inch heavy skillet over moderate heat until foam subsides, then cook 4 bread slices, turning over once, until almonds and bread are golden brown, 5 to 6 minutes total. Add remaining 1½ tablespoons butter and cook remaining 4 slices in same manner. Transfer French toast to a baking sheet as cooked and keep warm in oven.

TRUFFLED TOAST WITH RADICCHIO AND EGG

SERVES 4
ACTIVE TIME: 20 MIN START TO FINISH: 20 MIN

- 1 lb radicchio (preferably di Treviso), cored and coarsely chopped
- ½ teaspoon salt
- ¼ teaspoon black pepper
- 2 tablespoons olive oil
- 1 teaspoon distilled white vinegar
- 4 large eggs
- 4 (¼-inch-thick) slices country-style bread, cut in half crosswise
- 4 teaspoons truffle butter (see Sources)
- 5 oz thinly sliced Italian Fontina

▸ Preheat broiler.

▸ Cook radicchio with salt and pepper in oil in a deep 10-inch skillet over moderate heat, stirring, until just tender, 2 to 3 minutes. Transfer to a bowl and keep warm, loosely covered. Wipe skillet clean.

▸ Fill skillet with 1¼ inches cold water. Add vinegar and bring to a simmer.

▸ Break 1 egg into a cup, then slide egg into simmering water. Repeat with remaining 3 eggs, spacing them in skillet, and poach at a bare simmer until whites are firm but yolks are still runny, 2 to 3 minutes.

▸ Toast bread, then spread one side of each piece with truffle butter and cover with cheese. Broil toast on a baking sheet 4 to 6 inches from heat until cheese is just melted.

▸ Divide toast among 4 plates, then top with radicchio and poached eggs. Season with salt and pepper.

COOKS' NOTE: The eggs in this recipe are not fully cooked, which may be of concern if salmonella is a problem in your area. You can substitute pasteurized eggs (in the shell) or cook eggs until yolks are set.

OKA CHEESE FONDUE

SERVES 8 TO 10

ACTIVE TIME: 30 MIN   START TO FINISH: 30 MIN

1¼ cups heavy cream
½   cup dry white wine (preferably Riesling)
½   cup ice wine (preferably Canadian)
3   tablespoons all-purpose flour
1   lb Oka cheese or Port-Salut, rind removed and cheese
    coarsely grated (4 cups)

SPECIAL EQUIPMENT: **a fondue pot with long-handled forks**
ACCOMPANIMENTS: **cubed baguette; apple and pear wedges**

▶ Whisk together cream, wines, and flour in a 2-quart heavy saucepan until smooth, then bring to a boil over moderate heat, stirring constantly, until thickened and silky, about 5 minutes. Add half of cheese and stir gently until almost melted, then add remaining cheese and cook, stirring, until cheese is melted and fondue is smooth, about 3 minutes. Serve in fondue pot.

KITCHEN NOTE

IN THE 1880S, **OKA CHEESE** EMIGRATED WITH TRAPPIST MONKS FROM THE BRITTANY REGION OF FRANCE TO AN AREA JUST OUTSIDE MONTREAL. THE SEMISOFT COW'S-MILK CHEESE IS STILL AGED IN THE TRAPPIST CELLARS FOR ABOUT TWO MONTHS BEFORE BEING SOLD. ITS ROBUST FLAVOR AND MILD AROMA MAKE IT A GREAT CHOICE FOR ANY CHEESE PLATE AND ARE REASON ENOUGH TO DIG OUT THE FONDUE POT.

SANDWICHES

CROQUES-MONSIEUR

SERVES 2

ACTIVE TIME: 20 MIN   START TO FINISH: 20 MIN

1   cup sharp Cheddar, coarsely grated
3   oz Canadian bacon, sliced
4   slices firm white bread
2   large eggs
¼   teaspoon salt
⅛   teaspoon black pepper
2   tablespoons unsalted butter

▶ Arrange half of cheese, then all of bacon on 2 slices of bread. Top with remaining cheese and bread.
▶ Beat eggs with salt and black pepper in a shallow dish. Dip sandwiches in egg mixture, carefully turning over several times and pressing lightly, until all of egg mixture is absorbed.
▶ Heat butter in a 10-inch skillet over moderate heat until foam subsides. Transfer sandwiches with a spatula to skillet and cook until golden brown on bottom, 3 to 4 minutes. Turn over sandwiches, pressing lightly, and cook until golden brown on bottom, 3 to 4 minutes more.

CROISSANT EGG SANDWICHES

SERVES 4

ACTIVE TIME: 10 MIN   START TO FINISH: 20 MIN

16 paper-thin slices Genoa salami (4 inches in
    diameter; ¼ lb)
4   croissants, halved horizontally
8   large eggs
¾   cup whole milk
¼   cup whipped cream cheese
½   teaspoon salt
¼   teaspoon black pepper
1   tablespoon olive oil
4   cups baby arugula (about 2 oz)

SPECIAL EQUIPMENT: **parchment paper**

▶ Put oven rack in middle position and preheat oven to 325°F.
▶ Arrange salami slices in 1 layer on a large baking sheet lined with parchment paper. Bake until edges are crisp and beginning to curl, 10 to 12 minutes.
▶ Transfer salami to a rack to cool, arranging it in 1 layer. (Slices will crisp as they cool.) Leave oven on and discard parchment.
▶ Arrange croissants, cut sides up, on same baking sheet and toast in oven until just golden, 3 to 5 minutes.
▶ While croissants toast, whisk together eggs, milk, cream cheese, salt, and pepper until eggs are combined well (cream cheese won't blend into egg mixture completely).
▶ Heat oil in a 12-inch nonstick skillet over moderately high heat until hot but not smoking. Pour in egg mixture and cook, scraping up cooked egg with a heatproof rubber spatula and letting raw egg run underneath, until egg is set, about 3 minutes. Season eggs with pepper.
▶ Assemble croissant sandwiches with arugula, eggs, and salami.

WE RARELY USE CANNED WHITE TUNA PACKED IN WATER BECAUSE IT LACKS FLAVOR. INSTEAD, WE USE **TUNA PACKED IN OLIVE OIL** (NOT VEGETABLE OIL). IT'S THE STAR OF A CLASSIC SALADE NIÇOISE, AND IT'S ALSO TERRIFIC FLAKED OVER SEASONED COOKED WHITE BEANS AND ADORNED WITH MINCED PARSLEY.

TUSCAN TUNA-AND-BEAN SANDWICHES

SERVES 4

ACTIVE TIME: 30 MIN   START TO FINISH: 30 MIN

FOR BEANS

- 1 (14- to 15-oz) can cannellini beans, rinsed and drained
- 2 garlic cloves, finely chopped
- 1 tablespoon fresh lemon juice
- 2 tablespoons olive oil
- 2 tablespoons chopped fresh flat-leaf parsley or basil
- ¼ teaspoon salt
- ¼ teaspoon black pepper

FOR TUNA SALAD

- 2 (6-oz) cans Italian tuna in oil (see Sources), drained
- 2 tablespoons finely chopped fresh basil or flat-leaf parsley
- ¼ cup pitted Kalamata or other brine-cured black olives, finely chopped
- 1 celery rib, finely chopped
- 2 tablespoons finely chopped red onion
- 2 tablespoons olive oil
- 1 tablespoon fresh lemon juice
- ¼ teaspoon salt
- ⅛ teaspoon black pepper

FOR SANDWICHES

- 8 (⅓-inch-thick) slices rustic Italian bread (from a round crusty loaf) or 4 (4-inch-long) oval *panini* rolls
- 1 cup loosely packed trimmed watercress sprigs

PREPARE BEANS:

▶Coarsely mash beans with a fork in a bowl, then stir in garlic, lemon juice, oil, parsley, salt, and pepper.

MAKE TUNA SALAD:

▶Flake tuna in a bowl with a fork, then stir in basil, olives, celery, onion, oil, lemon juice, salt, and pepper until combined.

ASSEMBLE SANDWICHES:

▶Spoon one fourth of bean mixture on 1 slice of bread, then top with one fourth of tuna salad, some watercress, and a slice of bread. Make 3 more sandwiches in same manner.

GRILLED OPEN-FACE EGGPLANT AND SMOKED-GOUDA SANDWICHES

SERVES 4

ACTIVE TIME: 1¼ HR   START TO FINISH: 1¼ HR

- 1 lb tomatoes, finely chopped (2½ cups)
- ¼ cup finely chopped fresh flat-leaf parsley
- ½ cup plus 2 tablespoons extra-virgin olive oil
- 1 tablespoon white-wine vinegar
- ½ teaspoon black pepper
- 1¼ teaspoons salt
- 1 (8-oz) piece smoked cheese such as Gouda, mozzarella, or *scamorza*
- 4 (¾-inch-thick) slices country-style bread (from an 8-inch round loaf)
- 2 (1-lb) eggplants

▶Prepare grill for cooking over direct heat with medium-hot charcoal (moderate heat for gas); see Tips, page 8.

▶While coals are lighting, stir together tomatoes, parsley, 2 tablespoons oil, vinegar, pepper, and ¾ teaspoon salt in a medium bowl.

▶With a cheese plane or vegetable peeler, shave half of cheese into thin slices (if using mozzarella, thinly slice half of it with a knife) and cover slices with plastic wrap, reserving remaining piece for another use.

▶Brush bread on both sides with 1 tablespoon oil per slice.

▶Trim off top and bottom of each eggplant, then cut 2 (1-inch-thick) slices lengthwise from center of each eggplant, discarding remainder. Brush cut sides with 3 tablespoons oil (total) and sprinkle with remaining ½ teaspoon salt.

▶Lightly oil grill rack, then grill eggplant slices, covered only if using a gas grill, loosening with a metal spatula and turning over occasionally to avoid overbrowning, until very tender, 8 to 10 minutes. While eggplant is grilling, grill bread, turning over once, until grill marks form, 1 to 2 minutes total, then transfer to a large platter.

▶Transfer eggplant to platter, then top evenly with sliced cheese. Return to grill and cook, covered for charcoal or gas, without turning, until cheese begins to melt, about 1 minute. Transfer eggplant with spatula to platter.

▶Transfer grilled bread to 4 plates and spoon tomato mixture on top. Drizzle evenly with remaining tablespoon oil and top with eggplant. Season with pepper.

GRILLED SAUSAGE SANDWICHES WITH FENNEL AND SWEET ONION

SERVES 4

ACTIVE TIME: 10 MIN START TO FINISH: 20 MIN

The idea of cooking small individual coils of sausage for plenty of crispy outer edges comes from Frances Foley—mother of Gourmet*'s freelance photography assistant, Stephanie Foley.*

- 1 lb coiled thin Italian sausage (sometimes called *luganega*)
- ½ fennel bulb (sometimes labeled "anise"), thinly sliced
- ½ medium sweet onion, such as Vidalia or Walla Walla, thinly sliced
- 1½ tablespoons olive oil
- ¼ teaspoon salt
- ⅛ teaspoon black pepper
- 4 hamburger buns

SPECIAL EQUIPMENT: **4 (6- to 8-inch) wooden skewers; a well-seasoned large (2-burner) ridged grill pan (preferably cast iron)**
ACCOMPANIMENT: **mustard**

▶ Uncoil sausage and cut into 4 equal lengths. Re-coil each piece into a round and secure with a skewer by threading it horizontally through coil.
▶ Toss together fennel, onion, oil, salt, and pepper in a bowl.
▶ Lightly oil grill pan and heat over moderately high heat until hot but not smoking. Arrange sausages and fennel and onion in grill pan (vegetables can be in a shallow pile). Grill, turning sausages over once and tossing vegetables occasionally, until vegetables are softened and charred, 8 to 10 minutes. Transfer vegetables to a bowl and continue to grill sausages until cooked through, 2 to 5 minutes more.
▶ Remove skewers and serve sausages, topped with fennel and onion, on buns.

ARUGULA AND RICOTTA CALZONES

SERVES 4

ACTIVE TIME: 25 MIN START TO FINISH: 45 MIN

- 1 large garlic clove, minced
- 2 tablespoons extra-virgin olive oil
- 5 oz baby arugula (about 8 cups packed)
- 6 oz whole-milk ricotta (⅔ cup)
- 3 oz whole-milk mozzarella, coarsely grated
- 2 tablespoons finely grated Parmigiano-Reggiano (see Tips, page 8)
- 1 large egg yolk
- ¼ teaspoon salt
- ⅛ teaspoon black pepper
- 1 lb frozen pizza dough, thawed

SPECIAL EQUIPMENT: **an oiled 17- by 12-inch heavy baking sheet**

▶ Put oven rack in lower third of oven and preheat oven to 450°F.
▶ Cook garlic in oil in a 12-inch heavy skillet over moderate heat, stirring frequently, until golden, 1 to 2 minutes. Add arugula and cook, stirring frequently, until wilted, 2 to 3 minutes. Transfer to a sieve and press hard on arugula to squeeze out as much excess liquid as possible, then coarsely chop.
▶ Stir together ricotta, mozzarella, Parmigiano-Reggiano, yolk, salt, and pepper until blended, then stir in arugula.
▶ Quarter dough, then roll out each piece into an 8-inch round with a rolling pin. Put one fourth of cheese filling (about ⅓ cup) in center of 1 round and fold dough in half to enclose filling and form a semicircle. Press edges together to seal. Beginning at 1 end and working toward the other, stretch sealed edge outward, pinching and rolling edge to form a rope. Transfer to baking sheet. Make 3 more calzones in same manner, transferring to baking sheet.
▶ Bake calzones until golden and puffed, 12 to 15 minutes. Cool on baking sheet 5 minutes before serving.

PASTA AND GRAINS

PASTA

COUSCOUS WITH OLIVES AND LEMON

SERVES 4 (SIDE DISH)
ACTIVE TIME: 15 MIN START TO FINISH: 20 MIN

Serve this fast, garlicky couscous with grilled chicken or Italian sausages.

1½ teaspoons minced garlic
 3 tablespoons olive oil
1¾ cups water
 Rounded ¼ teaspoon salt
1½ cups couscous (10 oz)
 16 oil-cured black olives, pitted and coarsely chopped
 ⅓ cup chopped fresh flat-leaf parsley
1½ teaspoons finely grated fresh lemon zest (see Tips, page 8)

▶ Cook garlic in oil in a wide 2- to 3-quart heavy saucepan over moderate heat, stirring frequently, until golden, 1 to 2 minutes. Add water and salt and bring to a boil. Stir in remaining ingredients, then cover pan and remove from heat. Let stand, undisturbed, 5 minutes. Fluff with a fork.

COOKS' NOTE: Taste your olives before you start cooking; if they are very salty, reduce the salt in this recipe.

SHRIMP SCAMPI PASTA

SERVES 4 (MAIN COURSE)
ACTIVE TIME: 10 MIN START TO FINISH: 20 MIN

 ¼ cup olive oil
 1 lb peeled and deveined large shrimp (raw; 20 to 25 per lb)
 4 large garlic cloves, left unpeeled and forced through a garlic press
 ½ teaspoon dried hot red-pepper flakes
 ½ cup dry white wine
 1 teaspoon salt
 ½ teaspoon black pepper
 5 tablespoons unsalted butter
 ¾ lb *capellini* (angel-hair pasta)
 ½ cup chopped fresh flat-leaf parsley

▶ Bring a 6- to 8-quart pot of salted water (see Tips, page 8) to a boil.
▶ Meanwhile, heat oil in a 12-inch heavy skillet over moderately high heat until hot but not smoking, then sauté shrimp, turning over once, until just cooked through, about 2 minutes. Transfer with a slotted spoon to a large bowl. Add garlic to oil remaining in skillet along with red-pepper flakes, wine, salt, and pepper and cook over high heat, stirring occasionally, 1 minute. Add butter to skillet, stirring until melted, then stir in shrimp. Remove skillet from heat.
▶ Cook pasta in boiling water until just tender, about 3 minutes. Reserve 1 cup pasta-cooking water, then drain pasta in a colander. Toss pasta well with shrimp mixture and parsley in large bowl, adding some of reserved cooking water if necessary to keep moist.

ORZO WITH ARTICHOKES AND PINE NUTS

SERVES 4 (SIDE DISH)
ACTIVE TIME: 15 MIN START TO FINISH: 15 MIN

1½ cups orzo (10 oz)
 3 tablespoons pine nuts
 1 (14-oz) can whole artichoke hearts (not marinated)
 ¼ cup extra-virgin olive oil
 2 tablespoons red-wine vinegar
 ¾ teaspoon salt
 ½ teaspoon black pepper
 ½ cup finely chopped fresh flat-leaf parsley
 1 teaspoon finely grated fresh lemon zest (see Tips, page 8)

▶ Cook orzo in a 4- to 5-quart pot of boiling salted water (see Tips, page 8) until al dente. Drain in a colander.
▶ While orzo cooks, lightly toast pine nuts in a dry small skillet over moderate heat, stirring, until pale golden, about 2 minutes. Remove from heat and cool 1 minute, then coarsely chop.
▶ Drain artichoke hearts in a large sieve and rinse well. Pull off leaves from bases of hearts and quarter bases. Rinse leaves and bases well, then drain thoroughly.
▶ Stir together oil, vinegar, salt, and pepper in a large bowl. Add orzo, pine nuts, artichokes (leaves and bases), parsley, and zest and toss to combine.

WILD-MUSHROOM PASTA

SERVES 6 (FIRST COURSE) OR 4 (MAIN COURSE)
ACTIVE TIME: 40 MIN   START TO FINISH: 40 MIN

This pasta dish is made for the culinarily creative—feel free to use your favorite mushrooms for a recipe all your own.

- ⅔ oz dried morel or porcini mushrooms
- 1¾ cups boiling-hot water
- 5 tablespoons unsalted butter
- ½ lb fresh cremini mushrooms, trimmed and sliced ¼ inch thick
- ¾ lb mixed fresh wild mushrooms, such as oyster, chanterelle, or porcini, trimmed and sliced lengthwise ¼ inch thick
- 1 large garlic clove, minced
- ¾ teaspoon salt
- ¼ teaspoon black pepper
- ½ lb dried egg fettuccine
- ¼ cup chopped fresh chives
- 2 tablespoons chopped fresh flat-leaf parsley
- 1½ teaspoons finely grated fresh lemon zest (see Tips, page 8)
- ½ teaspoon fresh lemon juice

ACCOMPANIMENT: **grated Parmigiano-Reggiano**

▶ Soak dried mushrooms in boiling-hot water in a bowl until softened, about 20 minutes. Drain in a paper-towel-lined sieve set over a bowl and reserve soaking liquid, then rinse soaked mushrooms. Pat dry and finely chop.

▶ Heat 3 tablespoons butter in a 12-inch heavy skillet over moderately high heat until foam subsides, then sauté fresh mushrooms with garlic, salt, and pepper, stirring occasionally, until liquid mushrooms give off is evaporated and mushrooms are browned, 5 to 7 minutes. Stir in chopped soaked mushrooms and reserved mushroom-soaking liquid and simmer 1 minute, then remove from heat.

▶ Cook pasta in a 6- to 8-quart pot of boiling salted water (see Tips, page 8) until al dente, about 5 minutes. Ladle out and reserve ¼ cup pasta-cooking water. Drain pasta in a colander, then add it to mushrooms in skillet. Add remaining 2 tablespoons butter and cook over moderately high heat, tossing and adding some reserved cooking water if necessary to lightly coat, 1 minute. Add chives, parsley, lemon zest, and juice, then toss well. Serve immediately with cheese and pepper to taste.

COOKS' NOTE: Fresh hen-of-the-woods, beech (also called *shimeji*), or any other wild mushrooms can be substituted for the mixed fresh wild mushrooms.

GRATINÉED GNOCCHI WITH SPINACH AND RICOTTA

SERVES 4 (MAIN COURSE)
ACTIVE TIME: 10 MIN   START TO FINISH: 20 MIN

- 1 (1-lb) package potato gnocchi
- ⅔ cup heavy cream
- ½ teaspoon all-purpose flour
- ½ teaspoon salt
- ½ teaspoon black pepper
- ⅛ teaspoon ground nutmeg
- 3 (5-oz) packages baby spinach
- ½ cup whole-milk or part-skim ricotta
- ⅔ cup shredded mozzarella

▶ Preheat broiler.

▶ Cook gnocchi in a 5-quart pot of boiling salted water (see Tips, page 8) according to package instructions (gnocchi will float to surface when done). Drain in a colander.

▶ Whisk together cream, flour, salt, pepper, and nutmeg in a 12-inch ovenproof skillet, then bring to a boil over moderate heat, whisking. Continue to boil, whisking frequently, until reduced by half, about 2 minutes. Add spinach in handfuls, tossing with tongs, and cook until wilted, 2 to 4 minutes. Remove from heat, then stir in gnocchi. Spoon ricotta over gnocchi in 5 large dollops and sprinkle with mozzarella.

▶ Broil 4 to 6 inches from heat until cheese is browned and bubbling in spots, about 2 minutes. Season with pepper.

KITCHEN NOTE

TO MAKE HOMEMADE **FRESH RICOTTA**, COMBINE 2 QUARTS WHOLE MILK, 1 CUP HEAVY CREAM, AND ½ TEASPOON SALT IN A 6-QUART HEAVY POT. SLOWLY BRING TO A ROLLING BOIL OVER MODERATE HEAT, STIRRING OCCASIONALLY TO PREVENT SCORCHING. ADD 3 TABLESPOONS FRESH LEMON JUICE, THEN REDUCE HEAT TO LOW AND SIMMER, STIRRING CONSTANTLY, UNTIL MIXTURE CURDLES, ABOUT 2 MINUTES. POUR THE MIXTURE INTO A LARGE CHEESECLOTH-LINED SIEVE SET OVER A LARGE BOWL AND LET IT DRAIN 1 HOUR. AFTER DISCARDING THE LIQUID, CHILL THE RICOTTA, COVERED; IT WILL KEEP IN THE FRIDGE 2 DAYS.

SPAGHETTI WITH BROCCOLI RABE AND GARLIC

SERVES 4 TO 6 (MAIN COURSE)

ACTIVE TIME: 15 MIN   START TO FINISH: 30 MIN

1   lb spaghetti
1   (1-lb) bunch broccoli rabe, hollow stems discarded and
      leaves and remaining stems cut into 2-inch pieces
5   garlic cloves, finely chopped
½   to ¾ teaspoon dried hot red-pepper flakes (to taste)
¾   teaspoon salt
½   cup olive oil

ACCOMPANIMENT: **grated Parmigiano-Reggiano**

▶ Cook pasta in a 6- to 8-quart pot of boiling salted water (see Tips, page 8) according to package instructions. When pasta is 5 minutes from finished, add broccoli rabe to pot and continue to cook until pasta is al dente. Drain in a colander and transfer to a large serving bowl.

▶ Meanwhile, cook garlic, red-pepper flakes, and salt in oil in a small heavy skillet over moderate heat, stirring frequently, until garlic is pale golden, 3 to 4 minutes. Pour over pasta and toss to combine.

ASIAN NOODLES WITH CHICKEN AND SCALLIONS

SERVES 4 (MAIN COURSE)

ACTIVE TIME: 10 MIN   START TO FINISH: 25 MIN

1   lb chicken tenders (not coated or cooked)
1   lb fresh or frozen broccoli florets
1   lb dried *udon* (thick wheat noodles)
½   cup premium oyster sauce (preferably Lee Kum Kee)
2   tablespoons hoisin sauce (preferably Lee Kum Kee)
1   tablespoon Asian sesame oil
2   teaspoons Chinese chile garlic paste (preferably Lan Chi;
      see cooks' note, below), or to taste
½   cup chopped scallions (from 1 bunch)
2   teaspoons roasted sesame seeds (optional)

▶ Cook chicken in a 6-quart pot of boiling unsalted water, covered, until just cooked through, about 3 minutes. Transfer to a large bowl with a slotted spoon.

▶ Add broccoli to boiling water and cook, uncovered, stirring occasionally, until just tender, 3 to 5 minutes. Transfer with slotted spoon to a colander to drain, then transfer to another large bowl.

▶ Return water to a boil and cook noodles until tender (check often; cooking time on package may not be accurate). Reserve 1 cup cooking water, then drain noodles in colander and rinse under hot water.

▶ While noodles cook, tear chicken into chunks.

▶ Add oyster and hoisin sauces, sesame oil, chile garlic paste, half of scallions, and ⅓ cup cooking water to chicken and stir to combine.

▶ Divide noodles, broccoli, and chicken mixture among 4 bowls and sprinkle with sesame seeds and remaining scallions. Serve immediately, stirring just before eating. If noodles become dry, moisten with some of reserved cooking water.

COOKS' NOTE: If you have to substitute an Asian chile paste without garlic for the chile garlic paste, start with ½ teaspoon and add to taste.

LINGUINE WITH ZUCCHINI AND MINT

SERVES 4 (MAIN COURSE)

ACTIVE TIME: 40 MIN   START TO FINISH: 40 MIN

2   lb zucchini (3 large)
1   cup olive oil
4   garlic cloves, finely chopped
1   lb dried linguine
¾   cup chopped fresh mint
1   tablespoon finely grated fresh lemon zest (see Tips, page 8)
1   teaspoon salt
¼   teaspoon black pepper

SPECIAL EQUIPMENT: **an adjustable-blade slicer**

▶ Slice zucchini very thinly with slicer.

▶ Heat oil in a 12-inch heavy skillet over moderately high heat until hot but not smoking, then fry zucchini in 3 batches, stirring occasionally, until softened and very pale golden, 3 to 4 minutes per batch. Transfer as fried with a slotted spoon to a baking pan lined with paper towels to drain. Keep zucchini warm, covered with foil.

▶ Add garlic to oil in skillet and cook over moderately high heat, stirring, until very pale golden, about 30 seconds. Remove skillet from heat.

▶ Cook pasta in a 6- to 8-quart pot of boiling salted water (see Tips, page 8), uncovered, until al dente. Reserve 1 cup pasta-cooking water. Drain pasta in a colander and transfer to a large shallow bowl.

▶ Toss pasta with garlic oil, zucchini, mint, zest, salt, and pepper. Add some of reserved cooking water to moisten if necessary.

PENNE WITH BUTTERNUT-SAGE SAUCE

SERVES 4 TO 6 (MAIN COURSE)

ACTIVE TIME: 10 MIN START TO FINISH: 25 MIN

1 lb peeled butternut squash pieces
1 small onion, quartered
½ stick (¼ cup) unsalted butter
1 tablespoon finely chopped fresh sage
1½ cups water
¾ teaspoon salt
½ teaspoon black pepper
2 oz finely grated Parmigiano-Reggiano (1 cup; see Tips, page 8) plus additional for serving
1 lb penne rigate

▶ Process squash and onion in a food processor until finely chopped, about 1 minute.

▶ Heat butter in a 5- to 6-quart heavy pot over moderately high heat until foam subsides, then cook sage until fragrant, about 15 seconds. Add chopped squash mixture, water, salt, and pepper and simmer, uncovered, stirring occasionally, until water is evaporated and squash is very tender, 8 to 10 minutes. Stir in cheese and remove from heat.

▶ While squash mixture simmers, cook penne in a 6- to 8-quart pot of boiling salted water (see Tips, page 8) until al dente. Reserve 1 cup pasta-cooking water, then drain pasta in a colander. Add ½ cup cooking water to squash mixture, then add drained pasta, tossing to combine.

▶ Thin with additional cooking water as desired and serve with additional cheese.

FETTUCCINE WITH SAUSAGE AND KALE

SERVES 4 (MAIN COURSE)

ACTIVE TIME: 30 MIN START TO FINISH: 30 MIN

3 tablespoons olive oil
1 lb hot turkey or pork sausage, casings discarded and sausage crumbled
½ lb kale, tough stems and center ribs discarded and leaves coarsely chopped
½ lb dried egg fettuccine
⅔ cup reduced-sodium chicken broth
1 oz finely grated Pecorino Romano (½ cup; see Tips, page 8) plus additional for serving

▶ Heat oil in a 12-inch heavy skillet over moderately high heat until hot but not smoking, then cook sausage, breaking up any lumps with a spoon, until browned, 5 to 7 minutes.

▶ Meanwhile, blanch kale in a 6-quart pot of boiling salted water (see Tips, page 8), uncovered, 5 minutes. Remove kale with a large sieve and drain. Return cooking water in pot to a boil, then cook pasta in boiling water, uncovered, until al dente. Reserve 1 cup pasta-cooking water, then drain pasta in a colander.

▶ While pasta cooks, add kale to sausage in skillet and sauté, stirring frequently, until just tender, about 5 minutes. Add broth, stirring and scraping up any brown bits from bottom of skillet, then add pasta and ½ cup reserved cooking water to skillet, tossing until combined. Stir in cheese and thin with additional cooking water if desired.

▶ Serve immediately, with additional cheese on the side.

PASTA WITH SPEEDY ROMESCO SAUCE

SERVES 4 (MAIN COURSE)

ACTIVE TIME: 10 MIN START TO FINISH: 20 MIN

This streamlined version of a complex Catalan sauce makes for a gratifying weeknight supper—and a welcome alternative to pasta with marinara.

1 lb corkscrew pasta such as *rotini*
1 slice firm white sandwich bread, toasted
1 (7-oz) jar roasted red peppers, drained
¼ cup roasted salted almonds (not smoked)
1 large garlic clove
½ cup reduced-sodium chicken broth
¼ cup extra-virgin olive oil
1 teaspoon Sherry vinegar, or to taste
¾ teaspoon salt, or to taste
¼ teaspoon dried hot red-pepper flakes, or to taste
1 (10-oz) package frozen baby peas (2 cups)
¼ cup finely grated Parmigiano-Reggiano plus additional for serving

▶ Begin to cook pasta in a 6- to 8-quart pot of boiling salted water (see Tips, page 8).

▶ Meanwhile, tear toast into pieces and blend with peppers, almonds, garlic, broth, oil, vinegar, salt, and red-pepper flakes in a blender until smooth, about 2 minutes. Transfer to a 12-inch heavy skillet and bring to a simmer.

▶ When pasta is barely al dente, add peas and continue to cook until peas are just tender, about 2 minutes. Reserve ½ cup pasta-cooking water, then drain pasta and peas in a colander. Add pasta and peas to sauce along with cheese (¼ cup) and toss to combine. Add some reserved cooking water to thin if necessary. Serve immediately.

GRAINS

KASHA WITH BROWNED ONIONS AND WALNUTS

SERVES 4 (SIDE DISH)

ACTIVE TIME: 20 MIN   START TO FINISH: 35 MIN

In Russia and eastern Europe kasha is most often made into thick gruel. Instead, we turned the roasted buckwheat kernels into a fantastic side dish studded with butter-toasted walnuts and browned onion.

- 1   cup coarse kasha (roasted buckwheat groats)
- 1   large egg, lightly beaten
- 2   cups boiling-hot water
- ¾   teaspoon salt
- ½   teaspoon black pepper
- ¾   cup walnuts (3 oz), coarsely chopped
- 1½ tablespoons unsalted butter
- 2   tablespoons olive oil
- 1   medium onion, coarsely chopped
- 2   teaspoons fresh thyme leaves
- 3   tablespoons chopped fresh flat-leaf parsley

▶ Stir together kasha and egg until coated well, then cook in a dry 3½- to 4-quart heavy saucepan over moderate heat, stirring constantly, until grains smell toasty and begin to separate, about 2 minutes. Add boiling-hot water, ½ teaspoon salt, and ¼ teaspoon pepper and simmer, covered, over low heat until kasha is barely tender and most of water is absorbed, about 12 minutes. Remove from heat and let stand, covered, 10 minutes.

▶ While kasha simmers, toast walnuts in 1 tablespoon butter in a 12-inch heavy skillet over moderate heat, stirring frequently, 5 minutes. Transfer nuts to a plate, then add oil and remaining ½ tablespoon butter to skillet and heat over moderate heat until foam subsides. Add onion and thyme and cook, stirring occasionally, until softened and browned, about 15 minutes.

▶ Stir kasha into onion along with walnuts, parsley, and remaining ¼ teaspoon salt and ¼ teaspoon pepper.

BAY LEAF RICE PILAF

SERVES 4 (SIDE DISH)

ACTIVE TIME: 10 MIN   START TO FINISH: 35 MIN

- 3   Turkish or 1½ California bay leaves
- 1   tablespoon olive oil
- 1   garlic clove, finely chopped
- 1¼ cups long-grain white rice
- ¼   teaspoon salt
- ½   teaspoon black pepper
- 1   cup water
- ¾   cup reduced-sodium chicken broth (6 fl oz)

▶ Cook bay leaves in oil in a 1½- to 2-quart heavy saucepan over moderate heat, turning over occasionally, until leaves are lightly browned, 2 to 3 minutes. Add garlic and cook, stirring, until pale golden, about 30 seconds. Add rice, salt, and pepper and cook, stirring gently to avoid breaking bay leaves, 1 minute. Add water and broth and bring to a full boil, uncovered, over high heat. Cover with a tight-fitting lid, then reduce heat to low and simmer until water is absorbed and rice is tender, about 15 minutes.

▶ Remove from heat and let stand, undisturbed, 5 minutes. Fluff rice with a fork and discard bay leaves.

FRIED RICE WITH CANADIAN BACON

SERVES 4 (SIDE DISH)

ACTIVE TIME: 20 MIN   START TO FINISH: 25 MIN

- 3   tablespoons peanut oil
- 2   tablespoons minced peeled fresh ginger
- ¼   teaspoon salt
- 1   bunch scallions, chopped
- 3   cups cold cooked white rice
- 1   (6-oz) piece Canadian bacon, cut into ½-inch cubes (1¼ cups)
- 1   cup frozen baby peas, thawed
- 2   cups fresh mung bean sprouts
- 3   tablespoons oyster sauce
- ¼   cup water
- ¼   teaspoon Asian sesame oil

▶ Heat peanut oil in a wok or 12-inch heavy skillet (not nonstick) over moderately high heat until smoking. Add ginger, salt, and ¼ cup scallions and stir-fry 1 minute. Add rice and stir-fry until beginning to brown, 7 to 10 minutes. Add remaining ingredients (including scallions) and stir-fry until liquid is absorbed, about 2 minutes. Season with pepper.

QUICK PAELLA

SERVES 6 (MAIN COURSE)
ACTIVE TIME: 10 MIN   START TO FINISH: 25 MIN

This version may not be strictly traditional, but garlic, kielbasa, shrimp, clams, and saffron bring the flavors of paella together in a satisfying way.

- 3 tablespoons olive oil
- 3 garlic cloves, chopped
- 1 cup frozen onions and bell peppers (6 oz)
- ¼ lb kielbasa (not low-fat), quartered lengthwise and cut crosswise into ¼-inch-thick slices (1 cup)
- 2 cups instant long-grain white rice such as Uncle Ben's
- ¼ cup dry white wine
- 1¼ cups reduced-sodium chicken broth (10 fl oz)
- ⅛ teaspoon crumbled saffron threads
- 20 frozen cleaned raw medium shrimp such as Contessa brand
- 1¼ lb cockles or other very small (1-inch-wide) hard-shelled clams, scrubbed
- 1 cup frozen peas
- ½ cup small pimiento-stuffed green olives

▶ Heat oil in a 12-inch heavy skillet over high heat until just smoking, then sauté garlic and frozen onions and bell peppers, stirring, until garlic and onions are golden, about 2 minutes. Add kielbasa and cook, stirring, until kielbasa is lightly browned, about 2 minutes. Add rice, wine, broth, saffron, and shrimp and cook, covered and undisturbed, over high heat until most of liquid is absorbed and shrimp are cooked through, about 6 minutes. Stir in cockles, peas, and olives and cook, covered, until cockles open wide, 2 to 4 minutes. (Discard any cockles that remain unopened after 4 minutes.) Remove from heat and let stand, covered, until all liquid is absorbed, about 5 minutes.

KITCHEN NOTE

LEFTOVER WHITE RICE IS A GREAT THING TO HAVE ON HAND FOR MAKING A QUICK SUPPER OR SIDE DISH OF FRIED RICE. WHEN YOU ORDER CHINESE TAKEOUT, ALWAYS ASK FOR AN EXTRA CONTAINER OF RICE. OR, WHEN COOKING YOUR OWN, MAKE EXTRA TO SET ASIDE.

WILD RICE WITH ROASTED PEPPERS AND TOASTED ALMONDS

SERVES 8 (SIDE DISH)
ACTIVE TIME: 30 MIN   START TO FINISH: 1¾ HR

- ¼ lb shallots (about 4 medium), thinly sliced crosswise into rounds
- 4 garlic cloves, thinly sliced crosswise
- 2 tablespoons olive oil
- 2 cups wild rice (11 oz), rinsed and drained
- 3½ cups reduced-sodium chicken broth (28 fl oz)
- 3½ cups water
- 2 red bell peppers
- 1 tablespoon unsalted butter
- 1 cup sliced almonds with skins (3½ oz)
- 1 teaspoon salt
- ¼ teaspoon black pepper
- 1 tablespoon Sherry vinegar

▶ Cook shallots and garlic in oil in a 4- to 5-quart heavy pot over moderately low heat, stirring occasionally, until golden brown, about 10 minutes. Add rice and cook, stirring, until it releases a nutty aroma, about 3 minutes. Add broth and water and bring to a boil, stirring occasionally, then reduce heat and simmer, covered, until rice is tender (grains will split open), about 1¼ hours.

▶ Meanwhile, preheat broiler. Halve bell peppers lengthwise, then discard stems and seeds. Put peppers, cut sides down, in 1 layer in an oiled shallow baking pan. Broil 2 inches from heat until charred and softened, 15 to 18 minutes. Transfer to a bowl. Cover and let steam 15 minutes. Peel, then cut into ½-inch pieces.

▶ Melt butter in a 12-inch heavy skillet over moderate heat, then add almonds and cook, stirring, until golden, 5 to 8 minutes.

▶ Remove rice from heat and drain well, then return to pot. Stir in salt, pepper, red peppers, almonds, and vinegar. Transfer to a serving dish.

COOKS' NOTE: Rice can be cooked (without draining) and peppers roasted and diced 1 day ahead. Cool rice completely, uncovered, then chill rice and peppers separately, covered. Reheat rice in a heavy pot, covered, over low heat, 10 to 15 minutes, then drain before adding seasonings, peppers, almonds, and vinegar.

VEGETABLES

DRY-CURRIED GREEN BEANS

SERVES 4

ACTIVE TIME: 5 MIN   START TO FINISH: 15 MIN

- 1 lb green beans, trimmed
- 1 cup water
- 2 tablespoons unsalted butter
- ¾ teaspoon curry powder
- ½ teaspoon salt
- ⅛ teaspoon black pepper
- ⅛ teaspoon cayenne

▸ Bring all ingredients to a boil in a 12-inch heavy skillet, then simmer briskly, partially covered, stirring occasionally, until beans are crisp-tender and liquid is reduced to about 2 tablespoons, 6 to 9 minutes.

ASPARAGUS GRATIN

SERVES 6

ACTIVE TIME: 25 MIN   START TO FINISH: 25 MIN

- 2 lb asparagus, trimmed and cut diagonally into 1½-inch pieces
- 2 tablespoons olive oil
- 2 tablespoons unsalted butter, cut into bits
- ½ cup finely chopped shallots (about 2 large)
- 4 slices firm white sandwich bread, cut into ¼-inch pieces
- ¼ cup pine nuts (1¼ oz)
- ¼ teaspoon black pepper
- 2 oz finely grated Parmigiano-Reggiano (1 cup; see Tips, page 8)
- ½ teaspoon salt
- ½ cup mascarpone cheese

▸ Butter a 2- to 2½-quart shallow ceramic flameproof baking dish.

▸ Cook asparagus in a 5- to 6-quart pot of boiling salted water (see Tips, page 8), uncovered, until crisp-tender, about 4 minutes. Drain in a colander, then transfer to baking dish and keep warm, tightly covered with foil.

▸ Meanwhile, heat oil and butter in a 12-inch heavy skillet over high heat until foam subsides, then cook shallots, stirring occasionally, until pale golden, about 3 minutes. Add bread pieces and pine nuts and cook, stirring, until browned in spots, about 5 minutes. Transfer to a bowl and add pepper, ½ cup Parmigiano-Reggiano, and ¼ teaspoon salt, tossing to combine.

▸ Preheat broiler.

▸ Toss warm asparagus with mascarpone, remaining ½ cup Parmigiano-Reggiano, and remaining ¼ teaspoon salt until combined well.

▸ Sprinkle bread-crumb mixture evenly over asparagus. Broil 5 to 7 inches from heat until topping is golden brown, 1 to 2 minutes.

BROCCOLI WITH HOT BACON DRESSING

SERVES 4

ACTIVE TIME: 25 MIN   START TO FINISH: 35 MIN

- 2 lb broccoli, trimmed and cut into 1-inch-wide florets (reserving stems)
- ¼ lb sliced bacon (about 4 slices), cut crosswise into ¼-inch-wide strips
- 1 garlic clove, finely chopped
- ⅓ cup raisins
- ¼ cup distilled white vinegar
- 2 tablespoons olive oil
- ½ teaspoon salt
- ¼ teaspoon black pepper

▸ Peel broccoli stems with a vegetable peeler, then cut crosswise into ¼-inch slices.

▸ Cook bacon in a 12-inch heavy skillet over moderate heat, stirring occasionally, until browned and crisp, 4 to 5 minutes. Transfer bacon with a slotted spoon to several layers of paper towels to drain, reserving fat in skillet.

▸ Add garlic and raisins to fat in skillet and cook over moderate heat, stirring, until garlic is pale golden, about 1 minute. Stir in vinegar, oil, salt, and pepper, then remove from heat.

▸ Meanwhile, cook broccoli florets and stems in a large pot of boiling salted water (see Tips, page 8) until just tender, 4 to 5 minutes. Drain broccoli well and transfer to a bowl.

▸ Bring dressing to a simmer, then cook, stirring, 1 minute. Pour hot dressing over broccoli and sprinkle with bacon, tossing to combine.

SAUTÉED BROCCOLI RABE AND PEAS

SERVES 4 TO 6

ACTIVE TIME: 10 MIN   START TO FINISH: 20 MIN

- 1 (¾- to 1-lb) bunch broccoli rabe
- 10 oz frozen peas (about 2 cups)
- ¼ cup extra-virgin olive oil
- 3 large garlic cloves, peeled and lightly smashed with side of a large knife
- ½ teaspoon salt
- ½ teaspoon black pepper

▶ Trim stem ends from broccoli rabe and discard. Cut remainder crosswise into 1½-inch pieces.

▶ Cook broccoli rabe and peas in a 4- to 6-quart pot of boiling salted water (see Tips, page 8) until broccoli rabe is wilted and stems are crisp-tender, 2 to 3 minutes. Drain well in a colander.

▶ Heat oil with garlic in a 12-inch heavy skillet over moderately high heat, turning garlic frequently, until garlic is golden, 1 to 2 minutes, then discard garlic.

▶ Add broccoli rabe, peas, salt, and pepper to skillet and sauté, stirring, until well coated with garlic oil, about 2 minutes.

BABY BRUSSELS SPROUTS WITH BUTTERED PECANS

SERVES 6 TO 8

ACTIVE TIME: 40 MIN   START TO FINISH: 40 MIN

If you find it difficult to get excited about Brussels sprouts, then it's likely you've never sampled baby ones. The tiny sprouts—less than an inch across—lack the bitterness of their full-grown counterparts.

- ½ cup pecan halves, cut crosswise into thirds
- 3 tablespoons unsalted butter
- ¾ teaspoon salt
- 2 lb baby Brussels sprouts, trimmed
- ½ tablespoon minced garlic
- 1 teaspoon fresh lemon juice, or to taste
- ¼ teaspoon black pepper

▶ Put oven rack in middle position and preheat oven to 350°F.

▶ Spread pecan pieces in 1 layer in a shallow baking pan and toast in oven until fragrant and a few shades darker, about 10 minutes. Add ½ tablespoon butter and ¼ teaspoon salt to nuts and toss until butter is melted and nuts are coated.

▶ While nuts toast, cook Brussels sprouts in a 6- to 8-quart pot of boiling salted water (see Tips, page 8), uncovered, until just

tender, 5 to 6 minutes. Transfer to a bowl of ice and cold water to stop cooking. Drain sprouts in a colander and pat dry.

▶ Melt remaining 2½ tablespoons butter in a 12-inch heavy skillet over moderate heat, then cook garlic, stirring, until fragrant, about 1 minute. Increase heat to moderately high, then add sprouts and sauté, stirring occasionally, until browned in patches, about 5 minutes. Add lemon juice, pepper, and remaining ½ teaspoon salt, then stir in pecans.

COOKS' NOTES: If you can't find baby Brussels sprouts, you can use 2 lb regular Brussels sprouts, quartered.
• Pecans can be toasted and buttered 1 day ahead, then kept at room temperature, covered.
• Brussels sprouts can be boiled 1 day ahead and chilled in a sealed plastic bag lined with a paper towel.

QUICK SAUTÉED ENDIVE, ESCAROLE, AND FRISÉE

SERVES 8

ACTIVE TIME: 35 MIN   START TO FINISH: 35 MIN

- 1 lb Belgian endives (2 to 4), cut crosswise into 1-inch pieces, discarding cores (4 cups)
- 1 lb frisée, trimmed of tough or discolored leaves and remainder cut crosswise into 1-inch pieces (about 10 cups)
- 1 (1-lb) head escarole, trimmed of any tough or discolored leaves and remainder (including ribs) cut crosswise into 1-inch pieces (about 10 cups)
- 6 tablespoons extra-virgin olive oil
- 1 teaspoon salt
- ½ teaspoon black pepper
- 4 teaspoons fresh lemon juice

▶ Toss greens together, then divide into 2 batches.

▶ Heat 3 tablespoons oil in a 12-inch nonstick skillet over moderately high heat until hot but not smoking, then add 1 batch of greens, ½ teaspoon salt, and ¼ teaspoon pepper and sauté, tossing with 2 wooden spatulas or tongs, until evenly wilted but still crunchy, about 2 minutes. Remove from heat and add 2 teaspoons lemon juice, tossing to coat. Transfer to a serving dish.

▶ Repeat procedure with remaining oil, greens, salt, pepper, and lemon juice.

COOKS' NOTE: Greens can be cut and tossed together 1 day ahead, then chilled in two sealed plastic bags lined with paper towels.

RED WINE AND MAPLE-GLAZED CARROTS

SERVES 6

ACTIVE TIME: 20 MIN   START TO FINISH: 45 MIN

- 3 tablespoons unsalted butter
- ¾ cup thinly sliced shallots (2 large)
- 1 teaspoon chili powder (not pure)
- ¾ teaspoon salt
- ¼ teaspoon black pepper
- 2 lb carrots, cut diagonally into 3-inch pieces
- ⅓ cup pure maple syrup
- 1 cup dry red wine
- 2 teaspoons cider vinegar
- 2 tablespoons chopped fresh dill

▶ Heat butter in a 12-inch heavy skillet over moderate heat until foam subsides, then cook shallots, stirring occasionally, until softened, about 4 minutes.

▶ Add chili powder, salt, and pepper and cook, stirring, until chili powder is very fragrant, about 1 minute.

▶ Add carrots, maple syrup, and wine and simmer, covered, stirring occasionally, until carrots are tender, about 20 minutes.

▶ Add vinegar and boil, uncovered, until liquid is reduced to a glaze, 3 to 5 minutes.

▶ Remove from heat and stir in dill.

CAULIFLOWER WITH HORSERADISH SAUCE

SERVES 4 TO 6

ACTIVE TIME: 10 MIN   START TO FINISH: 25 MIN

- 1 (2½- to 3-lb) head of cauliflower, cut lengthwise into 8 wedges
- 2 tablespoons bottled horseradish (not drained)
- ¼ cup water
- ¼ cup chopped fresh dill
- ⅔ cup sour cream
- ½ teaspoon salt

▶ Bring 1 inch of water to a boil in a wide 5-quart heavy pot. Steam cauliflower in a steamer rack set over boiling water in pot, covered, until just tender, about 12 minutes.

▶ Meanwhile, whisk together remaining ingredients in a bowl.

▶ Serve cauliflower topped with sauce.

BRAISED FENNEL AND POTATOES

SERVES 4 TO 6

ACTIVE TIME: 15 MIN   START TO FINISH: 35 MIN

- 1 large fennel bulb (sometimes labeled "anise") with fronds
- 1 large onion, halved lengthwise, then cut lengthwise into ¼-inch-thick slices (2 cups)
- ¼ teaspoon black pepper
- 1 teaspoon salt
- 3 tablespoons extra-virgin olive oil
- 1 lb red boiling potatoes
- ½ cup water

▶ Chop enough fennel fronds to measure 2 tablespoons, then cut off and discard stalks from bulb. Quarter bulb lengthwise and core, then cut lengthwise into ¼-inch-thick slices.

▶ Cook fennel, onion, pepper, and ½ teaspoon salt in oil in a 12-inch heavy skillet over moderate heat, covered, stirring occasionally, until onion is softened, about 5 minutes.

▶ Meanwhile, cut potatoes crosswise into ¼-inch-thick slices.

▶ Add potatoes and remaining ½ teaspoon salt to fennel mixture and cook, uncovered, stirring frequently, 3 minutes. Add water and cook, covered, stirring once, until potatoes are tender, 10 to 12 minutes more. Stir in fennel fronds before serving.

SMASHED POTATOES AND PEAS

SERVES 4

ACTIVE TIME: 15 MIN   START TO FINISH: 30 MIN

- 1 cup whole milk
- 1 lb large red boiling potatoes (about 4), scrubbed well and cut into 1-inch pieces
- 2 garlic cloves, quartered
- 2 (4-inch) sprigs fresh thyme
- 1¼ teaspoons salt
- ¼ teaspoon black pepper
- 1 (10-oz) package frozen peas (not thawed)
- 2 tablespoons unsalted butter

▶ Briskly simmer milk, potatoes, garlic, thyme, salt, and pepper in a 2-quart saucepan over moderate heat, partially covered, 10 minutes (do not let boil).

▶ Add peas and cook, partially covered, until potatoes are tender, about 5 minutes. Remove from heat, then add butter and let stand, covered, until melted, about 1 minute. Discard thyme.

▶ Coarsely mash mixture with a potato masher or large fork. Thin with additional milk if desired.

PARSNIPS WITH BLACK-TRUFFLE BUTTER

SERVES 8
ACTIVE TIME: 40 MIN   START TO FINISH: 45 MIN

- 4   lb parsnips (8 medium), peeled, quartered lengthwise, and cores cut out if woody
- 2½ oz black-truffle butter (5 tablespoons; see Sources) at room temperature
- ¾   teaspoon salt, or to taste
- ¼   teaspoon black pepper, or to taste

GARNISH: **chopped fresh chives**

▶ Cut parsnips crosswise into 1- to 1½-inch pieces, then cook in a large pot of boiling salted water (see Tips, page 8), uncovered, until tender, 4 to 5 minutes. Drain in a colander, then transfer to a bowl and gently toss with truffle butter, salt, and pepper.

KITCHEN NOTE

A DAB OF **TRUFFLE BUTTER** TRANSFORMS MASHED POTATOES OR GRILLED STEAKS. INDEED, BUTTER IS THE PERFECT VEHICLE FOR TRUFFLES—THE FAT ABSORBS THE INTOXICATING AROMA, SO HOME COOKS CAN GET THE FLAVOR SO FAMILIAR IN RESTAURANT DISHES WITHOUT SHELLING OUT FOR A WHOLE TRUFFLE.

PEPPERS WITH ALMOND-GARLIC BREAD CRUMBS

SERVES 4 TO 6
ACTIVE TIME: 25 MIN   START TO FINISH: 1 HR

- ½   cup slivered almonds (2 oz), lightly toasted (see Tips, page 8)
- 1   (5-inch) section of baguette, cut into 1-inch cubes
- 1   large garlic clove
- 3   tablespoons chopped fresh flat-leaf parsley
- 5   tablespoons extra-virgin olive oil
- ¾   teaspoon salt
- ¼   teaspoon black pepper
- 2   lb mixed red and yellow bell peppers, tender-roasted (see Tips, page 8)

▶ Put oven rack in middle position and preheat oven to 400°F.
▶ Pulse almonds, bread, and garlic in a food processor until finely chopped. Transfer to a bowl and stir in parsley, oil, ½ teaspoon salt, and ⅛ teaspoon pepper.

▶ Put half of bell peppers, alternating colors, in an oiled 9-inch glass or ceramic pie plate and sprinkle with remaining ¼ teaspoon salt and ⅛ teaspoon pepper. Sprinkle with half of almond mixture. Repeat layering with remaining bell peppers (do not season) and almond mixture, then bake until hot and crumbs are golden, 20 to 25 minutes.

WINTER SQUASH SOUFFLÉ

SERVES 6
ACTIVE TIME: 20 MIN   START TO FINISH: 1 HR

- 3   tablespoons unsalted butter plus additional for greasing
- 3   tablespoons all-purpose flour
- 1½ cups whole milk
- 1   (12-oz) package frozen winter squash purée, thawed
- 1   cup coarsely grated Swiss cheese (¼ lb)
- 1   tablespoon packed brown sugar
- ¾   teaspoon salt, or to taste
- ¼   teaspoon cayenne
- ⅛   teaspoon freshly grated nutmeg
- 3   large egg yolks
- 4   large egg whites
       Coarsely ground black pepper for serving

▶ Generously butter a 2-quart shallow ceramic or glass baking dish.
▶ Put oven rack in middle position and preheat oven to 425°F.
▶ Melt butter (3 tablespoons) in a 2-quart heavy saucepan over moderate heat until foam subsides, then add flour and cook roux, whisking, 2 minutes. Add milk in a slow stream and boil, whisking, then reduce heat and simmer, whisking occasionally, until thickened, about 3 minutes. Whisk in squash, cheese, brown sugar, salt, cayenne, and nutmeg until combined (mixture may not be completely smooth), then transfer to a large bowl and whisk in yolks.
▶ Beat whites with a pinch of salt in another bowl with an electric mixer until they just hold stiff peaks. Fold one fourth of whites into squash mixture to lighten, then fold in remaining whites gently but thoroughly. Spoon into baking dish and bake, uncovered, 15 minutes. Loosely cover top with foil and bake until puffed, golden brown, and just set, 25 to 30 minutes. Serve immediately, with freshly ground pepper.

CORN AND TOMATO GRATIN

SERVES 6 TO 8

ACTIVE TIME: 45 MIN   START TO FINISH: 1¾ HR

This hearty gratin resembles a savory bread pudding. Tomatoes, aromatic basil, and parmesan cheese give it an Italian flair.

1½ lb red or yellow tomatoes (4 medium), cut crosswise into
 ½-inch-thick slices
 2 teaspoons salt
 1 teaspoon black pepper
 4 cups fresh corn kernels (from 6 to 8 ears)
 1 cup whole milk
 ½ cup heavy cream
 2 cups coarse fresh bread crumbs (preferably from a day-old
 baguette; an 8-inch piece, including crust)
 ½ cup chopped fresh basil
 1 oz finely grated Parmigiano-Reggiano (½ cup; see Tips,
 page 8)
 ¾ stick (6 tablespoons) unsalted butter, cut into small pieces,
 plus additional for buttering pan

▶ Arrange tomato slices in 1 layer on a rack set in a shallow baking pan and sprinkle on both sides with 1 teaspoon salt and ½ teaspoon pepper. Let drain 30 minutes.

▶ While tomatoes drain, bring corn, milk, cream, and ¼ teaspoon salt to a simmer in a 2- to 3-quart heavy saucepan over high heat, then reduce heat and simmer, partially covered, until corn is tender, about 5 minutes. Cool slightly, uncovered.

▶ Put oven rack in upper third of oven and preheat oven to 375°F. Butter a shallow 2-quart baking dish.

▶ Toss together bread crumbs, basil, cheese, and remaining ¾ teaspoon salt and ½ teaspoon pepper in another bowl.

▶ Arrange one third of tomato slices in baking dish, then cover evenly with one third of bread-crumb mixture and dot with one third of butter. Spoon half of corn mixture over bread crumbs, then repeat layering with half of remaining tomatoes, bread crumbs, and butter, and all of corn. Arrange remaining tomatoes over corn, then top with remaining bread crumbs and dot with remaining butter.

▶ Bake, uncovered, until top is golden and gratin is bubbling all over, 40 to 45 minutes. Cool slightly on a rack, about 15 minutes, before serving.

COOKS' NOTE: **Gratin can be assembled (but not baked) 4 hours ahead and chilled, covered. Bring to room temperature, about 30 minutes, before baking.**

SWISS CHARD, RAISIN, AND PINE NUT TART

SERVES 8 (SIDE DISH OR LIGHT MAIN COURSE)

ACTIVE TIME: 40 MIN   START TO FINISH: 4¼ HR (INCLUDES MAKING PASTRY AND COOLING TART)

The flavors of this tart are remarkably balanced—it's a bit savory and a bit sweet. (In fact, in the south of France, where it's known as tourte aux blettes, *you'll often see the pastry served for dessert.) Paired with a salad, it makes a satisfying light dinner.*

½ cup golden raisins
 1 cup water
 2 lb green Swiss chard, stems and center ribs discarded
 1 large egg
 ½ cup heavy cream
1½ tablespoons granulated sugar
 ½ teaspoon finely grated fresh orange zest (see Tips, page 8)
 ⅓ cup pine nuts (1½ oz), toasted (see Tips, page 8)
 Pastry dough for a double-crust pie (page 275)
 2 teaspoons confectioners sugar

SPECIAL EQUIPMENT: **an 11- by 8- by 1-inch rectangular tart pan with a removable bottom**

▶ Bring raisins and water to a boil in a 1-quart heavy saucepan, then remove from heat and let stand, covered, 1 hour. Drain in a colander, then pat dry with paper towels.

▶ Put oven rack in middle position and preheat oven to 400°F.

▶ Blanch chard in a large pot of boiling salted water (see Tips, page 8), uncovered, stirring occasionally, until tender but still bright green, about 5 minutes. Transfer chard with a slotted spoon to a large bowl of ice and cold water to stop cooking. Drain chard in a colander, then squeeze out excess water by handfuls. Coarsely chop chard.

▶ Whisk together egg, cream, granulated sugar, zest, and a pinch of salt in a large bowl. Stir in pine nuts, raisins, and chard until combined.

▶ Roll out larger piece of dough on a lightly floured surface with a lightly floured rolling pin into a 15- by 11-inch rectangle and fit into tart pan (do not trim edges). Chill shell while rolling out top.

▶ Roll out smaller piece of dough on a lightly floured surface with lightly floured rolling pin into a 12- by 9-inch rectangle. Spread chard filling evenly into shell, then top with second rectangle of dough. Using a rolling pin, roll over edges of pan to seal tart and trim edges, discarding scraps. Cut 3 steam vents in top crust with a paring knife, then put tart (in pan) on a baking sheet. Bake until top is golden, about 1 hour. Transfer pan to a rack and cool 10 minutes, then remove side of pan. Cool to room temperature, about 1 hour. Dust with confectioners sugar.

SPINACH WITH TAHINI

SERVES 4
ACTIVE TIME: 15 MIN   START TO FINISH: 15 MIN

In the Middle East, this dish is made with dandelion greens or Swiss chard. Here, spinach substitutes, and the tahini takes care of the exotic flair.

- 1   medium garlic clove, chopped
- 3   tablespoons well-stirred tahini (Middle Eastern sesame paste)
- 1½   to 2 tablespoons fresh lemon juice (to taste)
- ¼   teaspoon salt
- ¾   cup water
- 15   oz baby spinach (24 cups loosely packed)
- 2   teaspoons sesame seeds (optional), toasted (see Tips, page 8)

▶ Blend together garlic, tahini, lemon juice, salt, and ¼ cup water in a blender until smooth.

▶ Bring remaining ½ cup water to a simmer in a 12-inch skillet over moderately high heat. Add spinach in handfuls, tossing with tongs, and cook until wilted, about 5 minutes. Drain in a large sieve set over a bowl, pressing to extract any excess liquid.

▶ Discard liquid and wipe bowl dry, then stir together spinach and tahini mixture in bowl. Sprinkle with sesame seeds.

ZUCCHINI MASH

SERVES 4 TO 6
ACTIVE TIME: 15 MIN   START TO FINISH: 35 MIN

Toss aside the mashed potatoes and welcome this appealing alternative.

- 1   medium green bell pepper, finely chopped (1 cup)
- 2   tablespoons extra-virgin olive oil
- 2   tablespoons unsalted butter
- 1   large garlic clove, finely chopped
- 6   medium zucchini (1¾ lb), halved lengthwise, then thinly sliced crosswise
- ½   cup water
- ¾   teaspoon salt
- ½   teaspoon black pepper
- ⅓   cup chopped scallion greens

▶ Cook bell pepper in oil and 1 tablespoon butter in a wide 4-quart heavy pot over moderately low heat, stirring occasionally, until softened, 4 to 6 minutes. Add garlic and cook, stirring,

1 minute. Add zucchini, water, salt, and pepper and bring to a boil over moderately high heat, then cook at a brisk simmer, covered, 6 minutes. Remove lid and simmer until most of liquid is evaporated and zucchini is soft, about 6 minutes.

▶ Coarsely mash zucchini with a potato masher. Add scallion greens and remaining tablespoon butter, stirring, until butter is incorporated.

SUCCOTASH

SERVES 6
ACTIVE TIME: 35 MIN   START TO FINISH: 45 MIN

Tender lima beans and fresh corn kernels straight off the cob team up to create a beautiful—and delicious—side dish that's perfect with almost any meal.

- 2   bacon slices (2 oz), cut crosswise into ¼-inch-wide strips
- 1   tablespoon unsalted butter
- 2   cups fresh corn kernels (from 3 to 4 ears)
- 1   lb fresh lima beans in pods, shelled (1½ cups), or 1 (10-oz) package frozen baby lima beans, thawed
- ½   cup diced (⅓ inch) green bell pepper
- 1   bunch scallions, cut crosswise into ⅓-inch pieces, keeping white and pale green parts separate from greens
- ¾   cup heavy cream
- ¼   cup water
- ½   teaspoon salt
- ½   teaspoon black pepper

▶ Cook bacon in a 10-inch heavy skillet over moderate heat, stirring frequently, until crisp, about 5 minutes. Transfer bacon with a slotted spoon to paper towels to drain, then add butter to fat in skillet and melt over moderate heat. Add corn, lima beans, bell pepper, and white and pale green parts of scallions and cook, stirring, 2 minutes. Add cream, water, salt, and pepper, then simmer, partially covered, until vegetables are tender, 10 to 15 minutes. Stir in bacon, scallion greens, and salt and pepper to taste.

SALADS

MAIN COURSE SALADS

WHEAT-BERRY AND SMOKED-CHICKEN SALAD

SERVES 6 TO 8

ACTIVE TIME: 40 MIN   START TO FINISH: 1¾ HR

The nutty flavor and firm bite of wheat berries make them a perfect addition to salads.

- 1   cup hazelnuts (4½ oz)
- 2   cups wheat berries (¾ lb)
- 4   medium red bell peppers
- 1   medium garlic clove
- 3   tablespoons Sherry vinegar
- ¾   teaspoon salt
- ½   teaspoon black pepper
- 5   tablespoons olive oil
- 1½ lb smoked chicken breast, skin discarded and meat cut crosswise into ¼-inch-thick slices
- 3   oz baby arugula (8 cups loosely packed)

▶ Put oven rack in middle position and preheat oven to 350°F.

▶ Toast hazelnuts in a shallow baking pan in oven, shaking pan occasionally, until golden, about 10 minutes. Cool slightly, then rub off any loose skins with a kitchen towel. When nuts are cool enough to handle, coarsely chop.

▶ Preheat broiler.

▶ Cook wheat berries in a 4-quart pot of unsalted boiling water, partially covered, until tender, 1 to 1½ hours. Drain well in a large sieve.

▶ While wheat berries cook, broil bell peppers on a baking sheet or broiler pan 4 to 5 inches from heat, turning occasionally with tongs, until skins are blackened in spots, 10 to 15 minutes. Transfer to a bowl, then cover and let steam 10 minutes. Peel peppers, discarding stems and seeds, and cut into 1-inch pieces.

▶ Mince and mash garlic to a paste with a pinch of salt using a large heavy knife. Transfer garlic paste to a large bowl and add vinegar, salt, and pepper. Add oil in a steady stream, whisking until combined well. Add wheat berries, hazelnuts, bell peppers, chicken, and arugula and toss gently to combine. Serve at room temperature.

BRESAOLA CARPACCIO WITH GRIBICHE VINAIGRETTE

SERVES 4

ACTIVE TIME: 30 MIN   START TO FINISH: 30 MIN

Bresaola—*a beef lover's prosciutto equivalent—gives this virtually no-cook dish a bright platform with deep flavor.*

- 2   hard-boiled large eggs, quartered
- ½   cup minced radishes (about 4)
- 2   tablespoons drained capers (in brine), rinsed and chopped
- 2   tablespoons minced cornichons or pickles (not sweet)
- 2   tablespoons chopped fresh chives
- 1½ tablespoons fresh lemon juice
- ½   teaspoon salt, or to taste
- ¼   teaspoon black pepper, or to taste
- 3   tablespoons extra-virgin olive oil
- 10 oz thinly sliced air-dried beef such as *bresaola* or *Bundnerfleisch*, or prosciutto (see Sources)
- 5   oz baby arugula (8 cups loosely packed)
- 2   tablespoons finely grated Parmigiano-Reggiano (see Tips, page 8)

▶ Force eggs through a medium-mesh sieve into a small bowl using back of a spoon.

▶ Add radishes, capers, cornichons, and chives to eggs, then gently toss to combine.

▶ Whisk together lemon juice, salt, and pepper in a large bowl, then add oil in a slow stream, whisking until emulsified.

▶ Arrange slices of bresaola, overlapping slightly, to cover 4 large plates. Drizzle all but ½ tablespoon vinaigrette over meat, then sprinkle generously with egg mixture.

▶ Add arugula and cheese to remaining vinaigrette in bowl and toss to coat lightly. Mound salad in center of each plate.

KITCHEN NOTE

THE SAVORY AIR-DRIED BEEF CALLED *BRESAOLA* ("BREZSH-*OWL*-AH"), COMMON IN THE MOUNTAINS OF NORTHERN ITALY, IS A SMART THING TO HAVE ON HAND. IT ABLY ROUNDS OUT A SIMPLE MEAL: PAPER-THIN SLICES ARE DELICIOUS WITH NOTHING MORE THAN LAVISH SHAVINGS OF PARMIGIANO-REGGIANO OR JUST A DRIZZLE OF OLIVE OIL AND LEMON JUICE.

CHIPOTLE CHICKEN SALAD

SERVES 6

ACTIVE TIME: 10 MIN   START TO FINISH: 10 MIN

Corn chips add crunch to this Southwest-influenced salad.

  1 rotisserie-cooked chicken (2 lb) at room
       temperature
  1 medium white onion, chopped
  1 (15- to 19-oz) can black beans, rinsed and drained
  ½ cup packed fresh cilantro sprigs
  1 rounded tablespoon canned chipotles in *adobo*,
       or to taste
  ⅓ cup olive oil
  ⅓ cup fresh lime juice
  ¾ teaspoon salt
  ¾ teaspoon black pepper
  2 firm-ripe California avocados, halved, pitted,
       and left unpeeled
  3 oz corn chips such as Fritos (1½ cups)
  1 heart of romaine, separated into leaves

▶ Remove chicken from bone in large chunks, with some skin if desired, and toss together with onion and black beans in a large bowl.

▶ Purée cilantro, chipotles, oil, lime juice, salt, and pepper in a blender. Add to chicken mixture along with corn chips and toss to combine.

▶ Cut avocado into ½-inch cubes, without cutting through peel, then scoop into chicken mixture with a spoon, separating cubes.

▶ Serve salad on romaine leaves.

SALAD WITH CANADIAN BACON AND POACHED EGGS

SERVES 4

ACTIVE TIME: 20 MIN   START TO FINISH: 20 MIN

  1 teaspoon Dijon mustard
  ¼ teaspoon salt
  2 tablespoons minced shallots
  1 tablespoon finely chopped fresh flat-leaf parsley
  5½ teaspoons red-wine vinegar
  4 tablespoons extra-virgin olive oil
  6 oz sliced Canadian bacon, cut into 1- by ¼-inch pieces
  ½ teaspoon black pepper
  4 large eggs
  6 cups torn frisée (French curly endive)

▶ Whisk together Dijon mustard, salt, shallots, parsley, and 4½ teaspoons vinegar in a large bowl. Add 3 tablespoons oil in a slow stream, whisking until emulsified.

▶ Heat remaining tablespoon oil in a 12-inch heavy skillet over high heat and brown bacon with pepper, stirring, 1 to 2 minutes.

▶ Fill a deep 10-inch skillet with 1½ inches cold water. Add remaining 1 teaspoon vinegar and bring to a simmer. Break 1 egg into a cup, then slide into water. Repeat with remaining 3 eggs, spacing them evenly. Poach at a bare simmer until whites are firm but yolks are still runny, 2 to 3 minutes. Transfer eggs to paper towels and season with salt and pepper.

▶ Toss frisée with dressing. Serve topped with bacon and eggs.

COOKS' NOTE: The egg yolks in this recipe are not fully cooked, which may be of concern if salmonella is a problem in your area.

WHITE-BEAN AND ASPARAGUS SALAD

SERVES 4

ACTIVE TIME: 10 MIN   START TO FINISH: 20 MIN

Lemony asparagus and beans make a lively vegetarian meal.

  1 lb medium asparagus, trimmed
  ¼ cup extra-virgin olive oil
  ½ teaspoon finely grated fresh lemon zest (see Tips, page 8)
  2 tablespoons fresh lemon juice
  ½ teaspoon salt
  ¼ teaspoon black pepper
  2 (15- to 19-oz) cans white beans, rinsed and drained well
       (3 to 3½ cups)
  4 slices country-style bread
  1 (½-lb) piece Parmigiano-Reggiano
  ¼ cup chopped fresh flat-leaf parsley
  2 tablespoons unsalted butter, softened
  1 garlic clove, halved crosswise

▶ Cut asparagus on a diagonal into ⅛-inch-thick slices.

▶ Bring oil, zest, lemon juice, salt, and pepper to a simmer in a 4-quart heavy pot, then stir in beans and asparagus. Remove from heat and let stand, uncovered, 10 minutes. While beans stand, toast bread until golden. Meanwhile, remove enough cheese from piece with a vegetable peeler to measure about ½ cup shavings. Add shavings to beans along with parsley, then toss.

▶ Spread hot toast with butter, then rub buttered side of each with cut side of garlic clove. Season toasts with salt and halve.

▶ Serve bean salad with toasts.

SIDE SALADS

PARMESAN CAULIFLOWER AND PARSLEY SALAD

SERVES 4

ACTIVE TIME: 35 MIN   START TO FINISH: 40 MIN

Fried with a parmesan coating, humble cauliflower takes on a whole new appeal in this side salad; lots of parsley makes it aromatic and refreshing.

FOR SALAD

- 1   teaspoon finely grated fresh lemon zest (see Tips, page 8)
- 2   tablespoons fresh lemon juice
- ½   teaspoon salt
- ¼   teaspoon black pepper
- ¼   cup extra-virgin olive oil
- 6   oz white mushrooms, thinly sliced
- 5   cups loosely packed fresh flat-leaf parsley leaves (from 2 large bunches)

FOR CAULIFLOWER

- 2   large eggs
- ¼   teaspoon salt
- ⅛   teaspoon black pepper
- 2   (10-oz) packages frozen cauliflower florets, thawed and patted dry
- 2   oz Parmigiano-Reggiano, finely grated with a rasp (2 cups)
- ⅓   cup olive oil

MARINATE MUSHROOMS FOR SALAD:

▶ Stir together zest, lemon juice, salt, and pepper in a large bowl. Whisk in oil until combined, then stir in mushrooms and marinate while panfrying cauliflower.

PANFRY CAULIFLOWER:

▶ Lightly beat eggs with salt and pepper in a medium bowl. Add cauliflower and toss until coated well. Put cheese in a large bowl. Lift cauliflower out of egg mixture with a slotted spoon and transfer to cheese, tossing to coat.

▶ Heat oil in a 10-inch heavy skillet over moderate heat until hot but not smoking, then panfry cauliflower in 3 batches, turning occasionally, until golden on all sides, about 3 minutes per batch. Transfer with a slotted spoon to paper towels to drain.

FINISH SALAD:

▶ Add parsley and cauliflower to mushroom mixture, tossing to combine.

ORANGE AND ENDIVE SALAD WITH MAPLE CHIPOTLE VINAIGRETTE

SERVES 4

ACTIVE TIME: 20 MIN   START TO FINISH: 20 MIN

The textural contrast of juicy ripe oranges and crisp endives is enhanced by a surprisingly complex vinaigrette containing sweet, spicy, and smoky flavors.

- ¼   cup fresh orange juice
- 2   tablespoons dark amber or Grade B maple syrup
- 2   tablespoons extra-virgin olive oil
- 1   tablespoon Sherry vinegar
- 1   tablespoon finely chopped red onion
- 1   teaspoon fresh lemon juice
- 1   teaspoon chopped canned chipotle chile in *adobo* plus 1 teaspoon *adobo* sauce
- ½   teaspoon salt
- 3   navel oranges
- 4   large Belgian endives, ends trimmed

▶ Whisk together orange juice, syrup, oil, vinegar, onion, lemon juice, chipotle with *adobo* sauce, and salt in a bowl until combined well.

▶ Remove peel and any white pith from oranges with a sharp knife. Cut oranges crosswise into ¼-inch-thick slices. Separate endive leaves and arrange with oranges on a platter, then drizzle with vinaigrette.

PEAR, ARUGULA, AND PANCETTA SALAD

SERVES 4

ACTIVE TIME: 20 MIN   START TO FINISH: 20 MIN

FOR VINAIGRETTE

- 1   tablespoon Champagne vinegar
- 1   tablespoon mild honey
- ½   tablespoon fresh lemon juice
- ⅛   teaspoon salt
- ⅛   teaspoon coarsely ground black pepper
- 3   tablespoons olive oil

FOR SALAD

- 2   oz thinly sliced pancetta (Italian unsmoked cured bacon; 4 to 5 slices)
- 1   tablespoon olive oil
- 2   firm-ripe pears
- 4   cups loosely packed baby arugula or torn larger arugula (2 oz)
- 3   oz ricotta salata, thinly shaved with a vegetable peeler

MAKE VINAIGRETTE:

▶ Whisk together vinegar, honey, lemon juice, salt, and pepper in a salad bowl. Add oil in a slow stream, whisking until combined well.

MAKE SALAD:

▶ Cook pancetta in oil in a 10-inch heavy skillet over moderate heat, turning frequently, until just crisp, about 5 minutes. Transfer to paper towels to drain (pancetta will crisp as it cools). Tear into bite-size pieces.

▶ Halve pears lengthwise, core, and cut lengthwise into ¼-inch-thick slices. Add pears to dressing along with arugula, cheese, and pancetta, tossing to coat.

WARM NEW POTATO SALAD WITH GRAINY MUSTARD

SERVES 4

ACTIVE TIME: 15 MIN   START TO FINISH: 30 MIN

  2 lb small (1- to 1½-inch) potatoes (preferably new potatoes)
1½ teaspoons salt
  3 tablespoons finely chopped shallots (about 2)
  ½ tablespoon Dijon mustard
  1 tablespoon whole-grain mustard
  1 tablespoon white-wine vinegar, or to taste
  ½ teaspoon black pepper
  3 tablespoons olive oil
  2 tablespoons chopped fresh flat-leaf parsley

▶ Cover potatoes with water by 1 inch in a 3- to 4-quart saucepan, then bring to a boil with 1 teaspoon salt. Simmer, partially covered, until potatoes are tender, about 10 minutes, then drain.

▶ Whisk together shallots, mustards, vinegar, pepper, and remaining ½ teaspoon salt in a large bowl, then add oil in a slow stream, whisking until emulsified.

▶ When potatoes are just cool enough to handle, halve them, then add to vinaigrette along with parsley and toss to combine. Serve warm or at room temperature.

KITCHEN NOTE

NEW POTATOES ARE SIMPLY YOUNG SPUDS OF ANY VARIETY THAT HAVEN'T CONVERTED ALL THEIR SUGAR TO STARCH. WE LIKE THEM BECAUSE THEY ARE SMALL ENOUGH TO BE COOKED WHOLE AND ARE EXCELLENT BOILED OR PAN-ROASTED.

CELERY, SESAME, AND TOFU SALAD

SERVES 4

ACTIVE TIME: 15 MIN   START TO FINISH: 15 MIN

  1 (14-oz) block of firm tofu
  2 tablespoons vegetable oil
  ¾ teaspoon Asian sesame oil
  2 teaspoons rice vinegar (not seasoned)
  1 teaspoon soy sauce
  ½ teaspoon black pepper
  4 large celery ribs
  2 teaspoons sesame seeds, toasted (see Tips, page 8)

▶ Rinse tofu and pat dry, then cut crosswise into ¼-inch-thick slices. Arrange slices in 1 layer on a triple thickness of paper towels, then cover with another triple thickness of paper towels. Put a small baking sheet on top of tofu and weight with 3 (1-lb) cans (this removes excess moisture), 10 minutes.

▶ Meanwhile, whisk together oils, vinegar, soy sauce, and pepper in a large bowl. Trim celery, then peel with a vegetable peeler and slice very thin diagonally. Cut tofu crosswise into ¼-inch-wide sticks and transfer to a bowl. Toss gently with dressing, celery, sesame seeds, and salt to taste.

NAPA CABBAGE, TOMATO, AND AVOCADO SALAD

SERVES 6

ACTIVE TIME: 15 MIN   START TO FINISH: 15 MIN

  1 teaspoon finely grated fresh lemon zest (see Tips, page 8)
  1 tablespoon fresh lemon juice
  1 teaspoon Dijon mustard
  ¼ teaspoon salt
  ½ teaspoon black pepper
  ¼ cup extra-virgin olive oil
  1 (1-lb) Napa cabbage
  1 (6- to 8-oz) firm-ripe avocado
  ¾ lb cherry or grape tomatoes, halved

▶ Whisk together zest, juice, mustard, salt, and pepper in a bowl until smooth, then add oil in a stream, whisking until emulsified.

▶ Tear enough cabbage leaves from ribs into bite-size pieces to measure 7 cups, reserving thick ribs and remaining leaves for another use.

▶ Quarter avocado lengthwise, then pit and peel. Cut into ½-inch pieces.

▶ Toss cabbage leaves, avocado, and tomatoes in a large bowl with just enough dressing to coat.

MEDITERRANEAN EGGPLANT AND BARLEY SALAD

SERVES 8 (SIDE DISH) OR 4 (MAIN COURSE)
ACTIVE TIME: 45 MIN   START TO FINISH: 1½ HR

Vegetarians can substitute water for the chicken broth and still enjoy this lush and hearty dish.

1½   lb eggplant, cut into ½-inch cubes
¾   lb zucchini, cut into ½-inch cubes
10   tablespoons extra-virgin olive oil
1   teaspoon salt
1   teaspoon black pepper
1   cup chopped scallion (from 1 bunch)
1½   teaspoons ground cumin
½   teaspoon ground coriander
¼   teaspoon cayenne
1¼   cups pearl barley (8 oz)
1   (14-oz) can reduced-sodium chicken broth (1¾ cups)
¾   cup water
2   tablespoons fresh lemon juice
1   garlic clove, minced
¼   teaspoon sugar
½   lb cherry tomatoes, quartered
⅓   cup Kalamata or other brine-cured black olives, pitted and halved
½   cup thinly sliced red onion, rinsed and drained if desired
1   cup chopped fresh flat-leaf parsley
½   cup chopped fresh mint

ACCOMPANIMENT: 1 (½-lb) piece ricotta salata, cut crosswise into thin slices

ROAST EGGPLANT AND ZUCCHINI:
▶ Put oven racks in upper and lower thirds of oven and preheat oven to 425°F.
▶ Toss eggplant and zucchini with 5 tablespoons oil, ¾ teaspoon salt, and ¾ teaspoon pepper in a bowl, then spread in 2 oiled large shallow (1-inch-deep) baking pans. Roast vegetables in oven, stirring occasionally and switching position of pans halfway through baking, until vegetables are golden brown and tender, 20 to 25 minutes total. Combine vegetables in 1 pan and cool, reserving other pan for cooling barley.

COOK BARLEY:
▶ Heat 2 tablespoons oil in a 3- to 4-quart heavy pot over moderately high heat until hot but not smoking, then cook scallion, cumin, coriander, and cayenne, stirring, until fragrant, about 1 minute. Add barley and cook, stirring until well coated with oil, 2 minutes more. Add broth and water and bring to a boil. Reduce heat and simmer, covered, until all of liquid is absorbed and barley is tender, 30 to 40 minutes. Remove from heat and let stand, covered, 5 minutes. Transfer to reserved shallow baking pan and spread to quickly cool, uncovered, to room temperature, about 20 minutes.

MAKE DRESSING AND ASSEMBLE SALAD:
▶ Whisk together lemon juice, garlic, sugar, and remaining ¼ teaspoon salt, ¼ teaspoon pepper, and 3 tablespoons oil in a large bowl. Add barley, roasted vegetables, and remaining ingredients to bowl with dressing and toss until combined well. Serve with cheese slices.

COOKS' NOTE: Salad can be made 1 day ahead and chilled, covered. Return to room temperature before serving.

KITCHEN NOTE

ALL YOU NEED TO **PIT OLIVES** IS A COMFORTABLY LARGE KNIFE. LINE UP A FEW OLIVES ON A CUTTING BOARD AND PRESS THEM WITH THE FLAT SIDE OF THE KNIFE. THEY'LL SPLIT OPEN, EXPOSING THE PITS, WHICH YOU CAN THEN JUST SLIDE RIGHT OUT. GREEN OLIVES ARE LESS RIPE AND THUS FIRMER THAN BLACK OLIVES, SO YOU MAY HAVE TO CUT THEM OFF THE PIT WITH A SMALLER KNIFE.

MELON AND MINT TABBOULEH

SERVES 4
ACTIVE TIME: 15 MIN   START TO FINISH: 35 MIN

Removing the typical cucumber from tabbouleh leaves plenty of room for fresh honeydew or any cool, sweet melon in this summer-inspired departure.

1   cup boiling-hot water
¾   cup fine bulgur (5 oz)
1½   cups loosely packed fresh mint leaves
⅓   cup olive oil
3   tablespoons fresh lime juice
1   (½-lb) piece firm-ripe honeydew, rind discarded and fruit cut into ½-inch pieces (1 cup)
½   cup very thinly sliced red onion (from 1 small)
½   teaspoon salt

▶ Pour boiling water over bulgur in a bowl, then cover bowl tightly and let stand 30 minutes. Drain in a sieve if watery.
▶ Meanwhile, purée mint with oil in a blender until smooth.
▶ Toss bulgur with mint oil, lime juice, honeydew, onion, and salt.

CHOPPED SALAD

SERVES 10 TO 12

ACTIVE TIME: 45 MIN   START TO FINISH: 1 HR

- 10 oz frozen black-eyed peas (not thawed)
- 1 lb zucchini, trimmed
- 1 medium fennel bulb (sometimes labeled "anise"), stalks discarded
- ½ cup finely chopped scallions (about 4)
- 2 tablespoons finely chopped fresh dill
- 3 tablespoons cider vinegar
- 2 tablespoons fresh lemon juice
- 1 tablespoon coarse-grain mustard
- ½ teaspoon black pepper
- ¼ teaspoon cayenne
- 2 tablespoons salt
- ⅓ cup extra-virgin olive oil
- 2¾ cups fresh corn (from about 4 ears)
- 1 lb frozen shelled *edamame* (not thawed)

▶ Bring 3 quarts water to a boil in a 5- to 6-quart pot, then cook black-eyed peas, partially covered, until tender, about 20 minutes.

▶ While peas are cooking, cut zucchini and fennel bulb into ¼-inch dice. Whisk together scallions, dill, vinegar, lemon juice, mustard, pepper, cayenne, and 1½ teaspoons salt in a large bowl. Add oil in a slow stream, whisking until emulsified.

▶ Add zucchini and fennel to dressing.

▶ When peas are tender, transfer with a slotted spoon to a sieve set over a large bowl, reserving cooking water in pot, and cool peas slightly, then add to salad.

▶ Return water to a boil and add remaining 1½ tablespoons salt, then cook corn and *edamame*, uncovered, until tender, 6 to 7 minutes. Transfer to sieve to cool slightly, then add to salad and stir to combine. Cool salad completely and serve chilled or at room temperature.

ZUCCHINI CARPACCIO SALAD

SERVES 4 TO 6

ACTIVE TIME: 15 MIN   START TO FINISH: 35 MIN

A meat-free carpaccio, this crisp mix of zucchini and arugula gets a boost from olive oil and salty cheese.

- 1½ lb zucchini (about 3 large)
- 1¼ teaspoons salt
- ½ lb arugula, stems discarded and leaves cut into ½-inch-wide strips (6 cups)
- 1 oz Parmigiano-Reggiano, coarsely grated (on large holes of a box grater; ½ cup)
- 3 tablespoons extra-virgin olive oil
- ¼ teaspoon black pepper

SPECIAL EQUIPMENT: **an adjustable-blade slicer**

▶ Cut zucchini crosswise into paper-thin slices with slicer.

▶ Toss zucchini slices with 1 teaspoon salt in a large colander set over a bowl and let drain 20 minutes.

▶ Rinse zucchini slices well, then drain, pressing gently on slices to extract any excess liquid. Pat zucchini slices dry with a kitchen towel.

▶ Put greens in a large bowl. Sprinkle with ¼ cup cheese and remaining ¼ teaspoon salt, then drizzle with 1½ tablespoons oil and toss.

▶ Arrange zucchini slices over arugula, then drizzle with remaining 1½ tablespoons oil. Sprinkle with pepper and remaining ¼ cup cheese.

CONDIMENTS AND SAUCES

CONDIMENTS

PLUM APPLESAUCE

MAKES ABOUT 6 CUPS

ACTIVE TIME: 15 MIN   START TO FINISH: 1½ HR

This vibrant red applesauce complements roast meats and makes a wonderful dessert on its own.

- 2 lb Gala or McIntosh apples, quartered and seeded (left unpeeled)
- 2 lb red or black plums, quartered and pitted
- ¼ cup water
- ¼ cup sugar

▶ Cook all ingredients in a 4- to 5-quart heavy pot, covered, over moderately low heat, stirring occasionally, until fruit is very tender and falling apart, 1 to 1¼ hours. Force mixture through a large medium-mesh sieve set over a bowl using a rubber spatula, discarding peels.

COOKS' NOTE: Plum applesauce keeps, cooled completely, uncovered, then chilled, covered, 1 week.

TART CRANBERRY-ONION RELISH

MAKES ABOUT 3½ CUPS

ACTIVE TIME: 5 MIN   START TO FINISH: 8½ HR

- 1 (12-oz) package fresh or unthawed frozen cranberries
- 1 (¾-lb) sweet onion, chopped (2 cups)
- 1 (12-oz) jar red-currant jelly
- ¼ cup cider vinegar
- 2 to 4 tablespoons sugar (to taste)

▶ Stir together all ingredients in a 2- to 3-quart heavy saucepan, then bring to a boil, covered. Remove lid and reduce heat, then simmer until cranberries have burst, about 5 minutes. Transfer to a bowl and cool, uncovered. Chill, covered, at least 8 hours for flavors to meld. Serve at room temperature.

COOKS' NOTE: Relish can be chilled up to 1 week.

CHAI-POACHED APRICOTS AND PLUMS

MAKES ABOUT 4 CUPS

ACTIVE TIME: 5 MIN   START TO FINISH: 1 HR (INCLUDES COOLING)

More elegant than jam but just as handy, this compote goes with almost everything from yogurt and granola to pork chops.

- ¾ cup sugar
- ½ vanilla bean
- 6 oz dried Angelino plums (see Sources; 1¼ cups)
- 6 oz dried California apricots (see Sources; 1¼ cups)
- 2 chai tea bags

▶ Combine sugar and 3 cups water in a 3- to 4-quart saucepan. Halve vanilla bean lengthwise with a paring knife and scrape seeds into pan, then add pod. Bring mixture to a boil, stirring occasionally until sugar is dissolved.
▶ Add plums and simmer, uncovered, 3 minutes. Add apricots and tea bags and return to a simmer. Cook fruit, gently stirring once or twice, 5 minutes, then remove from heat.
▶ Allow tea bags to steep with fruit in syrup 15 minutes (fruit will continue to soften as it steeps), then remove bags, gently squeezing liquid from them into syrup. Transfer compote to a bowl or jar and cool to room temperature, gently stirring occasionally, about 30 minutes.

COOKS' NOTE: Compote keeps, covered and chilled, 2 weeks.

RED-PEPPER MAYONNAISE

MAKES ABOUT 1 CUP

ACTIVE TIME: 15 MIN   START TO FINISH: 45 MIN

- 1 large garlic clove
- ½ teaspoon salt
- 1 lb red bell peppers, tender-roasted (see Tips, page 8)
- ¼ cup mayonnaise
- ¼ teaspoon fresh lemon juice, or to taste

▶ Mince garlic and mash to a paste with salt using a large heavy knife. Transfer to a blender with bell peppers. Purée until smooth. Add mayonnaise and lemon juice and blend until combined.

COOKS' NOTE: Mayonnaise keeps, covered and chilled, 1 week.

PICKLED MUSHROOMS

MAKES ABOUT 3 CUPS

ACTIVE TIME: 15 MIN   START TO FINISH: 9 HR

- 2 cups dry white wine
- 1 teaspoon whole coriander seeds
- ½ teaspoon whole black peppercorns
- ¾ teaspoon salt
- 1 Turkish or ½ California bay leaf
- 3 garlic cloves, peeled and smashed
- 1 lb small (1-inch) white or cremini mushrooms, trimmed
- ¼ cup extra-virgin olive oil

▶ Boil wine, spices, salt, bay leaf, and garlic in a deep 10-inch heavy skillet 5 minutes. Add mushrooms and oil, then reduce heat and gently simmer, uncovered, until mushrooms are barely tender, about 15 minutes. Transfer to a bowl and cool mushrooms in liquid, uncovered. Chill, covered, at least 8 hours for flavors to meld. Discard bay leaf and whole spices. Serve at room temperature.

COOKS' NOTE: Pickled mushrooms can be chilled up to 1 week.

SPICED SHALLOTS AND PRUNES

MAKES ABOUT 3 CUPS

ACTIVE TIME: 20 MIN   START TO FINISH: 9 HR

- 1¼ lb small shallots (about 24)
- ½ lb pitted prunes (1½ cups)
- 1½ cups ruby Port
- ¼ cup balsamic vinegar
- 1 (3-inch) cinnamon stick
- ½ teaspoon whole black peppercorns
- ¼ teaspoon whole allspice

▶ Blanch shallots (not peeled) in boiling water 2 minutes, then drain in a colander and rinse under cold water to cool. Peel shallots, then combine with remaining ingredients in a 10-inch heavy skillet. Simmer, uncovered, over moderate heat, stirring occasionally, until shallots are tender, 20 to 25 minutes. Transfer to a bowl and cool completely, uncovered. Chill, covered, at least 8 hours for flavors to meld. Discard whole spices. Serve at room temperature.

COOKS' NOTE: Relish can be chilled up to 1 week.

SAUCES

BLUEBERRY COMPOTE

MAKES ABOUT 1½ CUPS

ACTIVE TIME: 5 MIN   START TO FINISH: 15 MIN

- ½ cup water
- ½ cup sugar
- 2 (3- by ½-inch) strips fresh lemon zest (see Tips, page 8)
- 2 cups blueberries (10 oz)
- 1½ tablespoons fresh lemon juice

▶ Boil water, sugar, and zest in a 1-quart heavy saucepan, uncovered, 5 minutes. Discard zest. Stir in blueberries and simmer, stirring occasionally, until blueberries begin to burst, 3 to 5 minutes. Remove from heat and stir in lemon juice. Serve warm or at room temperature.

COOKS' NOTE: Compote keeps, cooled completely, uncovered, then chilled, covered, 3 days.

MOCHA CARAMEL SAUCE

SERVES 4

ACTIVE TIME: 15 MIN   START TO FINISH: 15 MIN

- 1 cup heavy cream
- 3½ teaspoons instant-espresso powder
- ½ cup sugar
- 4 oz fine-quality bittersweet chocolate (no more than 60% cacao if marked), finely chopped
- ⅛ teaspoon salt

▶ Stir together cream and espresso powder.
▶ Cook sugar in a dry 2-quart heavy saucepan over moderately high heat, undisturbed, until it begins to melt, about 2 minutes. Continue to cook, stirring occasionally with a fork, until sugar is melted into a deep golden caramel, 1 to 2 minutes.
▶ Remove from heat and carefully pour in espresso cream (mixture will steam and bubble vigorously), then cook over low heat, stirring, until caramel is dissolved, 1 to 2 minutes. Add chocolate and salt and cook, stirring, until sauce is smooth. Serve warm or at room temperature.

DESSERTS

CAKES

CRANBERRY CUPCAKES WITH DULCE DE LECHE PECAN FROSTING

MAKES 1 DOZEN

ACTIVE TIME: 20 MIN   START TO FINISH: 50 MIN

   1   cup all-purpose flour
1½   teaspoons baking powder
⅛   teaspoon salt
¾   stick (6 tablespoons) unsalted butter, softened
½   cup sugar
   1   large egg
½   teaspoon pure vanilla extract
½   cup whole milk
¾   cup dried cranberries (3 oz), finely chopped
   5   tablespoons cream cheese, softened
½   cup *dulce de leche* (see Sources)
½   cup pecans (2 oz), finely chopped, toasted (see Tips, page 8), and cooled

SPECIAL EQUIPMENT: **12 paper muffin-cup liners; a muffin pan with 12 (⅓- to ½-cup) muffin cups**

▶ Put oven rack in middle position and preheat oven to 350°F. Put liners in muffin cups.
▶ Whisk together flour, baking powder, and salt in a bowl.
▶ Beat together butter and sugar in a large bowl with an electric mixer at high speed until pale and fluffy, about 4 minutes. Beat in egg and vanilla. Reduce speed to low and add flour mixture and milk alternately in batches, beginning and ending with flour mixture and mixing just until incorporated. Fold in cranberries.
▶ Divide batter among muffin cups. Bake until pale golden and a wooden pick or skewer inserted into center of a cupcake comes out clean, 20 to 25 minutes. Turn cupcakes out onto a rack and cool 15 minutes.
▶ Meanwhile, beat cream cheese in a bowl with cleaned beaters until smooth, then add *dulce de leche* and a pinch of salt and beat until combined well. Stir in half of pecans.
▶ Spread frosting generously on cooled cupcakes and sprinkle with remaining pecans.

PEAR KUCHEN

SERVES 8

ACTIVE TIME: 30 MIN   START TO FINISH: 3¾ HR

Kuchen, a German yeast cake, acts as a golden pillow for ripe pears and a cinnamon, sugar, and hazelnut topping.

FOR DOUGH
⅓   cup warm milk (105–115°F)
⅓   cup plus 1 teaspoon sugar
1½   teaspoons active dry yeast (from a ¼-oz package)
1½   cups all-purpose flour plus additional for dusting
   1   whole large egg
   1   large egg yolk
½   teaspoon pure vanilla extract
½   teaspoon salt
   7   tablespoons unsalted butter, cut into pieces and softened
FOR TOPPING
   3   firm-ripe Bosc pears (about 1½ lb total)
   2   tablespoons unsalted butter, melted
¼   cup packed dark brown sugar
   2   tablespoons plain fine dry bread crumbs
   3   tablespoons hazelnuts, toasted (see Tips, page 8) and chopped
½   teaspoon cinnamon

SPECIAL EQUIPMENT: **a stand mixer fitted with paddle attachment; a 9- to 9½-inch (24-cm) springform pan**

MAKE DOUGH:
▶ Stir together milk and 1 teaspoon granulated sugar in bowl of mixer. Sprinkle yeast over mixture and let stand until foamy, about 5 minutes. (If yeast doesn't foam, discard and start over with new yeast.)
▶ Add ¼ cup flour, beating at medium speed until combined. Add whole egg, yolk, vanilla, salt, and remaining ⅓ cup sugar and beat until combined. Reduce speed to low and gradually mix in 1¼ cups remaining flour. Increase speed to medium and add butter, then continue beating, stopping and scraping down side of bowl once or twice, until dough is shiny and forms strands from paddle to bowl, about 3 minutes. (Dough will be very soft and sticky.)
▶ Transfer dough to a lightly oiled bowl and cover with plastic wrap. Let rise in a warm, draft-free place until doubled in bulk, about 1½ hours.

▸ Put oven rack in middle position and preheat oven to 400°F.

▸ Peel pears, cut lengthwise into eighths, and core. Toss pears with melted butter and 2 tablespoons brown sugar in a 13- by 9-inch glass or ceramic baking dish and arrange in 1 layer.

▸ Roast pears, gently turning and stirring occasionally, until just tender and lightly caramelized, about 45 minutes. Transfer pears to a plate with a slotted spatula. Stir bread crumbs into baking dish, scraping up all brown bits and butter, then transfer to a bowl. Stir hazelnuts, cinnamon, and remaining 2 tablespoons brown sugar into bread crumbs.

ASSEMBLE AND BAKE KUCHEN:

▸ Reduce oven temperature to 350°F.

▸ Transfer dough to springform pan and spread evenly with a rubber spatula to cover bottom.

▸ Sprinkle half of crumb mixture over dough, leaving a 1-inch border. Gently toss roasted pears with remaining crumb mixture and scatter pears over dough. Let rise, covered with plastic wrap, in a warm, draft-free place, 30 minutes.

▸ Bake, uncovered, until firm to the touch and deep golden brown, about 40 minutes. Cool in pan on a rack, 20 minutes, then carefully remove side of pan. Cool to barely warm or room temperature.

COOKS' NOTE: Cake can be baked 1 day ahead and cooled completely, then chilled, wrapped in plastic wrap. Reheat gently, uncovered.

CHOCOLATE HAZELNUT TORTE

SERVES 8

ACTIVE TIME: 25 MIN   START TO FINISH: 2½ HR (INCLUDES COOLING)

FOR CAKE

- 1 stick (½ cup) unsalted butter plus additional for buttering pan
- 1 cup hazelnuts (5 oz)
- 6 oz fine-quality bittersweet chocolate (no more than 60% cacao)
- 2 tablespoons potato starch
- ¼ teaspoon salt
- ½ cup sugar
- 4 large eggs, separated, at room temperature for 30 minutes
- 1 teaspoon pure vanilla extract

SPECIAL EQUIPMENT: a 9- to 9½-inch (24-cm) springform pan; parchment paper

GARNISH: confectioners sugar or Passover confectioners sugar if using for Passover (recipe follows)

▸ Put oven rack in middle position and preheat oven to 350°F.

▸ Generously butter bottom and side of springform pan, then line bottom with a round of parchment paper and butter parchment.

▸ Toast hazelnuts in a shallow baking pan in oven, shaking pan once or twice, until golden, about 12 minutes. Place nuts in a kitchen towel and rub off any loose skins while nuts are still warm, then cool nuts completely.

▸ Reduce oven temperature to 325°F.

▸ While nuts cool, melt butter and chocolate together in a heatproof bowl set over a pot of simmering water.

▸ Pulse hazelnuts in a food processor with potato starch, salt, and ¼ cup sugar until finely ground. (Be careful not to grind to a paste.)

▸ Whisk together yolks and 2 tablespoons sugar in a large bowl. Whisk in chocolate mixture, then add nut mixture and vanilla and whisk until combined (mixture will be slightly grainy).

▸ Beat whites with a pinch of salt in another bowl with an electric mixer at medium speed until they hold soft peaks. Add remaining 2 tablespoons sugar a little at a time, beating, and beat until whites just hold stiff peaks. Fold one fourth of whites into chocolate mixture to lighten, then fold in remaining whites gently but thoroughly. Pour batter into springform pan, and bake until a wooden pick or skewer inserted in center of torte comes out with a few moist crumbs adhering, 35 to 40 minutes. Transfer to a rack and cool completely in pan, about 1 hour. Run a knife around edge of torte to loosen, then remove side of pan. Dust with Passover confectioners sugar (recipe follows).

COOKS' NOTE: Torte can be made 1 day ahead and cooled completely, then kept in pan, covered with plastic wrap, at room temperature.

PASSOVER CONFECTIONERS SUGAR

MAKES ABOUT ½ CUP

ACTIVE TIME: 5 MIN   START TO FINISH: 5 MIN

This simple, two-ingredient blend yields a soft, powdery sugar perfect for sprinkling over desserts.

- ⅓ cup granulated sugar
- ½ teaspoon potato starch

SPECIAL EQUIPMENT: an electric coffee/spice grinder

▸ Grind together sugar and potato starch in grinder until powdery.

LEMON OLIVE-OIL CAKE

SERVES 8

ACTIVE TIME: 30 MIN   START TO FINISH: 2½ HR (INCLUDES COOLING)

Using extra-virgin olive-oil results in a fruitier, more pronounced flavor, while regular olive oil yields a lighter taste, but both are delicious.

- ¾ cup olive oil (extra-virgin if desired) plus additional for oiling pan
- 1 large lemon
- 1 cup cake flour (not self-rising)
- 5 large eggs, separated, reserving 1 white for another use
- ½ teaspoon salt
- ¾ cup plus 1½ tablespoons sugar

SPECIAL EQUIPMENT: **a 9- to 9½-inch (24-cm) springform pan; parchment paper**

▶ Put oven rack in middle position and preheat oven to 350°F. Oil springform pan, then line bottom with a round of parchment paper. Oil parchment.
▶ Finely grate enough lemon zest to measure 1½ teaspoons (see Tips, page 8) and whisk together with flour. Halve lemon, then squeeze and reserve 1½ tablespoons fresh lemon juice.
▶ Beat together yolks and ½ cup sugar in a large bowl with an electric mixer at high speed until thick and pale, about 3 minutes. Reduce speed to medium and add olive oil (¾ cup) and reserved lemon juice, beating until just combined (mixture may appear separated). Using a wooden spoon, stir in flour mixture (do not beat) until just combined.
▶ Beat egg whites (from 4 eggs) with salt in another large bowl with cleaned beaters at medium-high speed until foamy, then add ¼ cup sugar a little at a time, beating, and continue to beat until egg whites just hold soft peaks, about 3 minutes.
▶ Gently fold one third of whites into yolk mixture to lighten, then fold in remaining whites gently but thoroughly.
▶ Transfer batter to springform pan and gently rap against work surface once or twice to release any air bubbles. Sprinkle top evenly with remaining 1½ tablespoons sugar. Bake until puffed and golden and a wooden pick or skewer inserted in center of cake comes out clean, about 45 minutes. Cool cake in pan on a rack 10 minutes, then run a thin knife around edge of cake to loosen and remove side of pan. Cool cake to room temperature, about 1¼ hours. Remove bottom of pan and peel off parchment, then transfer cake to a serving plate.

COOKS' NOTE: Cake can be made 1 day ahead and wrapped well or stored in a cake keeper at room temperature.

KITCHEN NOTE

THE TANGY ZEST OF CITRUS FRUITS CAN MAKE A WORLD OF DIFFERENCE TO SAVORY DISHES AS WELL AS SWEET ONES. WHEN ZESTING LEMONS, IT'S ALWAYS A GOOD IDEA TO USE FRUIT THAT'S FRESH, COLD, DRY, AND FIRM ENOUGH TO PEEL OR GRATE EASILY. **TO GRATE ZEST** WE RECOMMEND USING A RASPLIKE MICROPLANE ZESTER WHICH RESULTS IN A FLUFFIER ZEST. PACK TO MEASURE. WHEN YOU'VE FINISHED ZESTING, BE SURE TO GLEAN EVERY RASPING FROM BOTH THE OUTSIDE AND THE INSIDE OF THE GRATER WITH A PASTRY BRUSH.

LEMON CURD MARBLED CHEESECAKE

SERVES 10

ACTIVE TIME: 30 MIN   START TO FINISH: 8 HR (INCLUDES CHILLING)

FOR LEMON CURD
- 1 teaspoon finely grated fresh lemon zest (see Tips, page 8)
- ½ cup fresh lemon juice
- ½ cup sugar
- 3 large eggs
- ½ stick (¼ cup) unsalted butter, cut into small pieces

FOR CRUST
- 1⅓ cups finely ground graham cracker crumbs (5 oz)
- ⅓ cup sugar
- ⅛ teaspoon salt
- 5 tablespoons unsalted butter, melted

FOR FILLING
- 3 (8-oz) packages cream cheese, softened
- 1 cup sugar
- 3 large eggs
- ¾ cup sour cream
- 1 teaspoon pure vanilla extract

SPECIAL EQUIPMENT: **a 9- to 9½-inch (24-cm) springform pan**
ACCOMPANIMENT: **blueberries**

MAKE LEMON CURD:

▶ Whisk together lemon zest, lemon juice, sugar, and eggs in a 2-quart heavy saucepan. Add butter and cook over moderately low heat, whisking frequently, until curd is thick enough to hold marks of whisk and first bubbles appear on surface, about 6 minutes.
▶ Force lemon curd through a fine-mesh sieve into a wide shallow dish, scraping bottom of sieve, then cover surface with wax paper. Cool completely, stirring occasionally, about 30 minutes.

MAKE AND BAKE CRUST:

▶ Put oven rack in middle position and preheat oven to 350°F. Invert bottom of springform pan (to make it easier to slide cake off bottom), then lock on side.

▶ Stir together crust ingredients in a bowl, then press onto bottom and 1 inch up side of springform pan. Place springform pan in a shallow baking pan and bake 10 minutes, then cool crust completely in springform pan on a rack.

MAKE FILLING AND BAKE CHEESECAKE:

▶ Reduce oven temperature to 300°F.

▶ Beat together cream cheese and sugar in a bowl with an electric mixer at medium speed until smooth, 1 to 2 minutes. Reduce speed to low and add eggs 1 at a time, beating until incorporated. Beat in sour cream and vanilla until combined.

▶ Pour two thirds of cream cheese filling into crust, then spoon half of lemon curd over filling and swirl curd into filling with a small knife. (Avoid touching crust with knife to prevent crumbs getting into filling.) Repeat with remaining filling and curd.

▶ Bake cheesecake until set 1½ inches from edge but center trembles when pan is gently shaken, about 45 minutes. (Center of cake will appear very loose but will continue to set as it cools.) Transfer springform pan to a rack and immediately run a knife around top edge of cake to loosen. Cool completely, about 2 hours, then chill, uncovered, at least 4 hours. Remove side of springform pan before serving.

COOKS' NOTES: Lemon curd can be made 1 week ahead and chilled, covered.

• Crust, without filling, can be made 1 day ahead and kept, covered, at room temperature.

• Cheesecake can be chilled, loosely covered, up to 2 days. Cheesecake must be completely chilled before covering to prevent condensation on its surface.

KITCHEN NOTE

TRANSFERRING A CHEESECAKE FROM SPRINGFORM PAN TO SERVING PLATE IS EASY IF YOU TURN THE BOTTOM OF THE PAN OVER BEFORE YOU FILL IT, SO THE LIP IS UPSIDE DOWN; WITH THE LIP OUT OF THE WAY, THE CAKE ALSO IS EASIER TO CUT. TO ENSURE CLEAN SLICES, USE A THIN SHARP KNIFE AND WIPE IT OFF BETWEEN SLICES. DIPPING THE KNIFE INTO HOT WATER BETWEEN SLICES CAN ALSO BE EFFECTIVE, BUT BE ESPECIALLY CAREFUL TO WIPE IT OFF BEFORE CUTTING SO YOU DON'T ADD MOISTURE TO THE PIECES OF CAKE.

COOKIES, BARS, AND CONFECTIONS

TEA-AND-HONEY CRISPS

MAKES ABOUT 6 DOZEN (4-INCH) COOKIES
ACTIVE TIME: 1½ HR   START TO FINISH: 1½ HR

These buttery, crisp tuiles are made with tea and honey—the Earl Grey lends a sophisticated note of bergamot—and taste wonderful with an afternoon cuppa.

1 stick (½ cup) unsalted butter, softened
1 cup confectioners sugar
¼ cup mild honey
2¼ teaspoons decaffeinated Earl Grey tea leaves (from 2 to 3 tea bags; see cooks' note, below)
2 large egg whites
1 cup all-purpose flour

SPECIAL EQUIPMENT: **disposable Styrofoam plates; a small sharp knife such as an X-Acto; a 17- by 11-inch nonstick bakeware liner such as Silpat; a small offset spatula**

▶ Draw desired shape of cookie on a Styrofoam plate, then cut out shape with X-Acto knife and discard shape. If desired, cut out additional shapes from same plate. Trim plate, leaving a 1-inch border around stencil(s). Make more stencils with more plates if desired.

▶ Put oven rack in middle position and preheat oven to 350°F. Line a large baking sheet with nonstick liner.

▶ Beat together butter, confectioners sugar, honey, and tea leaves in a large bowl with an electric mixer at medium speed until combined well. Add egg whites 1 at a time, beating well after each addition. Reduce speed to low, then mix in flour until just combined.

▶ Place stencil on liner and spread batter with spatula over stencil to completely cover opening. Carefully lift stencil from liner and stencil more cookies in same manner about 1 inch apart. Bake until edges are deep golden brown, 6 to 9 minutes. Cool cookies 1 minute on sheet, then transfer with spatula to a rack to cool completely. (To curl cookies, drape while hot over handles of wooden spoons or rolling pins to cool.) Stencil and bake more cookies with remaining batter.

COOKS' NOTES: If using loose tea, finely crush before measuring.

• Cookies keep in an airtight container at room temperature 1 week.

MIXED-NUT SHORTBREAD

MAKES 18 BARS

ACTIVE TIME: 15 MIN   START TO FINISH: 45 MIN

An amalgamation of chopped nuts adorns this deep golden butter-rich cookie that offers an intense caramel-like flavor.

  1 stick (½ cup) unsalted butter, softened
  ⅓ cup plus 1 tablespoon sugar
  ½ teaspoon pure vanilla extract
  1 cup all-purpose flour
  ¾ cup salted and roasted mixed cocktail nuts,
      coarsely chopped

▶ Put oven rack in middle position and preheat oven to 375°F.

▶ Stir together butter and ⅓ cup sugar in a medium bowl with a wooden spoon until combined well. Stir in vanilla, then add flour and mix with your hands just until a dough forms.

▶ Transfer dough to a lightly greased baking sheet and spread evenly with your fingers to form an 8-inch square. Sprinkle nuts evenly over dough, pressing down to help them adhere.

▶ Sprinkle remaining tablespoon sugar over nuts and bake until shortbread is deep golden, 20 to 25 minutes.

▶ Cool on baking sheet on a rack, 10 minutes. Cut into 18 (roughly 3- by 1½-inch) bars.

COOKS' NOTE: If you have only unsalted nuts on hand, sprinkle them with a generous ¼ teaspoon salt in addition to the 1 tablespoon sugar.

ALMOND THUMBPRINT COOKIES

MAKES ABOUT 2 DOZEN

ACTIVE TIME: 20 MIN   START TO FINISH: 1½ HR

These delicate little almond cookies are perfect for Passover or any time you entertain.

  ¾ cup sliced blanched almonds, toasted (see Tips, page 8)
      and cooled
  ⅔ cup sugar
  ⅔ cup matzo cake meal
  ¼ teaspoon salt
  1 stick (½ cup) unsalted butter, melted and cooled slightly
  1 large egg, lightly beaten
  ½ teaspoon pure vanilla extract
  ¼ teaspoon pure almond extract
      About 2 tablespoons fruit jam such as raspberry, strawberry,
      or apricot

▶ Pulse almonds, sugar, matzo cake meal, and salt in a food processor until finely ground. (Be careful not to grind to a paste.) Transfer to a bowl and stir in butter, egg, and extracts until combined well. Chill dough, covered, until firm, about 30 minutes.

▶ While dough chills, put oven rack in middle position and preheat oven to 350°F.

▶ Drop level tablespoons of dough 1 inch apart onto 2 ungreased baking sheets. Roll dough into balls, then chill until slightly firm, about 10 minutes. Make a ½-inch-wide (⅓-inch-deep) indentation in center of each ball using your thumb, index finger, or the rounded end of a wooden spoon. Fill each indentation with ¼ teaspoon jam and bake, 1 sheet at a time, until tops are pale golden and undersides are golden, 10 to 12 minutes. Transfer cookies to a rack and cool completely.

APRICOT WALNUT BARS

MAKES 32 BARS

ACTIVE TIME: 15 MIN   START TO FINISH: 1 HR (INCLUDES COOLING)

These buttery fruit-and-nut bars taste like rugelach but are much easier to make.

 1⅓ cups all-purpose flour
  ⅔ cup sugar
  ½ teaspoon cinnamon
  ½ teaspoon salt
 1½ sticks (¾ cup) cold unsalted butter, cut into
      tablespoon pieces
  2 large egg yolks
  1 teaspoon pure vanilla extract
  ½ cup apricot preserves
  ¾ cup chopped walnuts (3 oz)

▶ Put oven rack in middle position and preheat oven to 425°F. Butter a 9-inch square baking pan and line with 1 sheet of foil, leaving a 2-inch overhang on 2 opposite sides, then butter foil.

▶ Pulse flour, sugar, cinnamon, and salt in a food processor until combined. Add butter and pulse until mixture resembles coarse meal with some small (roughly pea-size) butter lumps. Add yolks and vanilla and pulse just until clumps of dough form, about 30 seconds.

▶ Press three fourths of dough evenly onto bottom of pan, then spread with apricot preserves. Crumble remaining dough over preserves and sprinkle evenly with walnuts.

▶ Bake until top is golden brown and preserves are bubbling, 20 to 25 minutes. Cool in pan on a rack. Lift from pan by grasping both ends of foil. Cut into 32 bars and lift bars off foil with a spatula.

COCONUT CHOCOLATE BITES

MAKES 32 (1-INCH) CANDIES

ACTIVE TIME: 15 MIN   START TO FINISH: 30 MIN

These confections are like miniature candy bars—only better.

- ¾ cup sweetened flaked coconut
- ¾ cup unsweetened dried coconut
- ⅓ cup sweetened condensed milk
- 3½ to 4 oz fine-quality bittersweet chocolate (preferably 70% cacao), finely chopped

SPECIAL EQUIPMENT: **a small offset metal spatula; 32 paper candy cups (optional)**

▶ Line bottom and 2 opposite sides of an 8-inch square metal baking pan with a sheet of wax paper, leaving a 2-inch overhang on both sides.
▶ Mix together flaked and dried coconut and condensed milk with your fingertips until combined well, then firmly press into pan in an even layer with offset spatula. Chill, uncovered, 5 minutes.
▶ Melt chocolate in a metal bowl set over a saucepan of barely simmering water or in top of a double boiler, stirring until smooth. Spread chocolate evenly over coconut layer with offset spatula and chill until firm, 5 to 7 minutes.
▶ Lift confection onto a cutting board using overhang and halve confection with a sharp knife. Sandwich halves together, coconut sides in, to form an 8- by 4-inch rectangle, then discard wax paper. Cut rectangle into 32 (1-inch) squares. Arrange paper cups (if using) on a platter and fill with candies. Chill, covered, until ready to serve.

COOKS' NOTE: Candies keep, covered and chilled, 1 week.

KITCHEN NOTE

WHEN **MELTING CHOCOLATE,** YOUR UTENSILS MUST BE PERFECTLY DRY—A SINGLE DROP OF WATER WILL MAKE THE CHOCOLATE SEIZE UP. WHEN USING A DOUBLE BOILER, MAKE SURE THE WATER IN THE BOTTOM PAN ISN'T TOUCHING THE TOP PAN, AND CHECK THE WATER OCCASIONALLY—IT SHOULDN'T GO ABOVE A BARE SIMMER. IF USING A METAL BOWL SET OVER A SAUCEPAN OF WATER, SELECT A BOWL AND PAN COMBINATION WIDE ENOUGH SO THAT THE PART OF THE BOWL HOLDING THE CHOCOLATE IS COMPLETELY WITHIN THE MOUTH OF THE PAN.

SALTED CHOCOLATE CARAMELS

MAKES ABOUT 64 CANDIES

ACTIVE TIME: 45 MIN   START TO FINISH: 3½ HR (INCLUDES COOLING)

It's sea salt that really takes these caramels over the top, teasing out the creamy richness of the buttery chocolate.

- 2 cups heavy cream
- 10½ oz fine-quality bittersweet chocolate (no more than 60% cacao if marked), finely chopped
- 1¾ cups sugar
- ½ cup light corn syrup
- ¼ cup water
- ¼ teaspoon salt
- 3 tablespoons unsalted butter, cut into tablespoon pieces
- 2 teaspoons flaky sea salt such as Maldon (see cooks' note, below)
  Vegetable oil for greasing

SPECIAL EQUIPMENT: **parchment paper; a candy thermometer**

▶ Line bottom and sides of an 8-inch straight-sided square metal baking pan with 2 long sheets of crisscrossed parchment.
▶ Bring cream just to a boil in a 1- to 1½-quart heavy saucepan over moderately high heat, then reduce heat to low and add chocolate. Let stand 1 minute, then stir until chocolate is completely melted. Remove from heat.
▶ Bring sugar, corn syrup, water, and salt to a boil in a 5- to 6-quart heavy pot over moderate heat, stirring until sugar is dissolved. Boil, uncovered, without stirring but gently swirling pan occasionally, until sugar is deep golden, about 10 minutes. Tilt pan and carefully pour in chocolate mixture (mixture will bubble and steam vigorously). Continue to boil over moderate heat, stirring frequently, until mixture registers 255°F on thermometer, about 15 minutes. Add butter, stirring until completely melted, then immediately pour into lined baking pan (do not scrape any caramel clinging to bottom or side of saucepan). Let caramel stand 10 minutes, then sprinkle evenly with sea salt. Cool completely in pan on a rack, about 2 hours.
▶ Carefully invert caramel onto a clean, dry cutting board, then peel off parchment. Turn caramel salt side up. Lightly oil blade of a large heavy knife and cut into 1-inch squares.

COOKS' NOTES: If desired, additional sea salt can be pressed onto caramels after cutting.
• Caramels keep, layered between sheets of parchment or wax paper, in an airtight container at cool room temperature 2 weeks.
• Caramels can be wrapped in 4-inch squares of wax paper; twist ends to close.

PIES AND TARTS

RUSTIC APPLE TARTS WITH CALVADOS WHIPPED CREAM

MAKES 4 SMALL TARTS
ACTIVE TIME: 30 MIN   START TO FINISH: 50 MIN

FOR TARTS
- ⅓ cup plus ½ tablespoon sugar
- ½ cup apple cider or apple juice
- 1 tablespoon cider vinegar
- 1 lb small Gala apples (about 4; left unpeeled)
- 1 frozen puff pastry sheet (from a 17¼-oz package), thawed
- 3 tablespoons unsalted butter
- 1 tablespoon Calvados

FOR CALVADOS WHIPPED CREAM
- ½ cup chilled heavy cream
- 1 teaspoon sugar
- 1 teaspoon Calvados

SPECIAL EQUIPMENT: **an adjustable-blade slicer**

MAKE TARTS:

▶ Put oven rack in lower third of oven and preheat oven to 425°F.

▶ Cook ⅓ cup sugar in a dry 10-inch heavy skillet over moderate heat, undisturbed, until it begins to melt. Continue to cook, stirring occasionally with a fork, until sugar is melted into a pale golden caramel. Tilt skillet and carefully pour in cider and vinegar (caramel will harden and steam vigorously). Simmer over moderately low heat, stirring occasionally, until caramel is dissolved.

▶ While syrup simmers, cut apples into ⅛-inch-thick slices with slicer, rotating around core of each (discard cores). Add apple slices to hot syrup in skillet, gently tossing to coat. Remove from heat and let stand, stirring occasionally, until apples are wilted by syrup, 5 to 10 minutes.

▶ While apples stand, roll out puff pastry sheet into a 12-inch square on a lightly floured surface with a floured rolling pin. Cut into quarters, forming 4 (6-inch) squares and brush off excess flour from both sides.

▶ Transfer squares to a large shallow baking pan, overlapping if necessary (squares will fit without touching after edges are folded in later).

▶ Drain apples in a sieve set over a bowl (reserve syrup), then mound slices decoratively on each square, leaving a ¾-inch border all around. Fold border over apples along edges, pinching edges together as necessary, then dot tops of apples with a total of 1 tablespoon butter and remaining ½ tablespoon sugar.

▶ Bake tarts until apples are tender, pastry is puffed, and edges and undersides are golden brown, 25 to 30 minutes.

▶ While tarts bake, boil reserved syrup in skillet with Calvados and remaining 2 tablespoons butter until thickened and reduced to about ⅓ cup. Brush or drizzle hot syrup over tarts.

MAKE CREAM:

▶ Beat cream with sugar and Calvados in a chilled bowl with a whisk or electric mixer until cream holds soft peaks.

▶ Serve tarts warm or at room temperature with cream.

COOKS' NOTE: Tarts can be baked 3 hours ahead and cooled, uncovered, then kept at room temperature. Reheat in a preheated 350°F oven until hot, 10 to 15 minutes.

BLACKBERRY HAND PIES

MAKES 12 SMALL PIES
ACTIVE TIME: 40 MIN   START TO FINISH: 3 HR (INCLUDES MAKING DOUGH AND COOLING PIES)

Eating one of these individual pies is quite different from your basic fork-and-plate experience. A bite through the crisp pastry, sparkling with sugar, reveals a thick filling of sweet-and-tart fruit.

- 2 cups blackberries (¾ lb)
- 1 large Golden Delicious apple, peeled and coarsely grated
- 2 tablespoons plus 1 teaspoon semolina flour (see Sources)
- ¼ teaspoon cinnamon
- 8 tablespoons sugar
- Pastry dough (recipe follows) for a double-crust pie
- 2 tablespoons milk

SPECIAL EQUIPMENT: **2 large (17- by 12-inch) baking sheets; parchment paper**

▶ Cook blackberries, apple, semolina flour, cinnamon and 6 tablespoons sugar in a 2-quart heavy saucepan over moderate heat, stirring frequently, until mixture just boils and is thickened, about 5 minutes. Transfer to a shallow bowl to cool.

▶ Put oven racks in upper and lower thirds of oven and preheat oven to 375°F. Line baking sheets with parchment paper.

▶ Roll out half of dough ⅛ inch thick on a lightly floured surface with a lightly floured rolling pin into a 16- by 11-inch rectangle (keep remaining dough chilled), then trim into a 15- by 10-inch rectangle, reserving scraps. Cut into 6 (5-inch) squares. Place a heaping tablespoon of fruit filling in center of 1 square. Moisten edges of square with milk and fold into a triangle, pressing edges to seal. Transfer to a lined baking sheet and press tines of a fork around edges of triangle. Make 5 more triangles in same manner, arranging them 1 inch apart on baking sheet. Repeat with remaining dough and filling, rerolling all of the scraps together once to make 12 triangles total.

▶ Brush triangles with milk and sprinkle with remaining 2 tablespoons sugar. Bake, switching position of sheets halfway through baking, until pies are golden, about 30 minutes total. Transfer pies to racks to cool.

PASTRY DOUGH
ACTIVE TIME: 20 MIN   START TO FINISH: 1¼ HR

FOR A SINGLE-CRUST PIE
1¼ cups all-purpose flour
¾ stick (6 tablespoons) cold unsalted butter, cut into ½-inch cubes
2 tablespoons cold vegetable shortening (preferably trans-fat-free)
¼ teaspoon salt
3 to 4 tablespoons ice water

FOR A DOUBLE-CRUST PIE
2½ cups all-purpose flour
1½ sticks (¾ cup) cold unsalted butter, cut into ½-inch cubes
¼ cup cold vegetable shortening (preferably trans-fat-free)
½ teaspoon salt
5 to 7 tablespoons ice water

SPECIAL EQUIPMENT: **a pastry or bench scraper**

▶ Blend together flour, butter, shortening, and salt in a bowl with your fingertips or a pastry blender (or pulse in a food processor) just until mixture resembles coarse meal with some small (roughly pea-size) butter lumps. Drizzle 3 tablespoons ice water for a single-crust pie or 5 tablespoons for a double-crust pie evenly over mixture and gently stir with a fork (or pulse) until incorporated.

▶ Squeeze a small handful of dough: If it doesn't hold together, add more ice water ½ tablespoon at a time, stirring (or pulsing) until incorporated. (Do not overwork dough, or pastry will be tough.)

▶ Turn out dough onto a work surface. For a single-crust pie, divide dough into 4 portions; for a double-crust pie, divide dough into 8 portions. With heel of your hand, smear each portion once or twice in a forward motion to help distribute fat. Gather all dough together with pastry scraper. For a single-crust pie, press into a ball, then flatten into a 5-inch disk. For a double-crust pie, divide dough into 2 pieces, with one slightly larger, then form each into a ball and flatten each into a 5-inch disk. If dough is sticky, dust lightly with additional flour. Wrap each disk in plastic wrap and chill until firm, at least 1 hour.

COOKS' NOTES: For sweet pastry dough (single crust), add 2 tablespoons sugar to flour mixture and proceed with recipe as directed.
• Pastry dough can be chilled up to 2 days.

PLUM GALETTE
SERVES 8
ACTIVE TIME: 45 MIN   START TO FINISH: 3 HR (INCLUDES MAKING DOUGH AND COOLING PIE)

The beauty of plums becomes all the more evident when they are displayed in a galette. Accompanied by sweetened Armagnac crème fraîche, this makes a wonderfully sophisticated dessert.

Pastry dough (recipe precedes) for a single-crust pie
2 tablespoons semolina flour (see Sources)
8 tablespoons granulated sugar
5 large black or red plums (1½ lb), halved, pitted, and each cut lengthwise into 8 wedges
1 tablespoon confectioners sugar
¾ cup crème fraîche or sour cream
1 tablespoon Armagnac or Cognac (optional)

SPECIAL EQUIPMENT: **parchment paper; a pastry brush**

▶ Put oven rack in middle position and preheat oven to 375°F. Line a large (17- by 12-inch) baking sheet with parchment paper.
▶ Roll out dough on a lightly floured surface with a lightly floured rolling pin into a 13-inch round. Transfer to lined baking sheet.
▶ Stir together semolina flour and 2 tablespoons granulated sugar and spread evenly over dough, leaving a 1-inch border. Arrange plums, skin sides down, in 1 layer on top of sugar mixture, then sprinkle plums with 3 tablespoons granulated sugar. Fold in edge of dough to cover outer rim of plums, pleating dough as necessary.
▶ Bake galette, loosely covered with a sheet of foil, 40 minutes. Remove foil and bake until fruit is tender and juices are bubbling, about 5 minutes more.
▶ Transfer galette on baking sheet to a rack and immediately brush hot juices over plums with pastry brush. Dust hot galette with confectioners sugar (sugar will melt and help glaze galette). Cool to warm or room temperature, about 30 minutes.
▶ While galette cools, stir together crème fraîche, Armagnac (if using), and remaining 3 tablespoons granulated sugar in a bowl until sugar is dissolved. Serve galette with Armagnac cream.

DEEP-DISH WILD BLUEBERRY PIE

SERVES 8 TO 10

ACTIVE TIME: 40 MIN   START TO FINISH: 7¼ HR (INCLUDES MAKING
DOUGH AND COOLING PIE)

*If you've never had pie made from wild blueberries before, you'll
be bowled over by the intensity of this one. If you can't find
fresh wild blueberries in your area, frozen ones also yield
excellent results.*

1¼ cups packed light brown sugar
5 tablespoons quick-cooking tapioca
6 cups fresh wild blueberries or 3 (10-oz) packages frozen
     (not thawed)
1 tablespoon fresh lemon juice
     Pastry dough (page 275) for a double-crust pie
1 tablespoon unsalted butter, cut into small pieces
1 large egg, beaten with 1 tablespoon water

SPECIAL EQUIPMENT: **a 9½-inch deep-dish pie plate (6-cup
capacity); small decorative cookie cutters (optional)**

▸ Put a large baking sheet on oven rack in middle position and
preheat oven to 425°F.
▸ Whisk together brown sugar and tapioca and toss with
blueberries and lemon juice in a large bowl.
▸ Roll out larger piece of dough (keep remaining piece chilled)
on a lightly floured surface with a lightly floured rolling pin into
a 13-inch round. Fit into pie plate. Trim excess dough, leaving a
½-inch overhang. Chill shell while rolling out dough for top crust.
▸ Roll out remaining dough on a lightly floured surface with
lightly floured rolling pin into an 11-inch round. Cut out 5 or
6 small holes with small decorative cookie cutters or use a small
knife to slash steam vents toward center.
▸ Spoon filling with any juices accumulated in bowl into shell,
dot with butter, and cover with top crust. Trim top crust with
kitchen shears, leaving a ½-inch overhang. Fold overhang of top
crust under bottom pastry and press against rim of pie plate to
reinforce edge, then crimp decoratively and brush with egg wash.
▸ Bake pie on hot baking sheet in oven 30 minutes, then cover
edge with a pie shield or foil to prevent overbrowning. Reduce
oven temperature to 375°F and continue to bake until crust is
golden and filling is bubbling, 45 to 50 minutes more.
▸ Cool pie completely on a rack, about 4 hours (filling will be
runny if pie is still warm).

COOKS' NOTE: We like our fruit filling on the soft side. If you
prefer a firmer set, increase the tapioca to 6 tablespoons.

LEMON BRÛLÉE TART

SERVES 6 TO 8

ACTIVE TIME: 25 MIN   START TO FINISH: 4¾ HR (INCLUDES MAKING
PASTRY AND COOLING TART)

*This pie is ideal after a heavy meal. Just a bit of additional sugar
allows the bright flavor of lemon to shine through.*

     Sweet pastry dough for a single-crust pie (see recipe and
         cooks' note, page 275)
⅔ cup heavy cream
⅔ cup plus 1 tablespoon sugar
1 teaspoon finely grated fresh lemon zest (see Tips, page 8)
½ cup fresh lemon juice
4 large egg yolks
1 whole large egg

SPECIAL EQUIPMENT: **a 9½-inch round fluted tart pan (1 inch
deep) with a removable bottom; pie weights or raw rice; a small
blowtorch**

▸ Roll out dough into a 13-inch round on a lightly floured surface
with a lightly floured rolling pin. Fit into tart pan and trim edges.
Chill shell until firm, about 30 minutes.
▸ Put oven rack in middle position and preheat oven to 375°F.
▸ Lightly prick bottom of shell all over with a fork, then line with
foil and fill with pie weights. Bake until side is set and edge is
pale golden, 18 to 20 minutes. Carefully remove and weights
and foil bake shell until deep golden, 15 to 20 minutes more.
Remove from oven and reduce oven temperature to 300°F.
▸ Whisk together cream, ⅔ cup sugar, zest, juice, yolks, and
whole egg until combined.
▸ Put tart shell (in tart pan) on a large baking sheet and transfer
to oven. With oven rack extended, carefully pour filling into
tart shell (custard will still have bubbles on top), then carefully
slide rack into oven. Bake tart until custard is set 3 inches from
edge but trembles slightly in center when gently shaken, 25 to
35 minutes. Remove from baking sheet and cool in pan on a
rack 30 minutes, then remove side of pan and cool tart to room
temperature, about 1¼ hours more.
▸ Just before serving, sprinkle remaining tablespoon sugar evenly
over top of tart. Move blowtorch flame evenly back and forth just
above top of tart, avoiding crust, until sugar is caramelized and
slightly browned (be careful not to burn sugar). Let tart stand
5 minutes before serving.

COOKS' NOTE: Tart, without caramelized top, can be baked and
cooled 1 day ahead, then chilled in an airtight container. Very
gently blot any moisture from surface of tart with paper towels
before sprinkling with sugar and caramelizing top.

MACADAMIA COCONUT TART

SERVES 8 TO 10

ACTIVE TIME: 25 MIN   START TO FINISH: 5½ HR (INCLUDES MAKING PASTRY AND COOLING TART)

Think of this pretty tart as a tropical version of traditional pecan pie. The sweet, buttery filling bakes up like a custard, and each slice is packed with macadamia nuts and sweetened coconut.

	Pastry dough for a single-crust pie (page 275)
3	large eggs
1¼	cups packed light brown sugar
½	teaspoon pure vanilla extract
¼	teaspoon salt
½	stick (¼ cup) unsalted butter, melted and cooled slightly
1½	cups dry-roasted macadamia nuts (7 oz), toasted (see Tips, page 8) and coarsely chopped
1	cup sweetened flaked coconut (2¾ oz)

SPECIAL EQUIPMENT: **a 10-inch fluted tart pan (1 inch deep) with a removable bottom; pie weights or raw rice**

▶ Roll out dough on a lightly floured surface with a lightly floured rolling pin into a 13-inch round. Fit into tart pan and trim edges. Chill shell until firm, about 30 minutes.

▶ Put oven rack in middle position and preheat oven to 375°F.

▶ Lightly prick bottom of shell all over with a fork, then line with foil and fill with pie weights. Bake until side is set and edge is pale golden, about 20 minutes. Carefully remove weights and foil and bake shell until deep golden, 10 to 15 minutes more. Leave oven on.

▶ Whisk together eggs, brown sugar, vanilla, and salt until combined, then whisk in melted butter, nuts, and coconut. Pour filling into tart shell and bake until set in center, 25 to 30 minutes. Cool in pan on a rack 30 minutes, then remove side of pan and cool tart to room temperature, 1½ to 2 hours more.

COOKS' NOTE: Tart can be made 1 day ahead and cooled completely, then kept, covered loosely with foil, at room temperature.

KITCHEN NOTE

IF, WHEN YOU'RE MAKING A **PIE DOUGH**, IT TAKES LONGER THAN YOU HAD EXPECTED TO CUT THE FATS INTO THE DRY INGREDIENTS, JUST POP THE BOWL INTO THE FREEZER FOR A FEW MINUTES TO CHILL.

FROZEN DESSERTS

POMEGRANATE GELATO

MAKES 1 QUART

ACTIVE TIME: 15 MIN   START TO FINISH: 3½ HR (INCLUDES CHILLING AND FREEZING)

This frozen sweet has a beautiful blush-pink color, and the tanginess of the fruit cuts the richness of the dairy.

1½	cups heavy cream
½	cup whole milk
¾	cup sugar
1½	tablespoons cornstarch
⅛	teaspoon salt
1¼	cups bottled pomegranate juice
⅓	cup pomegranate liqueur such as PAMA
1	teaspoon fresh lemon juice

SPECIAL EQUIPMENT: **an ice cream maker**
GARNISH: **pomegranate seeds**

▶ Whisk together cream, milk, sugar, cornstarch, and salt in a 2½- to 3-quart heavy saucepan. Bring to a boil over moderate heat, whisking occasionally, then boil, whisking, 2 minutes. Remove from heat and whisk in remaining ingredients.

▶ Transfer to a bowl and chill, uncovered, until cold, at least 1 hour.

▶ Freeze in ice cream maker, then transfer to an airtight container and put in freezer to harden, at least 2 hours.

▶ Soften gelato slightly in refrigerator, about 20 minutes, before serving.

COOK'S NOTES: Cream mixture (before churning) can be chilled, covered, up to 1 day ahead.

• Gelato keeps 1 week.

STRAWBERRY SHAKES

MAKES 2 (16-OZ) SHAKES

ACTIVE TIME: 10 MIN   START TO FINISH: 10 MIN

3	cups premium vanilla ice cream
2	cups sliced strawberries (19 oz whole)
1	cup whole milk

▶ Purée all ingredients in a blender just until smooth.

BLACK-AND-WHITE MALTS

MAKES 2 (16-OZ) SHAKES
ACTIVE TIME: 10 MIN   START TO FINISH: 10 MIN

The flavors of a classic New York cookie make a deliciously nostalgic malted.

- 2 cups premium vanilla ice cream
- 2 cups premium chocolate ice cream
- 1½ cups whole milk
- ¼ cup malted milk powder

▸ Purée all ingredients in a blender just until smooth.

COFFEE AND DULCE DE LECHE SHAKES

MAKES 2 (16-OZ) SHAKES
ACTIVE TIME: 10 MIN   START TO FINISH: 10 MIN

We've created a creamier version of the blended frozen drinks offered at many coffee shops.

- 3 cups premium coffee ice cream
- 1 cup whole milk
- ⅓ cup *dulce de leche*
- 1 teaspoon instant-espresso powder

GARNISH: cinnamon for dusting

▸ Purée all ingredients with a pinch of salt in a blender just until smooth.

CALIFORNIA DATE SHAKES

MAKES 2 (16-OZ) SHAKES
ACTIVE TIME: 10 MIN   START TO FINISH: 10 MIN

Be sure not to overblend—the little bits of fruit add a pleasant textural contrast. The pitted dates available in supermarkets work well.

- 3 cups premium vanilla ice cream
- 1 cup whole milk
- 1 cup whole pitted dates

▸ Blend all ingredients in a blender just until smooth with some small bits of date.

ORANGE VANILLA SHAKES

MAKES 2 (16-OZ) SHAKES
ACTIVE TIME: 10 MIN   START TO FINISH: 10 MIN

- 4 cups premium vanilla ice cream
- 1 cup whole milk
- ½ cup plus 2 tablespoons frozen orange juice concentrate

▸ Purée all ingredients in a blender just until smooth.

KITCHEN NOTE

WHAT ICE CREAM MAKES THE BEST MILKSHAKE? SUPERPREMIUM ICE CREAMS, SUCH AS HÄAGEN-DAZS AND BEN & JERRY'S, CONTAIN AT LEAST 14 PERCENT MILK FAT. THEY ALSO HAVE LESS AIR CHURNED INTO THEM THAN DO MORE TRADITIONAL ICE CREAMS, OFTEN LABELED "PREMIUM," LIKE BREYERS. BUT THESE FANCY BRANDS, WHICH WE LOVE TO EAT ON THEIR OWN, RESULT IN A SHAKE THAT'S SOUPY, NOT THICK. SO STICK WITH A TUB OF PREMIUM WHEN MAKING SHAKES.

CHOCOLATE AND PEPPERMINT CANDY ICE CREAM SANDWICHES

MAKES 8 SANDWICHES
ACTIVE TIME: 35 MIN   START TO FINISH: 3½ HR (INCLUDES FREEZING)

- 1 pt superpremium vanilla ice cream, softened slightly
- ¼ teaspoon pure peppermint extract
- 1 cup finely crushed peppermint hard candies (¼ lb)
- 16 chocolate wafers such as Nabisco Famous

SPECIAL EQUIPMENT: a ¼-cup ice cream scoop

▸ Stir together ice cream (reserve pint container), extract, and ½ cup crushed candy in a bowl until combined. Transfer mixture to pint container and freeze until just firm enough to scoop, about 1 hour.
▸ Working very quickly, scoop ice cream onto flat sides of 8 wafers (1 scoop per wafer), then top with remaining 8 wafers, flat sides down. Wrap each sandwich individually with plastic wrap and freeze until firm, about 1 hour. Unwrap sandwiches and roll edges in remaining ½ cup crushed candy. Rewrap and freeze until firm, about 1 hour.

COOKS' NOTE: Ice cream sandwiches keep 3 days.

PEANUT BUTTER AND BANANA SUNDAES

SERVES 4

ACTIVE TIME: 20 MIN   START TO FINISH: 25 MIN

1⅔ cups half-and-half
½ cup packed light brown sugar
1 tablespoon light corn syrup
¼ teaspoon salt
¾ cup creamy peanut butter (not natural)
1½ pt premium vanilla ice cream
2 firm-ripe bananas, cut crosswise into ¼-inch-thick slices

GARNISH: coarsely chopped chocolate toffee candy such as a Heath bar

▸ Bring half-and-half, brown sugar, corn syrup, and salt to a boil in a 2-quart heavy saucepan over moderately high heat, whisking until smooth. Remove from heat and whisk in peanut butter until smooth. Transfer to a glass measuring cup or small heatproof pitcher and cool slightly, about 5 minutes.
▸ Divide ice cream among 4 bowls, then top each serving with some banana slices and 3 tablespoons peanut butter sauce. (You will have some sauce left over.)

COOKS' NOTE: Sauce keeps, cooled completely, uncovered, then chilled in an airtight container 1 week. Reheat before using.

FRUIT FINALES

BALSAMIC BLUEBERRIES AND PEACHES

SERVES 4

ACTIVE TIME: 15 MIN   START TO FINISH: 45 MIN

2 tablespoons balsamic vinegar
3 tablespoons sugar, or to taste
3 cups blueberries (about 1 lb)
1 lb peaches or nectarines, sliced
½ teaspoon black pepper (optional)

▸ Boil vinegar, 3 tablespoons sugar, and 1 cup blueberries in a 1- to 1½-quart heavy saucepan, stirring, 1 minute. Remove from heat.
▸ Combine remaining 2 cups blueberries with peach slices in a large bowl. Toss with hot blueberry syrup and black pepper (if using), then add sugar to taste. Let stand, tossing occasionally, until cool, about 30 minutes.

STRAWBERRY PROSECCO SOUP

MAKES ABOUT 4 CUPS

ACTIVE TIME: 10 MIN   START TO FINISH: 1¼ HR

1 lb strawberries, chopped (3 cups)
1 cup Prosecco
2 teaspoons chopped fresh tarragon
⅛ teaspoon salt
2 to 3 tablespoons sugar
¾ cup vanilla yogurt

GARNISH: cracked black pepper

▸ Toss chopped strawberries with Prosecco, tarragon, salt, and 2 tablespoons sugar. Let macerate, covered and chilled, 1 hour.
▸ Purée mixture in a blender until smooth, then reserve 1 cup purée. Blend remaining mixture with yogurt and sugar to taste. Serve soup drizzled with reserved purée.

STRAWBERRIES WITH CHOCOLATE CARAMEL SAUCE

SERVES 4

ACTIVE TIME: 15 MIN   START TO FINISH: 15 MIN

This rich, creamy chocolate sauce is so versatile it might also be just what your favorite dessert has been missing.

¼ cup sugar
½ cup heavy cream
2 oz fine-quality bittersweet chocolate (no more than 60% cacao), coarsely chopped
⅛ teaspoon salt
1 tablespoon unsalted butter
1 lb strawberries, halved if large

ACCOMPANIMENT: lightly sweetened whipped cream

▸ Cook sugar in a dry 1-quart heavy saucepan over moderately high heat, undisturbed, until it begins to melt, about 2 minutes. Continue to cook, stirring occasionally with a fork, until sugar is melted into a deep golden caramel, 1 to 2 minutes.
▸ Remove from heat and carefully pour in cream (mixture will steam and bubble vigorously). Once bubbles begin to subside, return pan to moderate heat and cook, stirring constantly, until caramel is dissolved.
▸ Remove from heat, then add chocolate and salt and stir until chocolate is melted. Add butter and stir just until melted.
▸ Cool sauce slightly, then drizzle over strawberries.

PORT-AND-SPICE POACHED PEARS WITH GRANITA

SERVES 4

ACTIVE TIME: 15 MIN   START TO FINISH: 9¼ HR (INCLUDES STEEPING AND FREEZING)

- 4 firm-ripe Bosc pears
- 2 cups unsweetened white grape juice
- 2 cups ruby Port
- ¼ cup sugar
- 6 green or white cardamom pods (see Sources), smashed
- 1 (1-inch) piece cinnamon stick
- 2 whole cloves
- 1¼ cups water
- 3 tablespoons fresh lemon juice
- ⅔ cup crème fraîche, well stirred

SPECIAL EQUIPMENT: **parchment paper**

▸Peel pears, leaving stems intact. Cut a round of parchment paper to fit inside a wide 4-quart heavy pot.

▸Bring grape juice, Port, sugar, spices, and 1 cup water to a boil in pot over moderate heat, stirring until sugar is dissolved. Add pears, arranging them on their sides in 1 layer (pears will not be covered by liquid). Cover pears directly with round of parchment. Reduce heat to low and poach pears, turning occasionally, until just tender when pierced with a sharp knife, about 25 minutes. Remove from heat and let pears steep in liquid, covered with parchment, turning occasionally, at least 2 hours and up to 3.

▸Carefully transfer pears with a slotted spoon to a shallow dish, reserving poaching liquid. Let pears stand at room temperature or chill, covered with parchment.

▸Pour poaching liquid through a fine-mesh sieve into a bowl (discard spices) and return to pot. Boil, uncovered, until liquid is reduced to about 2½ cups, 25 to 30 minutes. Remove from heat and stir in lemon juice and remaining ¼ cup water. Pour liquid into an 8- to 9-inch square baking pan (not nonstick).

▸Freeze liquid 1½ hours, then scrape and stir with a fork, crushing any lumps. Repeat, scraping every hour until evenly frozen, about 4 hours more.

▸If chilled, bring pears to room temperature before serving, about 30 minutes.

▸Cut a thin slice from bottom of each pear, then stand pears upright on chilled plates. Scrape granita, then serve pears with granita and crème fraîche.

COOKS' NOTE: Pears and granita can be made 2 days ahead. Scrape granita with a fork before serving.

TWO-BERRY SHORTCAKES

SERVES 6

ACTIVE TIME: 20 MIN   START TO FINISH: 35 MIN

FOR BISCUITS
- 2 cups all-purpose flour
- 2 tablespoons sugar
- 2 teaspoons baking powder
- ½ teaspoon baking soda
- ½ teaspoon salt
- 5 tablespoons cold unsalted butter, cut into bits
- 1 cup well-shaken buttermilk

FOR FILLING
- 12 oz raspberries (about 3 cups)
- 6 oz blackberries (about 1½ cups)
- 2 tablespoons sugar

FOR CREAM
- 1 cup well-chilled heavy cream
- 1 tablespoon sugar

MAKE BISCUITS:

▸Put oven rack in middle position and preheat oven to 450°F.

▸Whisk together flour, sugar, baking powder, baking soda, and salt in a large bowl. Blend in butter with your fingertips until mixture resembles coarse meal with some small (roughly pea-size) butter lumps. Add buttermilk and stir just until a soft, sticky dough forms.

▸Drop dough in 6 mounds about 2 inches apart on an ungreased large baking sheet and bake until golden, 12 to 15 minutes. Transfer biscuits to a rack and cool to warm, about 10 minutes.

MAKE FILLING WHILE BISCUITS BAKE:

▸Gently mash half of berries with sugar in a bowl, then stir in remaining berries.

MAKE CREAM AND ASSEMBLE SHORTCAKES:

▸Beat together cream with sugar in a large bowl with an electric mixer until it holds soft peaks.

▸Carefully cut biscuits in half horizontally and arrange 1 bottom half, split side up, on each of 6 plates. Top each with berries, whipped cream, and other half of biscuit.

GELATINS, CUSTARDS, AND PUDDINGS

PASSION-FRUIT GELÉE WITH BASIL CREAM

SERVES 4

ACTIVE TIME: 45 MIN   START TO FINISH: 3 HR (INCLUDES CHILLING)

Though this recipe owes a debt to that icon of childhood desserts, Jell-O with whipped cream, the interplay of floral passion fruit and herbal basil is nothing if not elegant.

FOR GELÉE

- 1¾ teaspoons unflavored gelatin (from a ¼-oz envelope)
- ¼ cup water
- 2 cups passion-fruit nectar (preferably Looza brand)

FOR CREAM

- ½ cup loosely packed fresh basil leaves
- ½ cup sugar
- 1½ cups well-chilled heavy cream
- 1 teaspoon unflavored gelatin (from another ¼-oz envelope)
- 2 tablespoons water

SPECIAL EQUIPMENT: 1 empty egg carton; 4 (6- to 8-oz) slender clear glasses (not stemmed)

GARNISH: 4 fresh basil leaves (optional)

MAKE GELÉE:

► Sprinkle gelatin over water in a small saucepan and let stand 1 minute to soften. Cook over low heat, stirring, until gelatin is dissolved, 1 to 2 minutes. Remove from heat and whisk in 1 tablespoon passion-fruit nectar at a time until gelatin mixture is cool, then whisk in remaining nectar.

► Transfer to a metal bowl and set bowl into a larger bowl half-filled with ice and cold water. Let stand, stirring occasionally, until gelée is consistency of raw egg white, 15 to 25 minutes.

► Put egg carton in a shallow baking pan and arrange glasses in carton, then tilt glasses to a 45-degree angle. Divide gelée among glasses. Carefully transfer pan with glasses (in carton) to refrigerator and chill until gelée is set, at least 1 hour.

MAKE CREAM WHEN GELÉE HAS SET:

► Pulse basil, sugar, and a pinch of salt in a food processor until finely chopped, then transfer to a bowl and add cream, stirring just until sugar is dissolved.

► Sprinkle gelatin over water in a small saucepan and let stand 1 minute to soften. Cook over low heat, stirring, until gelatin is dissolved, 1 to 2 minutes. Remove from heat and whisk in 1 tablespoon basil cream at a time until gelatin mixture is cool, then whisk in remaining cream. Pour through a fine-mesh sieve into a metal bowl, pressing hard on and then discarding solids.

► Set bowl in a larger bowl half-filled with ice and cold water and let stand, stirring occasionally, until cream is consistency of raw egg white, 15 to 25 minutes.

► Holding 1 glass of gelée at a 45-degree angle, slowly fill glass with basil cream, gradually righting glass as filled. Fill remaining glasses in same manner. Chill, covered, until set, at least 1 hour.

COOKS' NOTE: Gelées with cream can be chilled up to 2 days.

MAPLE CUSTARD CUPS

MAKES 6

ACTIVE TIME: 15 MIN   START TO FINISH: 1½ HR

Maple syrup and maple sugar infuse a simple vanilla custard with a rich caramelized flavor.

- 2 whole large eggs plus 2 large yolks
- 1½ cups whole milk
- ½ cup heavy cream
- ¼ cup dark amber or Grade B maple syrup
- 2 tablespoons granulated maple sugar (see cooks' note, below, and Sources)
- ½ teaspoon pure vanilla extract
- ¼ teaspoon salt

SPECIAL EQUIPMENT: a 13- by 9-inch baking pan; 6 (6-oz) custard cups or ramekins

► Put oven rack in middle position and preheat oven to 350°F.

► Whisk together all ingredients in a large bowl until sugar is dissolved, then pour through a fine-mesh sieve into a 1-quart glass measure. Divide custard evenly among cups, then transfer cups to baking pan. Bake in a hot water bath (see Tips, page 8), pan covered loosely with foil, until custards are just set and a knife inserted in center of one comes out clean, 35 to 40 minutes.

► Carefully transfer cups to a rack and cool to warm, about 30 minutes.

COOKS' NOTES: Custard is best when eaten immediately, but can be made 1 day ahead and chilled, covered.

• Maple sugar is usually sold granulated, but if you find a brand sold as very large granules, pulse the sugar in a blender until it becomes more finely granulated.

RICOTTA PUDDINGS WITH GLAZED RHUBARB

MAKES 6

ACTIVE TIME: 15 MIN   START TO FINISH: 1 HR

Delicate and creamy, these tender individual desserts taste equally good served warm or at room temperature.

FOR PUDDINGS

- 1 cup whole-milk ricotta (8¾ oz)
- 1 whole large egg plus 1 large yolk
- ¼ cup sour cream
- 2 tablespoons sugar
- 2 tablespoons heavy cream
- 2 tablespoons mild honey
- ⅛ teaspoon salt
- ½ teaspoon finely grated fresh lemon zest (see Tips, page 8)

FOR GLAZED RHUBARB

- 3½ tablespoons sugar
- ½ teaspoon cornstarch
- ½ lb fresh rhubarb stalks (about 2), cut diagonally into ¼-inch-thick slices

SPECIAL EQUIPMENT: a muffin pan (preferably nonstick) with 6 (½-cup) muffin cups

MAKE PUDDING BATTER:

▶ Put oven rack in middle position and preheat oven to 325°F. Lightly oil muffin cups.

▶ Blend together all pudding ingredients in a blender until smooth, then divide batter among muffin cups.

PREPARE RHUBARB:

▶ Stir together sugar and cornstarch in a 9- to 10-inch glass or ceramic pie plate. Add rhubarb and toss to coat, then spread in one layer.

BAKE PUDDINGS AND RHUBARB:

▶ Bake puddings and rhubarb, side by side, carefully turning rhubarb over once halfway through baking, until puddings are just set and edges are pale golden, 35 to 45 minutes. Remove puddings and rhubarb from oven at the same time. Set rhubarb aside and cool puddings in muffin pan on a rack 5 minutes (puddings will sink slightly).

▶ Run a thin knife around edge of each pudding, then invert a platter over pan and invert puddings onto platter. Transfer puddings, right side up, to plates and serve topped with rhubarb and its juices.

COOKS' NOTE: A spoonful of your favorite jam can be used in place of the glazed rhubarb.

YOGURT AND BROWN-SUGAR PANNA COTTAS WITH GRAPE GELÉE

MAKES 6

ACTIVE TIME: 30 MIN   START TO FINISH: 8½ HR (INCLUDES CHILLING)

FOR GELÉE

- 1 teaspoon unflavored gelatin (from a ¼-oz envelope)
- 1 cup all natural Concord grape juice
- 1 tablespoon fresh lemon juice
- 1 cup red and green seedless grapes (6 oz), thinly sliced crosswise
- 1 tablespoon grappa
  Vegetable oil for greasing ramekins

FOR PANNA COTTAS

- 2 teaspoons unflavored gelatin (from another ¼-oz envelope)
- 1 cup heavy cream
- ½ cup packed dark brown sugar
- 2 cups low-fat plain yogurt
- 2 tablespoons grappa
- ⅛ teaspoon salt

SPECIAL EQUIPMENT: 6 (8-oz) ramekins

MAKE GELÉE:

▶ Sprinkle gelatin over ¼ cup grape juice in a 1-quart heavy saucepan and let stand 1 minute to soften. Bring to a simmer, stirring until gelatin is dissolved. Remove from heat and stir in remaining ¾ cup grape juice with lemon juice, grapes, and grappa.

▶ Lightly oil ramekins and put in a shallow baking pan. Divide grape mixture among ramekins and chill in freezer until just set, about 30 minutes.

MAKE PANNA COTTA MIXTURE WHILE GELÉE SETS:

▶ Stir together gelatin and ¼ cup cream in cleaned 1-quart heavy saucepan and let stand 1 minute to soften. Bring to a simmer over moderate heat, stirring until gelatin is dissolved. Add remaining ¾ cup cream with brown sugar and return to a simmer, stirring until sugar is dissolved.

▶ Whisk together yogurt, grappa, and salt until smooth in a large measuring cup, then pour in cream mixture and whisk until combined well.

CHILL PANNA COTTAS:

▶ Pour mixture into ramekins (over set gelée) and chill (in refrigerator), covered, until firm, at least 8 hours.

▶ To unmold, run a thin sharp knife along edge of each ramekin to loosen, then dip in a small bowl of very warm water 6 seconds. Invert a plate over each ramekin, then invert panna cotta with gelée onto plates, gently lifting off ramekins.

BANANA ESPRESSO BREAD PUDDING

SERVES 4

ACTIVE TIME: 15 MIN START TO FINISH: 1¼ HR

- 16 (½-inch-thick) slices day-old baguette
- 3 cups half-and-half
- 6 large egg yolks
- ¾ cup plus 1 tablespoon sugar
- 3 tablespoons instant-espresso powder
- 3 firm-ripe bananas, halved crosswise, then halved lengthwise
- 1½ tablespoons unsalted butter

▶ Put oven rack in middle position and preheat oven to 325°F.

▶ Arrange bread in 2 layers in a 2-quart (8-inch square) baking dish.

▶ Whisk together half-and-half, yolks, ¾ cup sugar, and instant-espresso powder, then pour over bread and soak 10 minutes.

▶ Cook bananas in butter in a 12-inch heavy skillet over moderate heat, turning over once, until golden brown, about 6 minutes total. Lay bananas, cut sides up, over bread and sprinkle evenly with remaining tablespoon sugar.

▶ Bake, uncovered, until custard is set, 50 minutes to 1 hour. Serve warm.

ESPRESSO SAMBUCA TAPIOCA PUDDING

SERVES 4

ACTIVE TIME: 10 MIN START TO FINISH: 1 HR

- 2¾ cups whole milk
- ⅓ cup sugar
- 3 tablespoons instant tapioca
- 5 teaspoons instant-espresso powder
- 1 large egg, lightly beaten
- 1 tablespoon Sambuca or anisette

ACCOMPANIMENT: lightly sweetened whipped cream

▶ Stir together milk, sugar, tapioca, espresso powder, and egg in a 2- to 3-quart heavy saucepan and let stand 5 minutes. Heat over moderately low heat, stirring, just until pudding reaches a simmer. Stir in Sambuca and cool pudding, its surface covered directly with wax paper. Serve at room temperature or chilled.

BROWN-SUGAR PUDDING

SERVES 6

ACTIVE TIME: 25 MIN START TO FINISH: 25 MIN

- 2 cups half-and-half
- ¾ cup packed dark brown sugar
- 2 tablespoons cornstarch
- 2 large egg yolks
- ¼ teaspoon salt
- 1 tablespoon unsalted butter
- ½ teaspoon pure vanilla extract
- ½ cup chilled heavy cream
- ¼ cup chilled sour cream

▶ Stir together half-and-half, brown sugar, and cornstarch in a 2- to 3-quart heavy saucepan and heat over moderate heat, stirring occasionally, until sugar is dissolved and mixture is heated through (do not let boil).

▶ Whisk together yolks and salt in a medium bowl until smooth, then add hot half-and-half mixture in a slow stream, whisking. Return mixture to saucepan and cook over moderate heat, whisking, until mixture just reaches a boil, then boil, whisking, 1 minute (mixture will thicken). Immediately pour through a fine-mesh sieve into a clean bowl and stir in butter and vanilla until butter is incorporated. Set bowl in a larger bowl of ice and cold water and chill, stirring frequently, until pudding is cool, about 10 minutes.

▶ Beat heavy cream with sour cream in a bowl with a whisk until mixture just holds stiff peaks.

▶ Divide pudding among 6 small bowls, then top each serving with a generous dollop of cream.

SOURCES

INGREDIENTS

Agar—Japanese markets, natural foods stores, and Uwajimaya (800-889-1928).

Asian dried tangerine peel—some Asian markets.

Asian egg or spring roll wrappers—Asian markets, some supermarkets, and Uwajimaya (800-889-1928).

Beef *shabu-shabu*—Asian markets.

Black mustard seeds—Kalustyan's (212-685-3451; kalustyans.com).

Black-truffle butter—specialty foods shops and D'Artagnan (800-327-8246; dartagnan.com).

Blackberry syrup—CoffeeAM.com (800-803-7774) and Kalustyan's (212-685-3451; kalustyans.com).

Bresaola* or *Bundnerfleisch—Italian markets, specialty foods shops, and many supermarkets.

Candied citron—economycandy.com and Kalustyan's (212-685-3451; kalustyans.com).

Canned sweet red beans—Uwajimaya (800-889-1928).

Cavi-art (caviar alternative)—caviart.us.

Cheeses such as Banon, Bouc Émissaire, Brick Chaput, and Chaput Pont Couvert—artisanalcheese.com.

Chinese black vinegar—Kam Man Food Products (212-571-0330).

Chinese fermented black beans—asiafoods.com.

Chinese mustard—Asian section of most supermarkets.

Chinese roast pork (*char siu*)—Asian markets.

Confit duck legs—D'Artagnan (800-327-8246; dartagnan.com).

Curry leaves—Kalustyan's (212-685-3451; kalustyans.com).

Doña Maria jarred *mole poblano*—mexgrocer.com.

Dried ancho, *mulatto*, and *pasilla* chiles—Latino markets and Kitchen/Market (888-468-4433; kitchenmarket.com).

Dried Angelino plums—nutsonline.com.

Dried bean curd skins—Asian markets.

Dried black mushrooms—Kam Man Food Products (212-571-0330).

Dried California apricots—apricot-farm.com.

Dried New Mexico and *guajillo* red chiles—Latino markets and Kitchen/Market (888-468-4433; kitchenmarket.com).

Dried pitted Chinese jujubes—Asian markets.

Dried scallops—Kam Man Food Products (212-571-0330).

Dulce de leche—specialty foods shops.

Finely grated unsweetened coconut—Kalustyan's (212-685-3451; kalustyans.com).

Gingko nuts—Asian markets.

Gorgonzola *dolce*—specialty cheese shops and Murray's Cheese (888-692-4339; murrayscheese.com).

Granulated maple sugar—The Baker's Catalogue (800-827-6836; bakerscatalogue.com).

Green or white cardamom pods—Indian markets and Kalustyan's (212-685-3451; kalustyans.com).

Italian tuna in oil—supermarkets and specialty foods shops.

Katsuo bushi (dried bonito flakes)—adrianascaravan.com.

Ketjap manis (Indonesian sweet soy sauce)—adrianascaravan.com.

Kombu (dried kelp)—adrianascaravan.com.

Krupuk (Indonesian shrimp crackers)—adrianascaravan.com.

Lady apples—Frieda's (800-241-1771; friedas.com).

Lavender honey—splendidpalate.com.

Lemon verbena—farmers markets in the summer months, plant shops, and nurseries.

Masa harina—Kalustyan's (212-685-3451; kalustyans.com).

Mirin—Asian markets, some supermarkets, and adrianascaravan.com.

Nigella seeds—Kalustyan's (212-685-3451; kalustyans.com).

Orange-flower water—Kalustyan's (212-685-3451; kalustyans.com).

Panko—many supermarkets and Uwajimaya (800-889-1928).

Pecorino Toscano—Murray's Cheese (888-692-4339; murrayscheese.com).

Quinoa—specialty foods shops and natural foods stores.

Rock sugar pieces—Kalustyan's (212-685-3451; kalustyans.com).

Sanding sugar—Sweet Celebrations (800-328-6722) and The Baker's Catalogue (800-827-6836; bakerscatalogue.com).

Seckel pears—melissasfarmfreshproduce.com.

Semolina flour—D. Coluccio & Sons, Inc. (718-436-6700; dcoluccioandsons.com).

Shanghai bok choy—Asian markets and specialty foods shops.

Smoked paprika—tienda.com.

Snails and sterilized escargot shells—Dean & DeLuca (212-226-6800).

Star fruit—many supermarkets.

Stock (duck and veal)—D'Artagnan (800-327-8246; dartagnan.com).

Sushi rice—Asian markets and specialty foods shops.

Swad (brand) **chutney**—indianblend.com.

Urad dal (white split lentils)—Kalustyan's (212-685-3451; kalustyans.com).

Usukuchi shoyu (Japanese light soy sauce)—adrianascaravan.com.

Veal demi-glace—D'Artagnan (800-327-8246; dartagnan.com).

Vegetarian oyster sauce—Asian markets.

Walkerswood Traditional Jamaican Jerk Seasoning—peppers.com, amazon.com, and cookscorner.net.

Walnut oil—latourangelle.com.

Wheat berries—some supermarkets and natural foods stores.

Winter melon—Asian markets.

EQUIPMENT

4- by 1¼-inch tartlet molds with removable bottoms—Bridge Kitchenware (800-274-3435; bridgekitchenware.com).

6-ounce ramekins (3½ inches across top and 2 inches deep)—Bridge Kitchenware (800-274-3435; bridgekitchenware.com).

Baba au rhum molds—Bridge Kitchenware (800-274-3435; bridgekitchenware.com).

Ice shaver—kitchenware stores and amazon.com.

Small melon-ball cutter—fantes.com.

INDEX

⊘ INDICATES RECIPES THAT CAN BE PREPARED IN 30 MINUTES OR LESS, ACTIVE TIME
Ⅴ INDICATES VEGETARIAN RECIPES

INDEX

TABLE SETTING ACKNOWLEDGMENTS

All items shown in photographs but not listed below are from private collections.

Front Jacket
Red bowl by Bo Jia—Middle Kingdom (800-560-2146).

Back Jacket
See South by Southwest below, page 70.

Table of Contents
Page 6: Bowl by Kenzo—fitzsu.com.

Sixty-Five Years, Sixty-Five Favorite Recipes
Page 50: Table—Eskandar (212-533-4200). Plywood chair—Vitra (212-929-3626). Dinner plates—Bernardaud (212-371-4300). Flatware by Astier de Vilatte—John Derian (212-677-3917). Candelabra by KleinReid—John Derian. Wineglasses and vase—Baccarat (212-826-2520; baccarat.com). Porcelain salad bowl—clio-home.com. Sand-colored ceramic dish—Joan Platt (212-876-9228).

Page 53: Bowl—Catherine Memmi (212-226-8200).

Page 59: Porcelain salad plate—Bernardaud.

Page 60, left: Leather bowl—Barneys New York (212-833-2070).

Page 60, right: White bowl—Catherine Memmi. Small bowl by MUD Australia—Global Table (212-431-5839).

Page 63: Gray plate—kilnenamel.com. Spoon—Eskandar.

The Menu Collection
Page 67: White bisque plates—murielgrateau.com. "Weathered Lined" red fabric—rlhome.polo.com.

South by Southwest
Page 68: Table—Amy Perlin Antiques (212-593-5756). Stoneware bowls by Rina Menardi—Christopher Fischer (212-965-9009).

Page 69: Cast-iron casserole by Timo Sarponava—MoMA Design Store (888-447-6662). Stoneware clay bowls—Joan Platt (212-876-9228).

Page 70: White vase—Alice Goldsmith (212-695-9607). Blue plate—Ralph Lauren (212-318-7000). Tumblers—Simon Pierce (212-334-2393). French bone-handled knives—Penine Hart Antiques & Art (212-226-2602). Wooden-handled cutlery—Dandelion (888-548-1968). Blue salad bowl—Ralph Lauren.

Page 73: Textured platter—Alice Goldsmith. Cup and saucer—Paula Rubenstein Ltd. (212-966-8954).

Meal of Fortune
Page 75: Table and chest—Jacques Carcanagues (212-925-8110). Chairs—M at Mercer (212-966-2830; m-mercer.com). Chinese vase—Leekan Designs (212-226-7226). Teapot—Pastec (212-219-3922). Ming Dragon plates—meissenusa.com. White bowls and red bowls by Bo Jia—Middle Kingdom (800-560-2146). Wineglasses by Joseph Hoffman—Takashimaya (212-350-0577).

Page 77: Green ceramic dish—Jacques Carcanagues.

Page 83: Spoon—Dandelion (888-548-1968). Red plate by Bo Jia—Middle Kingdom.

It Started in Naples
Page 97: French club chair—Suzanne Golden Antiques (212-421-3733). Table—Treillage (212-535-2288). Chairs—ABC Carpet & Home (212-473-3000).

Page 98: Platter—Joan Platt (212-876-9228).

Edible Odyssey
Pages 104–105: Dish towel—La Cafetière (646-486-0667). Seed box, "Soleil" wineglasses, and white "Rebecca" platter—Marston & Langinger (212-965-0434).

Take Your Pick
Page 118: Wineglass and violet Murano bowl—mossonline.com.

Page 119: Cut Wheat vessel—The Future Perfect (718-599-6278; thefutureperfect.com). Maple one-board pine-top table—Moon River Chattel (718-388-1121).

Page 123: "I Was Here" table—The Future Perfect. White dinner plate—karkula.com.

Fresh from the Farm
Page 125: Skirt by Hache—tessandcarlos.com. Bracelet by Sherzada—sherzada.com. Jeans by Levi's—levi.com. Shirt by J. Lindeberg—jlindeberg.com. Shoes by Bass—bassshoes.com. Necklace by R.J. Graziano—stylism.com. Bracelet by Ben Amun—ben-amun.com. Shirt by Strenesse—strenesse.com.

A Day in the Country
Pages 130–131: All glassware—Baccarat (212-826-2520; baccarat.com).

Into the Blue
Page 138: Outdoor table umbrella—Treillage (212-535-2288). Teak folding chairs—jojteak.com. Wood bench—tuckerrobbins.com.

Page 139: Ceramic plate—Nicole Farhi (212-223-8811; nicolefarhi.com). Small teacup—Takashimaya New York (800-753-2038).

Page 140 (left): Serving plate—Nicole Farhi. Gray napkin—Clio (212-966-8991; clio-home.com).

Page 143: Filo 03 Table—M at Mercer (212-966-2830; m-mercer.com).

A-Huntin' We Will Go
Page 144: "Dip" espresso cup and saucer—Nicole Farhi (212-223-8811; nicolefarhi.com).

Gathering Home
Pages 150–151: (left to right) Long-sleeve shirt—Fred Segal (323-651-1298). Brown pants by Dolce and Gabbana—neimanmarcus.com. Apron—nyvintage.com. Tank top—calvinklein.com. V-neck sweater by Dolce and Gabbana—neimanmarcus.com. Jeans—levi.com. Dress—nyvintage.com. White dress and light brown coat—marni.com. Gray T-shirt—Fred Segal. Plaid shirt and hooded sweater—marcjacobs.com. Pants—polo.com. Cardigan—nyvintage.com. Table runner—Andrianna Shamaris (212-388-9898). Glasses and cast-iron birds—Aero Ltd. (212-966-4700). Carafe—Moon River Chattel (718-388-1121).

TABLE SETTING ACKNOWLEDGMENTS

Page 153: Leather strapping—Andrianna Shamaris.

Page 154: Cast-iron chair—Paula Rubenstein Ltd. (212-966-8954). Napkin and cast-iron plate—Aero Ltd.

Page 157: Bowl—Golden Calf (718-302-8800).

Page 159: Forks and metal maritime signal—Paula Rubenstein Ltd. Napkin—Aero Ltd.

Just the Four of Us

Page 162: Plate—broadwaypanhandler.com.

Page 163: Bowl—Middle Kingdom (800-560-2146). Plate—Vietri (800-277-5933). Vase—Clio (212-966-8991; clio-home. com). Plate—davistudio (518-392-7308). Tumbler—Andrew O. Hughes Design (646-644-6861).

The Generous Table

Page 168: Serving platter and plates—heathceramics.com. Gray bowl—Moss (866-888-6677). Bowl—Catherine Memmi (212-226-8200).

Page 173: Wineglasses—Clio (212-966-8991; clio-home.com)

Morning Light

Page 180: Concrete candleholder—Just Scandinavian (212-334-2556).

Merry and Bright

Pages 186–187: Green goblets, decanter, and white glass bowl—The End of History (212-647-7598). Teak table—hipandhumble.com.

Page 188 (from left): Shirt—Prada (212-334-8888). Belt—clubmonaco.com. Green blouse—barneys.com. Patterned skirt—Prada. Ring—Tenthousandthings (212-331-9314). Silver bracelet—Gaffney (646-242-8668). Pants—barneyscoop.com.

Page 193: Dress—Prada. Silver coral bracelet—Tenthousandthings.

Crimson Tidings

Page 195: Red candlestick by Salviati—Gardner & Barr (212-752-0555; gardnerandbarr.com). Gray candlestick—Bardith Ltd. (212-737-3775; bardith.com). Hurricane—Ralph Lauren (212-318-7000). Silver flatware—James Robinson (212-752-6166). Silver-leafed fruit—Brilliant Surface (212-966-1506; brilliantsurface.com). Patterned fabric—Vaughan (212-319-7070). Wineglasses—Calvin Klein (212-292-9000). Castle Grey wall paint—Farrow & Ball (212-752-5544).

Page 196: Bowl—neuegalerie.org.

Page 198 (right): Red Leaf fabric—neuegalerie.org.

Page 201: Toy—yoyashop.com. Plate—Bardith. Glass—James Robinson. Fabric (front)—Vaughan.

CREDITS

We gratefully acknowledge the photographers listed below. With a few exceptions, their work was previously published in *Gourmet*.

Roland Bello: Just the Four of Us, pp. 162–167. The Generous Table, pp. 168–179. Morning Light, pp. 180–185. Merry and Bright, pp. 186–193. All Photographs © 2006.

Hans Gissinger: Take Your Pick, pp. 118–123. All Photographs © 2006.

Richard Jung: Let It Snow, pp. 90–95. All Photographs © 2006.

John Kernick: Chicken Hawaii, p. 22. Steak au Poivre, p. 24 (left). Butterscotch Chiffon Pie, p. 24 (right). Pommes de Terre Lorette, p. 26. Bouillabaisse of Peas, p. 30. Beet Consommé, p. 67. It Started in Naples, pp. 96–101. Fresh from the Farm, pp. 124–129. A Day in the Country, pp. 130–137. Crimson Tidings, pp. 194–203. All Photographs © 2006.

Marcus Nilsson: A-Huntin' We Will Go, pp. 144–149. All Photographs © 2006.

Gueorgui Pinkhassov: We Are Family, pp. 110–117. All Photographs © 2006.

Martyn Thompson: Edible Odyssey, pp. 102–109. Gathering Home, pp. 150–161. All Photographs © 2006.

Petrina Tinslay: Into the Blue, pp. 138–143. All Photographs © 2006.

Mikkel Vang: Black-Bean Shrimp with Chinese Broccoli, front jacket. Short Ribs Braised in Coffee Ancho Chile Sauce, p. 11. Grits and Bacon Roulade, p. 50. Warm Lentil Salad with Sausage, p. 53. Pho Bo, p. 54. Apple Charlotte with Calvados Crème Anglaise, p. 59. Mustard Cheddar Crackers, p. 60 (left). Pozole Rojo, p. 60 (right). Chocolate Soufflé Cake with Orange Caramel Sauce, p. 63. South by Southwest, pp. 68–73, back jacket. Meal of Fortune, pp. 74–83. Circle of Friends, pp. 84–89. All Photographs © 2006.

Romulo Yanes: Port-and-Spice Poached Pear with Granita, p. 2. Crisp Eggplant Chips, p. 6. Nasi Goreng, p. 12. Chinese Egg Rolls, p. 16. Sauternes and Sage Jelly, p. 17. Escargots à la Bourguignonne, p. 18. Maccheroni Quattro Formaggi Villa d'Este, p. 32. Sweetbreads Meunière, p. 36 (left). Chicken with Vinegar, p. 36 (right). Chawan Mushi, p. 39. Sesame Twists, p. 40. Kefta and Zucchini Kebabs, p. 42. Apricot Almond Tart, p. 43. Masala Dosas, p. 46 (left). Egg Noodles with Cabbage and Onions, p. 46 (right). Yellow Cake with Chocolate Frosting, p. 48. Coffee-Glazed Doughnuts, p. 205. All Photographs © 2006.